Pass Key to the GMAT

Bobby Umar, M.B.A.
GMAT Instructor and Consultant
President, Raeallan
Leadership Speaking and Training
Toronto, Canada

Carl S. Pyrdum, III, Ph.D.
GMAT Tutor
Ivory Tower Tutoring
Atlanta, Georgia

DISCARDED

®GMAT and Graduate Management Admissions Test are registered trademarks of the Graduate Management Admission Council (GMAC). The GMAC does not endorse, and is not affiliated with this product.

REFERENCE

About the Authors

Bobby Umar, MBA is a highly sought after GMAT instructor in North America. For almost 15 years, he has taught GMAT prep courses for Veritas Prep and Kaplan, global test prep companies, and his own company, Raeallan. In 2009–2010, he was awarded the "Worldwide Instructor of the Year" for Veritas out of 500+ instructors from 130 countries.

During his MBA studies at Degroote School of Business in Hamilton, Ontario, Bobby was President of the MBA Association, received awards in case competitions, academics, and leadership, and graduated at the top of his class as co-valedictorian. With a background in brand marketing, engineering, and the performing arts, he also draws on his diverse career to lead Raeallan, a transformational training and speaking company (*www.raeallan.com*). A four-time TEDx speaker, Bobby speaks about leadership, personal branding, networking, and social media. With his expertise about the GMAT, he has helped thousands of young leaders get into the best business schools.

You can connect with Bobby via Twitter, Linkedin or *www.GMATBobby.com*

Carl Pyrdum, Ph.D. is a long-time GMAT tutor, who opened his own tutoring company, Ivory Tower Tutoring in Atlanta, Georgia. He has worked as a teacher, tutor, and content developer for the GMAT, GRE, LSAT, SAT, and ACT for Barron's as well as for Kaplan. He has helped more than a thousand students improve their test scores and reach their undergraduate, graduate, and professional school goals.

Acknowledgment

The authors would like to acknowledge the valuable contribution of Sophia Glisch, who helped formulate a number of questions and answers in the book.

All inquiries should be addressed to:
Barron's Educational Series, Inc.
250 Wireless Boulevard
Hauppauge, New York 11788
www.barronseduc.com

Library of Congress Control Number: 2014930584

ISBN: 978-1-4380-0248-4

PRINTED IN THE UNITED STATES OF AMERICA
9 8 7 6 5 4 3 2 1

10% POST-CONSUMER WASTE
Paper contains a minimum of 10% post-consumer waste (PCW). Paper used in this book was derived from certified, sustainable forestlands.

Contents

The Basics

Officially, GMAT is an acronym that stands for The Graduate Management Admissions Test, the standardized computer-based test that the vast majority of business schools use in admissions decisions for their MBA programs.

The latest change in guard has, thankfully, done little to change the overall nature of the core test and its questions. True, some sections and question types have been dropped over the years, some added (the most recent, the Integrated Reasoning, added in 2012), but the underlying logic behind the test remains the same—and that's good news for prospective test takers like you! With the right guidance and a bit of hard work, the GMAT *can* be mastered, no matter how strange and difficult it might seem at the outset. There's not just a method to the GMAT's madness; there's a system of hidden rules and expectations that it always operates by that you can learn in order to secure the score you need to meet your admissions goals.

THE TEST'S STRUCTURE

When you sit down in front of your assigned computer on test day, you will face four scored sections in this order:

1. **ANALYTICAL WRITING ASSESSMENT SECTION (THE AWA).** In the AWA, you are given 30 minutes to write a response to an essay prompt, typing it into a simplified word processing interface. The prompt asks you to produce an "Analysis of an Argument," presenting a brief, fictitious argument from a made-up source and asking you to critique it.

2. **INTEGRATED REASONING SECTION (THE IR).** Here, you will be given 12 questions and 30 minutes to complete the section. IR questions ask you to use multiple sources of information—graphs, tables, charts, and short reading passages—and to employ both your math and your verbal knowledge and skills. Four types of questions are attached to these different sources of information: Graphics Interpretation, Two-Part Analysis, Table Analysis, and Multisource Reasoning.

3. **QUANTITATIVE SECTION (AKA "THE MATH" OR "THE QUANT").** The Quantitative Section contains 37 questions written in two different

formats, Problem Solving and Data Sufficiency (aka "the weird ones"). The questions will alternate between the two formats more or less at random. According to the test maker, both types of questions will require familiarity with arithmetic, elementary algebra, and "commonly known" concepts of geometry. You will have 75 minutes—an hour and a quarter—to answer all the questions.

4. **VERBAL SECTION.** As with the Quantitative Section, you have 75 minutes, but here you'll face 41 questions in three different formats (Reading Comprehension, Sentence Correction, and Critical Reasoning), also in no particular order. The Verbal questions require a basic understanding of the "rules" of arguments, the ability to read and organize information presented in both long (350- to 400-word) and short (100-word) passages, and familiarity with the grammatical rules of standard written English.

Section	# of Questions	Time	Question Types
AWA	1 essay prompt	30 minutes	Analysis of an Argument
Integrated Reasoning	12	30 minutes	Graphics Interpretation, Two-Part Analysis, Table Analysis, Multisource Reasoning
Short Break—up to 10 minutes			
Quantitative Section	37	75 minutes	Problem Solving, Data Sufficiency
Short Break—up to 10 minutes			
Verbal Section	41	75 minutes	Critical Reasoning, Sentence Correction, Reading Comprehension

YOUR 10 (YES, 10!) TEST SCORES

When all is said and done, you will receive a lot of different scores for the GMAT—ten in total! Usually, people will just refer to one, the Overall Score (as in "I got a 720" or "I heard you need a 712 to get into Harvard" or "You get 200 points just for writing your name down!"). In actual practice, your score will come back with a little chart that looks like this:

Test Date	Verbal	Quantitative	Total	Analytical Writing	Integrated Reasoning
23 June 20XX	40/90%	50/89%	690/89%	6/91%	7/82%

Actually, the scores you receive on the day of the test are considered Unofficial Scores, only becoming Official Scores when your score report appears in your e-mail inbox and on the Graduate Management Admissions Council (GMAC) website. It is rare for the numbers to change in between, so in practice most people don't use the "Official" and "Unofficial" distinction. Note, however, that most schools require you to have an Official Score to report *before* their application deadline!

Eight of your scores are calculated automatically on site, so you'll find them out on the day of your test. You have to wait a few weeks for the essays to be graded to receive the final two.

1. **OVERALL SCORE (YOUR SCALED SCORE).** This is that famous three-digit number, the first score in the Total column. It ranges from 200 to 800, in increments of 10. Two-thirds of test takers score between 400 and 600, and the median score is usually between 540 and 570. The scores are arranged on a bell curve, so scores below 300 or above 700 are relatively rare. This score is produced by a weighted average of your performance ONLY in the Quantitative and Verbal sections. (The AWA essay and the IR sections are tracked independently.) The average's weight skews toward the Math score, though the exact amount is a trade secret closely guarded by the test maker.

2. **OVERALL PERCENTILE SCORE.** The second score in the Total column, this one is actually more important than the three-digit number, although admittedly less iconic. It tells you what percentage of recent test takers your score bests. Thus, a 75th percentile scorer did better than 75 percent of people who've taken the test over the last three years. This score can change from year to year as the test taking population changes, though in practice it rarely moves more than a single point in either direction.

3. **QUANTITATIVE SUBSCORE.** Your performance in both the Math and Verbal sections is also tracked separately, on a range from 0 to 60, with increments of 1 point. Quantitative Subscores are typically in the 7 to 50 range (again, because of the test's built-in bell curve).

4. **QUANTITATIVE PERCENTILE SUBSCORE.** Like the Overall Score, your Quantitative Score will also be expressed as a percentile (the second score in the Quantitative column) and it, too, can change slightly from year to year. In most years, it takes a subscore of at least 52 to break into the 99th percentile.

5. **VERBAL SUBSCORE.** The first score in the Verbal column, this one's just like the Quantitative, but for Verbal: 0–60, 1 point increments. Most test takers will score between 9 and 44, which is, you might have noticed, a good bit smaller a range than in Math, with a lower top-end score as well.

6. **VERBAL PERCENTILE SUBSCORE.** The Verbal column's second score works just like the other percentiles, though the bell curve here is slightly more forgiving. A 99th percentile score can be had for the low, low price of a subscore of 45.

7. **INTEGRATED REASONING SCORE.** Calculated completely separately from any other section, the first score in your IR column will range from 1 to 8, with increments of one point. That means there are only eight possible scores for all people taking the test, and most of those scores are between 3 and 7, with a mean of 4. Interestingly, even though a score of 1 is theoretically possible, most years no one receives one.

8. **INTEGRATED REASONING PERCENTILE SCORE.** The second score in your IR column is also calculated only from your performance on the 12 IR questions and is also variable from year to year. The numbers here have jumped around quite a bit over this section's short history, although it seems to have stabilized around 94% as the top score, 46% the mean, and 17% the bottom.

9. **AWA SCALED SCORE.** Your essay scores will be calculated independently of all the other sections. The Scaled Score, first in the Analytical Writing column, has a theoretical range of 0–6, with increments of 0.5 (meaning it's possible to get a 4, a 4.5, or a 5, but not a 4.1 or a 4.8; however, in practice 0's are never given and more than 90% of test takers receive a score between 2 and 5.5. So, even though there are 11 possible scores in their range, the test maker only uses 7 regularly.

10. **AWA PERCENTILE SCORE.** Your final percentile score works like all the rest, though the top score of 6 translates to only the 91st percentile most years.

Of all these many scores, the one most important to your business school admissions goals remains that three-digit Overall Score. Though they are loathe to admit it, it's still the case that many schools have an Overall Score cutoff they use to winnow down the mountain of applications they receive each year. Fall under it, and your application goes to the circular file. Accordingly, the bulk of this book is dedicated to the principles and techniques that will allow you to raise that Overall Score to vault over whatever arbitrary bar you face.

WHAT THE CAT IS AND WHAT IT MEANS TO YOU

Now that you've got the basic who, what, where, and why of the GMAT down, it's high time we moved onto the how—as in, "How am I going to improve my score on the test?" The first step is to understand how this test differs from other tests you might have taken elsewhere, not the mundane details like number of questions and how to register but the real nitty-gritty that separates the GMAT from the SAT, GRE, and ABCs: the CAT.

The C in CAT is easy enough to understand, as is the T: we all know the GMAT is a **T**est that's only offered on a **C**omputer. It's that **A** that bears explaining. What does it mean for a test to be "**A**daptive"?

Back when the GMAT was administered on paper, every student in the room taking it faced exactly the same questions in exactly the same order. In general, the questions were organized with the easiest ones up front and the hardest toward the end, the idea being that a student who "deserved" a 540 would be able to work only a certain percentage of the test's questions, whereas one destined for a 740 would be able to work a much higher percentage, all but a few questions, and future 800s would be able to do them all.

The paper test could be administered only a few times a year because each administration requires the test makers to write an entirely new set of questions to keep those who took the February exam from telling those taking the test in April what questions they'd see. So if there were 100 questions on a test, each sitting meant a fresh 100.

Adaptive Features

An adaptive test is, instead, built from a single pool of questions much larger than the 41 Verbal and 37 Math questions a single student sees, and it's almost impossible that any two test takers would see the exact same 78 questions as any other. The pool of possible questions is organized into "tiers" of questions of similar difficulty. The first question the test taker sees is drawn from the middle tier of questions, ones that the test maker has designed to be doable by students who will end up with a score right in the fat part of the test's bell curve (and all those who exceed it) but not by those below it.

The next question drawn from the pool is determined by how the test taker performs on that first question. If the correct answer was picked, the next question will be from a slightly higher tier, and if one of the four incorrect choices picked, a slightly lower one. Another correct answer will mean the next question is more difficult still, while an incorrect one will dial the difficulty back a notch. As the test progresses, the jumps or falls in difficulty decrease in magnitude, so missing a question in the first ten will have a greater impact on the tier your questions are drawn from than missing one of the last ten.

The idea is that the test will be able to home in very quickly on the test taker's true skill level and only offer questions appropriate to that skill level. Whenever test takers get enough questions right to raise the difficulty up into a tier that's too hard for them, they'll start missing questions, lowering it right back down to their true skill level.

If the system worked perfectly, eventually test takers should expect to reach a point where they miss every other question, wobbling back and forth around their true skill level. In practice, as you might imagine, that sort of precision is seldom the case.

No Skipping Around

On a paper test you're free to flip back and forth from page to page, doing whichever questions strike you as easiest and quickest, leaving yourself more than an average question's allotted time to tackle the hardest ones. On the *adaptive* portions of the GMAT (Quantitative and Verbal), you have to answer all the questions in front of you before you are given the next.

You Have to Finish the Test

Because of the way GMAT's special proprietary score-calculation algorithm works, failing to complete a question counts against your score more than missing it does. Suppose two students missed exactly the same questions in the Math section and in their Verbal section up until question 39. If one student never answers question 40 and never sees question 41 whereas the other tries both but gets them both wrong, the second will get the higher score on the test.

You Must Maintain an Even, Consistent Pace

Because the test soon learns the level of difficulty liable to give you the most trouble, the temptation to slow down and give more time to each subsequent question grows as the test goes on. Beware of the "just *one* more minute" trap because one minute can easily become two or three. You have to be willing to give the occasional question more than the one and a half or two minutes you have, on average, for each question, but put emphasis on the word *occasional*. The GMAT isn't a test suited to either tortoises or hares: slow and steady fails just as surely as quick and careless. Aim instead for brisk but careful. As St. Augustine famously wrote, "Hurry, but hurry slowly."

You Can't Afford to Look Over Your Own Shoulder

Because test takers know that the test is adapting to their performance, many end up trying to gauge their performance on the test with each question. If a new question feels difficult, they silently fist-pump, but if it feels easier, they start to sweat, worried that means that they missed the question they just hit "confirm answer" on. The first problem with this approach is that the more time you spend assessing your performance, the less time you're spending on the question that's actually in front of you, the one that, because there's no going back or skipping ahead, is the only question that can actually improve your performance.

The other problem is that it's actually tricky determining the difficulty of a question because there's actually no such thing as an objectively easy question or an objectively hard one. When we speak about a question's difficulty, we have to use the only ranking tool that test makers have available to them: the percentage of students who, when given the question as an experimental question on a past GMAT, answered it correctly. We say a question is "hard" when a sizable number of those past GMAT students got the question wrong; when most of them got it right, it's an "easy" question. But the reason we put scare quotes in that last sentence is that no one, not even the master test makers employed by the GMAC, has any way of knowing why any particular student got a given question right or wrong.

So what if 88% of beta-testing students got a question wrong. If you were in the 12% of students who got it right, it probably felt pretty easy to you. The same goes for easy questions. Even if 94% of people knew how to solve an equation, the 6% who didn't would probably rank the question it appeared in as hard.

Nobody aligns perfectly with the statistical average, so the reason the question in front of you feels easier than the last may have absolutely nothing to do with your performance so far.

To Do Well, You Must Know Your Comfort Zone (And When You've Left It)

Even though an individual question may feel easy or hard for esoteric or personal reasons, after taking a few practice exams and studying for a while, you actually should be able to get a pretty good feel for whether you're headed toward the score you've gotten in the past over a stretch of about six or seven questions (instead of from question-to-question).

As we said before, the test is designed to feel hard for everyone, regardless of their ability level. With a little reflection, you should be able to recognize how it feels to do a stretch of hard questions and how that feeling differs from doing several easy ones in a row. Thus, when the test starts to consistently "feel hard," when you've left your comfort zone—that is, once you're in the difficulty tier that is just at the edge of your ability—you know you're on track. The better you get at the test, the later this feeling will kick in, the later you'll enter what we might call your "discomfort zone."

Moreover, how well you can recognize and manage your discomfort zone will determine how high your score can go. If you consistently "freak the heck out" (to use the clinical phrase) when the test gets to an uncomfortable level of difficulty, you'll fall back into your comfort zone, just as you would if you calmly executed a triage strategy to deal with a question you didn't understand, but after a freak out you'll probably also fall further, missing a couple of hard but still manageable questions that are on the high end of your comfort zone. That means you'll have to spend a few more questions climbing back to the edge of the zone, and you won't be able to climb as high in the end, leaving you 20 points shy of your peak performance.

WHAT THE GMAT *REALLY* TESTS . . . AND WHAT IT DOESN'T

Hopefully, it's becoming clear that the GMAT isn't like most of the tests you've taken before, and consequently the study habits and test-taking strategies you've used on other tests might not be as useful to you here. That's where the book in your hands comes in. Before we go any further, let's clear up one final misconception about the test. The GMAT tests your ability to take the GMAT. It's that simple.

The GMAT is not a test of your business knowledge. There are many successful executives and managers who would absolutely fail the test, and many has-beens and never-beens who could post near perfect scores.

The GMAT is also not an intelligence test. MENSA won't let you use it to prove your IQ, and securing a 740 doesn't mean you're smarter than your friend with the 700.

The GMAT isn't a very good predictor of your ultimate success in business school, either. Even though there is some positive correlation between a high GMAT score and good grades in the first year of business school, the correlation falls away after that.

The GMAT isn't even much of a math or English test. Certain mathematical concepts appear on the test, as do certain grammatical rules and basic principles of formal logic. Ultimately, however, neither your math skills nor your deftness with the subjunctive mood will translate directly to an impressive GMAT score. So what will affect your score?

How Can We Be So Sure the Test Hasn't Changed Recently?

That's easy. Both of the authors of this book (who tend to write in the royal "we") make their living as professional GMAT tutors, drawing clients from many different backgrounds and with score goals that run the gamut from 500 all the way to the top. The book you hold in your hands represents nearly 25 combined years of experience with the test in all its subtle nuances. What's more, with this brand-new *Pass Key* edition of the *Barron's GMAT,* the book has been completely revamped and written from the ground floor up, unlike some of those other books in your stack, which just change the number on the cover every year and call it a day. And it's loaded with helpful strategies for answering the various question types.

Let's face it: no book could cover every single facet of the test or provide the instruction to overcome every student's particular challenges—not if you want it to fit in a backpack, at least. So, think of this book as your comprehensive guide to GMAT preparation. While preparing, you'll still probably need to consult other sources for help on particular topics.

GATHER YOUR MATERIALS

As we all know, sometimes the difference between success and failure boils down to having the right tools for the job. In this, the GMAT is no different. You'll want to lay your hands on the following as soon as you can:

A Legal-sized Wet Erase Pad

For security reasons, the test center won't let you use paper for your scratch work. Instead, you get a noteboard, a spiral-bound booklet of six double-sided yellow legal-sized laminated sheets of graph paper. As much of a pain as it might be, you need to get used to working problems and taking notes on boards like these. Mock-ups are available from various online retailers (Amazon and the like); however, you can always have a print shop photocopy some graph paper lines onto appropriately sized pages, then laminate and spiral bind them. Either option will set you back less than $10.

A Stockpile of Wet Erase Pens

You also need the pens to go with your board, naturally. If you want to make your practice work as close to the test day experience as possible, you can even purchase the exact model that the testing centers all stock: the Staedtler Lumocolor Non-permanent #3119 Superfine black pen.

A Reliable Digital Timer

While there is great value to be had in working practice questions in untimed conditions, eventually you have to bite the bullet and add the pressure of the ticking clock to your efforts. Digital is preferable to analog, as the timer on the day of the test (found in the upper left corner of the GMAT's computer interface) will be digital.

Some Real Live People to Study With

Forget those dubious groupwork assignments from your undergrad days. Finding a study group of similarly dedicated future business school students can do wonders for your preparation. Even if you end up as the person in the group with the most advanced math knowledge, the one everyone's always asking to explain why it's important that pies aren't square, you'll still find that the very process of explaining it to someone else will further cement and deepen your own understanding of the material.

Simulate Test Day as Often as Possible

There's a reason we asked you to get a practice noteboard. On the day of the test, it's all you'll have to write on. Remember, too, that you should use it as you answer the questions in this book. Although it's perfectly acceptable for you to take notes as you study, the first time you work a question, resist the temptation to write on the page. You won't be able to underline a telling phrase in a Reading Comprehension passage on the day of the test, so don't ·give yourself that luxury in practice.

REGISTER FOR THE TEST, ALREADY!

It's all too easy to delay taking the GMAT, to give yourself "just a few more weeks" of study, to wait until after a looming deadline, an upcoming vacation, the end of the semester exam week, Christmas break, and the list can go on forever to "really get serious about the test."

The best way to forestall this stalling is to give yourself a deadline and put some money on the line. At $250, the GMAT isn't cheap. Schedule your GMAT for an appropriate time in the future; for most students, that's two or three months from now. Go ahead, you can sign up for the test right now. We'll wait here while you do.

Back? Good. Now you have a deadline and a $250 bet with yourself, a good reason to turn to the next chapter, where you'll begin learning about those predictable GMAT patterns and how best to turn them to your advantage. Sure, you could wait until later, but there's no time like the present . . .

The Analytical Writing Assignment | 2

INTRODUCTION

If you're an applicant from a country where English isn't the native tongue, there's some bad news. Your AWA essay will be scrutinized a bit more heavily than an applicant hailing from the United States or the United Kingdom because business schools want to make sure you're up to the challenge presented by courses given entirely in English. The AWA still won't overrule more important indicators—such as your TOEFL score—but it will be considered.

If, on the other hand, you're a native English speaker, your AWA score is likely to get the most cursory of glances, unless your academic experience suggests some sort of deficiency in your writing skills. In that case, the AWA does allow you the opportunity to answer some of those lingering questions.

What Does an AWA Score Look Like?

As discussed in the first chapter of this book, you'll receive two scores for the AWA, and you'll have to wait about three weeks to find out what they are. Your AWA Score and its accompanying percentile score will arrive only with your Official Score Report. Your primary AWA Score will be a number from 0 to 6, either a whole number or something point five—that is, in half-point increments. The test maker almost never awards a score of .5 to 1.5, and 0 is reserved for students who simply do not write anything. Most business school applicants' scores fall between 4 and 5.5, or across only 4 different possible scores—not a lot of room to distinguish one candidate from the next.

This score, as well as the actual essay you type on the day of the test, is made available to every business school that receives your overall score.

How High an AWA Score Do I Need?

As a rule of thumb, once your AWA score is above 4, you're in the clear. If it's 4 or below, the schools will probably look more closely at your application and possibly even at the essay you wrote itself.

How Is the AWA Score Generated?

The best indication of how much schools should value your AWA score is how the score is generated. If you have images of panels of old professorial types in tweed jackets with leather elbow patches all sitting around a table in a well-appointed study discussing the relative merits of your essay, which they all have annotated heavily with red pen, congratulations, you have an excellent imagination. Alas, the truth is, unless there's some sort of problem, your essay will be read by two graders only. One of them will be a part-time employee of ACT working in a massive cubicle farm. Your essay will pop up on their computer screen for 2 minutes total. At the end of that 2 minutes, the reader—usually a current or former humanities graduate student—will enter a score for the essay, from 0 to 6 in half-point increments.

During the typical work day, these human essay graders will see about 30 essays every hour over an 8-hour shift. You don't have to have a perfect Verbal Subscore to know that means about 240 essays each day and 1200 a week.

What the GMAT AWA Really Doesn't Test . . .

According to the GMAC's *Official Guide*, the best essays are those that exhibit:

- Exemplary critical thinking skills
- An organized argument with well-developed support
- Mastery of the language and diction of the professional English vernacular

But are those really things that you can tell about an essay that (1) is read for no more than 2 minutes and (2) is graded partially by a computer program nowhere near as sophisticated as the one that beat Kasparov? We don't think so, either.

There is, however, a silver lining underneath this cloud. All you need to do is learn the formula, and you will be the proud owner of a robot-approved AWA score between 4.5 and 6.

The vaunted E-Rater—a computer algorithm that utilizes a database with hundreds of responses to each essay—is only going to scan your essay looking at the following:

- Structural keywords and phrases that indicate organization
- Spelling and grammar mistakes
- The general difficulty of vocabulary used
- The number and average length of phrases, sentences, and paragraphs

Attempting to match the E-Rater's assessment, the human graders will be looking for mostly the same things. So, instead of the GMAC's impressive-looking list of requirements, your essay will instead be aiming for two main things:

Length: The essay has to be long enough to give the impression that it covers the topic thoroughly and in detail.

Appropriate Vocabulary: Words that might strike your college English teacher as superfluous are absolutely essential, so you're going to need lots of transition words like *first, next, consequently, on the other hand, moreover,* and *in conclusion.*

Also, a liberal (but not excessive) dusting of "five-dollar words" can make your fluency with English rate higher with both man and machine. There is one grain of salt this advice does need to be taken with. Since one-half of the grading team actually is a person, you can bolster your chances for a score over 4 by making sure that the essay is also:

Easy to Read: Their job is not an easy or glamorous one; do the readers a favor and make sure your essay, particularly the first paragraph, glides easily from point to point.

On Topic: Though the computer algorithm can't tell lightning from a lightning bug, human readers can, and so make sure the essay actually is on the topic indicated at the top of the computer screen.

Palatable: If you think something might be offensive or alienating, then err on the side of caution. You want your essay to be easy, breezy, and comfortable for the grader.

Note the one big thing left out through all of this: content. As long as you don't write an essay about how much you love your dog when the prompt calls for an analysis of whether a particular code of ethics is likely to bring about a change in the corporate culture at Company X, *what* you say is almost insignificant compared to *how* you say it.

Indeed, it's an open secret in the test prep industry that graders of GMAT essays like to talk about essays in terms of what they call "fourness." As long as an essay *looks* like one that answers the question without having anything else to say for it—a mediocre but acceptable by-the-numbers essay—then it gets a 4. If it has any easily spotted plus, that bumps it up to a 4.5 or 5. Sixes get reserved for essays that make a great first impression and don't look at a further glance like they've committed any big errors of style or diction.

On the other hand, if there's something weird or hard to follow in the first few lines, only then do the 2's and 2.5's come out.

ANATOMY OF AN AWA PROMPT

When you finally hit that Begin Test button on test day, you'll be greeted with something that looks like this on your computer screen:

> The following appeared as part of a newspaper editorial:
>
> "Five years ago the teachers at Bellville Heights Technical School introduced interactive computer displays to their refrigeration and air conditioning classes. The proportion of students enrolled at the school who later failed their licensing exams dropped substantially. What's more, the decline followed almost immediately upon the program's introduction. Clearly, if we wish to improve education throughout our post-secondary educational system, we must allocate a greater portion of our education budget to bringing innovative technological approaches to learning into all of our classrooms."
>
> Discuss how well reasoned you find this argument. In your discussion be sure to analyze the line of reasoning and the use of evidence in the argument. For example, you may need to consider what questionable assumptions underlie the thinking and what alternative explanations or counterexamples might weaken the conclusion. You can also discuss what sort of evidence would strengthen or refute the argument, what changes in the argument would make it more logically sound, and what, if anything, would help you better evaluate its conclusion.

Notice that, much like Critical Reasoning questions, there are essentially three parts to an AWA question:

The Three Parts of an AWA Prompt

1. **THE SOURCE.** Every AWA question includes a single short line ending in a colon that gives a purported source for the argument that follows. This isn't filler, exactly, though you don't have to consider the source in making your essay if you prefer. The source does give you a handy way to reference the argument, however. "As the editorial states," "the editorialist's position," or "the argument in the editorial" would all be handy to have.
2. **THE ARGUMENT.** Usually the argument is fewer than 100 words long and generally presents either a plan to accomplish something, a recommendation of a course of action, or an abstract evaluation of whether one thing is

more important than another (both in a general way that extends to many different circumstances or in a specific, given circumstance).

3. **THE INSTRUCTIONS.** Read them now, commit them to memory soon, and once you have, never look at them again. They're not going to change, and it'll save you precious seconds on test day.

OVERALL STRATEGY FOR THE AWA

Step 1: Assess the Argument

As we will soon see, a thorough assessment of an AWA argument is a lot like untangling a Critical Reasoning question. Identify the speaker's conclusion and make a jot list of all the points of evidence the speaker employs. Unlike in the Critical Reasoning section, you're almost certainly going to want to jot this information down. You can use the note board or the question's response box.

While assessing the argument, take note of the usual suspects, particularly differences in the words used in the evidence and the conclusion. If a survey, study, or sample group appears (and they often do), make sure to compare every piece of information given about them and line those pieces up with the group the conclusion concerns.

Finally, don't forget that source note that comes at the top of the page. Context is always useful.

Step 2: Brainstorm

Now that you have the moving parts of the argument arrayed before you and understand the gaps in the author's reasoning, it's time to come up with all the points you think you might want to make. Though the general direction of the AWA essay is almost always the same (the speaker's argument is not convincing), be careful not to prejudge which bits of the argument will make the best hay for your essay. Very often, you'll find that something that initially seems like it might anchor one of your body paragraphs turns out to be a dud, and the point you only wrote down for completion's sake turns out to barely fit in a single paragraph once you've thought it over.

Nothing is off limits during your brainstorm. Let your mind wander free. Your essay will be the better for it.

Step 3: Outline Your Main Points

Here's a spot of good news: the outline you write for a GMAT AWA essay response will likely be shorter than one that you'd write for a paper for college credit. Forget all that old business about Roman numerals, capital letters, and so on. This can be as detailed or as scanty as you need. Keep your eyes on the prize. No one but you will ever see the outline. The essay's the only thing that can influence your score.

There is one part of the GMAT AWA outline that will differ from other essays you've written, the prewriting. Since the readers are unlikely to give careful or prolonged attention to your prose, you want to make sure that the places they will actually look are as polished and powerful as you can make them. As you finish up your outlining, you will want to convert your notes into fully completed first sentences for each of your main paragraphs. If you reach for clever turns of phrase or powerful hooks, they'll be wasted buried any further in your work, so now's the time to work them out.

Step 4: Write the Essay

All told, you'll probably only spend about 15–20 of your 30 minutes typing out your essay, with the remainder devoted to the other steps, with the bulk of that time devoted to planning out the essay. Once you're all planned up, it's time to get those fingers dancing across the keys—just remember, there's no spellcheck and auto-correct, so perhaps finger-dance a slightly slower tempo than you would at home.

THE PLAN IN ACTION

Let's analyze the familiar prompt on page 16 step by step.

Step 1: Assess the Argument

Since AWA arguments follow the same rules as Critical Reasoning arguments in terms of structure, the first heavy lifting you'll have to do with an AWA prompt will be finding the argument's conclusion.

Here, the argument's conclusion is clearly flagged for us with the concluding keyword "clearly":

> "Five years ago the teachers at Bellville Heights Technical School introduced interactive computer displays to their refrigeration and air conditioning classes. The proportion of students enrolled at the school who later failed their licensing exams dropped substantially. What's more, the decline followed almost immediately upon the program's introduction. Clearly, if we wish to improve education throughout our post-secondary educational system, we must allocate a greater portion of our education budget to bringing innovative technological approaches to learning into all of our classrooms."

Whenever you're surveying the information in an argument, a good test of whether you've got it down is to reword the pieces in your own words. How would you rewrite this conclusion?

Write your rephrasing here:

_____

_____

One possible way you could have gone would be something like this:

> If you want to make all colleges/technical schools in the area better, spend higher % of $ in budget on classroom "technology"

Note a couple of key points:

The conclusion has a **qualification** attached; in other words, it's an **if/then** conclusion. We will need to be careful that we don't overstep the argument's conclusion in the essay and imply that our editorialist thinks that we have to follow this plan, period. It's only if we want to make the schools better that we need to spend this money. (Of course, it's not much of a qualification. Who doesn't want to make schools better?)

The scope of the argument is not just a greater **amount** of money, but a greater **percent** of the money in the budget. So, however big that budget becomes or however much it should shrink, the speaker is committed to the percentage increasing.

The reason we placed "technology" in scare quotes is that it's a relatively **vague term**. There's no way the author's evidence could possibly encompass all technological innovations, so this is an assumption waiting to happen.

Once you have the conclusion well in hand, it's time to characterize and track the evidence the author employs. With the argument less than 100 words, and so much of that taken up on that kind of lame qualification, there's not going to be much room to support the claim. That's intentional on the part of the test maker. If the argument were supported, what would you write?

A possible jot list might look something like this:

> Sample group: one school, type of class: AC/Refrig, 1 type of tech: interactive student displays, effect: lisc exams
> Effect is % of entire school; tech only in AC/Refrig. "substantial" decr
> Timeframe: Incr *immediately* after tech; 5 years of history

There's a lot going on here in the evidence; or, it might be more accurate to say that there are so many places where not enough is going on in the evidence.

The argument, like so many on the AWA, draws a conclusion from a **sample group**, raising the issue of **representativeness**.

There are numerous ways the sample group can be characterized (and none of them appear in the conclusion specifically). The test case is **one school** in the district and only **one type of class** offered at that school. Likewise, as we should have expected, only **one type of technology** was involved: "interactive student displays." The **timeframe of the survey** is also specified. We're only talking about 5 years of data here. Is that enough?

An even more interesting discrepancy crops up in the editorialist's description of the effect this tech had on the school. Only one type of improvement was tracked, naturally, but note that the effect is not calculated directly from the sample group. Instead of telling us that the qualifying exam scores improved for the AC and Refrigeration students—the ones in the class with the computer screens—the evidence concerns the school's students as a whole! Since we don't know how big a percent of the student body the AC students are, the possibility of both a **percent versus number** problem and an **alternate cause** emerges.

The extent of the effect is characterized as "substantial," a fairly **vague term**, all things considered. How much of an improvement will the school board or regents of this district be purchasing with their increased budget allocation?

And finally, the **timeframe** is a bit suspicious. Were the students in these classrooms that received the computers all on the verge of taking their licensing exam?

As is always the case with GMAT arguments, once you have the evidence laid out (either in your head, as is usually the case in Critical Reasoning, or on paper, as here), the argument's assumptions become clear, and we have highlighted them by bolding the words above. In order for this argument to be true, we need to believe a lot that we're not told explicitly. Jot your thoughts down below and compare against the model:

_____

_____

_____

_____

The following is not meant to be an absolutely exhaustive list, but it covers the high points. For AWA prompts, our analysis of the assumptions need not be complete in any case, as we're only going to have room to write one or two as it is.

> The assumptions in play:
>
> - Bellville Heights Technical School must be similar enough to a substantial proportion of the schools in the district; otherwise, it's not going to be a good test case for making educational decisions in general.
> - The students and classwork in the AC & Refrigeration courses also need to be typical, both of Bellville Heights' student body and of students in the district in general.
> - These "interactive computer displays" must be sufficiently similar to the types of educational technology the editorialists believes will be purchased. And whatever their role in that AC & Refrigeration classroom, it has to be similar enough to how technology could be used in other courses throughout the district. In short, there's nothing special about these displays.
> - The timeframe cited requires us to take an awful lot on faith. We must assume that the displays caused the increase in passing scores on the licensing exams and that there's nothing suspicious about how soon after their introduction the scores went up.
> - We must also be content to accept that 5 years of evidence is good enough to make a recommendation as large as the editorialist makes.
> - When the editorialist says "substantial" decreases in the licensing board failure rate is a big enough benefit to count as an improvement, particularly of the sort that would change the way classes should be conducted in however many schools there are in Belleville's area.
> - Since the author never discusses the actual dollar amounts, we're left to assume that however much new technology costs, it's within the budget's ability to accommodate and that moving the money around won't cause some sort of indirect harm.

The speaker in this argument sure did leave a lot of bases uncovered. And that's excellent news for us, as there are so many ways we could go with this essay. Indeed, we'd best be careful not to try chasing down each and every one of them in the next step. Though 30 minutes is a good long while to write an essay in, it's still only 30 minutes.

Step 2: Brainstorm

We've done so much in Step 1, how much could there be for us to do now? That's kind of the point, actually. If we take enough time to understand the argument, we really won't have much difficulty with the points we're going to raise in the essay.

On your whiteboard or in the text field of the GMAT CAT interface, you'd pick some assumptions and consider how best to frame them for the purposes of writing a 15- to 20-minute 500–1000 word essay.

> Representativeness! How big is Bellville? The AC dept? The school system? What types of schools? Are the same sort of places, students disciplines, etc.?
>
> Too soon? How could computers turn AC around? How do we know it's relevant at all? Maybe just happy to have $ thrown at them, happy students.
>
> Representativeness #2 What do "displays" do for AC? How useful in lit, history, brain surgery, law, race car mechanics?
>
> Show me the $$$ — How much do they have? How big a % of budget? Room to spare? Throwing $ at problem . . .

Step 3: Outline Your Main Points

If you wrote your notes on your dry erase board, it's now time to move them up to the text field of the CAT interface. If you wrote your notes there on the computer, now would be the time to start deleting the lines of thought that proved less promising and to polish up the ones that you're going to go with. Of course, before you do either, you'll also need to make some decisions. What are you going to structure your essay around? Look for related points, points that will be easy to explain, and points that will flow into one another easily as you move from body paragraph to body paragraph in Step 4.

If you'd produced something like the sample brainstorming notes from Step 2, the direction is clear. If you're aiming for three body paragraphs, then the line item labeled "Too Soon" might be the one to drop, as it's a bit complicated an explanation to make in limited space and time and doesn't necessarily mesh with the other points.

If you're shooting for two body paragraphs, or an essay structured around two major points, then representativeness is clearly the way to go. Let's say that's the direction we decided to head. Our essay will be primarily about how the sample group is in many and varied ways not necessarily the best group to use to make comprehensive educational reform decisions.

Remember also that this is the part of our essay where we'll be writing out the first sentence of each of the paragraphs we're going to have in our final essay. It may seem a little bit like a cheat, but let's face it, the readers aren't likely to read past that first line anyway, and they certainly won't want to if the first lines aren't compelling.

Before we produce a sample outline here, though, we need to discuss what sort of essay we're aiming to produce, not just here with the computers at Belleville but on any prompt we might encounter in the AWA.

Step 4: Write the Essay

To make sure that the reader understands the issue, the first paragraph should begin with a restatement of the argument and the situation it arises in—both should be given in your own words, though don't strain too hard to produce synonyms for every single word in the original question. There's bound to be some overlap in terminology, as there are some concepts that are hard to express any other way. After the issue has been clearly presented, it's time for the big reveal: you don't think the argument is a good one, and here's a quick sketch of why you don't.

Here are three sample first paragraphs we could write for this essay, arranged from "not quite good enough" (under 4) to "meh" (4–5), to "that'll do nicely" (6)—or, to put it in the test's argot: well under 4, 4–5, 6.

> This argument is not a good one. Its assumptions are weak and the evidence it gives is insufficient.

The good: OK, so there's not much good here. But this scant little two-sentence introductory paragraph does manage to accomplish one of our goals. It clearly lays out what the essay's main point will be: this isn't a good argument.

The bad: The biggest problem is there's no explanation of just what argument we're talking about. While there's no need for us to pretend that we're writing about school systems all through history or the higher truths of education itself, we should still take the effort to inform our reader of what we think the argument in the question says. At this rate, our hypothetical AWA writer is cruising for a 2 at best.

> This argument, an anonymous editorial's recommendations for educational policy, asks us to believe that the evidence drawn from a single school is enough to make big decisions about how a school district should spend its entire budget. It supports this claim by asking us to believe without adequate support that the many differences between the pilot program's specifics and the district are inconsequential. Further, its recommendations are based only on a single type of technology. Without the addition of serious extra support, the argument should not be taken as valid.

The good: We're getting closer, but we're not there just yet. The introduction gives more specifics about the situation and the argument, and is also clear about the overall thrust of the essay. This has the whiff of "fourness" about it, though it might have an outside shot at a 5 if there's something eye-catching to follow.

The bad: The presentation of the argument and the essay's thesis statement kind of bleed together, as the hypothetical essayist seems to want to say both things at once. Hopefully, this essayist doesn't intend to call the editorial writer out for vague terminology, as this introductory paragraph is general and vague where it could easily be specific. (Pots should not call kettles black.)

> This editorialist's argument recommending that an unnamed school district drastically change the allocation of money within its educational budget in order to incorporate more technology into the classrooms in its colleges and technical schools fails to convince. The main evidence offered to support the claim is quite limited, requiring us to assume that the educational improvement of students in a single schools' air conditioning and refrigeration program following the introduction of interactive computer displays will be repeated throughout the district so long as those in charge of its educational budget are willing to spend extra money on technology. No regard is given to possible differences in kinds of program, sizes of school, or even the type of technology that will be purchased as the program moves from its pilot school to the entire district.

The good: Obviously, this hypothetical student's essay is going to end up longer than the other two, but notice how that length is accomplished: specific references and concrete detail. The author gives the essay's main point in the first line, fleshes out the argument in the middle of the paragraph, and then returns at its end to a preview of the sorts of issues that will be raised in the body paragraphs. It's also clear that this writer took the time to make sure that the first line of the essay was well written back in their version of Step 3.

The bad: This test taker's version of the argument is so tightly condensed into just a few phrases that it might be a little hard for the grader to grab onto. The level of diction and overall organization will probably mitigate that, however, so it's not that big a problem.

Now it's time for all three of our students to tackle the body paragraphs. Granted, it'd be hard to believe that all three of them are working from the same outline as we produced. Student 1's introduction is probably scantier, Student 3's is more developed, but not necessarily. One skill that separates the 4's from the 5.5's is the ability to take an outline and run with it.

Let's check back in with Student 1:

> To begin, how do we know whether the students in the first school are like the students all over the district? It could be that the increases in passing scores weren't even that impressive. And even if they are, that's not reason to believe that these students aren't different somehow. They're AC & Refrigeration majors, after all, and that's not exactly brain surgery. Until we know more about these guys, it's not a good idea for us to accept the editorial's argument. I mean, how do we even know that this editorialist is good at telling real educational successes from what just looks like a success after five years. You can spend ten years thinking you're doing the right thing, and only later find out that you weren't. There are too many examples of this sort of thing to list, and that's not even considering the possibility that there are a lot of schools in this district where people study all kinds of things, not just how to make sure your house is cool in the summer and your cold cuts don't spoil.
>
> That's not the biggest problem with this argument, though. We need to know a lot more about how those computer screens were used in the AC classes even. What does "interactive" even mean, and how would it help you figure out which part of the air conditioner you need to bang on when it doesn't work. And it's not like you bang on the same part when you're doing brain surgery, at least I'd hope not.

The good: Even with an inauspicious beginning, this student is managing to bring up specific reasons why the argument's underlying assumptions might not be valid. The occasional bit of color like the cold cuts in paragraph two isn't a bad idea, truth be told, though banging on the brain might be a little *too* colorful.

Also, notice that the student does manage to use transitional keywords to make sure the reader knows when the subject is being changed.

The bad: A tendency to meander and lose sight of the paragraph's purpose is this student's main flaw. The language is a bit loose, yes, but disorganization will do much more to lower a score than a casual tone. The student's body paragraphs likely mean that a 3 is not out of the question, though it is likely the essay's ceiling.

Over at Student 2's computer, body paragraphs are coming along, too:

> The program that saw the "substantial" results that so impress the editorial writer and motivate the entire proposal seems far too specific and esoteric a subject matter to use to make any drastic or far-reaching decisions about educational spending priorities. Nothing against Air Conditioning and Refrigeration Repair students, but this doesn't tend to be the program that draws the best and brightest, even at a technical school like Belleville Heights Technical. It's not clear that the results of a technical college are even relevant to collegiate education in general. Whatever the new technological improvements did for the tech school students' licensing exams, we should not be so quick to change course on the basis of their example. It is certainly within the realm of possibility that the AC Repair program at BH Technical is a comparatively small program, even at the school itself. If this were the case, it would be inadvisable for a school board to make too much of their success, however "substantial."
>
> A more compelling issue is the exact nature of the technology and the question of whether it could be usefully applied in other programs at BHT and elsewhere. The drama majors at Belleville Heights Fine Arts Academy might not know what to do with an interactive computer display, even if the business majors at a different school could use them for PowerPoint presentations that were miles above the ones they'd been able to do with noninteractive displays.

The good: The introduction of the appropriately named Fine Arts Academy is a nice touch, as is the PowerPoint example in the second paragraph. Whenever you can incorporate specific, relatable examples into your discussion, your essay will be the better for it. Student 2 is also doing a fair job of showing how the unwarranted assumptions aren't necessarily wrong, and that it will all come down to specifics that the editorial writer doesn't provide in the argument.

The bad: The problem of different points getting a bit mixed together in this student's presentation continues here. Putting the focus on the technology itself in the middle of paragraph two does mean that paragraph three is a clear extension of the overall line of thought, the original point about the HVAC students' representativeness is getting overshadowed. When writing an AWA essay, it's imperative that you finish making one point before moving on to the next.

And what sort of masterpiece has our 6-bound student produced while these last two students were sweating away?

> The first and most glaring flaw with the editorial's argument is how little is told about the students in the pilot program. If the school district that contains Belleville Heights Technical is full of similar technical colleges that focus on subjects similar to air conditioning repair, we can be more confident that attempts to duplicate its success throughout the district will be met with success. On the other hand, if Belleville Heights is the only technical college in a sea of liberal arts schools, things might be different. Moreover, it is not even a certain thing that air conditioning repair itself represents a large proportion of the study body at the school in where the new computer technology was introduced. Though the drop in failure rates was substantial for students at the school in general, it is possible that the gains were found more in automobile repair or electrical engineering. The performance of the air conditioning repair students may well have gone down, for all the editorialist reveals.
>
> This brings another problem to mind. There is very little information in the editorialist's writings about how the new "interactive computer screens" were used in the air conditioning and refrigeration repair classrooms. Without such knowledge, there is no way to determine how big a part of the increased performance was due to the computers. It could even be the case that they weren't used at all, only introduced and left to gather dust in the corner. Similarly, without knowing if there exist comparable technological advancements that could enhance the other programs in the school district, it is not possible to say whether allocating more funds to purchasing technology will bring about any increase in performance there. What helps an air conditioning repair student pass a qualifying exam might hinder a poet from creating a portfolio to send out to graduate programs.

The good: Again, it's easy to tell this essay is going to do well from the length alone, even though it is not the length alone that will determine its fate. Rather, Student 3 has clearly taken the time to think through several different points within the larger topics that serve as the focus for each of the two body paragraphs. There is little to no repetition in this student's delivery, instead detail upon detail added to flesh out the specifics of the essay's argument.

The bad: There's not much to criticize, though do notice how hard this student is having to work to keep from using personal pronouns. One wonders whose mind the problem is being brought to in the second body paragraph. At other points the diction gets a little obtuse. Great pains are being taken to keep even from abbreviating "air conditioning." This likely will not drag the essay lower than a 5.5, but if the essay seems too off putting to the human grader, it may just block the possibility of a 6.

It's time for our three students to sum their positions up in a concluding paragraph. We return to Student 1 first:

> In conclusion, this argument cannot be accepted simply on the evidence that the editorial gives because we do not know enough about the other schools or about the computers the AC program used.

The good: Don't let the brevity sway your assessment too much. This is a perfectly serviceable conclusion. It wouldn't elevate an essay from a 3 to a 3.5, but it also wouldn't lower one from a 3.5 to a 3, either. In fact, Student 1 finally shows signs of clarity and focus, very cleanly reprising the two points of the body paragraphs—more clearly than the topics were presented originally, in fact.

The bad: We could easily wish for a longer conclusion, particularly one that mentions some way in which the editorialist might be able to improve the argument or answer the student's objections. Your essay on test day should avoid simply attacking the speaker's position.

Now back to Student 2, who was teetering on the edge of the acceptable score range with a rambling middle section.

> Until more information about the scarcity or abundance of other, nontechnical colleges in the editorial writer's school district, and until more can be learned about the kinds of technology that fall within the potentially expanded budget, it will be hard for anyone to go along with the proposal in the editorial. Whenever someone suggests moving money around, but can only provide one limited example to back their suggestion up, we are right to be skeptical. Otherwise, we might end up with a ballet classroom full of VR helmets but no pointe shoes.

The good: Once again, Student 2 manages to rescue a substandard paragraph with a final flourish. Though beginning with the possible strengtheners as this paragraph does is a solid way to begin bringing an AWA essay to a close.

The bad: Resisting the temptation to go meandering for a sentence or two is still this student's greatest challenge. Often these shifts in subject are accompanied by shifts in tone, so that the essay oscillates unevenly between formal and casual. It would be better if this hypothetical essayist were to write an entirely casual essay than to haphazardly attempt more professional or academic sounding diction.

In the final analysis, the occasional flourishes and sparks of wit might convince the human grader to bump this essay up to 4.5 or even 5 if feeling generous. The E-Rater would probably not be as impressed and would likely suggest a 4, meaning the student's 4.5 is all but secured. It's not the most impressive AWA score, but it is good enough.

Back at Student 3's terminal, we might expect that the keystrokes have all but died down as the student dutifully follows this book's advice and is proofreading away. But what is there to show for the effort?

> The holes in this argument are too many and too substantial that it remains difficult to take the editorialist seriously. Without further evidence confirming the representative quality of the air conditioning program and explaining how different technologies might improve the educational outcomes in all of the district's programs, whatever they may be, the proposal to reallocate funds to technology should be greeted with the utmost skepticism.

The good: This conclusion is perfectly serviceable, too, though not much more so than the short little conclusion that Student 1 gave. This is simply the wordy version, which is perfectly OK to do. The reader is adequately reminded of the essay's earlier points, and some suggestion for improvement is given, but there is also nothing particularly interesting or eye catching. The 6 is probably not going to happen, though Student 3 will almost certainly not score lower than a 5.5.

Step 5: Proofread

The sorts of things that our three hypothetical essayists might find on their proofreading runs won't be typos or spelling mistakes, but that does not mean that their essays could not have benefited from the time. Even Student 3's very polished essay could be further enhanced, little inconsistencies of language could be ironed out or the vocabulary choices touched up here and there. And at the very least, the time allocated to proofreading will ensure that no one's essay cuts off abruptly.

The Final Template

Our experience with the three essayists allows us to suggest a final, fleshed out version of the potential essay template. Feel free to use it as you will. Tweak it to your own strengths and tastes, but remember that you don't have to reinvent the wheel in order to secure an excellent AWA score.

Introductory Paragraph

- Present the argument from the question in your own words.
- Clearly announce that the argument is flawed and indicate why.
- Sketch out briefly the points that form the core of the essay body.

Body Paragraphs

- In each, develop a single idea, most often a single assumption or type of assumption.
- Begin with a clear statement of the assumption to be discussed.
- Provide specific details of how certain unknown facts could weaken, others strengthen the assumption.
- Transition to the remaining body paragraphs, if any.

Concluding Paragraph

- Begin with some indication of the sorts of evidence that might strengthen the argument.
- Proceed to reiterate your claim that the argument, as currently stated, is unconvincing.

STRATEGY TIPS, TWEAKS, AND OTHER CONSIDERATIONS
The "Fourth" Part of the AWA: the Interface

In general, we haven't spent too much time in this book discussing the GMAT CAT's interface, as it's not too hard to figure out that you use the mouse to move the cursor and the left-hand button to click on the answer buttons.

But with the AWA, many students do struggle a bit, spoiled by the robustness of the word processing software that they've become accustomed to using at home, at school, or on the job. The GMAT's AWA is not your old reliable word processor. You'd have to go back to the days when word processors were single-function devices that looked like fancy typewriters to find an interface this basic. It's got fewer features than Microsoft Notepad!

The most glaring lack is that function we most disdain day to day: the spell-check. No helpful red lines will appear under misspelled words, and no button will autocorrect them for you. The only buttons you'll have access to will be Cut, Copy, Paste, Undo, and Redo.

Does spelling count?!? Officially, no, spelling does not count. But do remember that one of your readers is only human, and you are trying to make a good impression; the grad students grading essays can't help but be influenced by your spelling to some degree. It might be the difference between a 5 and a 5.5.

The lack of your computerized spelling coach is very important to keep in mind when following the advice elsewhere to pepper your essay with a reasonable number of high syllable count words. You should only elevate your vocabulary to words that you are comfortable spelling. Misspelling those sorts of words will quickly give the reader the impression you're trying to manipulate them and may even assume your true facility with the language is lower than the rest of the essay might demonstrate.

You won't need to use those buttons if you don't want, however, as there are a few shortcuts "under the hood" that are nice to know about. The interface designers even decided to make their bare-bones word processor agnostic to the PC versus Mac divide. Windows types will recognize these shortcuts:

Ctrl + X = Cut   Ctrl + V = Paste   Ctrl + Y = Redo
Ctrl + C = Copy   Ctrl + Z = Undo

And Mac aficionados will welcome this complementary set:

Alt + T = Cut   Alt + A = Paste   Alt + R = Redo
Alt + C = Copy   Alt + U = Undo

The AWA prompt will always take up a good bit of your screen real estate, while you'll be left to make do with the lower half. If you don't want to move your hands from the keyboard to scroll that tiny window up and down, don't forget the helpful [Page Up] and [Page Down] keys.

In Conclusion, Conclude

The 30 minutes you have for the AWA essay is a hard limit. There's no way to signal the computer that you need just one more second to finish your last sentence. When the timer in the upper right-hand corner of your screen hits 0:00, the word processing interface closes itself and punts you right into the Integrated Reasoning instruction screen. So in actual practice, you have about 29 minutes and 50 seconds in which to write your essay.

Essays that break off mid-sentence or mid-paragraph do take a grading hit from the computer and human readers alike. Prepare for this by knowing what your conclusion is going to be and, if possible, have it typed out at the bottom of your essay screen *before* you've written some of the middle paragraphs. It's easy to delete a supporting paragraph if you realize you don't have time to finish it, and so long as you've got other supporting paragraphs, they can compensate for the loss. A lost conclusion sinks the essay.

I Didn't Forget the Other Side—It's Just Wrong

Here's a simple but effective way to make your essay seem more well-reasoned and convincing with minimal extra effort on your part. You'll always be lacing your essay with pieces of information that will both strengthen and weaken particular unwarranted or under-warranted assumptions in the argument. Simply include a gracious acknowledgment that the side you find most likely is not the only possible outcome and that, indeed, many thoughtful people have disagreed.

It all boils down to one magic phrase: "There are [those/many/some] who would [say/argue/contend]..."

Consider the following:

> Industry alone is not sufficient to spur job growth. The Soviet political machine learned this in the last quarter of the past century, when their single-minded focus on industrial growth left villages of starving and diseased men and women who once could have entered the workforce. If only the central planners realized that if agricultural development does not keep pace with industrial, the proportion of the workforce simply unable to work will surely swell, erasing job gains in the industry.

Now, back off of that stance just a touch:

> While there are certainly economists who contend that industry alone is always sufficient to spur job growth, such an approach has often proven inadequate, as those advising the Soviet political machine learned in the last quarter of the past century, when a single-minded focus on industrial growth left villages of starving and diseased men and women who once could have entered the workforce. If only the central planners realized that if agricultural development does not keep pace with industrial, the proportion of the workforce simply unable to work will surely swell, erasing job gains in the industry.

Just one minor tweak and the author of the argument seems more engaged and even-handed, without a single jot of extra evidence!

It's possible to take the acknowledgment of other sides so far that it becomes the complete rejection of your own authority on the subject. Remember that the whole reason you're acknowledging the other side is to prove to your reader that you considered *but rejected* it.

Don't Repeat Your Evidence

In the ever-present quest for an essay that is long enough for a 6, it can be tempting to belabor points because doing so does make the page so nice and full and paragraphs so nice and long. The problem is that human reader again. You don't want your one possibility of a sympathetic soul to turn his or her head in disgust the fourth time you pound out your example. So don't repeat your evidence.

That doesn't mean you should never repeat a structural point, however. The three phases of every successful essay boil down to the mantra *Tell them what you're going to tell them; tell them; then tell them you told them*. The structural glue of your essay might seem too repetitive, all that "first, second, third" and "for this reason, too, the argument fails to convince" isn't how the writers on *The New York Times'* best-seller list operate—but it is how the successful GMAT AWA essayist works.

Exterminate Weasel Words

A "weasel word" is a little qualifying tweak that adds wiggle room to an otherwise straightforward statement. This is not the same as saying, "There are those who say"; rather, it's putting those squishy little asides like "sort of," "kind of," "of a sort," "so to speak," and "seems to." No responsible reader assumes that direct, forthright sentences mean that the author is some sort of pig-headed absolutist unable to see nuance, and overworked as they may be, the graders the GMAT employs are still responsible readers.

High schoolers use weasel words because they think that they make their case more compelling. Journalists do it to avoid recrimination and libel. They're both wrong, and in this you should not seek to join them.

Where to Go from Here

Now that you have an essay template to work from, examples of possible essays to draw upon, and an understanding of the actual standards that will be used to evaluate your writing, you should begin to feel a bit more confident about this small essay that begins the test. If you're still worried, or simply want extra help, there are a few extra resources readily available to you that will undoubtedly meet your needs.

Integrated Reasoning | 3

The Integrated Reasoning section has a 30-minute time limit with 12 questions. Some of the questions may have several parts. A special online calculator is available for use on only this part of the GMAT. The Integrated Reasoning section will be scored separately from your GMAT score (from 200–800) and from your AWA score (from 0–6). This section will be scored on a scale from 1–8, in intervals of 1. There are no partial points given, which means that if a question has three Yes/No statements, you need to get all three correct in order to get credit.

The Integrated Reasoning section is designed to measure your ability to review data in multiple formats using various methods, to identify key issues and trends, to apply high-level reasoning, and to organize information in order to make an informed decision. For this, you will need to be comfortable with synthesizing information from charts, tables, graphs, spreadsheets, e-mails, and letters in paragraph form. As with the rest of the GMAT, you will not need prior business knowledge to answer Integrated Reasoning questions. The Integrated Reasoning section can be best summarized as a blend of the GMAT Quantitative and Critical Reasoning sections along with some argumentative logic, thus the use of the term integrated.

Note that the Integrated Reasoning section is not computer adaptive like the quantitative and verbal sections, which become easier or more difficult in response to your performance. This means the questions are preselected, just like in a simple paper and pencil test. Therefore, you should expect a diverse mix of question types and difficulty levels.

OVERALL STRATEGIES

The Integrated Reasoning section requires some of the same skills you will use on the overall GMAT. It also has a similar structure and format. Therefore, you can apply many of the strategies you would use on the overall GMAT.

1. **INVEST TIME TO UNDERSTAND THE QUESTION:** For every GMAT problem, including the quantitative and verbal sections, you must ask yourself "What's going on?" before you dive into solving the question. Make sure you understand the question and the information given. Get a general

35

sense of what the question is asking. Think about how you might set up your solution. Investing time up front to review the data and key insights before diving into the questions will save you from losing time by backtracking.

2. **AVOID THE TWO MOST COMMON ERRORS:** The most common errors that test takers make on the GMAT are misreading the question and making unnecessary calculation errors. Make sure you review the questions, the information, the passages, and the answer choices quickly but carefully. When you make calculations, be sure to keep your scratch work clean, structured, and error free.

3. **KNOW HOW EVERYTHING RELATES:** Try to get a sense of how all the information—variables, numbers, and text—relates to each other. The GMAC writers don't expect you to look at all the data in great detail. Therefore, look for certain themes or trends within the data that are obvious. Most of the information given in the questions tells you the "what." Your job is to figure out the "so what." Ask yourself, "What does this tell me?" and "Why is this so important?"

4. **YOU DON'T ALWAYS NEED THE CALCULATOR:** The Integrated Reasoning section provides a calculator, but that doesn't mean you should always use it. It is an awkward tool. Most of the time, you can set up your questions to keep its use to a minimum. Most GMAT math problems can be solved conceptually and with minimal calculations. Even though you can solve all quantitative problems with a step-by-step process, there are always shortcuts. Do some mental calculations, simplify your work, and estimate whenever possible. You will be surprised by how little you need the online calculator.

5. **DON'T SKIM, SYNTHESIZE INSTEAD:** Skimming will not help you in this section. You are being tested on your ability to analyze and synthesize the data. That doesn't mean you have to look at every single detail. However, you do need to watch for important key words, note titles, headings, labels, and subject lines, along with units and key numbers.

6. **PRACTICE DATA SHUFFLING:** Since much of the navigation in Integrated Reasoning requires using tabs, scrolling, and sorting, you can practice much of this using spreadsheet software like Microsoft Excel. You can also try using a calculator on your computer for practice. Don't let the need to navigate slow you down.

7. **LEVERAGE CURRENT GMAT STRATEGIES:** Use the theory and strategies you learned in the Quantitative and Verbal sections of this book to help you. Many of the typical GMAT strategies use processes and methodologies that are transferable to the Integrated Reasoning section. You can

apply similar skills to answering all the questions—quantitative analysis, algebra, deductive reasoning, argumentative logic and structure, identifying conclusions, and anticipating questions.

8. **LOOK FOR ALL THE HIDDEN CLUES:** The GMAT test developers like to hide clues to questions in many places. You need to know where these clues are. Start with the questions and answer choices themselves. They can give you an idea of where to look in a question and what to look for. You can also use your work from previous questions within a section; you can use your work cumulatively to solve the next problem. Don't forget to look within the charts, tables, graphs, and paragraphs. They contain key numbers, labels, and words that provide more insight to the problem than you might originally realize. Digest every piece of the puzzle. With practice, you will begin to know what you should look for and what you can ignore.

9. **YOU DON'T NEED TO MEMORIZE:** Since you are given so much data and information, the test writers at the GMAC cannot expect you to memorize everything, nor should you try. Devote your time and energy to understanding the problem, navigating effectively, outlining a solution path, and getting to the answer. If you need to refer back, the data is always available.

10. **CONFIDENCE IS KEY:** Just like with the rest of the GMAT, confidence goes a long way to your success. When you are confident, you look at problems as a fun challenge and have the determination to solve them correctly. When you lack confidence, you second-guess yourself and you spend too much time focused on the wrong things. You use many of the skills tested on the Integrated Reasoning section every day in your professional and personal lives. Approach problems knowing that the theory, structure, and strategies you have internalized will help you succeed on the Integrated Reasoning section and on the rest of the GMAT.

THE FOUR QUESTION TYPES

The new Integrated Reasoning section contains four types of questions:

1. **GRAPHICS INTERPRETATION:** You will analyze a graphical image and then select options in a drop-down menu in order to create accurate statements.

2. **TABLE ANALYSIS:** You will receive a sortable table of information, similar to a spreadsheet, that you must analyze to answer questions in true/false, yes/no, or other formats.

3. **TWO-PART ANALYSIS:** You will receive a paragraph of information and then answer a question in a two-part format. This requires you to look at data in two different ways in order to solve the question.

4. **MULTI-SOURCE REASONING:** You are given two to three sources of information presented in various forms—including text, charts, and graphs—on tabbed pages. You then have to answer questions in either a yes/no format or in a select one out of five format.

Following are the four Integrated Reasoning question types, along with strategies and sample questions for each.

GRAPHICS INTERPRETATION

True to its name, this section will require you to interpret graphics. The basic idea is this:

Look at this graph. Understand what it is trying to say. Extract some key information.

You will be given a graphical image—scatter plot, graph with variables, Venn diagram, bar chart, statistical curve distribution, or pie chart—and some explanatory text. There will be several statements you will need to complete using choices from a drop-down menu.

Skills Tested

- Assimilating, analyzing, and interpreting data in graphical forms
- Identifying and extracting key information
- Interpreting past events and predicting future outcomes

Graphics Interpretation Strategies

1. **START WITH WHAT YOU KNOW:** As with any GMAT question, ask yourself "What's going on?" before attempting to answer. Invest the time to get the gist of the graph. Try to look at it from a high-level perspective and to understand the information it is trying to convey. Think of an appropriate title for the graph in your own words (IYOW) if none is given.

2. **MAKE SURE YOU CATCH EVERYTHING:** Now focus on the details. Look at any titles, axis labels, symbols, legends, or units of measurements given. Is the graph displaying data in thousands or millions, in inches or feet, and so on? Investing time up-front to understand the graph thoroughly will save you from having to analyze everything again later.

3. **IDENTIFY TRENDS AND RELATIONSHIPS:** Look for any key trends or relationships among the variables, the *x*-axis, and *y*-axis. Are there any direct or indirect relationships? Do certain areas of the graph have spikes, a greater concentration of points, or either a positive or a negative slope? This is where we interpret the data and extract the key information.

4. **USE THE STATEMENTS TO HELP YOU:** Just like in the rest of the GMAT, the answer choices can provide you with some great insights. If the statements talk about slope, familiarize yourself with the slopes of any lines shown on the graph. The statements will mention certain key words that are relevant to answering the question. If you identify enough, you will be able to "connect the dots" and solve the puzzle. In other words, you can piece together all the different aspects of the graph and what it is trying to say.

5. **ANTICIPATE THROUGHOUT THE QUESTION:** Throughout your first read of the material, try to anticipate what the relevant information is and what the questions are going to ask. Once you see the questions, you can try to figure out what the answer is before you open up the drop-down menu. It's a great confidence booster if you see the answer you anticipated in the drop-down menu. If you don't see your answer there, it's a good indicator that you may have made some oversights.

TABLE ANALYSIS

In this section, you will be required to analyze tables. The basic idea is this:

Look at this detailed table. Sort the information to answer statements about it.

You will be given a table or spreadsheet that has sorting ability, much like a Microsoft Excel worksheet. Some text will be included to explain the table. The questions will have varying types of statements—yes/no, true/false, would help to explain/would not help to explain, or inferable/not inferable. You will have to select one choice for each statement. Every column in the table is sortable either numerically or alphabetically.

Skills Tested

- Assimilating, analyzing, and interpreting data tables
- Sifting through and organizing a mass of information
- Identifying trends and patterns
- Extracting meaningful information to make decisions
- Understanding how data can be used to satisfy certain conditions or support either a hypothesis or principle

Table Analysis: Strategies

1. **START WITH WHAT IS GIVEN:** Look at the table and the headings. Invest the time up-front to get the gist of the table. Get a sense of the data given, sorting options, rankings, columns, and highest and lowest items in the table. Think of an appropriate title for the table in your own words (IYOW) if none is given.

2. **USE THE QUESTIONS OR STATEMENTS TO HELP YOU FOCUS:** The questions will give you a good idea of what kind of information needs to be extracted from the table. Yes/no and true/false are usually easy to figure out. However, watch out for the more abstract "would help explain" questions. Ask yourself if sorting a particular column would point you toward a solution.

3. **IDENTIFY TRENDS AND RELATIONSHIPS:** Look for any key trends or relationships among the numbers given. Look at how the numbers or rankings change among columns. Do you see some obvious disparities? Are there direct, indirect, or inverse relationships? This is where you interpret the data and extract the key information. Do not spend an undue amount of time going through each piece of data. Rather, you need to get an overall sense of the table. Remember, you can always look back at the table for reference, so there is no need to memorize anything.

4. **DON'T OVERANALYZE; BE EFFICIENT:** These questions contain a lot of information. You can easily get lost on some of the larger spreadsheets and forget about the clock. If you practice sorting beforehand using a spreadsheet program, you can get a better understanding of how sorting works. When you look at numbers, you can **estimate** or use very rough numbers (for example, $23,846 is better thought of as $24k). Remember again that the questions will refer you to which columns to look at. So take the time to determine what would be the best sort to find the answer.

TWO-PART ANALYSIS

This section requires you to do two-part analysis. The basic idea is this:

Analyze a problem with two components and solve for two components.

You will be given a problem that is structured with two components. The question could be either a typical GMAT quantitative problem (two-variable, rate, or work problems), a verbal problem (two opinions on an issue, two separate aspects of research), or a combination of both. The problem will have two issues, variables, or aspects under consideration. The question will also have two components, usually as columns in a chart, with several possible answers in rows. These answer components may or may not be related. Your job is to select the one correct answer for each column.

Skills Tested

- Solving complex or multilayered problems
- Recognizing relationships between two entities
- Solving simultaneous equations
- Thinking and reasoning
- Weighing trade-offs and making decisions with more than one aspect

Two-Part Analysis: Strategies

1. **START WITH WHAT YOU KNOW AND UNDERSTAND:** Write down what you know from the question, especially for multilayered or complex problems. This includes what you know and what is implied by the statements in the question. This is your starting point and helps you figure out what's going on before diving deeper.

2. **STRUCTURE WITH CHARTS OR DRAWINGS:** Typically, the more complex a GMAT problem is, the more important it is to add structure to it. Lay out the data in a more organized form or use a drawing to visualize the information. Using a structure also keeps your scratch work clean, makes your scratch work easy to follow, and helps you to extract key aspects of the problem.

3. **ALGEBRA IS YOUR BEST FRIEND:** In many of the more quantitative problems, algebra is a great tool. Algebra is the language of math. It can help you simplify the problem, understand what's going on, and unlock keys to the solution.

4. **DETERMINE THE KEY ISSUES:** In complex problems, several issues, aspects, or constraints are at play. Spend some time identifying and understanding what they are. Then you might be able to look at the answer choices and see which ones meet the question's criteria.

5. **PLUG AND PLAY:** Once you have a strong understanding of the problem, you can start trying some of the answer choices given. Many of the Two-Part Analysis problems have dependent variables. Plugging in one answer may lead to what the other answer should be. If the other answer choice is there, that is great. If not, try another answer choice and see if you can find a match.

MULTI-SOURCE REASONING

For the final question type in the Integrated Reasoning section, you will be required to use multi-source reasoning. The basic idea here is:

Look at multiple sources of information, and pull the relevant data to solve problems.

You will be given two or three tabs that contain a large amount of information, either in text form (such as e-mails and research articles) or in table form. The idea is to give you more information than you need. Your job is to pull the relevant information from the sources and solve problems. Some of the more wordy problems resemble GMAT Reading Comprehension or lengthy Critical Reasoning questions. You may be required to use quantitative skills, verbal skills, or both. You will also have to use either deductive or inductive reasoning. Questions may be in a yes/no or a multiple-choice format.

Skills Tested

- Assimilating voluminous amount of data and extracting relevant content
- Using both deductive and inductive reasoning
- Integrating various types of information from different sources to make a decision
- Dealing with information overload
- Using both quantitative and qualitative information simultaneously
- Analyzing a case study

Multi-Source Reasoning: Strategies

1. **DETERMINE THE SCOPE OF THE QUESTION:** First determine whether the question is more quantitative or verbal, as this will determine which strategies and tactics are appropriate for the question. If the question is more verbal, first think about what the key aspect or topic is of the entire case study. Then look at each tabbed section and identify its key aspect or topic. This will help you get a better understanding of the pieces of the puzzle and the puzzle as a whole. If the question is more quantitative, make sure you know what the basic objective of the question is and what variables are at play.

2. **DETERMINE THE "SO WHAT?":** Each section, particularly for the verbal-type questions, will have conclusions, inferences, and purposes from which you can extract deductions or use inductive reasoning. Think about what each section's purpose is and what the writer is trying to conclude. Again, you should do this both in context and in your own words (IYOW). Most of these questions will ask you to draw a conclusion, so understanding each section is key. The writer of each section will give you the "what," but you need to determine the "so what?"

3. **USE EACH QUESTION FOR DIRECTION:** Each question will give you a good idea of what issues or areas to focus on. The question should align with the scope and purpose you have already identified. If you are confused with all the information, you can first determine the main gist of the information and then look at the question. Depending on the question, you should be able to determine which section will be the best place to start.

4. **STRUCTURE YOUR INFORMATION:** Whether the question is qualitative, quantitative, or both, you will have to digest a lot of information. Write down the key pieces of information from each section, or create a chart that helps you sort out the issues or the math. Take the time to determine what would be the best tab to find the answer.

5. **LOOK AT THE STATEMENTS, AND ASK YOURSELF WHETHER THAT IS TRUE:** For every inference or conclusion you have to make, you will find support in the content. As a quick check, you can try two options. The first is to find the specific support from the statements. If you can find support, then you know the answer is correct. However, if you cannot find the support, the answer cannot be correct. The second option is to ask yourself whether the answer is true based on the statements. If you can find a plausible alternative inference, perhaps the statement is false or the answer is no.

Quantitative Section: An Introduction

4

T he good news about the quantitative or math section of the GMAT is that you've seen it before, probably in grade 11 or earlier. The chapters ahead review the fundamentals along with some of the more commonly tested topics. Go through at your own pace, making sure you have a solid understanding of each section because the learning is cumulative. The further you go, the more you build up a GMAT quantitative bag of tricks. Eventually, you will have several tools and tactics in your arsenal to defeat the GMAT—and isn't victory fun?

PROBLEM-SOLVING STRATEGY, METHODS, AND TACTICS

We will cover several comprehensive strategies and tools for conquering the GMAT problem-solving questions. Below is a summary of what we will explore in more detail in the problem-solving chapter.

Problem-Solving Fundamentals

- Careless errors be gone!
- The secret is out about minimal or no calculations.
- The math is clean.
- Know how they deceive you.

Problem-Solving Strategies

- You need strong fundamentals.
- Invest in your immediate future.
- Harvest the garden of answer choices.
- Try this concept—conceptual thinking! Simplicity is the Ultimate Sophistication.
- Carry 3 big sticks—picking numbers, algebra, and number properties.

Problem-Solving Methods

Use the know-want-approach method:
1. What do you know?
2. What do you want?
3. What is your approach?

Problem-Solving Tactics

1. Pick numbers . . . wisely.
2. Use your best friends (algebra and number properties) . . . forever.
3. Don't break your back solving, try backsolving.
4. Construction, construction, what's your function?
5. Break it down!
6. Estimate, guess-timate, approximate to elucidate.
7. Process of elimination (POE): return of the friend.
8. Don't get tricked. Become a trickster.
9. Stop staring!
10. Let it go.

DATA SUFFICIENCY DIRECTIONS FOR THE GMAT

Below are the official directions from the GMAC that appear before your first data sufficiency problem on the GMAT.

DIRECTIONS: This problem consists of a question and two statements, labeled (1) and (2), in which certain data are given. You have to decide whether the data given in the statements are sufficient for answering the question. Using the data given in the statements plus your knowledge of mathematics and everyday facts (such as the number of days in July or the meaning of counterclockwise), you must indicate whether:

A. Statement (1) ALONE is sufficient, but statement (2) alone is not sufficient to answer the question asked;
B. Statement (2) ALONE is sufficient, but statement (1) alone is not sufficient to answer the question asked;
C. BOTH statements (1) and (2) TOGETHER are sufficient to answer the question asked, but NEITHER statement ALONE is sufficient;
D. EACH statement ALONE is sufficient to answer the question asked;
E. Statements (1) and (2) TOGETHER are NOT sufficient to answer the question asked, and additional data specific to the problem are needed.

Numbers: All numbers used are real numbers.

Figures: A figure accompanying a data sufficiency problem will conform to the information given in the question but will not necessarily conform to the additional information in statements (1) and (2).

Lines shown as straight can be assumed to be straight, and lines that appear jagged can also be assumed to be straight.

You may assume that positions of points, angles, regions, etc., exist in the order shown and that angle measures are greater than zero.

All figures lie in a plane unless otherwise indicated.

Note: If the data sufficiency problem asks you for the value of a quantity, the data given in the statements are sufficient only when it is possible to determine exactly one numerical value for the quantity.

DATA SUFFICIENCY STRATEGY, METHODS, AND TACTICS

We will cover several comprehensive strategies and tools for conquering the GMAT data sufficiency section. Below is a summary of what we will explore in more detail in the data sufficiency chapter.

1. **INVEST UP FRONT, AND MAKE IT COUNT.**
   - Avoid misreading the question and statements
   - Understand the macroquestion, and know what data sufficiency type it is
   - Determine what you know, want, and need.

2. **MANAGE THE INFORMATION IN A STRATEGIC AND TIMELY WAY**
   - Every statement implies something.
   - Know what you *know,* both direct and implied.
   - Avoid making assumptions.
   - Do not carry information from statement 1 into statement 2.

3. **LEVERAGE THE CONSTRUCT TO YOUR ADVANTAGE.**
   - Do not do calculations unless you have to.
   - Start with the easier statement.
   - Statements 1 and 2 never contradict.
   - Determine sufficiency by proving insufficiency.

4. **DON'T LET THE GAME FOOL YOU.**
   - The tests put the same info in each statement.
   - Do not forget that "no" can mean sufficient.
   - Watch out for the easy C.
   - When the tests asks for $a + b$, you do not need individual values.

5. **USE YOUR KNOWLEDGE OF GMAT THEORY, STRATEGIES, AND METHODOLOGIES TO SIMPLIFY.**
   - Manipulate the equations.
   - You always have your two BFF's (algebra and number properties).
   - Do not forget about 0 (zero).
   - Pick numbers.

Arithmetic | 5

The best way to deal with math is to have fun with it. One of the reasons why the quantitative section proves challenging for students is that they likely have not done this kind of math in several years. If you do a practice test and score less than 25% on the quantitative section, you are probably missing many fundamental math skills. Even if you score above the 80th percentile, you may still have some gaps in basic definitions. Regardless, know that the math concepts on the GMAT are mostly grade 11 level or earlier. You have already "been there, done that" with success. Now you can do it again and hopefully have fun in the process. This section will introduce you to the basic definitions and arithmetic fundamentals that you need for your GMAT quantitative journey.

ARITHMETIC DEFINITIONS AND OPERATIONS

INTEGER: Any whole number that is not a fraction or decimal. It can be positive or negative. For example, –1200, –43, –2, –1, 0, 1, 2, 28, and 1462 are integers, and –0.6, $\frac{1}{2}$, and π are not integers.

EVEN INTEGER: Any integer that, when divided by 2, gives you another integer. For example, –4, –2, 0, 2, 4, 6, 8, and 10 are even integers.

ODD INTEGER: Any integer that, when divided by 2, gives you a noninteger. For example, –3, –1, 1, 3, 5, and 7 are odd integers.

REAL NUMBER: Any number on the number line. This includes (but is not limited to) positives and negatives, integers, rational and irrational numbers, roots, and π (pi). For example, –4.5, $-\frac{1}{3}$, 0, 2, $\frac{7}{37}$, $\sqrt{139}$, and $3.2 \cdot 10^{87}$ are real numbers. The only numbers that are not real are called complex or imaginary numbers (e.g. $\sqrt{-1}$), and they are not tested on the GMAT.

DIVISOR OR FACTOR: For an integer N, the divisor is a positive integer that can divide into N without creating a remainder. For example, 1, 2, 3, 4, 6, and 12 are divisors of 12 while 0, 1.5, 5, and 10 are not divisors of 12.

MULTIPLE: A multiple of integer N results from multiplying N with another integer. For example, –7, 0, 7, 140, and 28,007 are multiples of 7 while –5, 1, 8, 139, and 28,005 are not.

PRIME NUMBER: An integer that is divisible by **only** itself and 1. Prime numbers have exactly 2 factors. For example, 2, 3, 5, 7, 29, and 31 are prime numbers while 4, 10, 15, and 35 are not prime numbers. Note that 0 and 1 are not prime numbers. Note also that 2 is the smallest prime number and the **only** even prime number.

DIVISION: If we look at the simple expression $\frac{7}{3} = 2$, r1, we find several terms used in division: 3 is the **divisor**, 2 is the **quotient**, 7 is the **dividend**, and 1 is the **remainder**.

STRATEGIES FOR CALCULATION SHORTCUTS

Test takers often make computational errors on the GMAT. You are expected to know all aspects of mathematical calculations and operations including addition, subtraction, multiplication, and division of integers, decimals, and fractions. You also have to do these computations quickly and efficiently but without sacrificing accuracy. The good news is that most GMAT quantitative questions require a conceptual approach with little need for calculations. Still, it is important that you master the beginner concepts.

Calculation Shortcuts

Many students have trouble with time management. Although most questions in the GMAT math section require few calculations, you can expect some. These provide you with an opportunity to save time by employing shortcuts. The seconds that you shave off each calculation will add up to minutes of extra time that you can apply to the harder questions.

For example, if you can reduce your average time per question by even 20 seconds, you will save $37 • 20 = 740$ seconds $= 12\frac{1}{3}$ minutes saved on the quantitative section!

MULTIPLICATION TABLES: To save time, you should **memorize** the classic times table.

x	1	2	3	4	5	6	7	8	9	10
1	1	2	3	4	5	6	7	8	9	10
2	2	4	6	8	10	12	14	16	18	20
3	3	6	9	12	15	18	21	24	27	30
4	4	8	12	16	20	24	28	32	36	40
5	5	10	15	20	25	30	35	40	45	50
6	6	12	18	24	30	36	42	48	54	60
7	7	14	21	28	35	42	49	56	63	70
8	8	16	24	32	40	48	56	64	72	80
9	9	18	27	36	45	54	63	72	81	90
10	10	20	30	40	50	60	70	80	90	100

You should also **memorize** these commonly seen multiples.

Perfect Squares		Powers of 2	Cubes and Fourths
$1^2 = 1$	$11^2 = 121$	$2^3 = 8$	$3^3 = 27$
$2^2 = 4$	$12^2 = 144$	$2^4 = 16$	$3^4 = 81$
$3^2 = 9$	$13^2 = 169$	$2^5 = 32$	$4^3 = 64$
$4^2 = 16$	$14^2 = 196$	$2^6 = 64$	$4^4 = 256$
$5^2 = 25$	$15^2 = 225$	$2^7 = 128$	$5^3 = 125$
$6^2 = 36$	$20^2 = 400$	$2^8 = 256$	$5^4 = 625$
$7^2 = 49$	$25^2 = 625$	$2^9 = 512$	$6^3 = 216$
$8^2 = 64$		$2^{10} = 1024$	
$9^2 = 81$			
$10^2 = 100$			

Multiplying and Dividing Larger Numbers

Remember that the mathematical operations on the GMAT are generally clean. That is, you will not be expected to manipulate complicated numbers. Instead, the numbers can usually be broken down for simpler computations. You can also use certain tricks to help you do the math in your head.

What is 32 • 15?

Solution: You can break this down to 30 • 15 = 450 plus 2 • 15 = 30 and add them together to get 480. You can also break this down to 32 • 10 = 320 plus 32 • 5 = 160 and add them together to get 480. Note that 32 • 5 is half of 32 × 10.

What is 651 ÷ 7?

Solution: To break this down, think of the multiple of 7 closest to 651 that you can quickly figure out in your head. In this case, 7 × 90 = 630. What is left over is 21 = 7 • 3. Therefore, the answer will be 90 + 3 = 93.

Simplify when you can: Look to simplify mathematical expressions whether at the beginning, middle, or end of a calculation.

$$144x = \frac{12y}{5}$$

Simplification: Instead of multiplying 5 • 144, divide 12 out of both sides to get $12x = \frac{y}{5}$, which simplifies to $y = 60x$.

Estimate where you can: Sometimes the answer choices are such that you don't need to calculate everything, you can just estimate.

701 • 52

The correct answer is going to be just a little bit more than 700 × 50 = 35,000, so look for that value among the choices. Furthermore, we know the correct answer will have a unit digit of 2 due to properties of numbers (discussed later in this book).

LEVERAGE FRACTIONS: Since you don't have a calculator, many decimal and percent calculations are much easier when you use fractions.

33.3% of 24 multiplied by 0.25 becomes $\frac{1}{3} \cdot 24 \cdot \frac{1}{4} = \frac{24}{12} = 2.$

FRACTIONS

In GMAT math, using fractions is especially important since no calculators are allowed. A fraction is made up of 2 numbers: the numerator divided by the denominator.

$$\frac{\text{numerator}}{\text{denominator}}$$

Definitions and Properties

PROPER FRACTION: When the numerator is less than the denominator. For example, $\frac{1}{2}, \frac{1}{4}, \frac{5}{13}$, and $\frac{15}{114}$.

IMPROPER FRACTION: When the numerator is greater than the denominator. For example, $\frac{2}{1}, \frac{5}{4}, \frac{13}{5}$, and $\frac{114}{15}$.

MIXED NUMBER: When a whole number and a fraction are combined. For example, $2\frac{1}{2}, 3\frac{3}{4}$, and $7\frac{1}{3}$.

A fraction cannot have 0 as a denominator because this would make the number undefined. Integers can be expressed as fractions. For example, $12 = \frac{12}{1}$ and $5 = \frac{5}{1}$.

Fraction Operations

Addition and Subtraction

Fractions need to have the same or common denominator. You can multiply all the denominators together to find a common denominator. Instead, you can find the least common multiple (LCM) for all denominators, which is sometimes easier depending on the complexity of your calculations.

$$\frac{1}{2} + \frac{1}{8} - \frac{1}{5}$$

In this case, the common denominator is $2 \cdot 8 \cdot 5 = 80$. However, you may notice that the least common denominator is 40, so let's use that.

$$\frac{20}{40} + \frac{5}{40} - \frac{8}{40} = \frac{(20+5-8)}{40} = \frac{17}{40}$$

Multiplication and Division

When multiplying 2 fractions, multiply the two numerators on top and then the two denominators on the bottom. When dividing 2 fractions, convert the equation to a multiplication problem by flipping the 2nd fraction.

$$\frac{3}{4} \cdot \frac{2}{7} = \frac{(3 \cdot 2)}{(4 \cdot 7)} = \frac{6}{28} = \frac{3}{14}$$

$$\frac{3}{4} \div \frac{2}{7} = \frac{3}{4} \cdot \frac{7}{2} = \frac{(3 \cdot 7)}{(4 \cdot 2)} = \frac{21}{8}$$

Fraction Conversions

On the GMAT, you will often need to convert decimals or percents into fractions. You will also need to convert fractions from one form to another.

$$225\% = 2.25 = 2\frac{1}{4} = \frac{9}{4}$$

All of these numbers are expressing similar values.

Converting Mixed Numbers

The following diagram shows the basic process.

$$3 \xleftrightarrow[\text{multiply}]{\text{add}} \frac{3}{5} \qquad 3\frac{3}{5} = \frac{18}{5}, \text{ but how?}$$

1. Multiply the denominator by the integer of the fraction: $5 \cdot 3 = 15$.
2. Add this result to the numerator: $15 + 3 = 18$.

3. Set this result above the numerator: $\frac{18}{5}$.

Converting Decimals

Each fraction is a division problem, one number divided by another or one numerator divided by a denominator. The GMAT is not going to give you very complicated decimals that require conversion. However, learning to convert either way is helpful in calculations. So it's much easier simply to **memorize** the most commonly occurring decimal/fraction equivalents. Some of the following are approximations.

$\frac{1}{5} = 0.5$ $\frac{1}{6} = 0.167$ $\frac{4}{9} = 0.444$

$\frac{1}{3} = 0.333$ $\frac{5}{6} = 0.833$ $\frac{5}{9} = 0.555$

$\frac{2}{3} = 0.666$ $\frac{1}{7} = 0.143$ $\frac{7}{9} = 0.777$

$\frac{1}{4} = 0.25$ $\frac{1}{8} = 0.125$ $\frac{8}{9} = 0.888$

$\frac{3}{4} = 0.75$ $\frac{3}{8} = 0.375$ $\frac{1}{10} = 0.1$

$\frac{1}{5} = 0.2$ $\frac{5}{8} = 0.625$ $\frac{3}{10} = 0.3$

$\frac{2}{5} = 0.4$ $\frac{7}{8} = 0.875$ $\frac{7}{10} = 0.7$

$\frac{3}{5} = 0.6$ $\frac{1}{9} = 0.111$ $\frac{9}{10} = 0.9$

$\frac{4}{5} = 0.8$ $\frac{2}{9} = 0.222$ $\frac{1}{11} = 0.0909$

Note that we left out such fractions as $\frac{2}{6}$ or $\frac{4}{10}$ because they reduce to $\frac{1}{3}$ and $\frac{2}{5}$, respectively. We also didn't include all of the sevenths as you will likely need only the first $\frac{1}{7}$ fraction.

Reducing Fractions

To simplify your calculations, you will often have to reduce a fraction. A fraction is reduced to its lowest term when the numerator and denominator have no common factors.

$$\frac{1000}{1200} = \frac{10}{12} = \frac{5}{6}$$

The 5 and 6 have no common factors, so you cannot reduce further.

The key to reducing fractions with large numbers is to find large common factors. In the example above, we could have divided by 2 a few times, but that would've taken more time. Instead, we divided by 100 right away to save time.

If you aren't sure if there are any common factors, you can either break down each number into prime factors or memorize and use divisibility rules. Here is a list of the most common divisibility rules.

DIVISIBILITY RULES FOR NUMBERS

Number	Divisibility Rule	Example
2	The number is even	108 is even, 108 = 54 • 2
3	The sum of the digits is divisible by 3	108, sum of digits is 1 + 0 + 8 = 9, which is a multiple of 3, 108 = 3 • 36
4	The last 2 digits of the number are divisible by 4	108, last 2 digits are 08, which are divisible by 4, 108 = 4 • 27
5	The last digit of the number is either a 0 or a 5	1050 ends with a 5, 1050 = 5 • 210
7	Take the last digit of the number, double it, and then subtract it from the rest of the digits of the original number; if the result is divisible by 7, the original number is divisible by 7	1050, last digit is 0, double it we get 0, subtract that from the rest of the digits, we get 105 – 0 = 105, since 105 = 7 • 15, then 1050 is divisible by 7, 1050 = 7 • 150
10	The last digit of the number is a 0	1050, last digit Is 0, 1050 = 10 • 105
11	Take the difference between sums of alternate digits; if the result is divisible by 11, the original number is divisible by 11	4,862, we get 4 + 6 = 10 and 8 + 2 = 10; 10 – 10 = 0, which is divisible by 11; so 4,862 = 11 • 442
25	The last 2 digits of the number are divisible by 25	1050, last digits are divisible by 25, 1050 = 25 • 42

Another shortcut is to find the closest multiple that is easy to calculate. For an awkward number like 7, this works nicely. For example, what if we want to determine if 1050 is divisible by 7? We know that 700 is divisible by 7. If we subtract 1050 – 700, we get 350. We know that 350 is a multiple of 7; therefore 1050 is divisible by 7.

DECIMALS

Although fractions are easier to use in GMAT calculations than decimals, you still need to understand decimals. Some of the most common things to remember are below.

TERMINATING DECIMAL: Any decimal that has a finite number of nonzero digits. For example, $\frac{2}{5} = 0.4$.

NONTERMINATING DECIMAL: Any decimal that has an infinite number of nonzero digits. For example, $\frac{3}{11} = 0.2727\ldots$

Addition or Subtraction of Decimals

When adding or subtracting two numbers with decimal places, make sure you line up the decimal points. You may need to add zeros to help you.

$$134.6 - 3.547 = \,?$$

$$
\begin{array}{r}
134.600 \\
- 3.\,547 \\
\hline
131.053
\end{array}
$$

Multiplication of Decimals

When multiplying two numbers with decimal places, the number of decimal places in the answer must equal the sum of all the decimal places in the numbers being multiplied. Be sure to place the number with the fewest digits on the bottom.

$$\text{What is } 1.8 \times 0.1212$$

$$
\begin{array}{r}
0.1212 \\
\times \quad 1.8 \\
\hline
9696 \\
+ \,12120 \\
\hline
0.21816
\end{array}
$$

Division of Decimals

When dividing numbers that have decimal points, always remove the decimal points before calculating. Determine which number has the most decimal places. Then move the decimal point to the right in both numbers as many times as is necessary to remove the decimal places.

$$\text{Divide } 0.0024 \text{ by } 0.008.$$

Since 0.0024 has the most decimal places, we need to move the decimal point to the right 4 times in each number. This gives us $\frac{24}{80} = 0.3$

FACTORS AND MULTIPLES

Prime Numbers

Understanding prime numbers is essential for GMAT questions that involve factorization, fractions, and properties of numbers.

PRIME NUMBER: Any positive number that has exactly 2 factors, itself and 1. For example, 2, 3, 5, 7, 11, 13, 17, 19, 23, 29, 31, 37, 41, 43, and 47 are prime numbers.

COMPOSITE NUMBERS: Numbers greater than 1 that are not prime numbers.

You should memorize all the prime numbers less than 50. They show up often on the GMAT and this will save you time.

If a number is not prime, it can be expressed as a multiple of 2 or more prime factors.

$$30 = 2 \cdot 3 \cdot 5.$$

Factor (or Divisor)

FACTOR: A positive integer that can be evenly divided into another integer, N, resulting in another integer.

30 has the factors 1, 2, 3, 5, 6, 10, 15, and 30.

Factors are always positive. Remember that 1 is a factor of all integers and 0 is never a factor.

The quickest way to determine the factors of a number, whether prime factors or all the factors, is to use a factor tree.

[30 broken down into 6, 5 and then the 6 broken down into 2, 3]

[280 broken down into 14, 20, then 7, 2 and 5, 2, 2, then 7, 2, 2, 5, 2]

When you factor a number, first try to break it down into factor pairs that are close to the square root. Note that the 280 could have been broken down into 140 • 2, but the process would have take longer.

If you are still unsure, you could check to see if 7 divides into 101, but it doesn't. There is no need to check 11 as a possible factor because $11^2 = 121$, a number greater than 101. This means that in order for 11 to be a factor of 101, it would have to be multiplied by a number smaller than itself. Since we know no other numbers less than 11 are factors except for 1, 101 must be a prime number.

GREATEST COMMON FACTOR (GCF): The largest number that divides evenly into each of the numbers given. The best way to determine the GCF is to look at the prime factors. The GCF is the product of all the prime factors the numbers have in common.

> The GCF of 42 (which is 2 • 3 • 7) and of 70 (which is 2 • 5 • 7) is 2 • 7 = 14

Multiples

MULTIPLE: A multiple of any number is that number multiplied by an integer.

> 6, 9, 12, 15 are all multiples of 3 because $3 \times 2 = 6$, $3 \times 3 = 9$, $3 \times 4 = 12$, and $3 \times 5 = 15$.

Note that if we multiply 2 and 3 to get 6, then 6 is a multiple of both 2 and 3. Conversely, 2 and 3 are factors of 6.

LEAST COMMON MULTIPLE (LCM): The smallest nonzero number that is a multiple of 2 or more given numbers. The key to finding the LCM involves prime factorization. You need to look at each individual number and make sure that the LCM includes the minimum required prime factors for each number.

> The LCM of 42 (which is 2 • 3 • 7) and of 56 (which is 2 • 2 • 2 • 7) is 2 • 2 • 2 • 3 • 7 = 168.

42 has 2, 3, and 7 as factors. 56 has 2, 2, 2 and 7 as factors. This means that the LCM must have at least one 7, one 3, but most importantly, it must have at least three 2s in order to be a multiple of 56.

PROPERTIES OF NUMBERS

Number properties determine how numbers work—how they increase, decrease, or change in value. For example, when you multiply two negative numbers, the result is a positive number. When you square a positive proper fraction, the number becomes smaller. Understanding number properties is essential for doing many GMAT questions. You will need them mostly on data sufficiency questions. However, with certain problem-solving questions, especially those that seem to require far too many calculations, you can use number properties to reduce your calculations and more quickly find a solution.

Even and Odd Integers

EVEN INTEGERS: Integers that are divisible by 2. For example, the integers $\{\ldots -6, -4, -2, 0, 2, 4, 6, \ldots\}$ form the set of even integers.

ODD INTEGERS: Integers that are not divisible by 2. For example, the integers $\{\ldots -5, -3, -1, 1, 3, 5 \ldots\}$ form the set of odd integers.

You should understand and **memorize** the following rules.

- The sum and difference of two even integers is even: $2 + 4 = 6$ and $6 - 4 = 2$.
- The sum and difference of two odd integers is even: $3 + 5 = 8$ and $5 - 3 = 2$.
- The sum and difference of an odd integer and an even integer is odd: $2 + 3 = 5$ and $5 - 2 = 3$.
- The product of two even integers is even: $2 \bullet 4 = 8$.
- The product of two odd integers is odd: $3 \bullet 5 = 15$.
- The product of an odd integer and an even integer is even: $3 \bullet 2 = 6$

Positive and Negative

Just like with odd and even numbers, positive (+) and negative (–) numbers have specific rules.

Multiplication

$(-) \bullet (+)$ or $(+) \bullet (-) = (-)$
$(-) \bullet (-) = (+)$
$(+) \bullet (+) = (+)$

Division

$(-) \div (+)$ or $(+) \div (-) = -$
$(-) \div (-) = +$
$(+) \div (+) = +$

Units Digit

As we saw in the section on decimals, the units digit of a number is the number just to the left of the decimal point and just to the right of the tens place. Understanding how the unit digit works can greatly increase your computation speed.

What is the unit digit of 6,797 • 13,473?

The GMAT does not expect you to do the long calculation. Rather, you can use properties of numbers. The first number has the unit digit 7, and the second number has the unit digit 3. Because 7 • 3 = 21, we know that the resulting number, no matter how huge it is, will end in a unit digit of 1.

Since you have already memorized your basic times table, you can calculate the unit digit for any multiple of large numbers.

PERCENTS

Understanding percent calculations will greatly increase your computation speed and minimize mindless errors. Your ability to maneuver quickly among fractions, decimals, and percents will be a key to success on test day.

Percent, Fraction, and Decimal Conversions

Percent	Fraction	Decimal
40%	$\frac{40}{100} = \frac{2}{5}$	0.4
320%	$\frac{320}{100} = \frac{16}{5}$	3.20
0.4%	$\frac{0.4}{100} = \frac{1}{250}$	0.004

"Percent" means per 100. For example, 20% means 20 per 100. Percents are used to measure or report the change in an amount. You hear it all the time in statements like "X stock rose 22% today in massive trading" or "24% of students failed that course." To determine percent increases and decreases quickly you need to know the basic formula:

$$\text{Percent change} = \left(\frac{(\text{Future value} - \text{Present value})}{(\text{Present value})} \right) \cdot 100$$

If you let *FV* mean "future value" and *PV* mean "present value" you can write the formula like:

$$\% \text{ change} = \left(\frac{(FV - PV)}{(PV)} \right) \bullet 100$$

The percent change from 12 to 15 is $\left(\frac{(15-12)}{12} \right) \bullet 100 = 25\%$.

You should also be able to calculate quickly percent increases and decreases algebraically using the formula:

Increase or decrease of a number

$$= \left(1 + \frac{(\text{percent increase or decrease})}{100} \right) \bullet (\text{The number})$$

If *x* increases by 30%, then you get $(1 + 0.3)x$ or $1.3x$.
If *x* decreases by 30%, then you get $(1 - 0.3)x$ or $0.7x$.

> Stock *x* goes up by 80% in year 1 but then decreases by 80% in year 2. By what percentage did the value of the stock change from the beginning to after year 2?

Solution: There are many ways to do this problem, but let's try using algebra.

We start at $x \rightarrow 1.8x$ after year 1 $\rightarrow (1.8) \bullet (0.2)x$ after year 2.

$1.8 = \frac{9}{5}$ and $0.2 = \frac{1}{5}$. Therefore we get $\frac{9}{5} \bullet \frac{1}{5}x = \frac{9x}{25}$, which is a decrease of $\frac{16x}{25}$ or 64%.

Another great strategy with percent questions is to pick numbers, especially 100. For this example, we would do the following.

We start with 100 $\rightarrow$ 180 after year 1 $\rightarrow$ 180 $\bullet$ 0.2 = 36 after year 2 or a 64% decrease.

Note that we would have gotten the same answer had the stock decreased first and then increased.

RATIOS

Ratio: A proportional relationship that compares two or more numbers. The ratio of x to y is written as $x : y$ or $\frac{x}{y}$, which is read as "x to y." It is a relationship of a part to a part or a part to a whole. Interpreting ratios properly is critical.

> In a GMAT class, the ratio of females to males is $\frac{1}{3}$.
> What proportion of the class is female?

Solution: Be careful when you write this out. You should get $\dfrac{\text{F:M:Total}}{1:3:4}$.

Note that we often need to keep track of the total of all the parts in order to interpret the question properly. In this case, the sum of the parts is 4. The proportion is now $\frac{1}{4}$ and not $\frac{1}{3}$ as many students might think.

> If the ratio of dogs, cats, and mice in a pet store is
> $\dfrac{\text{D:C:M:Total}}{2:3:5:10}$, then the percentage of dogs in the store
> would be $\frac{2}{10} = 20\%$.

ARITHMETIC: TARGETED REVIEW QUESTIONS

1. If y is an integer, is $\dfrac{3^y}{10,000} > 1$?

   (1) $\dfrac{100}{3^y} < 0.01$

   (2) $\sqrt{3^y} = 243$

2. At a business superstore, Stephen spends $\frac{1}{3}$ of his money on software, $\frac{1}{7}$ on accessories, and $\frac{1}{10.5}$ on paper products. If he spends the remaining \$90 on gift cards, how much did Stephen spend at the business superstore?

   (A) \$90
   (B) \$110
   (C) \$140
   (D) \$210
   (E) \$260

3. If r and s are positive integers and $900s = r^3$, which of the following must be an integer?:

   I. $\dfrac{s}{\left(3 \bullet 5 \bullet \left(2^3\right)\right)}$

   II. $\dfrac{s}{\left(\left(3^2\right) \bullet 5 \bullet 2^2\right)}$

   III. $\dfrac{s}{\left(3 \bullet 2^2 \bullet \left(5^2\right)\right)}$

   (A) I only
   (B) II only
   (C) II and III only
   (D) I and II only
   (E) None of the above

4. If x is an odd integer and y is an even integer, which of the following must be true?
   (A) y is not a factor of x.
   (B) xy is an odd integer.
   (C) x^2 is an even integer.
   (D) $y - x$ is an even integer.
   (E) x is a prime number.

5. What is the tens digit of the 2-digit positive integer x?
   (1) x divided by 20 has a remainder of 17.
   (2) x divided by 11 has a remainder of 0.

ANSWER KEY

1. **(D)**   3. **(E)**   5. **(C)**
2. **(D)**   4. **(A)**

SOLUTIONS

1. **(D)** We can manipulate the original question stem to ask if $3^y > 10{,}000$.

    Statement 1 can be manipulated by multiplying both sides by 3^y, which gives us $100 < 0.01(3^y) \rightarrow$ Multiply both sides by 100 to get $10{,}000 < 3^y$, which is exactly what the question is asking for. *Sufficient*

    Statement 2 tell us that if we square both sides, we will get $3^y = 243^2 = (3^5)^2$, which means we can solve for y and that $y = 10$. *Sufficient*

Each statement alone is sufficient.

2. **(D)** This is a fraction question. The key to doing this quickly is to recognize the common denominator. We get $\frac{1}{3} + \frac{1}{7} + \frac{1}{10.5}$ $= \frac{7}{21} + \frac{3}{21} + \frac{2}{21} = 12/21$ of the total. The rest of the amount, \$90, represents $\frac{9}{21}$ of the total. Therefore the total is $\$90 \cdot \frac{21}{9} = \$210$.

3. **(E)** This question tests your knowledge of prime factors. If we break down $900s$, we get

$$90 \cdot 10 \cdot s = 9 \cdot 10 \cdot 5 \cdot 2 \cdot s = 3 \cdot 3 \cdot 5 \cdot 2 \cdot 5 \cdot 2 \cdot s = r^3$$

    Since s and r are positive integers and $r^3 = 2 \cdot 2 \cdot 3 \cdot 3 \cdot 5 \cdot 5$, then each side of the expression is a perfect cube. Therefore, s must have minimally $2 \cdot 3 \cdot 5$ as factors in order for the expression to remain a cube. It could, for example, have $2 \cdot 3 \cdot 5 \cdot 7^3$ as factors because it is still a cube. However, we should look at the least possible value. If s was $2 \cdot 3 \cdot 5$, then none of the three expressions given would be an integer.

4. **(A)** One way to solve this properties of numbers question is to pick numbers to prove four of the statements false. Alternatively, you should be able to leverage your thorough understanding of number properties, especially since you should know the theory anyway.

    (A) If y is even, it cannot be a factor of x, which is odd. True
    (B) Odd $\cdot$ even is always even, just like $3 \cdot 2 = 6$. False
    (C) An odd number squared is still odd, e.g., $3^2 = 9$. False
    (D) Even $-$ odd $=$ odd, just like $6 - 3 = 3$. False
    (E) Most prime numbers are odd, except for 2. Regardless, if x is odd, it is not necessarily a prime number. False

5. **(C)** Start with what we **know**—x is a positive integer and has 2 digits. Then determine what we **want**—the tens digit and only one possible answer. Let's look at the statements to see if they give us what we **need**.

Statement 1 tells us that x could be 17, 37, 57, 77, or 97. 17 is here because when we divide 17 by 20, we get 0 and a remainder of 17. Regardless, we have multiple values for x. *Insufficient*

Statement 2 tells us that x could be any 2 digit multiple of 11, which means x = 11, 22, 33, 44, 55, 66, 77, 88 or 99. *Insufficient*

When we combine the statements, we now know that x could only be 77. *Sufficient*

Both statements together are sufficient.

Algebra

6

Often the biggest obstacle in algebra is translating word problems. Here are some of the common key words that you might see on the GMAT.

ALGEBRA TRANSLATION KEYWORDS

Addition	Increased by, more than, combined, together, total of, sum, added to
Subtraction	Decreased by, minus, less, difference between/ of, less than, fewer than
Multiplication	Of, times, multiplied by, product of, increased/ decreased by a factor of
Division	Per, out of, ratio of, quotient of, percent (divide by 100)
Equals	Is, are, was, were, will be, gives, yields, sold for

"Billy is three years older than twice Megan's age 5 years ago" translates to

$$B - 3 = 2(M - 5)$$

A rope 40 cm in length is cut into two pieces, a short piece and a long piece. The short piece is 8 cm shorter than the long piece. What is the length of the long piece?

Solution: We could let the variables be x and y or, better, s and l. However, the simplest way is to have just one variable, which we'll call L for the long piece of rope. The short piece of rope we can call $40 - L$. By using the 8 cm difference, we get:

$$L - 8 = 40 - L \rightarrow 2L = 48 \rightarrow L = 24 \text{ cm}$$

ABSOLUTE VALUE

The absolute value of a number is its value without regard to its sign. Another way to look at it is that the absolute value of a number is the measure of its distance to 0 on the number line.

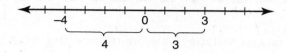

The absolute value of –4, denoted as |–4|, is 4. Similarly, |+3| = 3.

Strategies for Absolute Value

- When given multiple absolute value parentheses, start inward and work outward.

$$| 6 - (|-10|) | = | 6 - 10 | = | -4 | = 4$$

- Solving an equation with absolute value requires you to consider two cases. In case 1, you open the bracket normally and set everything equal. In case 2, you open the bracket and change the expression in the absolute value brackets to its negative form. (Do not change the side of the equation that isn't in absolute value brackets).

$$| x - 10 | = 20, \text{ solve for } x$$

Case 1: $x - 10 = 20$ $\rightarrow$ $x = 10$
Case 2: $-(x - 10) = 20$ $\rightarrow$ $-x + 10 = 20 \rightarrow x = -10$

- To avoid confusion when you have absolute values on both sides, try breaking down the equation by looking at the left-hand side (LHS) and the right-hand side (RHS) separately.

$$| x | = - | -x |, \text{ solve for } x$$

Try picking numbers. If $x = 2$, LHS = 2, RHS = –2. Doesn't work!
If $x = -2$, LHS = 2, RHS = –2. Doesn't work!
Don't forget about zero! If $x = 0$, LHS = 0, RHS = 0. This works. Therefore, $x = 0$.

Later on, we will see how to solve absolute value inequality problems.

EXPONENTS AND ROOTS

Exponents are involved in a large portion of the algebra questions on the GMAT. Let's look at the most common definitions and rules for exponents.

$$x^y = 16$$

In the above expression, x is called the **base** and y is the **exponent**. Sometimes we say "x to the **power** of y." In this particular example, if both x and y are positive integers, then either $x = 2$ and $y = 4$ or $x = 4$ and $y = 2$.

BREAKING DOWN EXPONENTS

Exponent	Expanded Expression	Base	Exponent	Value
5^3	$5 \cdot 5 \cdot 5$	5	3	125
2^6	$2 \cdot 2 \cdot 2 \cdot 2 \cdot 2 \cdot 2$	2	6	64
10^9	$10 \cdot 10 \cdot 10 \cdot 10 \cdot 10 \cdot 10 \cdot$ $10 \cdot 10 \cdot 10$	10	9	1,000,000,000

EXPONENT RULES

$x^0 = 1$	Any number to the zero power equals 1.
$x^1 = x$	Any number to the 1 power equals that number.
$x^{-n} = \dfrac{1}{x^n}$ $4^{-2} = \dfrac{1}{4^2} = \dfrac{1}{16}$	A negative exponent changes sign when you move it between the numerator and denominator.
$2^4 \cdot 2^2 = 2^6$ $2^{(4 + 2)} = 2^6$	Add the exponents when multiplying two powers of the same base.
$2^6 \div 2^2 = 2^4$ $2^{(6 - 2)} = 2^4$	Subtract the exponents when dividing a power by another power of the same base.
$(2^2)^3 = 2^6$ $2^{(2 \times 3)} = 2^6$	Multiply the exponents when you raise a power to a power via parentheses.
$6^3 = (2 \cdot 3)^3 = 2^3 \cdot 3^3$	The exponent can be distributed among the factors of a base.
$\left(\dfrac{10}{2}\right)^3 = \dfrac{10^3}{2^3} = 5^3$	When a fraction is raised to a certain power, you can distribute the exponent to the numbers or variables in the fraction.

PROPERTIES OF EXPONENTS

$\left(\dfrac{1}{3}\right)^2 = \dfrac{1}{9}$ $\left(\dfrac{2}{3}\right)^3 = \dfrac{8}{27}$	When you apply any positive exponent to a positive proper fraction, the number becomes smaller. In this case, $x^2 < x$.
$(-3)^2 = 9$ $(-2)^6 = 64$	Any positive or negative number with an even exponent is always positive. In this case, $x^2 > 0$ and $x^6 > 0$
$(-3)^3 = -27$ $(3)^3 = 27$	Any positive or negative number with an odd exponent could be positive or negative depending on the sign of the original number.
$x^3 = x$ $x^2 = x$	When $x = 0$ and x is the base, raising it to any power always results in 0, which is neither positive nor negative.
$2^1 = \underline{2},$ $\quad 2^5 = 3\underline{2},$ $2^2 = \underline{4},$ $\quad 2^6 = 6\underline{4}$ $2^3 = \underline{8},$ $\quad 2^7 = 12\underline{8}$ $2^4 = 1\underline{6},$ $\quad 2^8 = 25\underline{6}$	There is a repeating pattern for all unit digits raised to a certain power. For powers of 2, the unit digit pattern is 2, 4, 8, and 6 repeating. For powers of 3, the unit digit pattern is 3, 9, 7, and 1 repeating and so on.

Roots are similar to exponents because they can be expressed in the same way. Therefore, the rules will also apply the same way to roots as they do to exponents.

$$\sqrt{x} = x^{\frac{1}{2}}$$

In the above equation, 1 represents the exponent of x and the 2 represents the root of x.

You should be able to move back and forth between the radical form and the exponent form.

$$x^{\frac{2}{3}} = \sqrt[3]{x^2}$$

Note that by definition if no number is in the root, a square root is implied. Secondly, the root sign implies a positive value.

Multiplication and Division of Roots

When you multiply and divide roots, you can treat them like regular numbers.

$$\sqrt{2} \cdot \sqrt{3} = \sqrt{6} \quad \text{and} \quad \frac{\sqrt{10}}{\sqrt{2}} = \sqrt{5}$$

$$\sqrt{\left(\frac{x}{y}\right)} = \frac{\sqrt{x}}{\sqrt{y}} \quad \text{and} \quad \sqrt{(x \cdot y)} = \sqrt{x} \cdot \sqrt{y}$$

Addition and Subtraction of Roots

When you add or subtract roots, you generally need to remember two things:

1. As with variables and with adding or subtracting like terms, you can only add or subtract like roots.

$$\sqrt{2} + 3\sqrt{2} + 4\sqrt{3} - \sqrt{3} = 4\sqrt{2} + 3\sqrt{3}.$$

You cannot simplify this any further.

2. Certain roots can be reduced, which can help you find like roots. The key is to find a factor that is a perfect square and then take it out of the root.

$$\sqrt{2} + \sqrt{8} + \sqrt{98} = \sqrt{2} + \sqrt{4 \cdot 2} + \sqrt{49 \cdot 2} = \sqrt{2} + 2\sqrt{2} + 7\sqrt{2} = 10\sqrt{2}$$

You should **memorize** the most commonly occurring roots that can be reduced.

$\sqrt{8} = 2\sqrt{2}$	$\sqrt{12} = 2\sqrt{3}$	$\sqrt{20} = 2\sqrt{5}$	$\sqrt{27} = 3\sqrt{3}$
$\sqrt{50} = 5\sqrt{2}$	$\sqrt{75} = 5\sqrt{3}$	$\sqrt{98} = 7\sqrt{2}$	

ROOTS IN A DENOMINATOR: It is considered bad form to have roots in a denominator. Therefore, you may need to remove the root by multiplying the numerator and the denominator by the root found in the denominator. Example: $\dfrac{8}{\sqrt{2}}$ is not in standard form, so we need to remove the root in the denominator.

$$\frac{8}{\sqrt{2}} \cdot \frac{\sqrt{2}}{\sqrt{2}} = \frac{8\sqrt{2}}{2} = 4\sqrt{2}$$

PROPERTIES OF ROOTS

$\sqrt{16} = 4$ $\sqrt[6]{64} = 2$	All even roots of positive numbers result in another positive number.
	You cannot take an even root of a negative number. For example, you cannot solve $\sqrt{-16}$.
$\sqrt[3]{-27} = -3$ $\sqrt[5]{32} = 2$	Odd roots of real numbers can be negative, positive, or zero.
$\sqrt{\left(\dfrac{4}{9}\right)} = 2/3$ $\sqrt{25} = 5$	When you take the square root of a number between 0 and 1, the result is greater than the original number. When you take the square root of a number greater than 1, the result is less than the original number.

ALGEBRAIC CALCULATIONS AND OPERATIONS

Not only must you be very comfortable working with algebraic equations, expressions, and inequalities, you need to be quick with your calculations and flexible in applying the rules. These rules include simplifying, factoring, expanding, combining like terms, eliminating variables, and so on.

Order of Operations

The order in which you carry out calculations can be critically important in reaching the correct answer. For example, $3 + 5 \cdot 2$ may, at first glance, be seen as equivalent to $8 \cdot 2$. However, it is not. The correct simplification is $3 + 10$. PEMDAS is a useful acronym for remembering the correct order.

1. **P**arentheses: Work from the innermost to the outermost parentheses
2. **E**xponents: Work from left to right.
3. **M**ultiplication and **D**ivision: Work from left to right.
4. **A**ddition and **S**ubtraction: Work from left to right

$$3 + 4^2 \cdot 2 - 10 \div (5 - 3) = 3 + 16 \cdot 2 - 10 \div 2 = 3 + 32 - 5 = 30$$

Parentheses

The biggest challenge for test takers when dealing with parentheses occurs when you open them up. You might forget to change the sign or multiply an outside number by all of the terms in a set of parentheses.

Rule: $a(b + c) = ab + ac$

$$-2(x + (-6)) = -2x + 12$$

Rule: $(a + b)(c + d) = ac + ad + bc + bd$

You can use **FOIL** (**F**irst, **O**utside, **I**nside, **L**ast) to make sure you multiply every term of an expression in parentheses with every other term in the other set of parentheses.

$$(2x + y) \cdot (x - 3) = 2x^2 - 6x + xy - 3y$$

ALGEBRAIC EQUATIONS

There are three main types of algebraic equations.

1. **LINEAR EQUATIONS WITH ONE VARIABLE:** The variable has an exponent of degree 1.

2. **LINEAR EQUATIONS WITH MULTIPLE VARIABLES:** Every variable has an exponent of degree 1.

3. **QUADRATIC EQUATIONS:** One or more variables has an exponent of degree 2.

Linear Equations with One Variable

The following example shows the algebraic equation in its most basic form:

$$x + 7 = 3$$

To solve these equations, you generally need to isolate the variable. You follow several general steps to do this.

1. Eliminate any parentheses
2. Get rid of any fractions or denominators
3. Put all numbers on one side and all terms with the variable on the other side
4. Combine like terms
5. Isolate the variable by dividing by its coefficient (if there is one).

Solve for the expression $x + 2(x - 3) = \dfrac{2(x+1)}{3} - 4x$

Solution:

$x + 2x - 6 = \dfrac{2x}{3} + \dfrac{2}{3} - 4x$	(Open the parentheses)
$3x + 6x - 18 = 2x + 2 - 12x$	(Multiply both sides by 3 to eliminate the denominator)
$9x - 2x + 12x = 2 + 18$	(Gather all terms with the x variable on one side and all numbers on the other side)
$19x = 20$	(Combine like terms)
$x = \dfrac{20}{19}$	(Divide by 19 and solve)

Linear Equations with Multiple Variables

Most GMAT problems have more than one variable. When you have two variables in algebra, you need to have more than one equation in order to solve. The general rule is that you need N distinct equations for N unknowns. Therefore, if you have to solve for 5 variables, then you need 5 equations. This concept is often tested in data sufficiency type questions.

There are two ways to solve multiple equations, **substitution** and **addition/subtraction**.

Substitution Method

1. Express one variable in terms of everything else in the equation.
2. Plug this expression into one of the other equations.
3. Keep repeating until you solve for one of the variables. You can then substitute the solved value into the other equations. If possible, substitute into one of the original equations.

$$(1)\ x + y = 6$$
$$(2)\ x - y = 2$$

Solution:

Express equation (1) in terms of x	$\rightarrow$ (3) $x = 6 - y$
Substitute equation (3) into equation (2)	$\rightarrow$ $(6 - y) - y = 2$
Solve for the variable y	$\rightarrow$ $6 - 2y = 2$, $-2y = -4$, $y = 2$
Substitute $y = 2$ into equation (1)	$\rightarrow$ $x + 2 = 6$, $x = 4$

Addition/Subtraction Method

1. Line up the equations on top of each other.
2. Look for a variable to eliminate by adding or subtracting the two equations. You may have to multiply one or more equations by a constant number so that the variables will have the same coefficient but with opposite signs.
3. Add or subtract the equations so that the variables with the same coefficients will cancel out.
4. Solve for the variable that remains.
5. Substitute the solved variable back into one of the original equations if possible and repeat until you have all the variables.

$$(1)\ x + y = 6$$
$$(2)\ x - y = 2$$

Solution: This is the same question as the one we used in the substitution method. Since the variables all have coefficients of 1, we can easily eliminate either x or y. Let us add and so we get

$$2x + 0 = 8, \text{ therefore } x = 4$$

Substitute back into equation (1) to get $y = 2$.

Quadratic Equations

A quadratic equation takes the form $ax^2 + bx + c = 0$, where a, b, and c are numbers of any value.

These equations are solved by **factoring**, where you break apart the equation into two or more separate parts or factors.

$x^2 + 7x + 12 = 0$ factors into $(x + 3)(x + 4) = 0$, which means that $x = -3$ and $x = -4$.

In the previous example, -3 and -4 are also known as the **roots** of the equation. When you plug them into the original equation, the left side will equal zero. Although this equation has two distinct roots, some quadratic equations have only one distinct root. For example, $x^2 + 6x + 9 = 0$ breaks down into $(x + 3)^2 = 0$. Therefore the only root is $x = -3$.

You can use three ways to solve a quadratic equation on the GMAT:

1. **You can factor the equation by inspection**, which is likely the preferred and quickest way.
2. **You can plug in the answer choices**, which is not preferable as it is generally time consuming.
3. **You can use the quadratic equation**, but do this only as a last resort.

How to Factor

How did we solve the equation $x^2 + 7x + 12 = 0$ in the example above so quickly by inspection? The basic idea is to look for a pair of factors of $+12$ (because the number could be negative) that will add up to $+7$. The factors of 12 are 1 and 12, 2 and 6, 3 and 4. Note that we look at the factors in pairs. In this method, 3 and 4 stand out. We can then set up the factors as $(x + 3)$ and $(x + 4)$.

Quadratic Formula

The **quadratic formula** is $x = \dfrac{-b \pm \sqrt{b^2 - 4ac}}{2a}$ for any equation in the form $ax^2 + bx + c = 0$. In most quadratic equations, x usually has two solutions. Note that if $b^2 - 4ac < 0$, there is no real solution and if $b^2 - 4ac = 0$, the equation has only one solution. Sometimes you should check the value of $b^2 - 4ac$ before solving the entire formula. This check may solve you time.

Algebraic Factoring

As with any algebraic expression, you need to move back and forth between expanding expressions and factoring them. In other words, you can use FOIL to expand an expression and use factoring to bring the equation back to its pre-expanded form.

To help with your algebraic manipulation, you should **memorize** the 3 most common algebraic identities that are easily factored. You must be able to recognize these three factored forms and work quickly with them.

$$(a + b)^2 = (a + b)(a + b) = a^2 + 2ab + b^2$$
$$(a - b)^2 = (a - b)(a - b) = a^2 - 2ab + b^2$$
$$(a + b)(a - b) = a^2 - b^2 \quad \text{Also known as the } \textbf{difference of two}$$
squares

INEQUALITIES

Inequalities compare two statements with different values. They are very similar to typical algebraic expressions except that the equal sign (=) is replaced by several other possible symbols. There are five main types of inequalities:

x	$>$	y	x is greater than y
x	$\geq$	y	x is greater than or equal to y
x	$<$	y	x is less than y
x	$\leq$	y	x is less than or equal to y
x	$\neq$	y	x is not equal to y

Almost all of the rules for algebraic equations also apply to inequalities. Remember this key difference:

> **INEQUALITIES GOLDEN RULE**
>
> If both sides of an inequality are multiplied or divided by a negative number, then you must flip the inequality sign.

What is fascinating is that the inequalities golden rule drastically increases the difficulty level of inequalities for test takers. Most of this difficulty is just confusion about the rules and how to apply them. Note that the general rule above does not apply to addition or subtraction. So let's look at the main ways you need to address inequalities.

Addition and Subtraction of Inequalities

When you add or subtract a number to both sides of the inequality, the sign is not affected.

$$2x - 3 > x - 10$$

Subtract x from both sides and add -3 to both sides

$$x > -7$$

Note that the unknown variable and the negative number have no effect on the inequality sign.

Multiplication or Division of Inequalities

This is where the golden rule of inequalities comes into play. Remember these three tips.

1. If you multiply or divide by a positive number, there's no sign change. Treat the inequality as you would an equation.
2. If you multiply or divide by a negative number, change the direction of the inequality symbol.
3. If you multiply or divide by a variable, you need to ask the question, "Is this number positive, negative, or I don't know?" Once you confirm, then proceed according to the first two tips above.

$$\text{Is } x > y?$$

(1) $\frac{x}{y} > 1$ If this were an equation, you might try to multiply the y on both sides to get $x > y$. However, this is an inequality. You don't know if y is positive or negative. Therefore, you cannot manipulate this inequality to solve it. Insufficient

Solving Multiple Inequalities

As with equations, you can solve two or more inequalities together by adding or subtracting inequalities, or by using substitution. The key difference is that the inequality signs must be pointing in the same direction.

$x + y > 12$ and $x - y < 6$. Solve for x and y.

Solution: Set up the inequalities so that their signs are facing the same direction.

(1) $x + y > 12$

(2) $\underline{+\ \ -x + y > -6}$ (We did this by multiplying both sides by -1, thus changing the sign.)

$2y > 6 \rightarrow y > 3$ This means that $x > 9$ (via substitution into equation 1).

Inequalities with Absolute Value

The GMAT frequently increases the difficulty of problems by combining two separate concepts. Inequalities are often combined with absolute values, but the process to solve these is the same. You will again have to solve two separate cases.

$|x - 5| > 3$, solve for x

Solution: We need to look at two cases.

Case 1: $x - 5 > 3 \rightarrow x > 8$

Case 2: $-(x - 5) > 3 \rightarrow -x + 5 > 3 \rightarrow x - 5 < -3 \rightarrow x < 2$

So we get $x < 2$ or $x > 8$. If you have time, you can check numbers just to be sure.

FUNCTIONS, SYMBOLS, AND SEQUENCES

Functions are simply an alternate way to write an algebraic expression with one variable. Test takers find functions confusing because they are more abstract. A function comes in the form

$$f(x) = 2x + 3 \rightarrow \text{This is the same as saying} \rightarrow y = 2x + 3$$

The two expressions above are identical. In each case, when we have a specific value for x we simply plug it into the equation and solve. So if $x = 1$, then

$$f(1) = 2(1) + 3 = 5 \quad \text{OR} \quad y = 2(1) + 3 = 5$$

You can solve for functions in almost the same way as you solve for algebraic expressions. To illustrate further how similar they are, let's create a T-chart for a function and an equation.

$$g(x) = x^2 - 3 \rightarrow \text{which again is the same as} \rightarrow y = x^2 - 3$$

T-charts for both

$g(x)$	x
–3	6
–2	1
–1	–2
0	–3
1	–2
2	1
3	6

y	x
–3	6
–2	–1
–1	–2
0	–3
1	–2
2	1
3	6

As you can see, functions are the same as algebraic equations. Just as we would say $y = -2$ when $x = -1$ or $x = +1$, we can also say $g(-1) = -2$ or $g(1) = -2$. The **domain** of a function is the set of all possible values for the variable.

$$g(x) = \frac{\sqrt{x-3}}{x-5}$$

The variable x cannot be 5 because the denominator would be undefined. x also cannot be less than 3 because the radical would be undefined. Therefore, the domain of $g(x)$ is all values of x, as long as $x \geq 3$ and $x \neq 5$.

Function Symbol Problems

Symbol problems are challenging because of the use of unfamiliar symbols to define an expression. Despite this abstract nature, you just need to "plug and play" by inputting the values and carrying out the operations as you normally would. One effective strategy is to separate all the steps and operations with a clear and structured chart.

If the operation ¥ is defined for all a and b as the equation

$a ¥ b = \dfrac{ab}{2}$, then what is $2 ¥ (3 ¥ 4)$?

Solution: It's important to understand what the definition is. Simply put, whatever values of a and b we have, we plug them into the expression as defined. Using a chart can help here.

	a	b	$a ¥ b = \dfrac{ab}{2}$
$3 ¥ 4$	3	4	$\dfrac{3 \times 4}{2} = 6$
$2 ¥ (3 ¥ 4) = 2 ¥ 6$	2	6	$\dfrac{2 \times 6}{2} = 6$

Sequence Functions

Sequence problems are a particular kind of function question on the GMAT. In general, you are given a formula that defines the sequence, the domain, and some of the terms of the sequence. The formula is of the form: $a_n =$ (some equation with n as a variable). The terms of the sequence are: $a_1, a_2, a_3 \dots a_n$.

$a_n = n^2 - 1$, where $n > 1$. What is the value of a_5?

Solution: The quickest way to do this is to input $n = 5$ for a_5 to get $a_5 = 6^2 - 1 = 24$.

The GMAT asks 3 common types of sequence questions:

- **Sequence type 1**: Find the nth term of the sequence. (Solve by inputting values into the definition.)
- **Sequence type 2**: Find the nth term of the sequence when given two or more values for terms. (Solve using the definition to find the link.)
- **Sequence type 3**: Find the 1000th term of the sequence. (Solve by finding a pattern with the definition to figure out the far away term.)

Sequence Strategy

1. Make sure you understand the definition of the sequence.
2. Line up the terms in order vertically.

   - If you are given the value of a few terms, make sure to leave gaps for the terms that you do not know but may need to solve.
   - If you are not given any terms, try to input the first 3–5 terms of the sequence.
   - If you can't find any terms to put in, use algebraic terms.

3. Use the definition to fill in the gaps and solve.
4. If that doesn't work, try to find a pattern to help you solve the problem.
5. Make sure you do not violate any given domain.

ALGEBRA: TARGETED REVIEW QUESTIONS

1. If $3^x - 3^{x-2} = 2^3 \bullet 3^{17}$, what is x?
   - (A) 15
   - (B) 17
   - (C) 19
   - (D) 20
   - (E) 23

2. If the operation £ is defined by $q \; £ \; p = \dfrac{(q-p)}{(q+p)}$ for all positive integers q and p,

   then $3 \; £ \; (-4 \; £ \; 5)$ is
   - (A) −9
   - (B) −4.5
   - (C) −2.5
   - (D) 1.5
   - (E) 6

3. A convenience store bought an item for C dollars, then sold it for D dollars. The cost of the item was what percent of the gross profit that the convenience store realized?

   (1) $\dfrac{D}{C} - 1 = \dfrac{2}{3}$

   (2) $D - C = 8$

4. If the sequence S has 1000 terms, what is the 777th term of S?

   (1) The 4th term of S is –26.

   (2) The 977th term is 16,515, and each preceding term of S before the last is 17 less than the current term

5. If a and b are integers and $a = |b + 11| + |12 - b|$, does a equal 23?

   (1) $b < 12$

   (2) $b > -11$

ANSWER KEY

1. **(C)**   3. **(A)**   5. **(C)**
2. **(C)**   4. **(B)**

SOLUTIONS

1. **(C)** When you first look at this question, you may second-guess yourself because you're wondering why there is a 2 on the right side of the equation. The rules and tactics for exponent manipulation are the same, which are to reduce everything to a prime factor base (already done) and to factor out like terms when you see addition or subtraction. So in this question, let's take out 3^x from each term on the left-hand side

$$3^x(1 - 3^{-2}) = 3^x(1 - \frac{1}{3^2}) = 3^x(1 - \frac{1}{9}) = 3^x(\frac{8}{9}) = 3^x(\frac{2^3}{3^2})$$

Now we know where the 2^3 comes from. This gives us

$$3^x 2^3 3^{-2} = 2^3 \bullet 3^{17} \rightarrow 3^{x-2} 2^3 = 2^3 3^{17} \rightarrow \text{Thus } x - 2 = 17, x = 19.$$

2. **(C)** This is a symbol problem. The key is to make sure to structure it clearly, plug in the numbers correctly, and follow the order of operations.

$$q \pounds p = \frac{(q-p)}{(q+p)} \rightarrow \text{Thus } -4 \pounds 5 = \frac{(-4-5)}{(-4+5)} = -\frac{9}{1} = -9$$

$$3 \pounds -9 = \frac{(3-(-9))}{(3+(-9))} = \frac{(3+12)}{(3-9)} = \frac{15}{-6} = \frac{-5}{2} = -2.5.$$

3. **(A)** What we want in this question is the proportion of cost to gross profit on the item or $\frac{(D-C)}{D}$ or $1 - \frac{C}{D}$. So what we need is either 2 distinct equations or the ratio $\frac{C}{D}$.

Statement 1 tells us, with a bit of manipulation, that $\frac{D}{C} = \frac{5}{3}$. This is sufficient, because we can plug into $1 - \frac{C}{D}$ and get $1 - \frac{3}{5} = \frac{2}{5}$. *Sufficient*

Statement 2 gives us a distinct equation. However, there's no other information, such as another distinct equation, to help us solve or to manipulate in order to get the ratio $\frac{C}{D}$. *Insufficient*

Statement 1 alone is sufficient.

4. **(B)** In order to determine the 777th term of sequence S, we either need the definition of the sequence or some way to find a pattern.

Statement 1 gives us only one term. Therefore, there is no way to determine the pattern for the definition. *Insufficient*

Statement 2 gives us a term and a definition. This means we could take the number 16,515 and subtract 17 as many times as needed in order to get to the 777th term. The GMAT test makers don't expect you to calculate this number. You just have to know that you can. *Sufficient*

Statement 2 alone is sufficient.

5. **(C)** The best way to do this question is to pick numbers and prove insufficiency by finding one example that works and one that does not.

Statement 1 → If $b = -20$, then $a = |-20 + 11| + |12 - (-20)|$
$$= |-9| + |32| = 9 + 32 = 41$$

→ If $b = 11$, then $a = |11 + 11| + |12 - 11|$
$$= |22| + |1| = 22 + 1 = 23 \text{ Insufficient}$$

Statement 2 → If $b = 20$, then $a = |20 + 11| + |12 - 20|$
$$= |31| + |-8| = 31 + 8 = 39$$

→ If $b = 11$, then $a = |11 + 11| + |12 - 11|$
$$= |22| + |1| = 22 + 1 = 23 \ \textit{Insufficient}$$

When we combine statements 1 and 2 together, we know that $-11 < b < 12$. Pick numbers.

If $b = 11$, then $a = |11 + 11| + |12 - 11| = |22| + |1| = 22 + 1 = 23$

If $b = -10$, then $a = |-10 + 11| + |12 - (-10)| = |1| + |22| = 1 + 22 = 23$

Try a 3rd number if you are not convinced.

→ If $b = -1$, $a = |-1 + 11| + |12 - (-1)| = 10 + 13 = 23$

Both statements together are sufficient

Geometry | 7

Geometry is fun! Now you may wonder where our enthusiasm comes from. Simply put, geometry is all about making drawings and a bunch of rules. In other words, you get to doodle! Some students, having forgotten most of the rules, decide to skip geometry altogether, thinking they can make up their score with the other questions. This is a bad idea. As mentioned before, there is a finite amount of underlying theory on the GMAT. There is an end in sight. In addition, the tested quantitative theory is from high school or earlier. Geometry is often taught even earlier, likely in junior high or middle school (oh those fun, awkward years). So you may find it more difficult than other quantitative topics because you were exposed to it so long ago. Geometry makes up about 10% to 15% of the quantitative questions. This represents at least 4 to 6 GMAT questions that you should be getting right!

BASIC GEOMETRY STRATEGY

1. **KNOW ALL THE RULES:** Geometry is rule based. To solve geometry problems, you need to know the rules and be able to recognize which ones apply. You already know most of the rules, such as the area of a circle or the angles of a triangle. The key to success is to know the more obscure rules as well as the common ones.

2. **ALWAYS MAKE A DRAWING:** Visualizing will help you greatly in geometry. Even if the GMAT provides a diagram, you should draw it again on your scratch pad. Draw it neatly and large enough to work with effectively. In many cases, you will need to draw more than what you are given.

3. **LEVERAGE SPECIAL TRIANGLES:** Most quantitative problems have a key insight that helps you understand and solve the problem efficiently. In geometry, you will often find that the key insight involves special triangles such as isosceles triangles, equilateral triangles, Pythagorean right triangles, 30-60-90 triangles, and 45- 45-90 triangles.

LINES AND ANGLES

A **line** is defined as a geometric object that is straight and can be either finite or infinite.

A fixed portion of a line is often called a **line segment**, as is AB in the diagram below.

When 2 lines intersect, we create 2 pairs of angles. The angles opposite each other are equal. The sum of the angles on one side of the line is 180°.

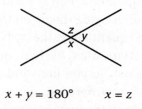

$$x + y = 180° \qquad x = z$$

Parallel and Perpendicular Lines

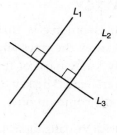

Parallel lines are those in the same plane that never intersect. As shown in the diagram, $L1$ and $L2$ are parallel.

Perpendicular lines are those that intersect, creating 90° angles. In the diagram, $L3$ is perpendicular to $L1$ and $L2$.

When two parallel lines are intercepted by a third line, as shown below, we create two sets of four identical angles. Again this case, $x + y = 180°$.

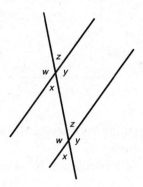

TRIANGLES

The GMAT test makers love to use triangles. In fact, you will find triangles in the majority of geometry questions. Special triangles are often the key to solving more difficult problems.

In the triangle below, the sum of the interior angles is always 180°, no matter what the shape. Therefore, when you know 2 angles, you can determine the 3rd angle.

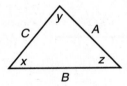

$$x + y + z = 180°$$

The perimeter of a triangle is the sum of the length of its sides. $P = A + B + C$

The area of a triangle is its base multiplied by its perpendicular height divided by 2.

$$A = \frac{B \times H}{2}$$

Note that any side can be the base. However, you must make sure that you use the perpendicular altitude from that base for the height.

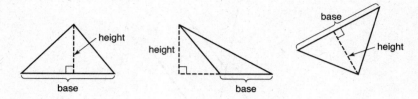

The shortest side of a triangle is opposite the smallest angle. The longest side is opposite the largest angle.

The sum of any 2 sides of a triangle must always be greater than the 3rd side.

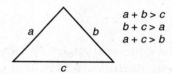

$$a + b > c$$
$$b + c > a$$
$$a + c > b$$

The exterior angle of a triangle is equal to the sum of the 2 interior angles of a triangle that are not next to that exterior angle.

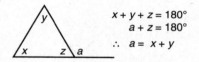

$$x + y + z = 180°$$
$$a + z = 180°$$
$$\therefore \quad a = x + y$$

Right Triangles

The most important triangle in the GMAT quantitative section is the right triangle. In a right triangle, one angle measures 90°. This angle is opposite the longest side of a triangle, which is known as the hypotenuse. We can calculate the length of the third side of a right triangle when given the length of the other two sides using Pythagoras's famous formula:

PYTHAGOREAN THEOREM

$$a^2 + b^2 = c^2$$

where c is the hypotenuse while a and b are the other two sides of a right triangle

---

The most well known Pythagorean triangle identity is the 3-4-5 triangle. Not only should you know this right triangle, but you should also know common multiples of it such as 6-8-10, 9-12-15, 15-20-25. There are also a few other common Pythagorean triangle identities shown below.

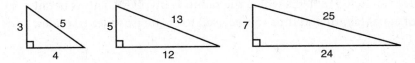

The Pythagorean theorem is a fundamental building block for everything about right triangles, but rarely would you need to use it in calculations. Knowing all of the different right triangle identities you will save time on your calculations.

Special Triangles

There are 4 special triangles that are critical to success in GMAT geometry:

1. **EQUILATERAL TRIANGLES**

2. **ISOSCELES TRIANGLES**

3. **45-45-90 TRIANGLES**

4. **30-60-90 TRIANGLES**

Equilateral Triangles

All sides of an equilateral triangle are the same length. All angles in an equilateral triangle are the same—60°. An equilateral triangle is also by definition an isosceles triangle. If you cut an equilateral triangle in half, you create 2 identical 30-60-90 right triangles. What is not commonly known about this special triangle is that you need only one side length to calculate the area by using the following formula.

$$A = \frac{s^2\sqrt{3}}{4}$$

These properties of equilateral triangles are key in both problem solving and data sufficiency type questions.

Isosceles Triangles

Isosceles triangles have 2 angles and 2 sides that are the same. So if 2 sides of a triangle have the same length, then the 2 opposite angles are also equal to each other and vice versa. Sometimes you will find isosceles triangles cleverly hidden in circle problems where the radius is involved. This is because 2 radii are of equal length and thus can be used to create isosceles triangles.

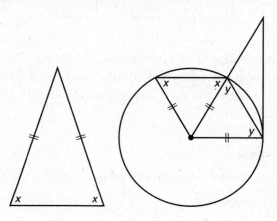

30-60-90 and 45-45-90 Triangles

These triangles are special because they have specific proportions for each side. You only need to know only the length of one side in order to find the length of the other 2 sides. This is especially important to know for data sufficiency type problems.

In a 30-60-90 triangle, the ratio of the lengths is fixed at $1:\sqrt{3}:2$. This means if the side opposite the 30° angle measures 1, the side opposite the 60° angle measures $\sqrt{3}$, and the hypotenuse measures 2. Note that you can also create this triangle when you split an equilateral triangle in half. When dealing with this type of triangle, the best way to calculate the other sides is to use a chart as shown on the next page.

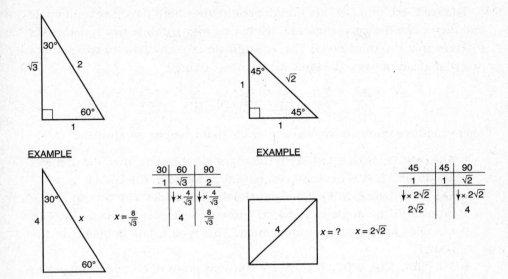

EXAMPLE

EXAMPLE

In a 45-45-90 triangle, the ratio of the side lengths is fixed at $1:1\sqrt{2}$. This means that if either leg measures 1, the hypotenuse measures $\sqrt{2}$. This triangle is also an isosceles right triangle. Note that 45-45-90 triangles are created when you split a square in half by the diagonal. You should also be familiar with common multiples of this ratio such as $\sqrt{2}$, $\sqrt{2}$, and 2.

Similar Triangles

Over the years, the GMAT has become more sophisticated and complex. The test makers use a variety of ways to complicate questions whether through tricky wording or by using advanced concepts more frequently. Similar triangles are one such area where savvy test takers need to have a better understanding.

When two triangles are similar, they share the same angles and thus share similar proportional properties. In other words, any two triangles with the same angles have their sides and heights in proportion.

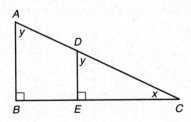

Triangles *ABC* and *DEC* are similar because they both have one right angle and they share the same angle at *C*. Note that we need only two equal angles to know that the third one is also equal. If we take any ratio of two sides of one triangle, it must be the same for the other triangle.

$$\frac{AB}{AC} = \frac{ED}{DC}, \frac{BC}{AB} = \frac{EC}{ED}, \text{ and } \frac{BC}{AC} = \frac{EC}{DC}$$

There are three standard ways to determine that triangles are similar.

- **AAA (ANGLE, ANGLE, ANGLE):** If the angles are the same, then the triangles are similar. This is the most common type found in the GMAT.
- **SAS (SIDE, ANGLE, SIDE):** If the triangles share two sides with corresponding ratios and the angle in between those two sides is the same in both triangles, these triangles are similar. This type is less frequent on the GMAT.
- **SSS (SIDE, SIDE, SIDE):** If there are constant ratios of corresponding sides for two triangles, then the triangles are similar. This type is rarely seen on the GMAT, usually because most geometry questions won't give you that much information (all the lengths of six different sides!).

The most common similar triangle identity you might see is the following.

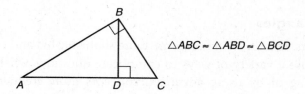

$$\triangle ABC \approx \triangle ABD \approx \triangle BCD$$

QUADRILATERALS

Quadrilaterals are 4-sided polygons. The four most commonly occurring quadrilaterals on the GMAT are the square, rectangle, parallelogram, and trapezoid.

QUADRILATERAL TYPES AND PROPERTIES

	Square	Rectangle
Properties	All opposite sides are parallel; All sides are the same length; All angles are 90°; Diagonals are the same length, intersect at 90°, and bisect each other; interior angles add up to 360°	All opposite side are parallel; Opposite sides are the same length; All angles are 90°; Diagonals are the same length and bisect each other; interior angles add up to 360°
Area	$A = s^2$	$A = l \bullet w$
Perimeter	$P = 4s$	$P = 2l + 2w$
Key shapes	Diagonals create two 45-45-90 isosceles right triangles	Diagonals create 2 right triangles

	Parallelogram	Trapezoid
Properties	All opposite side are parallel; Opposite sides are the same length; Opposite angles are equal; Diagonals bisect each other; interior angles add up to 360°	2 sides are parallel; Interior angles add up to 360°
Area	$A = b \bullet h$	$A = \frac{1}{2}(b + c)h$ or (Avg. base) $\bullet$ h
Perimeter	$P = 2a + 2b$	$P = a + b + c + d$
Key shapes	Right triangle needed to find the height	Right triangle needed to find the height

OTHER POLYGONS

Polygons are two-dimensional, closed plane figures that are bound by straight lines. You may see other polygons on the GMAT besides triangles and quadrilaterals such as pentagons, hexagons, or more complicated figures. You need to know a few things about polygons.

1. The sum of the interior angles of any polygon is $(n - 2) \cdot 180°$, where n is the number of sides.
2. A regular polygon is one where all sides are the same measure and all angles are the same measure.
3. All polygons can be broken down into smaller triangles, which can be a quick way to determine the sum of all interior angles.

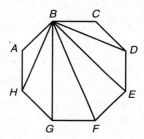

Here we have a regular octagon, with all sides and angles equal.

Sum of angles is $(8 - 2) \cdot 180° = 1080°$.

You can also see that we can draw 6 triangles within the octagon. Since triangles have interior angles that add up to 180°, then octagons have $6 \cdot 180 = 1080°$.

When you see an irregular polygon on the GMAT, the key is to break the shape down into polygons that you recognize and can solve. For example, a shape like the front of a house can be broken down into rectangles and triangles.

CIRCLES

A circle is an infinite set of points that are all equidistant from a point called the center. Circles are often involved in some of the harder geometry problems on the GMAT, mostly because test makers combine circles with other geometric shapes such as triangles and quadrilaterals. Circles also have a large number of properties that can be used for a variety of GMAT questions. Let's first understand the basic definitions.

Definitions

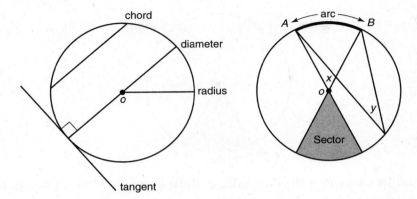

RADIUS: The distance from the center of the circle to the outside edge. The radius is usually the most important piece of information that you need for circle problems.

DIAMETER: The largest distance from one side of a circle to the other, going through the center. The diameter is twice the length of the radius.

CHORD: A line that connects any 2 points on circle. Note that the diameter is also a chord.

CIRCUMFERENCE: The distance around the circle, which has a standard formula $C = 2\pi r$, where r is the radius.

ARC: Any portion of the circumference. The points A and B on the diagram create 2 arcs, which are the minor arc (shorter length) and the major arc (longer length).

CENTRAL ANGLE: An angle with its vertex at the center of the circle. These angles are used to calculate arc lengths and sector areas. This is angle x in the diagram.

INSCRIBED ANGLE: An angle with its vertex on the circumference of the circle. This is angle y in the diagram.

SECTOR: A portion of the area of a circle, defined by 2 radii and an arc.

TANGENT: A line that touches a circle at just one point. This tangent line is perpendicular to the radius at the point of tangency.

Circle Formulas and Properties

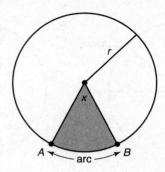

Your ability to connect the dots among all the geometry rules is a key factor to success. Therefore, you should know the main formulas in some of the commonly tested properties and relationships of circles. Know the following three most commonly used formulas for GMAT circles:

1. $A = \pi r^2$
2. $C = 2\pi r$
3. Arc length $= 2\pi r\left(\dfrac{x}{360°}\right)$

A = area, C = circumference, r = radius, and x = central angle measure.

Note that arc length is the proportion of the circumference where x represents the angular proportion. The total number of degrees of arc in the circle is 360°. You must know the relationship among arcs, inscribed angles, and central angles.

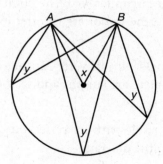

- **SIMILAR INSCRIBED ANGLES:** All inscribed angles that extend to the same arc or same 2 points on a circle are equal to each other. This can be seen with angles *y* in the previous diagram.

- **CENTRAL ANGLE VS. INSCRIBED ANGLE:** Any central angle that extends to the same arc or the same two points on a circle as does an inscribed angle is twice the size of the inscribed angle. Therefore as shown in the diagram, $x = 2y$.

- **TRIANGLES INSCRIBED IN A SEMICIRCLE:** Any triangle that is inscribed in a semicircle where the longest length is the diameter of the circle is always a right triangle.

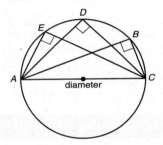

- **RADII CREATE ISOSCELES TRIANGLES:** Note that in some difficult circle problems, you can sometimes use 2 radii to create isosceles triangles and thus create 2 angles that are equal to each other.

VOLUMES AND 3-D FIGURES

The most common three-dimensional (3-D) figures in the GMAT geometry are cubes, rectangular solids, and cylinders. You may also see spheres, cones, or figures that are a combination of these. You will need to understand volumes, surface areas, and line segments within 3-D figures. A simple way to think of most volumes is that you are multiplying an area by a new dimension.

Volume = (Area of 2-D surface) × (Height)

The chart below outlines the most commonly needed formulas and properties of 3-D figures on the GMAT.

	Cube	**Rectangular Solid**
Visualize as	Dice	Box
Definitions	Faces, edges, vertices, bases, and heights	Faces, edges, vertices, bases, lengths, widths, and heights
Volume	$V = s^3$	$V = lwh$
Surface area	$SA = 6s^2$	$SA = 2lw + 2lh + 2hw$
Longest length within	$L = \sqrt{(3s^2)}$	$L = \sqrt{(l^2 + w^2 + h^2)}$

	Cylinder	**Sphere**
Visualize as	Soda Can	Ball
Definitions	Base, heights, radius	Radius, surface
Volume	$V = \pi r^2 h$	$V = \left(\dfrac{4}{3}\right) \pi r^3$
Surface area	$SA = 2(\pi r^2) + 2\pi rh$	$SA = 4\pi r^2$
Longest length within	$L = \sqrt{(4r^2 + h^2)}$	$L = 2r$

Note that a sphere would be considered a more unusual shape, as would be cones. However, we've added it to the chart because there have been a few sphere questions where the volume formula was not given. In general, the GMAT test makers will give you the formulas required for unusual shapes. If the question gives you a more complex figure, look for ways to break it down into more common 3-D shapes.

With your knowledge of basic geometry and areas, you should be able to calculate the volume of most 3-D figures such as the triangular solid below.

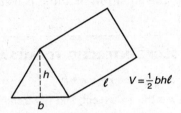

$$V = \frac{1}{2}bh\ell$$

COORDINATE GEOMETRY

Coordinate geometry is simply the mapping of points, lines, and shapes on a coordinate plane. It has become more important in recent years. Coordinate geometry questions are often combined with algebraic equations. Below we review the basic equations and properties of coordinate geometry.

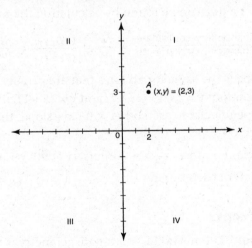

The figure is called the **coordinate plane**. The horizontal line is called the **x-axis**, and the vertical line is the **y-axis**. The point O is the **origin**. The axes divide the planes into four **quadrants**, 1, 2, 3 and 4 as shown on the chart. Every point in the plane has an **x-coordinate** and a **y-coordinate**, which is expressed (x, y).

Linear Equations

The line drawn in the diagram can be expressed using an algebraic equation. In coordinate geometry, the equation of a line is usually expressed using the slope-intercept formula.

SLOPE-INTERCEPT FORMULA

$$y = mx + b$$

where m is the slope, b is the y-intercept, and $\frac{-b}{m}$ is the x-intercept

---

Slope

The slope of a line is an expression of its steepness. In the slope-intercept formula, it is m. We can think of the slope from left to right as a hill, where uphill is positive and downhill is negative. A straight horizontal line, which would be no hill at all, has a slope of 0. A straight vertical line has an undefined slope. The slope of a line can be found by calculating the following:

$$\frac{\text{Change in } y\text{-coordinate}}{\text{Change in } x\text{-coordinate}} = \frac{\Delta y}{\Delta x} = \frac{(y_2 - y_1)}{(x_2 - x_1)} = \frac{rise}{run}$$

Note that the slope is the same for all lines that are parallel to each other. Lines with the equations $y = 2x$, $y = 2x + 7$, and $y = 2x + 11$ all have a slope of 2. Lines that are perpendicular to each other will have slopes that are the negative reciprocals of each other.

The lines $y = 3x - 1$ and $y = -\frac{1}{3}x + 7$ intersect at 90° because 3 and $-\frac{1}{3}$ are negative reciprocals of each other.

x– and y–Intercepts

The most important skill on GMAT coordinate geometry is finding the x- and y-intercepts of an equation quickly. The x-intercept is where a line crosses the x-axis and the y-intercept is where the line crosses the y-axis. One way to find the x- and y-intercepts is to use the formula $y = mx + b$. The other way is to set x or y equal to 0.

To find the y-intercept, set x equal to 0. Then solve for y.
To find the x-intercept, set y equal to 0. Then solve for x.

$$2x + 3y = 6$$

Solution: Set x equal to 0. $3y = 6$, therefore $y = 2$.

Set y equal to 0. $2x = 6$, therefore $x = 3$.

So, the x-intercept is 3, or at point (3, 0). The y-intercept is 2, or at point (0, 2). If needed, we can also calculate the slope using x- and y-intercept points.

$$m = \frac{(y_2 - y_1)}{(x_2 - x_1)} = \frac{(2-0)}{(0-3)} = -\frac{2}{3}.$$

Other Formulas and Properties

You will often be asked other types of coordinate geometry questions on the GMAT.

Calculate the Equation of the Line

Often in GMAT, coordinate geometry problems will ask you to determine the equation of the line. To do this, you will need any of the following:

1. Any 2 points on the line
2. Both x-and y-intercepts
3. The slope and either x- or y-intercept
4. One point on the line and the slope
5. One point on the line and the slope or equation of a line perpendicular or parallel to that line

Calculating Intersections

Whenever you are asked to calculate the intersection point of 2 lines, you need to set the equations equal to each other.

Calculate the intersection of $y = 3x - 2$ and $y = 5x - 6$.

Solution: Since both equations are set equal to y, set the equations equal to each other.

$$3x - 2 = 5x - 6$$

We get $4 = 2x$. Therefore $x = 2$. Now substitute $x = 2$ into either of the original equations.

$$y = 3(2) - 2 = 6 - 2 = 4$$

So $y = 4$.

If you use the other equation, you get the same answer.

$$y = 5(2) - 6 = 10 - 6 = 4$$

The intersection is at (2,4).

Distance Formula

When you have 2 points on a coordinate plane, you can usually find the distance between them using the Pythagorean theorem. (You can't use this formula for 2 points on the same axis.) The distance is found by drawing a right triangle between the 2 points.

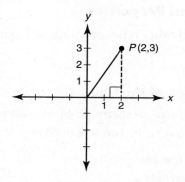

Distance between any 2 points (x_1, y_1) and (x_2, y_2) =

$$\sqrt{(\Delta x)^2 + (\Delta y)^2} = \sqrt{(x_1 - x_2)^2 + (y_1 - y_2)^2}$$

Midpoint Formula

When you have 2 points in the coordinate plane, you can find their midpoint, which can save you time on some of the more complex geometry questions. The basic idea is to calculate the average of the x- and y-coordinates.

$$\text{Midpoint} = \frac{(x_1 + x_2)}{(2)}, \frac{(y_1 + y_2)}{(2)}$$

Nonlinear Equations—Curved Lines and Circles

Sometimes on the GMAT you will see quadratic equations and circles in the coordinate plane. In these cases, your knowledge of intercepts and algebraic manipulation will be most useful.

$$y = x^2 - 3x + 2 \qquad \text{or} \qquad x^2 + y^2 = 100$$

When $x = 0$, the y-intercept is 2.

When $y = 0$, we get $(x - 2)(x - 1) = 0$; thus the x-intercepts are 1 and 2.

Note that this equation creates a circle of radius 10.

Using algebra, we can also calculate the x- and y-intercepts to be at ±10.

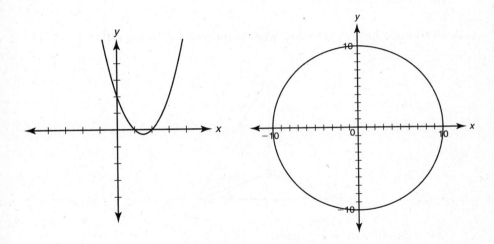

As you can see, graphing quadratic equations creates curved lines. If you still have trouble, try using a T-chart to get a better visual understanding. You can also use your knowledge of algebraic manipulation to simplify the equation.

GEOMETRY: TARGETED REVIEW QUESTIONS

1. If ℓ1 is perpendicular to ℓ2 and ℓ2 is perpendicular to ℓ3 in a three-dimensional space, what do we know about the relationship between ℓ1 and ℓ3?

   I.   ℓ1 ∥ ℓ3
  II.   ℓ1 ⊥ ℓ3
 III.   ℓ1 equal to ℓ3

  (A)   I only
  (B)   II only
  (C)   I and III only
  (D)   II and III only
  (E)   None of the above

2. In triangle ABC, if $BD = DC$, what is the value of angle BAD?

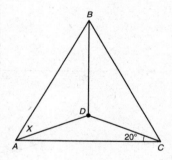

  (1)   Triangle ABC is equilateral.
  (2) AD bisects BDC.

3. If x and z are the centers of 2 circles x and y, respectively, what percent of the area of circle x is the area of circle z?

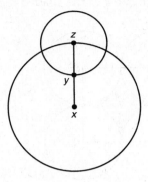

(1) $yz = \left(\dfrac{1}{2}\right)xz$

(2) The circumference of circle x is 49.

4. Rhombus $ABCD$ of side 6 has perpendicular line ED intersecting side AB. What is the area of trapezoid $BCDE$?

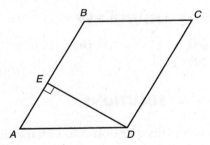

(1) $\dfrac{AE}{EB} = \dfrac{1}{1}$

(2) Angle EDA is 30°.

5. In the diagram below, the 4 circles intersect each other at a point tangent to their centers, forming a shaded region. Line *BD* has a length of $8\sqrt{2}$. What is the area of the shaded region?

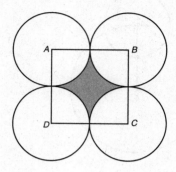

(A) $16 - 4\pi$
(B) $64 - 16\pi$
(C) $128 - 32\pi$
(D) $128 - 16\pi$
(E) 128

ANSWER KEY

1. **(E)**   3. **(A)**   5. **(B)**
2. **(A)**   4. **(D)**

SOLUTIONS

1. **(E)** The best way to solve this question is to visualize it with a drawing.

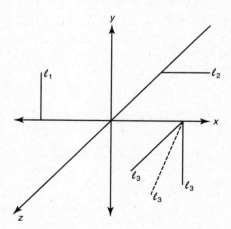

The trick here is to understand that perpendicular lines are not necessarily in the same surface plane. In other words, you should consider 3 dimensions instead of 2 dimensions. As you can see from the drawing, ℓ_3 is not necessarily parallel to or perpendicular to ℓ_1. It is also not necessarily the same length.

2. **(A)** In data sufficiency questions, we cannot assume that figures are drawn to scale. Even though it may look like an equilateral triangle, we cannot be certain unless information tells us so. We do know angles *DBC* and *DCB*.

Statement 1 confirms for us that the triangle *ABC* is an equilateral triangle. We are given angle *DCA* and thus can calculate angle *DCB* because the entire angle *ACB* must equal 60°. From this we get

$$\angle DCB = \angle DBC = 40° \rightarrow \angle DBA = 20° \rightarrow \angle BDC = 180° - 20° - 20° = 140°$$

Since triangle *ABC* is equilateral, $\angle DCB = \angle DBC$ and $BD = DC$. The point *D* is at the midpoint of line *BC* if it were to extend to *D*. This means that the line *AD* will bisect $\angle BDC$ (making statement 2 redundant).

$$\angle BDA = \angle ADC = \frac{(360° - \angle BDC)}{2} = \frac{(360° - 140°)}{2} = 110° \rightarrow$$

$$\angle BAD = 180° - 110° - 20° = 50° \quad \textit{Sufficient}$$

Statement 2 tells us that line *AD* bisects *BDC*. However, we don't know what $\angle DCB$ and $\angle DBC$ are so we cannot solve for any other angles. *Insufficient*

Statement 1 alone is sufficient.

3. **(A)** What we know is there are two circles, *x* and *z*. What we want is $\frac{A_z}{A_x}$. What we need is A_z and A_x, $\frac{A_z}{A_x}$, r_z and r_x, or $\frac{r_z}{r_x}$ because the radius will also give us the area.

Statement 1 tells us that the radius of *z* is half the radius of *x*, giving us $\frac{r_z}{r_x} = \frac{1}{2}$. *Sufficient*

Statement 2 gives us information about circle *x* but no information about circle *z*. *Insufficient*

Statement 1 alone is sufficient.

4. **(D)** Since this figure is a rhombus, we know that all four sides are of length 6. What we need to solve for the trapezoid is the length of the two bases *EB* and *CD* as well as the height *ED*. We already have *CD* = 6.

Statement 1 gives us the ratio of sides *AE* and *EB*, which means *AE* = 3 and *EB* = 3. Since triangle *AED* is a right triangle (and a 30-60-90 one too), we can also calculate the length of *ED* using the Pythagorean theorem.

$6^2 - 3^2 = ED^2 \rightarrow ED = \sqrt{36-9} = \sqrt{27} = 3\sqrt{3} \rightarrow$ We could have used the 30-60-90 ratios.

To find the area of a rhombus, A = (average base)(height) = $\left(\dfrac{(3+6)}{2}\right) \bullet$ $3\sqrt{3} = \dfrac{27\sqrt{2}}{2}$ *Sufficient.*

Statement 2 tells us that triangle *AED* is a 30-60-90 right triangle. Since we have the length of the hypotenuse, we can determine the other two sides using the ratio 1-$\sqrt{3}$-2. Sides *AE* and *ED* would be 3 and $3\sqrt{3}$, respectively. Now we can solve for the trapezoid as we did in statement 1 above. *Sufficient*

Each statement alone is sufficient.

5. **(B)** When a geometry problem seems complex, it's important to break it down into easier-to-manage steps. In order to calculate the shaded region, you need to take the area of the square and subtract the area of each sector of the 4 circles. More simply put, you just need to subtract the area of one circle from the area of the square. The problem gives the diameter of the square as $8\sqrt{2}$. Using the 45-45-90 right triangle ratio of 1-1-$\sqrt{2}$, you know that a hypotenuse of $8\sqrt{2}$ means you have a side of 8. Thus the radius of the circle is 4. This gives:

area of square – area of the circle = $s^2 - \pi r^2 = 8^2 - \pi 4^2 = 64 - 16\pi$

Statistics

8

Statistics is a topic that was very relevant to you even before you become a business school student. We see statistics cited every day in our professional and personal lives. Now here is your chance to appreciate them even more! If you are unfamiliar with statistics theory, know that you have to learn it for your MBA anyway, so you might as well start learning now. Mastering statistics will increase your confidence and will help you on some of the harder problems. The GMAT has lately been including more statistics problems. However, the depth of theory is not too complex. For example, you don't need to know how to calculate standard deviation, just how to maneuver it or understand its magnitude. You should expect to see at least a couple of statistics questions if not more.

AVERAGE (ARITHMETIC MEAN)

The **average** or the **mean** is the most common statistical concept on the GMAT. The basic formula is straightforward.

$$\text{Average} = \text{arithmetic mean} = \text{mean} = \bar{x} = \frac{\text{the sum of the terms in the set}}{\text{the number of terms in the set}}$$

> Billy's marks this term were 80, 85, 90, 95, and 60. What was his average mark?

Solution: There are five terms. If we plug them into the formula, we get

$$\frac{(60 + 80 + 85 + 90 + 95)}{5} = \frac{410}{5} = 82.$$

Note that you may see the words **average**, **arithmetic mean**, and **mean** used interchangeably on the GMAT. They all mean the same thing. The test makers are not likely to give you the sum of the terms and the number of terms. That would be way too easy. If you do get that, then you're probably doing pretty badly on the test. What you will likely see is any of the following:

- An average and a way to find the sum of the terms
- An average and a given number of terms
- An abstract mix of the sum of the terms and the number of terms

Strategies for the Arithmetic Mean

1. **LOOK AT THE ANSWER CHOICES FIRST.** The answer choices tend to give clues for many GMAT quantitative problems, but this is especially true for questions involving the mean.
2. **THINK CONCEPTUALLY.** Although this advice applies to most quantitative problems, it is particularly important for questions involving the mean. Look for a way to solve without calculations, especially if you see the key word "approximately" or "estimate" in the question stem.
3. **USE YOUR "BEST FRIENDS": ALGEBRA AND NUMBER PROPERTIES.** Understanding arithmetic mean problems may require you to set up algebraic equations or leverage number properties to unlock a shortcut or key insight.

SETS OF NUMBERS

A **set** is a collection of things. In math, a set usually refers to a set of numbers.

An **element** is one of the things or numbers in a set. A set can have a finite or an infinite number of elements.

If we take part of a set made up of elements, we have a **subset**.

> If set $S = \{-3, 2, 7, 10, 100\}$, and if set $T = \{2, 7, 10\}$, then
> T is a subset of S

Remember these few things about sets of numbers:

1. Rearrange the order of elements from smallest to largest. Not every set is given to you in the proper order. The first step when you see any set of numbers is to fix this.
2. When you multiply or divide a set by a constant, you must multiply or divide every element in the set.

3. Several commonly seen sets of numbers appear on the GMAT. Be familiar with them. Remember n is any interger.

- **CONSECUTIVE INTEGERS:** { –3, –2, –1, 0, 1, 2, 3). This can be written as $n, n + 1, n + 2, ...$
- **CONSECUTIVE EVEN INTEGERS:** {–10, –8, –6, –4, –2}. These can be written as $2n, 2n + 2, 2n + 4, ...$
- **CONSECUTIVE ODD INTEGERS:** {1, 3, 5, 7, 9, ...}. These can be written as $2n + 1, 2n + 3, 2n + 5, ...$
- **PRIME NUMBERS:** {2, 3, 5, 7, 11, 13, 17, ...}
- **CONSECUTIVE MULTIPLES** of any number: e.g., {7, 14, 21, 28, 35}

4. To find the number of elements in a larger set of consecutive numbers, you can do the following calculation: **(largest number) – (smallest number) + 1**

> How many numbers are there between 50 and 175, inclusive?

Solution: 175 – 50 + 1 = 126 numbers

Note that if we wanted the numbers between 50 and 175 but not including 50 and 175, we would take (largest number) – (smallest number) – 1 → 175 – 50 – 1 = 124 numbers.

5. To find the number of multiples in a set, use

$$\frac{(\text{l arg est number}) - (\text{smallest number})}{\text{multiple}} + 1.$$

Be careful that the largest and smallest numbers are actual multiples themselves so that they fit the criteria.

> How many even integers are between 520 and 300, inclusive?

Solution: $\dfrac{(520 - 300)}{2} + 1 = 111$ even integers.

If the question above had asked about even integers between 521 and 299, we still would need to use 520 and 300 in the equation. What if the questions wanted the number of multiples of 3 between 520 and 300 exclusive? You would get

$$\frac{(520 - 300)}{3} + 1 = \frac{220}{3} + 1 = 73\frac{1}{3} + 1$$

In this case, take 73 + 1 = 74 multiples of 3.

MEDIAN

The **median** is the middle value of a set of numbers when the numbers are arranged in order. If the set has an even number of terms, it is the average of the two middle terms in the set.

> The median of the set {2, 3, 5, 7, 11} is 5 because it is the middle term. The median of the set {2, 3, 5, 7, 11, 13} is 6 because the average of the two middle terms, 5 and 7, is 6.

Median and Mean

For consecutive sets, otherwise known as evenly distributed sets, the median and the mean are equal. This statistics concept is tested often on the GMAT. One great tactic to determine the mean and median of a consecutive set quickly is by taking the average of the first and last number.

> What is the mean and median of set Z: {6, 12, 18, 24, 30, 36, 42, 48}?

Using the first and last elements $\rightarrow \dfrac{(48+6)}{2} = 27$

RANGE

The **range** is the difference between the largest value of a set and the smallest value of a set.

> The range of the set {–7, –2, 6, 9, 10} is 17, which we get from $10 - (-7) = 17$.

Remember a few things about the range of a set.

1. The range is always a positive number.
2. If you add numbers to a set that are between the highest and lowest numbers, the range is not affected.
3. A range of zero means that all numbers in the set are the same, e.g. {3, 3, 3, 3}.

MODE

The **mode** is the most frequently occurring number in a set. A set can have multiple modes. If all the numbers in a set are distinct from each other, then there is no mode.

> *A*: {2, 4, 4, 8, 8, 10, 10, 12} has three modes: 4, 8, and 10.
> *B*: {2, 4, 4, 8, 10, 12} has only one mode: 4.
> *C*: {2, 4, 8, 10, 12} has no mode.

On their own, each statistics concept is relatively straightforward. So then how can the test makers create difficult questions? Often the GMAT will present statistics problems that combine concepts from mean, median, mode, and range.

STANDARD DEVIATION

Standard deviation is a measure of the **spread** of numbers in a set. Another way to say this is that it is the **dispersion** or **deviation** of numbers. More specifically, the standard deviation looks at how closely terms in a set are spread out around the set's mean. You will not have to calculate standard deviation on the GMAT. However, you should know how it is calculated, what exactly it stands for, and what aspects are tested on the GMAT.

1. Analyze and compare magnitudes of different sets and their standards deviations
2. Determine what happens to a standard deviation when changes are made to the elements of the set

Calculating Standard Deviation

The steps to calculating the standard deviation are in the following example.

$$\text{Set } S: \{2, 4, 9, 10, 15\}.$$

1. Calculate the mean of the set: $\frac{40}{5} = 8$.

2. Find the difference between each term and the mean. Then square that difference.

Term	Difference from Mean	Square of Difference
2	$(2 - 8) = -6$	$(2 - 8)^2 = 36$
4	$(4 - 8) = -4$	$(4 - 8)^2 = 16$
9	$(9 - 8) = 1$	$(9 - 8)^2 = 1$
10	$(10 - 8) = 2$	$(10 - 8)^2 = 4$
15	$(15 - 8) = 7$	$(15 - 8)^2 = 49$

3. Calculate the sum of the differences between each value and the mean squared:

$$36 + 16 + 1 + 4 + 49 = 106$$

4. Divide the previous sum by the number of terms:

$$\frac{106}{5} = 21.2 \rightarrow \text{This is also known as the } \textbf{variance,}$$
or the mean of the squares.

5. Take the square root of the previous value:

$$\sqrt{21.2} = 4.604$$

Here are some other things to keep in mind about the standard deviation.

- Standard deviation is never negative. If it is zero, this means that all numbers in the set are equal, such as in the set {2, 2, 2, 2, 2}.
- Adding or subtracting a constant to each number in a set does not change the standard deviation.
- If you multiply each term in a set by a number greater than 1, the standard deviation will increase. Conversely, if you divide each term in a set by a number greater than 1, the standard deviation will decrease.
- The variance is the square of the standard deviation.
- Numbers that are tightly clustered around an average have a smaller standard deviation than numbers that are spread out.
- When analyzing the standard deviation among sets, the first thing to look at is the relative spread of the numbers. This usually is enough. If you are still not sure, look at the range of the set as a tiebreaker. If you still aren't sure, then you may have to calculate the average and look at how spread the numbers are around the mean.

STATISTICS: TARGETED REVIEW QUESTIONS

1. A waitress serving customers throughout the day keeps track of the number of people she serves each hour. On Monday, the number of people she served in each of the hours during her shift was 6, 7, 5, 10, 7, 6, S, and T. If there is only one mode for the number of customers served in an hour on Monday, how many different numbers could be the mode?

   (A) 2
   (B) 3
   (C) 4
   (D) Greater than 4
   (E) It cannot be determined from the information given

2. The median monthly rental income of a commercial real estate property with 17 different stores is $5,000. If the average rental income increases by 20% in the next month, what will the median rental income in the real estate property be next month?

   (A) $5,000
   (B) $5,500
   (C) $6,000
   (D) $6,500
   (E) It cannot be determined from the information given

3. What is the standard deviation of the 4 integers a, b, c, and d?

   (1) $b = a + 2$, $c = b + 2$, and $d = a + 6$
   (2) $a = 6$, $b = 8$, and $d = 12$

4. For set T: {100, 102, 101, 103, 102, 100, 101, 103, Y}, which of the following values would increase the standard deviation the most?

   (A) 100
   (B) 101
   (C) 102
   (D) 103
   (E) 104

5. The median of the four terms a, b, $a + b$, and $b - a$ is 4. If $a > b > 0$, what is the arithmetic mean (average) of the four terms?

(A) 4

(B) $\dfrac{(2b + a)}{2}$

(C) $\dfrac{3b}{2} + a$

(D) $3 + \dfrac{(b - a)}{4}$

(E) $4 + \dfrac{(b + a)}{2}$

ANSWER KEY

1. **(C)**   3. **(A)**   5. **(D)**

2. **(E)**   4. **(E)**

SOLUTIONS

1. **(C)** In order to have only one mode, one of the numbers in the set must occur the most frequently. Currently, both 6 and 7 occur twice, but we don't know what S and T are. They could be anything. Let's write out the possible scenarios to see how many unique modes we can create

    Case 1: $S = 7$, $T = 7$ → 7 is the mode
    Case 2: $S = 6$, $T = 6$ → 6 is the mode
    Case 3: $S = 5$, $T = 5$ → 5 is the mode
    Case 4: $S = 10$, $T = 10$ → 10 is the mode

    If S and T were two other numbers, say $S = 8$ and $T = 8$, this would violate the fact that there can be only one mode. Therefore, we have 4 possible modes.

2. **(E)** Often our assumptions can trip us up. For example, just because the average rental increase was 20% doesn't mean that each property had a 20% increase on its rent. We are given 17 properties, so the median would be ranked 8th among the rental incomes, leaving us with 7 rental incomes on either side of the set. We could increase all the rental incomes by 20% and the median would become $6,000. However, we could also increase fewer or even one rental income by a much larger amount to

give us the same average increase. So we really don't know what the exact rental distribution is. There is no way to determine the answer to this problem.

3. **(A)** In order to determine standard deviation, we need to know the spread of all the numbers. If we jump ahead to statement 2, we don't have any value for c; therefore we cannot determine the standard deviation. *Insufficient*

   Statement 1 gives us enough information to determine that the integers in the set are a, $a + 2$, $a + 4$, and $a + 6$. Even though we don't have specific values, we do have the spread of numbers. No matter what the value of a is, the four integers will have the same distribution. *Sufficient*

   Statement 1 alone is sufficient.

4. **(E)** Standard deviation is a measure of the spread of numbers and, more specifically, the distribution of numbers around the mean. When we put the set above in correct order, we have {100, 100, 101, 101, 102, 102, 103, 103, Y}. Of the answer choices, the only number outside our current group is 104. Just to be sure, we can check the mean of this set, which is 101.5. The number that is most likely to affect the standard deviation will be the one that's farthest from the mean. The number 104 will make this set as widely distributed as possible.

5. **(D)** The first thing we need to figure out is how these numbers rank in value. We know that a and b are both positive and that $a > b$. This means that $a + b$ is the largest number and that $b - a$ is a negative number and thus the smallest. This gives us the ordered set {$b - a$, b, a, $a + b$}. Since the median is 3, we know that it is the average between a and b so

$$\frac{(a+b)}{2} = 3 \rightarrow a + b = 6$$

The arithmetic mean is the (sum of terms)/(number of terms), which gives us

$$\frac{((b-a)+(b)+(a)+(a+b))}{4} \rightarrow \frac{((b-a)+(a+b)+(a+b))}{4}$$

$$\rightarrow \text{substitute } a + b = 6$$

$$\frac{(b-a+6+6)}{4} = \frac{(12+b-a)}{4} = 3 + \frac{(b-a)}{4}$$

Data Sufficiency

9

WHAT IS DATA SUFFICIENCY?

Data sufficiency problems ask a simple question: are the data provided sufficient to solve the problem? Determining the answer may not be so simple. Data sufficiency problems test your mathematical knowledge in a unique way. Because the setup is somewhat abstract, many students are intimidated by this section. The good news is that once you understand the structure, data sufficiency problems are easy to break down. In addition, you don't always have to perform calculations in order to solve them. You only have to know whether you **can** solve a problem via calculations. Therefore, data sufficiency questions generally take less time to answer than problem-solving questions.

WHY DATA SUFFICIENCY?

It's important to understand why business schools want to test you on data sufficiency. As a future manager or leader, you will be required to do several things:

1. Sort through information or data
2. Identify key issues
3. Make decisions

Data sufficiency is designed to measure your ability to think critically, identify relevant information, extract key insights, and know when you have enough information to solve a problem. These skills are important for any business school graduate and future manager.

DATA SUFFICIENCY BREAKDOWN

Based on the structure, format, and directions of data sufficiency questions, there are a few things you need to know:

- Data sufficiency accounts for at least 15 of the 37 quantitative problems. However, in recent years, test takers have seen nearly half the questions as data sufficiency, depending on how well they are doing. The better you are doing on the quantitative section, the more data sufficiency questions you will get.

- Your job is to determine when you have enough information to solve the problem. However, you rarely need to solve the problem.
- The format of the answer choices is the same, so you should memorize what each answer choice represents to save time.
- Data sufficiency tests all the same math theory that problem-solving does—arithmetic, algebra, geometry, properties of numbers, probability, statistics, and combinatorics.
- For each statement, you have to ask yourself, "Do I have enough information to determine sufficiency?" This is very similar to the real world where business leaders ask, "Do we have enough information to make a decision?" The major difference here is that in the real business world, managers rarely make decisions with 100% of the information required (usually anywhere from 20%–80%) because getting all of the information would take too long. However, the principle remains the same.
- Data sufficiency questions have a fixed format and set rules. Knowing the rules and how to exploit them is key.

There are two types of data sufficiency questions: straight solve and yes/no. The chart below describes both.

DATA SUFFICIENCY QUESTIONS—STRAIGHT SOLVE VS. YES/NO

	Straight Solve	Yes/No
Description	The question asks you to solve for something.	The question asks you to answer either Yes or No.
Key words	Solve, find, calculate, what? e.g., "What is x?"	Is, does, can, will? e.g., "Is $x > y$?"
Key insight	You need only one quantity for sufficiency; multiple quantities would be insufficient	You may have multiple quantities but just need to answer either "Yes definitively" or "No definitively."
Example	Q. What is x? (1) $x^2 = 9$ Since x = 3 and –3, statement 1 is not sufficient.	Q. Is $x > 0$? (1) $(x + 3)(x + 2)(x + 1) = 0$ Since $x = -3, -2, -1$ and x is always negative, we can answer "No definitively," and therefore statement 1 is sufficient.

DATA SUFFICIENCY STRATEGIES

Strategy 1: Decision Tree Method

The most common strategy is to use a decision tree to answer the following questions:

1. Is statement 1 sufficient by itself to solve the problem?
2. Is statement 2 sufficient by itself to solve the problem?
3. Are statements 1 and 2, when taken together, sufficient to solve the problem?

Depending on your answer for each question, you can follow the decision tree below to determine the proper answer choice. Notice that you only have to ask the third question approximately 40% of the time. Make sure you understand why you answered "yes" or "no" to each question.

Data Sufficiency Decision Tree

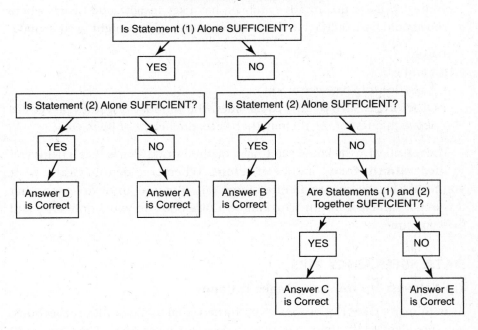

Strategy 2: Know-Want-Need Method

Another key strategy is to use the know-want-need method. It works well for a variety of quantitative topics—number properties, algebra, geometry, probability, weighted average, mixture, and word problems.

KNOW: What information do you know or have that is either directly given or implied? Do the statements themselves give you any extra insight about the problem?

WANT: What does the question ask for (i.e., what is the macro question)? Are there any specific units? Is this a straight solve or a yes/no question type? Do you need to be aware of any key words (ratio of, percent of, number of, etc.)?

NEED: This is the link between what we know and what we want. Data sufficiency, while seemingly complex at times, can always be simplified. You are looking for a statement that gives you what you need either directly or indirectly. Every quantitative problem has a key insight, and here is where you should try to extract it. Some common things you might need include:

- x or y
- x and y
- A relationship between x and y
- Other items such as two equal sides, the number of games played (as above in question 2), the rate that Alice, the height of Billy, etc.

The reason why the know-want-need method works well is that it helps you to **understand**, **focus**, and be **efficient**. When you identify clearly what you need, the statement will often jump out at you in an obvious way that it is either sufficient or not. This can be a nice boost to your confidence and save you time.

DATA SUFFICIENCY TIPS

Tip 1. Invest Up Front and Make it Count

As with many GMAT questions in both the verbal and quantitative sections, you should invest the time up front to understand the problem. The extra 15–30 seconds you invest to "get it" before you dive in can save you considerable time and mental energy. Make sure you:

- Avoid misreading the question and statements
- Understand the macro question and know what data sufficiency type it is
- Determine what you know, want, and need

Tip 2. Manage the Information in a Strategic and Timely Way

You can mine plenty of information from data sufficiency questions. The challenge is to know what to extract, when to extract it, and what not to extract. Keep in mind the following:

- **EVERY STATEMENT IMPLIES SOMETHING.** Determine the "what" and the "so what" for each statement. Ask yourself, "What is this telling me?" or "Why are you here?"

$$(1)\ x^5y^2 > 0$$

This statement implies that $x > 0$ because $y^2 > 0$.

- **KNOW WHAT YOU KNOW, BOTH DIRECT AND IMPLIED.** The question often has information embedded within it.
- **AVOID MAKING ASSUMPTIONS.** Use only explicit information from the question and statement. What's given is given, and what's not given is not given.

If y is an integer and $xy = 150$, is y a 2-digit number?

Note that the question stem mentions y to be an integer but makes no mention of x. You can be sure the test makers will try to make you assume that x is an integer, so be careful. *Insufficient*

- **DO NOT CARRY INFORMATION FROM STATEMENT 1 INTO STATEMENT 2.** You first need to look at each statement with a clean slate.

Tip 3. Leverage the Construct to Your Advantage

Data sufficiency questions have a certain construct. The test makers have to follow the logic and process of this structure. Therefore, if you know how they set up the questions, having this insight can give you certain advantages on test day.

- **DO NOT DO CALCULATIONS UNLESS YOU HAVE TO.** Many data sufficiency questions are conceptual and do not require solving. You just have to know that you can. Often the test makers will make you think you need to do calculations when you don't have to.

Drake's taxes were what portion of his salary?
(1) Drake received a year-end bonus of 7% of his salary.
(2) Drake's salary was $72,000.

Conceptually, you need to know Drake's tax rate. Since no information about the tax rate is given in either statement, you can't solve this. *Insufficient*.

The answer is E; both statements together are still not sufficient.

- **START WITH THE EASIER STATEMENT.** Since most test takers like to do things in order, the test makers will make statement 1 more complex than statement 2. Doing statement 2 first will not only eliminate some answer choices, but it might give you further insight into the problem and dealing with statement 1.

- **STATEMENTS 1 AND 2 NEVER CONTRADICT.** For example, in a straight solve type, if you find for statement 1 that $x = 2$ and for statement 2 that $x = 3$, you have made an error and need to redo your calculations. You could also use this information to gain extra insight.

> What is the value of x?
> (1) x is negative
> (2) $x^2 = 49$

If you thought here that $x = 7$, this would contradict what you learned in statement 1. This reminds you that $x = -7$ as well!

The answer is C.

- **DETERMINE SUFFICIENCY BY PROVING INSUFFICIENCY.** Sometimes you can focus on proving insufficiency by picking numbers to find both a scenario that works and another that doesn't work, thus proving insufficiency.

Tip 4. Don't Let the Game Fool You

Given the previous tip, the construct of data sufficiency also gives the test makers a variety of ways to trick you. There is almost a game to how the GMAT is tested or played. Arm yourself with the knowledge of some of the traps the test makers set up for you.

- **THEY PUT THE SAME INFO IN EACH STATEMENT.** It is very easy in math to say the same thing in completely different ways (e.g., positive integer, whole number, nondecimal number greater than zero, etc.). So if you were the GMAT test maker, why not do this in data sufficiency as a way to trick test takers? If this does happen, the answer can only be either D or E. If one statement works, the other has to work. If statement 1 doesn't work, then statement 2 won't work. Putting them together adds no new information.

Solve for x.
(1) $x - 3y = -7$
(2) $21 + 3x = 9y$

The equation in statement 2 is a manipulated version of the equation in statement 1. Therefore, we essentially have one equation and two unknowns. The equation cannot be solved. *Insufficient*

The answer is D.

- **DO NOT FORGET THAT "NO" CAN MEAN "SUFFICIENT."** A common thought process is to associate "No" with "Not sufficient." For yes/no data sufficiency questions, remember that if the answer to the macro question is "no, definitively," then that is sufficient.

  Is $x > 0$?
  (1) $(x + 3)(x + 2)(x + 1) = 0$

The statement tells us that $x = -3, -2,$ or -1. We know definitively that x is not greater than 0. *Sufficient*

- **WATCH OUT FOR THE EASY C.** If the question seems to lead you to think that both statements together are sufficient, think again! You should expect the same difficulty level of questions, so getting an easy one doesn't make sense. It is likely that one (or both) of the statements have some information embedded in them or there is something in the question stem that you missed. Alternatively, there may be a hidden reason why the statements don't work even when taken together.

  If $2x + y = 5z$, what is the value of y?
  (1) $3x = -1.5 + 7.5z$
  (2) $x = 2$

Upon first glance, statement 2 doesn't work. When combined with statement 1, though, you can plug in $x = 2$ and then solve for z and y because you have 2 equations and 2 unknowns. If you look closely at the question stem and statement 1, both can be manipulated to get ① $y = 5z - 2x$ and ② $7.5z - 3x = 1.5$, respectively. If we divide $7.5z - 3x = 1.5$ by 1.5, we get $5z - 2x = 1$. We can substitute this into ① and get an actual value for y. *Sufficient*

The answer is A.

- **WHEN THE TEST ASKS FOR a + b, YOU DO NOT NEED INDIVIDUAL VALUES.** Some data sufficiency questions seem to have too many algebraic variables, but you don't always need to solve for every variable. As long as you know what $a + b$ equals, you do not need to know what a and b are individually.

Tip 5. Use Your Knowledge of GMAT Theory, Strategies, and Methodologies to Simplify

Everything you learn in this book and externally is ammunition for beating the GMAT. All the skills and tips we share throughout the book will help you better process, understand, and approach all data sufficiency problems. You just have to leverage them when needed and be flexible whether doing data sufficiency questions conceptually or mathematically.

- **MANIPULATE THE EQUATIONS.** Just because an equation is given to you in a certain way, whether it is in the question stem or in the statement, this does not mean you can't manipulate it to serve your needs.

  Is $x - y > 0$?

  This is the same as asking if $x > y$

- **YOU ALWAYS HAVE YOUR TWO BFFS.** As we said earlier in the book, algebra and properties of numbers are your two "best friends forever" in data sufficiency as well as in all the quantitative questions. You can set up equations, simplify your work, unlock keys, break down the statements via conceptual understanding, and so much more!

- **DO NOT FORGET ABOUT 0 (ZERO).** It's so easy to forget about zero. It has unique qualities in terms of both usage and how it can change the dynamics of a question. Be wary of zero when dealing with inequalities, absolute value, and properties of numbers. Zero can also be a powerful number to use when picking numbers.

  Is $x > 0$?
  (1) $|x| = -x$

  This implies x is negative but also zero. *Insufficient*

- **PICKING NUMBERS.** We've saved the best for last and so can you (although you can try it first sometimes, too). This is the universal strategy taught by every test prep company in the world. We all can't be wrong! It helps you to understand the question better and to simplify the process. In a straight solve question type, you pick numbers to find more than one value. In a yes/no type problem, you pick numbers to find both a yes and a no answer.

If x and y are distinct prime numbers, is $x(y - 5)$ odd?
(1) $x < 3$

Statement 1 tells us that $x = 2$. Try any prime number for y ($y = 3, 5, 7, 11$, etc.). The equation $x(y - 5)$ is always even. *Sufficient*

DATA SUFFICIENCY: TARGETED REVIEW QUESTIONS

1. If t is the tens digit and u is the units digit of a two-digit number, what is the value of this number?
   (1) $t + u = 9$
   (2) $t - u = -5$

2. An organization is showcasing an outdoor play in a park. If over the course of a two-week run, it sells $3,200 worth of tickets, all at the same price, what is the price of one ticket?
   (1) If the price of each ticket were $1 more, the total revenue would be $800 more.
   (2) If the organization decreases the ticket price by $1 and sells 25% more tickets as a result, the total revenue would remain the same as before.

3. Milk carton A and milk jug B each contain milk. The capacity of jug B is 40% greater than that of carton A. How much more milk is in carton A than in jug B?
   (1) When full, container B holds 7 L of milk.
   (2) Container A is 4/5 full, and container B is 2/7 full.

4. If Aloysius had an appointment with his lawyer on a certain day, was his appointment on a Thursday?
   (1) The appointment was between 11 A.M. and 4 P.M.
   (2) Exactly 58 hours before the appointment, it was Tuesday.

5. If x_1 and x_2 are the number of schoolchildren and y_1 and y_2 are the number of schools in Country A and Country B, respectively, the ratio of the number of schoolchildren to the number of schools is greater for which of the two countries?

(1) $y_1 > y_2$
(2) $x_1 < x_2$

ANSWER KEY

1. **(C)**   3. **(C)**   5. **(C)**
2. **(D)**   4. **(C)**

SOLUTIONS

1. **(C)** You know that tu is a two-digit number. You want the value of both u and t. You need either u AND t (which of course test makers are not likely to give directly) or two equations with u and t that you can solve algebraically.

Statement 1 means that the number could be 18, 27, 36, 45, 54, 63, 72, 81, or 90. *Insufficient*

Statement 2 means that the number could be 16, 27, 38, or 49.

When you combine both statements, you have two distinct equations that can be solved for u and t. Furthermore, you know that the only possible value satisfying both statements is 27. *Sufficient*

Both statements together are sufficient.

2. **(D)** Using algebra, you know that $P \bullet n = 3200$, where P = the price of a ticket and n = the number of tickets. You want P. What you need is either P, or n, or another distinct equation with P and n.

Statement 1 means that $(P + 1)n = 3200 + 800. \rightarrow (P + 1)n = 4000$. This is another equation with P and n, thus giving you what you need. *Sufficient*

You don't have to solve this, rather just know that you can. However, just by inspection you know that a $1 increase per ticket leads to an $800 increase in overall sales. Therefore, the organization sold 800 tickets.

Statement 2 means that $(P - 1)(n \bullet 1.25) = 3200$. Again, this is another distinct equation with P and n. Therefore, you can solve it. *Sufficient*

Each statement alone is sufficient.

3. **(C)** Let's use the know-want-need method along with algebra.

know: $C_B = 1.4C_A$ → Jug B's capacity is 40% more than carton A's capacity.

want: $A - B$ → The amount of milk in A minus the amount of milk in B

need: A and B or a relationship among A, B, C_B, and C_A

Statement 1 means that $C_B = 7$. The trick here is that the statement says "when full" and does not say that the container is actually full. You still don't know the amount of milk in either container. *Insufficient*

Statement 2 tells how full the containers actually are. $A = \left(\dfrac{4}{5}\right)C_A$ and $B = \left(\dfrac{2}{7}\right)C_B$. However, you don't know the actual capacities of either container. Make sure you do not mistakenly take information from statement 1 and apply it to statement 2 by itself. *Insufficient*

When you combine both statements, you know the capacities of both containers and the amount of milk in each container. Therefore, you can solve. *Sufficient*

$$C_B = 7 \text{ and } C_B = 1.4C_A \text{ which means } 7 = \left(\dfrac{7}{5}\right) \bullet C_A \rightarrow C_A = 5$$

$$A = \left(\dfrac{4}{5}\right)C_A \rightarrow A = 4L \qquad B = \left(\dfrac{2}{7}\right)C_B \rightarrow B = 2L \rightarrow A - B = 4 - 2 = 2L$$

Both statements together are sufficient.

4. **(C)** The main trick on this GMAT question is that some test takers will forget about the 24-hour clock when it comes to determining the current day.

Statement 1 doesn't tell you anything about the day, so you cannot solve. *Insufficient*

Statement 2 says that 58 hours before the appointment was a Tuesday. This could be 11 P.M. Tuesday night, making the appointment fall on Friday at 9 A.M. Instead, the appointment could be 58 hours after 9 A.M. on Tuesday, making it fall on 7 P.M. on Thursday. Since you have no idea when on Tuesday the 58 hours before was, you cannot solve. *Insufficient*

When you combine both statements, you know that it is impossible to have an appointment on Friday between 11 A.M. and 4 P.M. You know this from statement 2 above where you looked at Tuesday at 11 P.M. in the late evening. Even if you went to 11:59 P.M. on Tuesday night, the latest you can extend it, the Friday appointment could be only as late as 9:59 A.M. Therefore, the appointment has to be on Thursday. *Sufficient*

Both statements together are sufficient.

5. **(C)** What you want to know is if $\frac{x_1}{y_1} > \frac{x_2}{y_2}$ or if ratio 1 > ratio 2.

Statement 1 says that the denominator of ratio 1 is larger than the denominator of ratio 2. This is not helpful because you don't know the numerators. Try picking numbers to visualize this.

If $y_1 = 10$ and $y_2 = 5$ and if $x_1 = x_2 = 1$, then $\frac{x_1}{y_1} < \frac{x_2}{y_2}$ because $\frac{1}{10} < \frac{1}{5}$.

If $y_1 = 10$ and $y_2 = 5$ and if $x_1 = 100$ and $x_2 = 1$, then $\frac{x_1}{y_1} > \frac{x_2}{y_2}$ because $\frac{100}{10} > \frac{1}{5}$. *Insufficient*

Statement 2 gives you the same dilemma as above. Now you know the numerators of ratio 1 and ratio 2, but you don't know the denominators. Thus you cannot compare the ratios. *Insufficient*

When you combine both statements, you know that $y_1 > y_2$ and $x_1 < x_2$. Ratio 2 now has both the larger numerator and smaller denominator. This means that it must be greater than ratio 1. Again, you can use numbers to verify this.

If $y_1 = 10$ and $y_2 = 5$ and if $x_1 = 5$ and $x_2 = 10$, then $\frac{x_1}{y_1} > \frac{x_2}{y_2}$ because $\frac{10}{5} < \frac{5}{10}$. *Sufficient*

Both statements together are sufficient.

Problem Solving

10

Problem solving accounts for up to 22 of 37 questions in the quantitative section of the GMAT. In recent years, some test takers have likely seen more data sufficiency questions if they were doing well. Based on this information, the number of problem-solving questions you face could reduce to about half. Problem-solving questions cover all of the theoretical topics including arithmetic, algebra, geometry, statistics, number properties, probability, and combinatorics. In this chapter, we will review the strategies, methods, and tactics for problem solving. Then we will dive deeper into the major word problems and question types.

PROBLEM SOLVING: WINNING THE WAR

The general strategy for problem solving is common among most test prep books.

1. **READ THE PROBLEM CAREFULLY.**
2. **MAKE SURE YOU ANSWER THE PROPER QUESTION.**
3. **PICK THE BEST APPROACH.** There are also dozens of tools and tactics you can use. These weapons are a significant part of your arsenal when dealing with GMAT problems. You need to be flexible, creative, and swift enough to handle any question. Below are some fundamentals, key strategies, methods, and tactics to keep in mind for problem solving on the GMAT.

Problem-Solving Fundamentals

Understanding how the GMAT test makers structure problem-solving questions will help you to process the question better and come up with a plan that works.

- **CARELESS ERRORS BE GONE!** The two most common errors test takers make are misreading and computational error. By being aware of these common errors and the fact that the test makers will try to exploit this, you can make every effort to try to avoid them.

- **THE SECRET IS OUT ABOUT MINIMAL OR NO CALCULATIONS.** Most GMAT problem-solving questions can be done conceptually or with several shortcut tactics that will be presented later in this chapter. This means that you should not have to do many calculations. You can often do calculations. However if you don't have to, you would be better off just selecting your answer and moving on.
- **THE MATH IS CLEAN.** If calculations are necessary, they will not be very complex. The numbers will work out smoothly. If they don't, you either have made a calculation error or have missed a shortcut such as simplifying, estimating, or algebra.
- **KNOW HOW THEY DECEIVE YOU.** The GMAT test makers can trick you in many ways. The most common are using clever wordplay, including misleading answer choices, and making you do unnecessary calculations. After going through all of the advice in this book, you should be able to spot the deceptions.

Problem-Solving Key Strategies

- **YOU NEED STRONG FUNDAMENTALS.** If you want to get a competitive MBA score, you must have a solid understanding of fundamentals. If you struggle to reduce fractions, manipulate exponents, or translate algebra, this will slow you down big time. The information covered in the first few chapters of this book (arithmetic, algebra, geometry) provides an essential foundation for your success.
- **INVEST IN YOUR IMMEDIATE FUTURE.** Many test takers dive right into the questions by doing calculations and then quickly get lost. However, you know that many questions require minimal or no calculations. You must invest the time up front to understand the question thoroughly before attempting to solve it. You should do this for all GMAT questions, both verbal and quantitative. Don't spend too much time, though. You have 15–30 seconds to understand the question and come up with a plan of attack. This investment will save you time in the immediate future (the next 1–2 minutes).
- **HARVEST THE GARDEN OF ANSWER CHOICES.** The answer choices provide more information than you realize. They narrow the field down to five possibilities. They tell you what kind of response is required. They give you extra insight into the question. For example, if every answer choice has a π or a $\sqrt{3}$ in it, this may tell you to exploit your knowledge of circles or special triangles. If you eliminate an answer choice,

you may be able to eliminate another choice or two for the same reason, allowing you to get rid of two or three answer choices at the same time.

- **TRY THIS CONCEPT—CONCEPTUAL THINKING!** As mentioned before, conceptual thinking is a big part of doing problem solving questions quickly and with minimal calculations. Most test takers, though, have not practiced this enough. So they go back to doing small calculations on the side. We know this is hard at first. However, the more you exercise your brain, the smarter, faster, and more confident you become.

- **"SIMPLICITY IS THE ULTIMATE SOPHISTICATION."** Leonardo da Vinci said it best. Sophisticated test takers simplify problems in many ways by leveraging conceptual thinking, algebra, and number properties and by breaking down the question. Simplify your calculations, your processes, and your thinking.

- **CARRY 3 BIG STICKS—PICKING NUMBERS, ALGEBRA, AND NUMBER PROPERTIES.** Although we will discuss these tactics below, leveraging these three biggest weapons in your arsenal really counts as a strategy on its own. Every GMAT test prep book, course, and successful student will champion picking numbers, algebra, and number properties. You should too.

Notice that for this problem, we needed the fundamentals of algebra and distance/rate/time. We had to think conceptually and combine it with a simplified approach to our calculations. Had we harvested the answer choices more deeply, we would have determined that the answer would have to be a multiple, thus eliminating B and C. Later in this chapter, we will spend time understanding how to find the best approach.

Problem-Solving Methods

We introduced this chapter with a basic three-step approach. We will now discuss a variety of methods and processes for some of the more common problem-solving question types later in the chapter. The main methodology you should use is the **know-want-approach method**.

When you encounter a problem-solving question on the GMAT, ask yourself the following questions:

1. **WHAT DO YOU KNOW?** You need to extract and digest everything you read.

   - What information has been given to you directly in the problem?
   - What extra information is implied?
   - What do the answer choices tell you about the question?

2. **WHAT DO YOU WANT?** You need to understand the scope clearly.

   - What is the problem specifically asking for?
   - Are there any particular keywords or hints to be aware of?
   - Are there any defined units in the question?

3. **WHAT IS YOUR APPROACH?** You need to come up with a plan of attack. For every problem-solving question, you should be able to identify the necessary components quickly.

   - What theory is being tested?
   - What relevant strategies, methods, and tactics do you have in your arsenal?
   - What is the key insight or catch of the problem? (Most quantitative questions require a special insight for doing the problem most effectively.)
   - Based on the above, what is the best approach, or mix of approaches, for you to apply?

The idea behind the **know-want-approach** method is a solid **understanding**, a strategic **focus** of your time and effort, and overall **efficiency**. In the initial stages of your GMAT studying, you may want to write down everything. Eventually, with practice, this method will become instinctive.

Problem-Solving Tactics

We've already mentioned a few tactics above in our fundamentals, strategies, and methods. However, let's look at some of the more effective and popular tactics for GMAT problem solving.

Tactic 1. Pick Numbers . . . Wisely

Picking numbers is one of the oldest tricks in the book. But it still remains one of the wisest tricks in the book. Almost every GMAT prep guide in the universe (OK, at least on planet Earth), with the ironic exception of the official guide, mentions this tactic. When you begin to work out your solution, you can pick numbers to understand the question better and to simplify your approach. As you proceed, you can pick numbers to make your calculations easier. Lastly, you can pick numbers to check your work. Just make sure you pick numbers that make sense for the question.

- In general, use simple numbers such as 2 or 3. You can also use 0 and 1 for certain problem types (such as inequalities and absolute value), although be mindful of their special properties. Don't forget about fractions, such as $\frac{1}{2}$ or $\frac{1}{3}$, or about negative values if the question allows for them.
- If the question involves a fraction with $\frac{1}{3}$, use a large multiple of 3 such as 30, 60, or 120. Similarly, if you see a $\frac{x}{5}$ or $\frac{y}{7}$ in a question, you should pick a number that is a multiple of 35.
- If the question involves percent changes in a stock, you might try using 100.
- The most likely questions where picking numbers can be a good tactic include percents, mixtures, ratios, or problems where algebraic expressions are in the answer choices.

> Company X's stock rose 30% in year 1 and declined 10% in year 2. How much did the stock increase from the beginning of year 1 to the end of year 2?

Solution: Pick 100 as your starting number → After year 1, you get 100 + 30 = 130. After year 2, you get 130 − 13 = 117. → The increase is 17%.

Tactic 2. Use your Best Friends (Algebra and Number Properties) . . . Forever.

As we have said before, algebra and properties of numbers are indeed your BFFs in math because they are always there to support you and bail you out of a messy situation. Algebra is the language of math, helping you to translate problems, unlock key insights, and simplify calculations on the majority (that's right, over half!) of quantitative questions. Properties of numbers are like the letters and words of math. These properties are how numbers work together and how they react to mathematical situations. Properties of numbers are often the key insight to questions that seem to require 10+ minutes of calculations, letting you figure things out in less than a minute.

> What is the unit digit of 2^{23}?

Solution: Clearly, multiplying the number 2 by itself 23 times is not the answer, as it would take an excessive amount of time. Properties of unit digits tell us that powers of 2 have a pattern of 2-4-8-6 as unit digits, looping every fourth power. This means that 2^4, 2^8, and thus 2^{24} have a unit digit of 6. Therefore, the looping pattern tells us that 2^{23} has a unit digit of 8.

Tactic 3. Don't Break Your Back Solving, Try Backsolving

If you get stuck on a problem and have already spent over a minute to no avail, backsolving or working backward from the answer choices can be a good last resort option (along with POE and guess-timating below). Start with answer choice C because almost all GMAT answer choices are in ascending order and you can likely get to the right answer within three tries. On certain GMAT questions, you should consider backsolving:

- If the problem gives you an end result and asks you to find the starting number
- When the answer choices are simple, clean, and thus easy to plug into the question
- When the math seems to get a bit too labor intensive
- When the algebra in a word problem is more complex than plugging in the answer choices or logically reasoning them out in the question

Tactic 4. Construction, Construction, What's Your Function?

The more complicated a question, the more important it is for you to add structure to the problem. There are many ways you can organize the information—charts, drawings, lists, arrows, matrix boxes, Venn diagrams, and headings such as before/after or year 1/year 2/year 3, etc. Adding structure allows you to see and process things more clearly. It can also provide a great method for solving a problem (e.g., distance-rate-time charts, seen later in this chapter). Lastly, if your scratch work on the given GMAT yellow pad is structured, clean, and easy to follow, you can easily track your work if the answer you get is not among the 5 choices.

Tactic 5. Break It Down!

This is an excellent GMAT tactic, aside from being one of the most common expressions sung by numerous musical artists over the years (MC Hammer leaps to mind). However, these words ring true for many questions, especially those that require structure as described in tactic 4. When you set up your approach to a problem, a high-level view shows you 2, 3, or sometimes even 4 steps to solve it. When you break down a problem, you separate each section into more easily solved pieces.

Tactic 6. Estimate, Guess-timate, Approximate to Elucidate

This tactic is not used enough. We know that most calculations are minimal. Therefore, some questions may test your ability to make reasonable approximations. You can approximate to simplify your calculations. You can estimate if the answer choice values are quite far apart from one another. You can guess-timate (intelligently of course!) if you are running out of time. For example, in geometry if you're stumped but you have a diagram drawn to scale, you can eyeball and guess the closest answer.

Tactic 7. POE: Return of the Friend

As we saw in the critical reasoning chapter, process of elimination (POE) is a very helpful tactic. Eliminating answer choices that are clearly incorrect increases the probability that any guesses, should you make them, will be correct. If you can get down to 2 possible answer choices, your chances are now 50% versus 20% had you not eliminated choices. While eliminating choices, you might just gain further insight to solve the problem. Again, this tactic should be considered among the last resort options. After all, we're hoping you will learn and retain all the theory and strategies to beat the GMAT.

Tactic 8. Don't Get Tricked: Become a Trickster

GMAT test makers have an unusually large bag of tricks from which to conjure smoke and mirrors and throw you off the scent of the correct answer. If you understand how and when they do this, you can become a magician yourself! You can then finesse any tricky question and pull that rabbit out of the hat. Watch for some of the common GMAT traps:

- Incorrect assumptions made when reading questions quickly
- Units of measurement that confuse you
- Wordy questions that ramble on to make you overthink
- Mixing a percent increase with an absolute percent, or misunderstanding the percent of a whole versus the percent of a part
- Good-looking answer choices that seem too easy but are meant to lead you astray
- Mistaking the distance remaining with the distance traveled
- Equation types that you are prone to set up incorrectly
- In geometry, confusing the area inside a figure with the area outside a figure
- Wasting time looking for the shortcut when sometimes you just have to do the math

Tactic 9. Stop Staring!

Many students will gaze at a question in bewilderment, trying to process where to begin. Meanwhile, an entire minute has gone by and they've done nothing. Write down what you know, redraw the diagram, put down a relevant question, and/or map out your know-want-approach method. Just get something on paper. You might find something in the visual scratch work.

Tactic 10. Let It Go

This is one of the hardest things for even the most advanced test takers to do. Letting go of a question is hard because you want so badly to get it right. You might even know that you're pretty close. There is no reason to ever spend more than 3 minutes on a question. Sometimes it's not working out. Sometimes you are just not getting it. It's OK. This happens. You can still get several questions wrong and earn a great score. So focus on the questions you know you can get right and let go of the ones you can't get right. Make sure you really let go of a question and aren't dwelling on it 5 questions later. You need the time and energy to get the doable questions right.

CONVERSION PROBLEMS

Some questions are categorized as conversion problems. In most cases, when other questions require you to make some type of the conversion, the conversion will be given to you in the problem. However, you should be quite familiar with a few conversions, especially converting imperial to metric units.

$$1 \text{ kg} = 2.2 \text{ lbs. (pounds)} \quad 1 \text{ mile} = 1.61 \text{ km} \quad 1 \text{ inch} = 2.54 \text{ cm}$$
$$1 \text{ meter} = 100 \text{ cm} = 1000 \text{ mm}$$

You should also know how to calculate conversions. The key is to figure out the end result and then determine which units you need to get rid of. Keep track of numerators and denominators. Use conversion equivalents to get rid of or change units.

20 mph is how many meters per second?

Solution: 20 miles/hour • 1 hour/60 min • 1 min/60 s • 1.61 km/1 mile • 1000 m/1 km

Note all the different units that cancel out

$$\left(\frac{20 \bullet 1.61 \bullet 1000}{3600}\right)\text{m/s} = \left(\frac{20 \bullet 1.61 \bullet 10}{36}\right)\text{m/s} = \left(\frac{50 \bullet 1.61}{9}\right)\text{m/s} = 8.944 \text{ m/s}$$

MIXTURE PROBLEMS

Most mixture problems involve two or more solutions mixed together or a solution with two or more parts going through changes. Often you'll need to create algebraic expressions to solve these problems. However, there are many shortcuts and tactics you can use.

1. **ALGEBRA.** If you can set up an algebraic equation to start, then do it. If the answer choices are in algebraic form, then this is a pure algebra question. You'll likely have to manipulate the equations.
2. **DRAWING.** It's easy to do mixture problems if you can visualize them with a drawing.
3. **TRACK EVERYTHING.** In many mixture problems, you need to keep track of units, amounts, percentages, total volumes, or a mix of all of them.
4. **CHARTS.** For mixtures that go through changes (e.g., adding 2 L of water to an existing solution), a chart is a good way to lay out the information clearly.
5. **WEIGHTED AVERAGE LINE GRAPH.** If two solutions are mixed together, the resulting solution may have a weighted average mixture. Thus, you can use the line graph to your advantage.
6. **MEASUREMENT PROBLEMS ARE OFTEN CONCEPTUAL.** Whenever you see a classic measurement problem, which is a form of mixture problem where "Jar A is half-full and half of it is poured into Jar B," your best bet is to solve conceptually by visualizing and using logic and reason to figure it out.

RATE PROBLEMS

Rate problems include mostly work/rate and distance/rate questions. The basic formula is

$$\text{Work} = \text{Rate} \cdot \text{Time or } W = RT$$

where W is the amount of work done, R is the speed or rate at which the work is done, and T is the time it takes to do the amount of work.

> Robert peels potatoes at a rate of 3.5 per minute. How many potatoes will he peel in 1 hour?

Solution: $W = (3.5 \text{ potatoes/min}) \cdot (60 \text{ min})$ Note that we converted 1 hour to 60 min = 210 potatoes

Whenever you deal with rate problems, here is what you need to know:

1. **KEEP TRACK OF UNITS.** Often in work/rate problems, several units are at play, which can often get lost in your calculations.
2. **ALWAYS CONVERT TO UNIT RATES OF COMPLETE JOBS.** If you're told that a machine can produce 300 papers in 2 hours, you should convert that to 150 papers per hour. For rate questions, the unit rate means you are converting to per hour (or per days, minutes, or seconds) or converting to per job. If you are given the time for a partial job, calculate the rate for the complete job.
3. **YOU CAN ADD RATES TOGETHER.** If you know the unit rates of 2 different people or 2 different machines, you can add them to come up with a combined rate of the 2 people or the 2 machines. This is another reason why it's important to convert to unit rates.
4. **WHEN STUCK, USE $W = RT$.** If the rate problem is unfamiliar to you, try starting with the basic equation and look for the pieces.
5. **CHART IT OUT!** For more complex rate problems and most distance/rate/time (DRT) problems, a chart is a great method for sorting the information and solving. We'll visit this further in the DRT section.

Work/Rate Problems

There are 3 main types of work/rate problems—single jobs, batch jobs, and triple aspect types. We will explore them all and work for a sample problem for each type.

Work/Rate Type 1: Single Jobs

> Hose A fills a pool in 3 hours, and hose B fills the pool in 4 hours. How long will it take hose A and hose B, working together, to fill the pool?

Solution: For this type of problem, there are 2 methods. We will show them side by side.

Method 1: Combine Unit Rates

Calculate the unit rates for each hose.

Hose A: unit rate = $\frac{1}{3}$ pool/hr

Hose B: unit rate = $\frac{1}{4}$ pool/hr

Add the rates to get the combined rate:
$\frac{1}{3} + \frac{1}{4} = \frac{7}{12}$ pool/hr

Flip the equation to get the total time

$\frac{12}{7}$ hours/pool.

Method 2: Use the Work/Rate Formula

The standard work/rate formula is

$$\frac{1}{A} + \frac{1}{B} = \frac{1}{Both}$$

where A = the time A takes to do something

B = the time it takes B to do something

Both = the time both A and B take to do something

Plugging in we get

$$\frac{1}{3} + \frac{1}{4} = \frac{1}{x} \quad \frac{7}{12} = \frac{1}{x}$$

Therefore $x = \frac{7}{12}$ hours

The big question is which method is better? Unfortunately the answer is, as always, it depends. The formula method is quicker if the test makers give you specific times for all the people or machines in the question. For more complex rate questions, tracking and combining unit rates might be better.

Work/Rate Type 2: Batch Jobs

> Machine A prints 350 newspapers in 7 hours, and machine B prints 2400 newspapers in 6 hours. How long will it take both machines working together to print 1800 newspapers?

Solution: For this type of question, you need to calculate unit rates. Depending on the question, you would either calculate a rate per hour or rate per thing, such as, per newspaper. Given the way that the question is laid out, you should calculate the hourly rate.

Machine A: unit rate = 50 newspapers/hr
Machine B: unit rate = 400 newspapers/hr

Therefore, the combined rate is 450 newspapers/hr. You should be able to see that the math works cleanly and the total number of hours is 4 hours. However, if you cannot see this, then use the formula

$$W = RT \rightarrow 1800 \text{ newspapers} = (450 \text{ newspapers/hr}) \bullet T$$

$$\rightarrow T = \frac{1800}{450} = 4 \text{ hours}$$

Work/Rate Type 3: Triple Aspect

A common format for this type is "*X* people can do *Y* things in *Z* hours. How long will it take *A* people to do *B* things?"

Here you have three aspects at play in the question, which makes it a bit harder. Let's look at a specific example.

> 10 people can paint 6 houses in 5 days. How long would it take 2 people to paint 3 houses?

Strategy for Type 3 Work/Rate Problems

1. **FOCUS ON 2 ASPECTS AT A TIME.** The work/rate problem asked above has 3 aspects. Look at 2 aspects, and decide which one you want to adjust. In this example, you may want to change the 10 people down to 5 people. When you do that, keep the 3rd aspect the same and calculate how the 2nd aspect changes.

10 people	paint 6 houses	in 5 days	becomes
↓ ÷2	↓ ÷2	↓	
5 people	paint 3 houses	in 5 days	

Notice that we changed the number of houses and people but kept the time constant.

2. **BE CAREFUL OF THE INVERSE RELATIONSHIPS.** In the previous step, the number of people and the number of houses had a direct relationship. So when we reduced the people by half, the number of houses also reduced by half. The amount of time, however, has an inverse relationship with both the number of people and the number of houses. At this point in the example, we have the correct number of houses but now we want to change the people from 5 to 2.

5 people	paint 3 houses	in 5 days	becomes
↓ • $\frac{2}{5}$	↓	↓ • $\frac{5}{2}$	
2 people	paint 3 houses	in 12.5 days	

Since the number of people versus days has an inverse relationship, we multiplied the second number by the inverse. In order to get from 5 people to 2 people, we had to multiply by $\frac{2}{5}$. Therefore, for the number of days, we had to multiply by $\frac{5}{2}$, which is the inverse (or the reciprocal).

3. **UNIT RATES CAN HELP.** Sometimes if the question is a bit more complex, it can be worthwhile to bring 2 of the 3 aspects to a unit rate. (It is unlikely you can get all 3 rates equal to 1). Using unit rates can be an easier starting point for your calculations. In the example, bringing two aspects to a unit rate would mean finding how many days it would take for 1 person to paint 1 house. Had we calculated this (feel free to have fun trying to calculate this), we would get 8.33 days.

Distance-Rate-Time (DRT) Problems

The basic formula for distance/rate problems is an offshoot of the work/rate formula:

$$\text{Distance} = \text{Rate} \cdot \text{Time} \rightarrow D = RT$$

If Jill travels 5 hours by car at a speed of 50 mph, the total distance she travels is $D = RT = (50 \text{ mph}) \cdot (5 \text{ hours}) = 250$ miles.

Most DRT problems will not be this simple. Instead, they will be broken down into 2 and sometimes 3 sections. Here are the 3 most common setups.

1. **THE MEET UP:** Alice travels from the west, and Billy travels from the east. They are a certain distance apart. When do they meet?

2. **THE OVERTAKE:** Alice travels from a certain point in a certain direction. Billy travels from the same point and same direction but a little bit later and at a faster speed. When will Billy overtake Alice?

3. **THE MIXED SPEEDS:** Alice travels at a certain speed during part of a trip but then travels at a different speed during another part of the same trip. What was Alice's average speed?

So how do the GMAT test makers make these questions more difficult?

- They make one or both persons start at different times.
- They make one or both persons have to stop or go slower for a short period of time.
- They throw in algebraic variables instead of actual numbers.
- They mix up the units, thinking that you might forget to convert them.

DRT Method: The DiRTy Chart

Regardless of the setup, the best way to deal with DRT problems is to use the "DiRTy chart method." Here's how it works.

	Route A	Route B	Total
D			
R			Average rate
T			

STEP 1 If it helps, you may want to draw a diagram to understand the question better.

STEP 2 Draw the DiRTy chart as per the diagram. Note that some DRT problems may split into 3 parts.

STEP 3 Input the values given in the question.

STEP 4 Determine what value you need to find, and let the variable equal this value. Input that variable into the chart.

STEP 5 Fill in the rest of the chart using your chosen variable.

STEP 6 Determine the key relationship that will help you create an equation to solve. In most cases, it will be:

- Total distance = $D_A + D_B$
- Total time = $T_A + T_B$
- D_A is equal to or is related to D_B
- T_A is equal to or is related to T_B
- Average rate = Total distance/Total time (The chart has been grayed out above so that you don't think that box might represent total rate, because it doesn't.) Calculating average rate is a special subtype of DRT problems that requires you to calculate total distance and total time in order to figure it out.

STEP 7 Solve for the equation or relationship to get your answer.

VENN DIAGRAMS AND MATRIX BOXES

Venn Diagrams and Matrix Box problems are very similar because they are a form of set theory. Simply put, these questions require you to organize information that relates to each other. They are almost like fun word puzzles! In many of these cases, when there are 2 sets of information, both of these methods work. What is important is to find the best method to use for the question in front of you. How do we tell them apart?

- Use Venn diagrams for overlapping groups and matrix boxes for complementary groups (parts add up to 100%). For example, if the group is made up of red and nonred boxes, this is a complementary group and should be solved with matrix boxes.
- For Venn diagrams, you will see key words such as "only," "exactly," "both," or "neither."
- If there are 3 sets or groups of information, you should use Venn diagrams.

In most cases, test takers seem to prefer the matrix box.

1. It tends to involve less work.
2. It has more spaces and so can represent more quantities explicitly.
3. Its rows and columns are nicely aligned for automatic addition/subtraction.

However, if you can fully grasp how Venn diagrams work, they are a much more powerful tool for the tougher problems. Of course, we recommend that you master both methods. Let's first look at Venn diagrams.

The Venn Diagram Method

The basic setup for Venn diagrams is as follows:

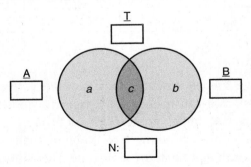

Venn formula 1: $T = a + b + c + N$
Venn formula 2: $T = A + B - c + N$

Depending on the question, you will be given values for either formula 1 or formula 2. Note that the c in formula 2 is subtracted because it was counted twice.

STEP 1 Fill in the total number of elements in the question if given. Label the 2 groups in the question.

STEP 2 Input values in the boxes or inside of circles only if they are specifically given.

STEP 3 Don't forget to consider the value of "neither" in the question. Quite often, this value is zero.

STEP 4 Determine which Venn formula is appropriate. If you are given a value for "a only," then you would use formula 1. If you are given a value for "all of A," then you would use formula 2. Make sure it is clear from the precise wording what the values are.

STEP 5 Manipulate the equation to solve.

The Matrix Box Method

For the matrix box, we use a similar input approach as we did for the Venn diagrams. Essentially, we create a 2 × 2 box to input our values. This is why it's often referred to as a double matrix. We also have a third column and a third row for our totals. When we combine that with another row and column for descriptive headings, we get the following matrix box.

MATRIX BOX

	Description A	Description B	Total
Aspect X			
Not aspect X			
Total			100%

Matrix Box Tactics

- You can have 2 separate descriptions, A or B (e.g. the animals are either dogs or cats). You can instead have aspect X and its complementary opposite (e.g., the animals are black or not black).
- The column and row headings have to be mutually exclusive. In other words, they cannot occur at the same time. Therefore, using our previous example, we cannot have a dog and a cat at the same time nor can we have a black and a nonblack animal at the same time.

- If the question gives you awkward percentages or fractions, try the Picking Numbers tactic. Start with a total number that makes sense, such as a number that is divisible by all the denominators, if you were given fractions in the question.
- Remember that the right-most columns must equal the sum of the columns to the left of them. Similarly, the bottom rows must equal the sum of the numbers above them.

MINIMUM/MAXIMUM PROBLEMS

A common requirement on GMAT problems is to find the maximum or minimum value. This can also be written as "least," "smallest," "most," and "largest" to name just a few synonyms.

> Harry is running for President of his club against two others, Stephen and Gillian. If 31 people are in the club, including Harry, what is the minimum number of votes with which he could actually win?

Solution: To find the minimum number of votes Harry needs, we need to find the minimum number of votes that Stephen and Gillian could get such that Harry would need only one extra vote. Ironically, if we think about the maximum spread of votes, we should just divide $\frac{31}{3}$ and get a spread of $10\frac{1}{3}$. This means that the maximum spread of votes would be 10, 10, and 11. Therefore, Harry needs a minimum of 11 votes.

Minimum/Maximum Strategies

- Figure out first whether you need to maximize or minimize and what variables are at play in the question.
- If you're asked to maximize something, you will usually need to minimize the remaining variables in the problem. If the problem asks you to minimize something, you will usually need to maximize the remaining variables.
- Even though most of the time you can use logic to understand these abstract questions better, you still should do the math and look at the scenarios that exploit the minimum or maximum values.

INTEREST RATE PROBLEMS

GMAT math questions involving interest rates fall into two categories: simple interest and compound interest. These are calculated on a starting loan or investment called the principal. Let's first understand the definitions.

INTEREST: The amount paid for the use of lent or invested money, usually given as a percentage.

PRINCIPAL: The amount of the loan or investment.

SIMPLE INTEREST: Interest that is calculated on only the original principal.

COMPOUNDED INTEREST: Interest that is calculated on the original principal *plus* all accumulated interest.

SEMIANNUAL: Twice a year.

BIANNUAL: Every other year.

SEMIMONTHLY: Twice a month.

BIMONTHLY: Every other month.

Simple Interest Rate Problems

Simple interest is the most basic type of interest rate question tested on the GMAT. The formula is

Interest earned = (Principal invested) • (interest rate) • (Time) = Pit

> If you invest $2000 at an annual interest rate of 8%, your interest earned at the end of year is 2000 • 0.08 • 1 = $160

Another way of looking at this calculation is using the more formal equation

$$A = P(1 + In)$$

where A = amount, P = principal, I = interest rate, n = number of periods

Total amount of investment
= Principal • (1 + (Interest) • (number of time periods))

Interest Rate Tactics

1. Make sure you express the rate of interest in decimals rather than percentage.
2. Make sure you are clear about whether you are solving for the interest or for the new amount due to the interest. These two different things can be easily confused.
3. When you deal with periods of the loan or investment that are not full years and if you adjust the time period, do not adjust the rate of interest or vice versa. For example, if the calculation is to be made on a semiannual basis, then adjust either the time period or the rate of interest, not both.
4. Know how to interpret between simple interest and compound interest. The key is to see how many periods the interest is paid. If interest is paid in one period, that is simple interest. If interest is paid on interest in multiple periods, that is compound interest.
5. Some questions can be solved conceptually by applying concepts such as weighted average or by backsolving.

Compound Interest Rate Problems

Often interest rates are compounded monthly, quarterly, or semiannually. This means that the interest at each period of compounding is added to the original principal. Compounded interest will yield a bigger return than does simple interest at the same rate. The standard formula is:

$$A = P(1 + \frac{r}{n})^{nt}$$

where

A = Amount currently in the investment (principal plus interest)
P = Original principal amount
r = Interest rate (yearly) in decimal format (i.e., 8% = 0.08)
n = Number of times per year the interest is compounded
t = Number of years

There are some common question types when it comes to compound interest rate problems.

Type A Example

> If Alice invests $2000 at an interest rate of 10%, how
> much money will she have at the end of a year?

Answer: $2000 • 1.10 = $2200

Type B Example

> If Alice invests $2000 at an interest rate of 10%,
> compounded semiannually, how much money will
> she have at the end of a year?

Since the annual interest rate is compounded twice during the year, you need to calculate interest at $\frac{10}{2}$ = 5% every 6 months. This is how compounding gets you more money on your investment than does simple interest.

STEP 1 At 6 months, the principal becomes $2000 • 1.05 = $2100.

STEP 2 At 12 months, the new principal balance of $2100 earns another 5% interest, or $2100 • 1.05 = $2205.

Type C Example

> If Alice invests $2000 at an interest rate of 12%,
> compounded quarterly (or bimonthly or monthly),
> how much money will she have at the end of a year?

You can take the step-by-step approach to solve for the 4 quarters, but it will take you time. The calculating would be even more time consuming for bimonthly or monthly compounding questions. This is where using the formula helps. Remember that 12% = 0.12.

$$\text{Quarterly compound: } A = P\left(1 + \frac{r}{n}\right)^{nt}$$

$$\rightarrow A = 2000 \cdot \left(\frac{1 + 0.12}{4}\right)^{4 \cdot 1} = 2000 \cdot (1.03)^4$$

The GMAT test makers won't require you to make lengthy calculations, so look for the answer choices to be in the format above.

PROFIT AND REVENUE

Profit, revenue, and cost questions are relatively common on the GMAT, usually in the form of arithmetic or algebra word problems. You need to know two main equations:

Profit = Revenue – Costs   or $\pi = R - C$

Revenue = Price • (Number of units sold)   or $R = P \cdot Q \rightarrow$

Note that $P = R/Q$

P stands for price, while π stands for profit, just so you can avoid any confusion. Other terms you might hear about include the following.

BREAK-EVEN POINT: The point when the profit is zero. If $\pi = 0$, then $R = C$.

GROSS PROFIT: This is Selling price – Cost, usually on a per unit basis.

PER UNIT: This is the most important GMAT trick to understand on these questions. Sometimes the test makers will give you values in cost per unit while revenue is expressed in total number of unit sales. Make sure you convert to per unit revenue or convert the unit cost to a total cost value.

DATA INTERPRETATION

Data interpretation questions are occurring less frequently on the GMAT. This is because some of the core skills are now being tested on the graphical interpretation section of integrated reasoning. However, you still may see some. If you do, here are some strategies to keep in mind.

- **FIRST, ANALYZE THE DATA CAREFULLY:** Note labels, units, and trends. Avoid misreading.
- **BE QUESTION DRIVEN:** Use the question given in the stem to ask yourself, "What data do I need to solve?"
- **ESTIMATE WHEN POSSIBLE:** Just as in the integrated reasoning section, the GMAT test makers don't expect you to make lengthy or precise calculations. Estimating will simplify your process and reduce the time you spend.

PROBLEM SOLVING: TARGETED REVIEW QUESTIONS

Rate Problems

1. Daniel can paint the fence in 10 hours. When Mr. Miyagi helps, they can both paint the fence in $3\frac{1}{3}$ hours. How long would it take Mr. Miyagi to paint half the fence by himself?

   (A) $2\frac{1}{3}$

   (B) $2\frac{1}{2}$

   (C) 3

   (D) 5

   (E) $6\frac{1}{6}$

2. Machine 1 produces 1000 bolts in 5 hours, while machine 2 can complete 75% of the same job in 3 hours. How much time is required for both machines to produce 1750 bolts if machine 2 stops producing after 3 hours?

   (A) 5

   (B) 5.75

   (C) 6

   (D) 7.5

   (E) 8

Venn Diagrams

3. 500 dormitory residents eat daily in a campus cafeteria with a prepurchased meal plan. On an average day, 320 residents have soup with their meal and 160 residents have salad with their meal. If at least 100 residents have neither soup nor salad, then the number of residents who have both soup and salad must be between:

   (A) 40 and 100

   (B) 80 and 120

   (C) 80 and 160

   (D) 100 and 160

   (E) 160 and 320

4. Molly's high school focuses on the performing arts. In her year, 40 students can sing, 60 students can dance, and 24 students can act. No student is a triple threat (someone who can sing, dance, and act). However, 16 students can sing and dance, 12 students can dance and act, and 8 students can sing and act. How many students have only one performing talent?

   (A) 44
   (B) 52
   (C) 60
   (D) 66
   (E) 72

Mixture/Measurement

5. In a lab experiment, the number of bacteria cells produces double the amount of new bacteria cells each day for each of the 4 days since initiation. If the total number of bacteria cells after 4 days is 54 million, how many bacteria cells did the experiment begin with?

   (A) 1.5 million
   (B) 2 million
   (C) 4 million
   (D) 5.5 million
   (E) 7 million

Matrix Boxes

6. At *A Magazine's* Oscar party, $\frac{7}{12}$ of the guests are its employees, and $\frac{1}{2}$ of the guests at the Oscar party are men. If $\frac{1}{5}$ of the guests are men who are not employees of *A Magazine*, what percent of the guests are male employees of *A Magazine*?

   (A) 12%
   (B) 20%
   (C) 24%
   (D) 30%
   (E) 36%

Minimum/Maximum

7. On a hot day in July, an ice cream man sold an average of 14 ice cream products per hour over 5 consecutive hours. If during each hour, this ice cream man sold at least 7 ice cream products, what is the greatest possible range of the number of ice cream products sold in any hour?

(A) 14
(B) 28
(C) 35
(D) 42
(E) 49

Interest Rates

8. Kumar's parents bought him a $5000 GIC investment that paid interest at an annual rate of 6 percent compounded semiannually. What was the total amount of interest paid on the investment in one year?

(A) $150
(B) $300
(C) $304.50
(D) $618
(E) $10,300

9. Just Lamps Inc. sells only lamps and bulbs. Lamp sales revenue was 8% higher in 2011 than in 2010 while bulb sales revenue was 12% lower. If Just Lamps Inc. saw its overall revenue decline by 2% during the same period, what was the ratio of lamp revenues to bulb revenues in 2010?

(A) 2 : 3
(B) 3 : 4
(C) 1 : 1
(D) 3 : 2
(E) 5 : 3

ANSWER KEY

1. **(B)**   4. **(B)**   7. **(E)**
2. **(A)**   5. **(B)**   8. **(C)**
3. **(C)**   6. **(D)**   9. **(C)**

SOLUTIONS

1. **(B)** Use the $\dfrac{\text{work}}{\text{rate}}$ standard formula:

$\dfrac{1}{10} + \dfrac{1}{M} = \dfrac{1}{\frac{10}{3}}$, where M is the number of hours Mr. Miyagi takes to paint the fence

$$\frac{1}{M} = \frac{3}{10} - \frac{1}{10} = \frac{2}{10} \rightarrow M = \frac{10}{2} = 5 \text{ hours}$$

However, you need Mr. Miyagi's time to paint half the fence, which is 2.5 hours.

2. **(A)** First determine unit rates

Machine 1 unit rate $= \dfrac{1000}{5} = 200$ bolts/hr

Machine 2 unit rate $= (75\%) \bullet \dfrac{(1000)}{3} = \dfrac{750}{3} = 250$ bolts/hr

The two machines' combined rate is $200 + 250 = 450$ bolts/hr

Now break down this problem into the first 3 hours and the rest of production.

In 3 hours, the machines produce $450 \bullet 3 = 1350$ bolts $\rightarrow$ leaving $1750 - 1350 = 400$ bolts.

Machine 1 can produce the rest of the 400 bolts in 400 bolts/200 bolts/hr $= 2$ hours. The total time is $2 + 3 = 5$ hours.

3. **(C)** Let's start by drawing a Venn diagram.

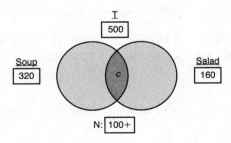

In this case, use the formula $T = A + B - c + N$, which gives

$$500 = 320 + 160 - c + (100+)$$
$$\rightarrow \text{By isolating the } c \text{, you get } c = 480 - 500 + (100+)$$

$c = 80+ \rightarrow$ The range is limited by the number of people who can have salad, which is 160.

4. **(B)** Because you have overlapping sets, this is a Venn diagram problem. However, this is a triple diagram since there are 3 different performing disciplines. Don't get too stressed out. The process is the same and the GMAT test makers typically make these triple Venn diagrams easier than the standard ones. First, fill in what you know

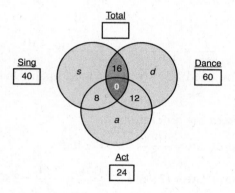

Now calculate the number of students with a single performing talent by subtracting the double threats from the whole of each performance type.

Singing: $40 - 16 - 8 = 16$
Dancing: $60 - 16 - 12 = 32$
Acting: $24 - 12 - 8 = 4$

This gives $16 + 32 + 4 = 52$ students with a single performing talent.

5. **(B)** Given that you are looking for a starting point number, this question could best be served by backsolving. Start with answer choice C.

Day 1	Day 2	Day 3	Day 4	Total	
4	$+ 8 = 12$	$+ 24 = 36$	$+ 72 = 108$	108	$\rightarrow$ Too high! Try a lower number
2	$+ 4 = 6$	$+ 12 = 18$	$+ 36 = 54$	54	$\rightarrow$ On target!

Algebraically, you could have let the starting amount be x, which would give you

$$x + 2x + 6x + 18x = 54 \rightarrow 27x = 54 \rightarrow x = 2 \text{ million}$$

The algebra here is relatively straightforward. In a harder question, though, it's good to have two different tactics up your sleeve.

6. **(D)** This is a matrix box problem because there are 2 • 2 elements at play and there is no overlap. Guests are either male/female or employee/nonemployee. Also, because of the fraction $\frac{7}{12}$, let's pick the number 120 total. Your box should look like this (**bold** is for original values: *italics* are calculated values):

	Male	**Female**	**Total**
Employee	36	34	70
Nonemployee	24	26	50
Total	60	60	120

From the matrix box, you can see that the number of male employees is 36 out of 120 or $\frac{36}{120}$, which reduces to $\frac{3}{10}$ or 30%.

7. **(E)** In order to find the greatest number of ice cream products sold in any hour, you need to minimize the number sold in all the other hours. This means that you should let the ice cream man sell 7 ice cream products in each of 4 different hours, or 7 • 4 = 28 ice cream products sold. You also need to look at the average for the 5 hours.

$$\text{Average} = \frac{\text{(Sum of terms)}}{\text{(Number of terms)}} \rightarrow 14 = \frac{(28+x)}{5}$$

$$70 = 28 + x \rightarrow x = 56 \rightarrow \text{You want the range,}$$
$$\text{though, which is } 56 - 7 = 49.$$

8. **(C)** You can use the formula $A = P\left(1+\frac{r}{n}\right)^{nt}$, where

A = the amount of money after t or 1 year
P = principal amount invested of \$5,000
r = the annual interest rate of 6% or 0.06
n = the number of times compounded, which is 2

$$5000\left(\frac{1+0.06}{2}\right)^{(2)(1)} = 5000(1.03)^2 = 5000(1.0609) = \$5304.50$$

Therefore the interest paid is \$5,304.50 – \$5,000 = \$304.50.

9. **(C)** Since you are given two different years, it's a good idea to sort out this information. Second, since you're dealing with percents and no actual numbers, picking numbers for one of the revenues would be a good tactic here. Use algebra for the rest. Use $100 for the starting bulb revenue in 2011 and x for the starting lamp revenue in 2011. When you draw a chart, you get

	2010	% chg	2011
Bulb revenue	100	−12	88
Lamp revenue	x	+0.08x	1.08x
Total revenue	100 + x	−0.02(100 + x)	0.98(100 + x)

Using the 2011 column gives the equation $88 + 1.08x = 0.98(100 + x)$

$$88 + 1.08x = 98 + 0.98x \rightarrow 0.1x = 10, x = 100$$

What this means is that in 2010, lamp revenues = bulb revenues, so the ratio is 1: 1.

You could also have used the weighted average line graph. Instead, you could have noticed that the overall decline of 2% (−2%) is exactly between +8% and −12%. It still is a good exercise to try this out and leverage algebra and picking numbers as a solid strategy.

Probability

11

Probability is the likelihood that a certain event or multiple events will occur. The questions that show up on the GMAT range from easy to very difficult. This topic is broken down into three main probability formulas along with several key topics that are used to increase the difficulty. Some basic elements to remember are the following:

- Probability values range from 0% to 100%, inclusive. You cannot have a probability of 150% to win a game (no matter what Kobe Bryant or other professional athletes might tell you).
- Probability can be measured in decimals, fractions, or percents. Be sure to check the answer choice format before starting to solve.
- Many probability questions use decks of cards, coin tosses, or dice rolls. So if you're not a card shark and have no idea how many aces or spades are in a deck of cards, you should probably buy a set or watch some Texas hold'em poker on TV.

BASIC PROBABILITY OF A SINGLE EVENT

The simplest probability question would ask, "What is the probability of rolling a six on one roll of a die?"

The answer, of course, is $\frac{1}{6}$. This realization stems from the basic formula for probability of a single event.

$$P(A) = \text{(The number of outcomes where } A \text{ occurs)/} \\ \text{(The total number of possible outcomes)}$$

This is the starting point for all probability questions. The difficulty of the questions is increased by adding further obstacles such as multiple events or restrictions.

PROBABILITY OF ONE EVENT OR ANOTHER

Although we gave you the basic formula for probability, there is also the general case formula for probability of one event or another.

$$P(A \text{ or } B) = P(A) + P(B) - P(A \text{ and } B)$$

MUTUALLY EXCLUSIVE AND COMPLEMENTARY EVENTS

The best way to explain and compare mutually exclusive and complementary events is with a chart.

MUTUALLY EXCLUSIVE AND COMPLEMENTARY EVENTS

Aspect	Mutually Exclusive Events	Complementary Events
Definition	Events that can never occur together; the occurrence of one event eliminates the possibility of the other event occurring	Events are complementary if one or the other must occur but they can never occur together
Examples	• Scoring both 780 and 800 score on the same GMAT test • Coming in 1st and 3rd place in an Olympics marathon • Getting both heads and tails on the same coin toss • The Miami Heat and the LA Lakers winning the NBA Championship in the same year	• Getting into the MBA school of your dreams or not • Winning the Olympics marathon or not • Getting heads or tails on the same coin toss • Winning at least one game of the NBA Championships or not winning any games
Why is this important?	If events are mutually exclusive, then you simply add the probabilities of each event.	The probability of complementary events always adds to zero, you can use the mirror rule to solve some difficult problems
How does this affect the general case formula?	$P(A \text{ and } B) = 0$	$P(A \text{ and } B) = 0$ $P(A \text{ or } B) = 1$
Other tips to consider	• Note that the probability of heads and tails in coin tosses is both complementary and mutually exclusive. • All complementary events are, by definition, also mutually exclusive	

PROBABILITY OF TWO OR MORE EVENTS

When you are trying to determine the probability of 2 or more events occurring, use this third formula. It is applicable to a large proportion of GMAT probability questions.

$$P(A + B) = P(A) \bullet P(B)$$

Let's look at this example.

What is the probability of rolling 2 sixes on two rolls of a die?

(A) $\dfrac{1}{36}$

(B) $\dfrac{1}{18}$

(C) $\dfrac{1}{6}$

(D) $\dfrac{7}{36}$

(E) $\dfrac{1}{3}$

Solution: $P(6 \text{ and } 6) = P(6) \bullet P(6) = \dfrac{1}{6} \bullet \dfrac{1}{6} = \dfrac{1}{36}$.

The answer is A.

INDEPENDENT AND DEPENDENT EVENTS

The best way to explain and compare independent and dependent events (also known as conditional probability) is with a chart.

INDEPENDENT AND DEPENDENT EVENTS

Aspect	Independent Events	Dependent Events
Definition	Events where the occurrence of one event does not affect the probability of the other	Events where the occurrence of one event affects the probability of another
Examples	• Coin tosses • Dice rolls • Winning money at the casino and getting hit by a truck on the way home • Picking balls out of jars/boxes with replacement • Picking cards out of a deck with replacement	• Picking balls out of jars/boxes without replacement • Picking cards out of a deck without replacement • The probability of getting the 3rd prize in a raffle after the first two prizes are given out
Why is this important?	If events are independent, then you can easily multiply events together to calculate probability	With dependent events, you need to determine how the new probabilities are conditional to previous outcomes
How does this affect the 3rd formula?	No effect	$P(A + B) = P(A) \bullet P(A/B)$ or $P(A + B) = P(A) \bullet P_A(B)$
Other tips to consider	• Watch for whether the question specifies "with" or "without" replacement when selecting objects • Dependent events can sometimes create two or more scenarios to consider • Whenever multiple events are said to be simultaneous, you can look at each event in turn	

MIRROR RULE PROBABILITY

Often the GMAT will ask you the probability of something "not happening" or of "at least one" thing happening. By using the complementary rules for probability, we get two equations that make the mirror rule.

$$P(A \text{ happens}) = 1 - P(A \text{ doesn't happen})$$
$$P(\text{at least one of } B \text{ happens}) = 1 - P(\text{no } B \text{ happens})$$

Let's look at the mirror rule strategy in an example.

A single coin is tossed four times. What is the probability that you will get at least one tail?

(A) $\dfrac{1}{16}$

(B) $\dfrac{1}{4}$

(C) $\dfrac{3}{8}$

(D) $\dfrac{5}{8}$

(E) $\dfrac{15}{16}$

Solution:

$P(\text{at least one tail}) = 1 - P(\text{no tails}) = 1 - P(4 \text{ heads})$

$= 1 - \dfrac{1}{2} \cdot \dfrac{1}{2} \cdot \dfrac{1}{2} \cdot \dfrac{1}{2} = 1 - \dfrac{1}{16} = \dfrac{15}{16}$

The answer is E.

Be sure you understand the complementary opposites of "will happen" and of "at least one happens."

In question 4, we could still have used conceptual thinking to help us narrow the choices. You are more likely to get at least one tail out of four tosses as opposed to three tails. Therefore, we can reason that the correct answer will be closer to 1 than it is to zero, leaving us with choices D and E as our possible picks.

PAIRS PROBABILITY

What if you are asked, "If you roll a die twice, what is the probability you will end up with a pair?" Let's draw.

P(die #1)

?/?

P(die #2)

?/?

A common mistake is to make the probability of the first die roll $\frac{1}{6}$.

The first roll can actually be any number from 1 to 6. The question is asking the probability that the second roll will match the first. This second probability is dependent on the first roll. No matter what the first die roll is, the probability of the second roll is the same. So we would actually get:

Die #1

6/6

Die #2

1/6

Probability(getting a pair in two die rolls) = $\frac{6}{6} \cdot \frac{1}{6} = \frac{1}{6}$

ADVANCED PROBABILITY

The GMAT creates more difficult and advanced questions by simply adding different elements of theory to the question. For example, the test makers have a probability question combined with algebra or take two probability concepts and put them both in the same question. So even though we've reviewed all the main topics of probability, the GMAT test makers will require your cumulative knowledge and adaptability in order to solve the tougher questions.

Joey and his friends played a new game that uses 20 playing cards made up of 2 suits of 10 cards each. The cards in each suit have values from 1 to 10. If Joey turns over 4 cards, what is the probability that he will find at least one pair of cards having the same value?

(A) $\frac{1}{5}$

(B) $\frac{99}{323}$

(C) $\frac{3}{5}$

(D) $\frac{224}{323}$

(E) $\frac{4}{5}$

Solution: This question is tough because it combines the mirror rule with pairs probability. Let's draw it out first.

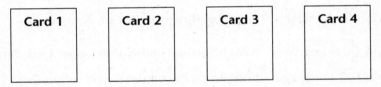

Note that this question uses the key phrase "at least one," which tells you to use the mirror rule. So you would get:

$$P\text{ (at least one pair)} = 1 - P\text{(getting no pairs)}$$

To solve P (getting no pairs), you need to make sure that for every card that gets picked, the next card cannot match the previous cards. This means you are going to have fewer cards to pick and a smaller number of cards to pick from each time.

$$\frac{20}{20} \cdot \frac{18}{19} \cdot \frac{16}{18} \cdot \frac{14}{17} = \frac{224}{323}$$

Finally, $1 - \frac{224}{323} = \frac{99}{323}$

The answer is D.

PROBABILITY: TARGETED REVIEW QUESTIONS

1. In a raffle that sells 3200 tickets, there is only one prize. What is the probability that a man who bought 40 tickets will win the prize?

   (A) $\dfrac{1}{3200}$

   (B) $\dfrac{1}{320}$

   (C) $\dfrac{1}{80}$

   (D) $\dfrac{3}{80}$

   (E) $\dfrac{1}{8}$

2. Teams A, B, and C compete in a baseball league but in separate divisions. Each team is vying to win at least 100 games against division rivals in the season. The probability of each team doing so is $\dfrac{1}{3}$, $\dfrac{2}{5}$, and $\dfrac{3}{8}$, respectively. What is the probability that teams A and B will win 100 games against division rivals while team C will not?

   (A) $\dfrac{1}{40}$

   (B) $\dfrac{1}{20}$

   (C) $\dfrac{1}{12}$

   (D) $\dfrac{2}{15}$

   (E) $\dfrac{5}{8}$

3. A number is selected from the first 40 positive 2-digit integers. What is the probability that the number is a multiple of 7 or 13?

   (A) 2.25%
   (B) 12.50%
   (C) 20.25%
   (D) 22.50%
   (E) 25.25%

4. A jug contains balls with colors and numbers. Each ball has one of three colors and one of five numbers on it. If one ball is selected from the jug, what is the probability of selecting a white ball with a 3 on it.

   (1) The probability of selecting a white ball or a ball with a 3 on it is $\frac{1}{5}$.

   (2) P(a white ball) – P(a ball with a 3 on it) = $\frac{1}{20}$

5. Sebastian draws x cards from a deck of cards. What is the probability that he draws at least one pair?

   (1) The probability of selecting one pair is $\frac{1}{16}$.

   (2) The probability of selecting no pairs is $\frac{5}{16}$.

ANSWER KEY

1. **(C)**   3. **(D)**   5. **(B)**
2. **(C)**   4. **(E)**

SOLUTIONS

1. **(C)** Using the basic formula for probability gives
$$\frac{40 \text{ tickets}}{(3200 \text{ tickets})} = \frac{4}{320} = \frac{1}{80}$$

2. **(C)** Each team's probabilities are independent from each other. However, we should make sure that we use $\frac{5}{8}$ for team C's probability of not winning 100 games. Thus the probability will be
$$\frac{1}{3} \bullet \frac{2}{5} \bullet \frac{5}{8} = \frac{1}{12}$$

3. **(D)** The set of numbers are 10 to 49 inclusive. There are 6 multiples of 7 and 3 multiples of 13 in this set. Therefore the probability is $\frac{9}{40}$ = 22.5%.

4. **(E)** If we use the classic probability formula, we will get

$$P(\text{white ball or a ball with a 3})$$
$$= P(\text{white ball}) + P(\text{a ball with a 3}) - P(\text{white ball with a 3})$$

Statement 1 gives us only one part of this equation, and we are missing the other two pieces. *Insufficient*

Statement 2 gives us two parts of the equation that seem helpful. If we look closely, though, we are given a different setup (subtraction instead of addition). There is no way to manipulate the equation to solve for anything useful. *Insufficient*

Because of the awkward setup of statement 2, there is no way to solve this when you combine both statements. *Insufficient*

Both statements together are still not sufficient.

5. **(B)** This question is a bit tricky because we don't know how many cards are drawn.

Statement 1 gives us the probability of selecting one pair, but we don't know how many pairs are actually drawn. *Insufficient*

Statement 2 gives us information that could be used with the mirror rule, which gives us

$$P \text{ (at least one pair)} = 1 - P \text{ (no pairs)} \rightarrow 1 - \frac{5}{16} = \frac{11}{16} \ \text{Sufficient}$$

Statement 2 alone is sufficient.

Permutations and Combinations

12

Combinatorics is one of the more difficult topics in the math portion of the GMAT. Basically, combinatorics is the number of ways we can arrange things. A simple example would be the number of ways to arrange 5 different pictures in a display or to arrange 6 guests around a dinner table. Although this content is considered advanced material, some basic problems may show up for every student.

PERMUTATIONS VS. COMBINATIONS

There are two types of combinatorics: permutations and combinations. The basic difference is that in permutations, the order of the arranged objects matters. In combinations, the order does not matter. The chart below summarizes some of the main differences.

PERMUTATION AND COMBINATION OVERVIEW

Aspect	Permutation	Combination
Does order matter?	Yes	No (anarchy!)
How do I check for order?	Switch two elements around and see if it creates a new arrangement. If it does, then you have a permutation	
Example of question types	Passwords, seating arrangements, license plates, anything where you arrange objects in a nonrepeating way	People in groups, sets of numbers
Key words	Arrangement, order, schedule, itinerary, display	Team, group, committee, set, numbers
Frequency of each type on the GMAT	Frequent	Not often
Standard formula where: N = the # of total elements K = the # of items being selected	$\dfrac{N!}{(N-K)!}$	$\dfrac{N!}{K!(N-K)!}$
Notation	$_NP_K$ or "N PICK K"	$_NC_K$ or "N CHOOSE K"

REPEATING VS. NONREPEATING COMBINATORICS

By definition, permutations and combinations require that you cannot have repetition. For example, in a race, you cannot have someone finish in both 1st and 2nd place. For the permutation and combination section, we will assume that there is no repetition. If repetition is specifically allowed, then it is sometimes just easier to draw the problem and solve by inspection. License plates offer a perfect example:

New York City wants to issue license plates with 4 letters and 3 numbers. If the numbers and letters are allowed to repeat, how many different license plates can be created?

(A) 456,976,000
(B) 258,336,000
(C) 388,800
(D) 26,000
(E) Infinite

Solution: Note that this question is by definition a nonpermutation problem. However, it is a combinatorics question because we are still counting the number of arrangements. If we draw it out and calculate the total *number of* possibilities for each group, we would get:

LETTERS   **NUMBERS**

Now we just multiply them all together to get 26 × 26 × 26 × 26 × 10 × 10 × 10 = 456,976,000 license plates. So it looks like New York has room to grow!

The answer is A.

PERMUTATIONS: BASIC AND WITH SELECTION

The most basic permutation is the number of ways to arrange N items when order matters and there is no repetition. This is calculated as $N!$ or "N factorial," where N is the total number of elements in the question. Factorials are calculated by taking the number N and multiplying it by every whole number below it all the way down to the number 1.

$$10! = 10 \times 9 \times 8 \times 7 \times 6 \times 5 \times 4 \times 3 \times 2 \times 1$$

$$0! = 1 \quad 1! = 1 \quad 2! = 2 \quad 3! = 6 \quad 4! = 24 \quad 5! = 120 \quad 6! = 720$$

Billy goes to the movies with 5 of his friends. There are 6 seats left in the front row. How many different seating arrangements can Billy and his friends create?

(A) 15,625

(B) 7,776

(C) 720

(D) 30

(E) 6

Solution: Since order matters, this is a permutation. The total number of elements is 6 people, so $N = 6$. The answer is $6! = 6 \times 5 \times 4 \times 3 \times 2 \times 1 = 720$.

The answer is C.

PERMUTATION WITH SCENARIOS

If the combinatorics question uses the key word or phrases "or," "at least," or "at most," you may be dealing with scenarios. In this case, you will have different values for K. To resolve this type of question, you first need to determine the scenarios. For each scenario, calculate the total number of arrangements and then sum them up.

Alice is creating head tables for a wedding party of 14 people. Excluding the bride and groom, she is trying to decide whether to go with tables that seat 4 or 6 people. How many different seating arrangements can Alice have for the first table only?

(A) $\dfrac{14!}{10!}$

(B) $\dfrac{14!}{8!}$

(C) $\dfrac{12!}{8!}$

(D) $\dfrac{14!}{10!} + \dfrac{14!}{8!}$

(E) $\dfrac{12!}{8!} + \dfrac{12!}{6!}$

Solution: This is a permutation because order matters with a seating arrangement. $N = 12$ because we do not include the bride and groom. The number we are selecting can be 4 or 6 so we are dealing with scenarios. For each scenario, the K will be different.

Scenario 1–4 person table

$N = 12, K = 4$

$$_NP_K = {_{12}P_4} = \frac{12!}{8!}$$

Scenario 2–6 person table

$N = 12, K = 6$

$$_NP_K = {_{12}P_6} = \frac{12!}{6!}$$

Now we add up the scenario totals, giving us $\dfrac{12!}{8!} + \dfrac{12!}{6!}$.

The answer is E.

COMBINATIONS

Combination calculations are very much the same as permutation calculations. The only differences are that order does not matter, and that the standard formula we use is different by a factor of $1/K!$

Combinations with Selection

Bobby is studying for the GMAT, and there are 8 other students in his class. He wants to create a study group with 3 others. How many different groups can he create?

(A) 40,320

(B) 336

(C) 56

(D) 24

(E) 6

Solution: Order does not matter here because we are creating groups and the order in which the group members are selected does not matter (unless of course we are dealing with easily bruised egos).

$$N = 8, K = 3$$

$$_NC_K = {_8}C_3 = \frac{8!}{(3!5!)} = \frac{(8\times7\times6)}{(3\times2)} = 56$$

The answer is C.

Combination with Scenarios

John has 8 friends and wants to have a series of dinner parties. How many ways can he have a dinner party with 1 guest, 2 guests, or 3 guests?

(A) 12,544

(B) 92

(C) 56

(D) 28

(E) 8

Solution: This is a combination since we are talking about people forming groups. Thus the order will not matter. As in permutations, the key word "or" says to us that we are dealing with scenarios. Since we are selecting from 8 guests, then $N = 8$.

Scenario 1:
One Guest
$N = 8, K = 1$

$$_NC_K = {_8}C_1 = \frac{8!}{(1!7!)}$$

$= 8$

Scenario 2:
Two Guests
$N = 8, K = 2$

$$_NC_K = {_8}C_2 = \frac{8!}{(2!6!)}$$

$= 28$

Scenario 3:
Three Guests
$N = 8, K = 3$

$$_NC_K = {_8}C_3 = \frac{8!}{(3!5!)}$$

$= 56$

Now we add up all the scenarios giving us $8 + 28 + 56 = 92$.

The answer is C.

COMBINATORICS METHOD

Follow this basic methodology for solving combinatorics problems:

1. **DRAW IT OUT:** If you can, use a drawing to set up the problem and understand it better.
2. **SOLVE BY INSPECTION:** Simpler problems, particularly ones that allow for repetition (and are not true permutations), can be solved by simply looking at the number of possibilities for each group and multiplying them together.
3. **CHECK FOR ORDER:** If you are not sure, you can use the check described in the first table in this chapter "Permutation and Combination Overview."
4. **DETERMINE *N*:** This is the total number of elements involved in the question.
5. **DETERMINE IF THERE IS A *K*:** In some examples, you will select a smaller amount from the larger amount *N*.
6. **CHECK FOR ANY SPECIAL CIRCUMSTANCES:** These are among the harder examples, so it's important to know which types will show up.

   - **CIRCLE:** Use $(N - 1)!$
   - **REPEATED ELEMENTS:** Use $N!/A!B!...$, where *A* and *B* are the number of repeated elements in the question.
   - **COUPLES OR GROUPS:** Treat each subgroup as a single element. Then calculate the overall number of arrangements multiplied by the number of arrangements for each subgroup.
   - **SCENARIOS:** If the question uses the key word or phrases "or," "at least," or "at most," you need to calculate each combinatorics scenario separately and then add up the totals.
   - **SPECIAL CONSTRAINTS:** The key is essentially to break them down into separate portions and calculate each piece accordingly.

7. **SET UP THE BASIC EQUATIONS:** You can set up your equations in the form $_NP_K$ (*N* Pick *K*) and/or $_NC_K$ (*N* Choose *K*).
8. **PLUG IN FORMULAS AND SOLVE:** Use the memorized formulas to calculate the total. Remember to review the answer choices to determine whether the form of the answer will be a number or a combinatorics notation.

PERMUTATIONS AND COMBINATIONS:
TARGETED REVIEW QUESTIONS

1. Wayne just received 5 vases in a set from his grandmother. Although he doesn't particularly like them, he decides to display them on the mantle behind his 50-inch plasma television. That way, he hopes they won't be noticed. All the vases look the same except that there are 2 vases colored green, 2 colored red, and the last one is colored blue. In how many ways can Wayne arrange the display in a row?

   (A) 6
   (B) 18
   (C) 30
   (D) 60
   (E) 120

2. Coach Will needs to get his glee team ready for sectionals by selecting a 6-person team of 3 men and 3 women. There are 5 men and 7 women vying for the spots. How many different ways can he arrange the teams?

   (A) 35
   (B) 70
   (C) 120
   (D) 140
   (E) 280

3. Mario's Pizzeria is offering a special. Students can order a medium pizza for only $6.99 by choosing one topping from each of 4 categories: meats, veggies, cheese, and bread. Mario's has 5 different meats, 7 veggies, 4 types of cheese, and 3 varieties of bread. How many different combinations of pizzas can Mario make?

   (A) 105
   (B) 140
   (C) 275
   (D) 420
   (E) 525

4. Billy and 10 of his friends are going to the movies. There are 2 couples who insist on sitting together and another group of 4 BFFs that always sit together. How many different ways can they arrange themselves in the front row of the movie theater?

   (A) 11!
   (B) $11! \times 2 \times 2 \times 4$
   (C) $6! \times 2! \times 2! \times 4!$
   (D) $6! \times 4!$
   (E) $6! \times 4 \times 2$

5. Robin Hood and 4 of his Merry Men decide to see the Renaissance Festival evening show. There are 5 seats in the front row reserved for them. Little John has told the group that he has to sit on the end so that he can stretch his long legs. In how many ways can the Merry Men arrange themselves in the front row?

   (A) 48
   (B) 64
   (C) 84
   (D) 96
   (E) 108

ANSWER KEY

1. **(C)**   3. **(D)**   5. **(A)**
2. **(B)**   4. **(C)**

SOLUTIONS

1. **(C)** This is an example of permutations with repeated elements. The formula for repeated elements is $\dfrac{N!}{A!B!}$ ... where A and B are the repeated elements. In this case, the repeated elements are the red and green vases. So $N = 5$, $A = 2$, $B = 2$ and the answer is $\dfrac{5!}{(2!)(2!)} = 30$.

2. **(B)** This is a combination question since we are dealing with teams and we also have selection. We should treat the men and women as separate groups. For the men, $N = 5$ and $K = 3$. For the women, $N = 7$ and $K = 3$. So using the notation $_NC_K$ we get

Men		**Women**
$_5C_3$	*	$_7C_3$
$\dfrac{5!}{(3!)(2!)} = 10$	*	$\dfrac{7!}{(3!)(5!)} = 7 = 10 \times 7 = 70$ possibilities

3. **(D)** Each ingredient can be treated as a separate piece in this simple combinatory problem. Since we are choosing only one ingredient from each category, the total number of pizzas is $5 \times 7 \times 4 \times 3 = 420$ pizzas.

4. **(C)** Normally we would say that $N = 11$. In this case, though, we treat each subgroup as a single element. We now have $N = 6$ (2 couples, 1 quartet, and 4 singles). We first calculate the number of ways to arrange the grouped elements, which is

$$N! = 6! = 720$$

We also have to calculate the number of arrangements within each subgroup.

Each couple is $2! = 2$. The quartet is $4! = 24$.

The total number of arrangements is $6! \times 2! \times 2! \times 4!$

5. **(A)** In this problem, we have a constraint where Little John wants to sit only on the end. This results in 2 scenarios. Little John will be either on the left side or on the right side. Since the calculation for each scenario will be the same, we can just calculate one of the scenarios and multiply by 2.

Scenario 1: Little John is sitting on the left-hand side. To calculate the number of arrangements for the rest, $N = 4$, so it will be $4!$

The answer will be $2 \times 4! = 48$.

Introduction to the Verbal Section | 13

THE GROUND RULES

In the Verbal section, you will have 75 minutes in which to answer 41 questions in three different formats: Sentence Correction, Critical Reasoning, and Reading Comprehension. All are multiple-choice questions.

There is no set order to the question formats, but the GMAT does keep track of number of each format you have seen in a single test sitting: 12 Critical Reasoning questions, about 13 Reading Comprehension questions, and about 16 Sentence Correction questions.

We have to say "about," because the test maker slips a few questions into the 41 that don't count toward your score, "experimental questions" of each of the three formants that you're essentially beta-testing for future tests. Don't worry about trying to figure out if a question is "experimental" or "real"—just know that it means you might have one 14 Reading Comprehension questions and only 11 Critical Reasoning.

What the GMAT *Says* the Verbal Section Tests

According the GMAC's official documents, the Verbal section of the GMAT tests your ability to do three things:

1. read and comprehend written material,
2. reason and evaluate arguments, and
3. correct written material to conform to standard written English.

But that's just an indirect way of saying, "There are three types of questions: Reading Comprehension, Critical Reasoning, and Sentence Correction." To be sure, these three broad conceptual areas are tested, just probably not in the way you expect.

PACING AND TIMING IN THE VERBAL SECTION

If you were to split your 75 minutes time evenly among the 41 questions, you'd be able to spend a hair under 2 minutes on each question. However, spending equal time on all the questions would be a terrible idea. Reading Comprehension will require by far the largest share of your time. For it you will need to budget in the time needed to read the four passages that go with the questions—two long ones (about 300 words on average) and two short ones (about 150 words). That will take most people at least 10 minutes, and that's not counting the time needed to answer the questions themselves.

Where can you get the extra time? Critical Reasoning questions require a bit of reading themselves (and much more careful reading than Reading Comprehension questions), so it's best not to steal time away from them. That leaves only Sentence Correction questions. Because of the demands elsewhere on your time, you can afford to give no more than a minute apiece to the Sentence Correction questions.

Your overall time budget will look something like this:

Verbal Section Time Allocation

Though the most numerous, Sentence Correction questions will account for a fifth of your time, whereas more than half of the 75 minutes will be spent tackling the Reading Comprehension questions. As a rough guideline:

Type of Question	# of Questions	Average Time Per Question
Sentence Correction	15–16	1 minute
Critical Reasoning	11–13	2 minutes
Reading Comprehension	13–14	Questions: 1–1.5 minutes
		Long Passages: 3–4 minutes
		Short Passages: 2–3 minutes

Two minutes per question can be useful, though, if used as a rough guide as you progress through the Verbal section. If you break your time into 25-minute thirds, you should be done with roughly the first 12 or so questions when 25 minutes have passed, and be on question 27 or 28 after 50 minutes. When the clock switches from counting down minutes to minutes and seconds (the 5:00 mark), you should be somewhere around question 39.

1st Third	Q's 1–12
2nd Third	Q's 13–28
3rd Third	Q's 29–38
Last 5 minutes	Q's 39, 40, & 41

HOW TO TACKLE VERBAL QUESTIONS

Because the three big question types can appear in any order, it might seem like you're going to have to "change gears" frequently as you move through the section, but on a fundamental level the questions are a lot alike. Whether the question throws a handful of grammar rules at you, an argument against changing the zoning ordinances in Uzbekistan, or a catalog of the challenges faced by the earliest European colonists in Australia, each one consists of a discrete amount of information. Your job is to sort through that (often purposely disorganized) information to find the nugget that will allow you to pick the one point-bestowing answer choice from the available five.

Step 1: Identify the Task

Most questions in the Verbal section contain specific language, certain repeated phrases and ideas that both tell you how closely you're supposed to read the text you're working with and give you specific hints about what the right answer should sound like.

For example, say you came across this Reading Comprehension question:

> The author mentions the findings of Dr. Johnson's laboratory regarding the impact of the craters in the third half of the last ice age primarily in order to ...

The most important words of all are the last three: "in order to." That's your cue that you're dealing with a **Function** question. From that, you'll know immediately that the right answer will describe the role that the tediously described detail in the middle of the question (all that business about craters and labs) plays in the author's overall argument in the passage as a whole.

You'll also know that many of the wrong answers will be tempting because they contain information that is true according to the passage, maybe even some near-direct quotes from what you just read. Since the question is *why* the author said the detail, not *what* the author said, those can all be safely eliminated.

The same thing can be said of Critical Reasoning questions. Look to the right place for the right keywords, and you can tell immediately what you are supposed to do. If you saw

> Which of the following, if true, most strongly supports the prediction that the plan will succeed?

you'd know immediately that "most strongly supports" means your task is to Strengthen the argument by making one of its unstated assumptions more plausible. You would proceed to the big chunk of text and look for the argument's conclusion.

Step 2: Process the Information

Everything that appears in a GMAT Verbal question is there for a reason—but that's not the same thing as saying that everything that appears in the question is necessary to finding the credited answer. Indeed, most of what's written exists either to distract you or to set up a trap that will make one of the wrong answers seem appealing.

Processing the information in a question doesn't just mean reading over the text to say you've read it. Every few lines you'll need to stop and ask yourself, "Do I understand what I just read?" and "How does this new bit relate to what I've already read?" and, most importantly, "How does this relate to the task at hand?"

Processing the information also means learning what bits of information the GMAT uses to make an answer right and what bits you should always pause to figure out. In each section that follows, you'll learn the most common ways the test makers tip their hand and how to quickly sort through the intentionally disorganized jumble of facts and claims.

Step 3: Plan Your Approach to the Answers

Before reading the answer choices, pause to ask yourself, "What is the right answer going to look like?" Lots of wrong answer choices are tempting because they are actually correct—they're just the right answer to a question you aren't currently being asked. Other times they're made to sound right because they remind you of something you just read or they remind you of something you know to be true in the real world.

In other words, the test maker wants you to have an "Aha!" moment for all the wrong reasons and miss what's actually going on. The best defense against this (and all the other little tweaks and twists you might encounter) is to know which "Aha!" you're aiming for.

Sometimes this will mean making a specific prediction to yourself, pre-phrasing the answer. "The flaw here is that the author confuses the cause with the effect" or "The author says the most important cause of the war was the economic depression in the years leading up to it." Other times it'll be a bit looser: "I know the right answer will have to mention 'contentment' or 'happiness'." In each case, though, you've got a target in mind as you read the answers. This alone will help you avoid a lot of the traps the GMAT has set for you.

Naturally, there are going to be times when your prediction is extremely tentative or a bit generic: "Uh... something about clay pots?" or "There's a lot of rules here, so I'm not sure what the inference they're looking for is." That's OK. It just means you'll have to be more careful with the answer choices. You still have some idea of what you're looking for, and that's better than just reading the answers and hoping something sticks out.

Step 4: Attack the Answers

One principle will guide you as you search for the right answer: There is no "best" answer.

Forget what you might have heard elsewhere about picking the better of two answer choices or weighing things that seem "kind of right" against each other. On the GMAT, right and wrong are all-or-nothing. There is no "kind of right." There are just four wrong answers and one right one.

Every wrong answer will have some sort of fatal flaw that the test makers could point to if an unhappy test taker were to challenge them on it, a poison pill that kills the answer choice dead, dead, dead. As you learn about the different types of questions, you'll get a better idea of what sorts of things kill answers in one type but not another and the things that are always deal breakers.

Be merciless with the answers, tearing into them until you find that fatal flaw that will let you eliminate it. And once an answer choice has been eliminated, you *stop reading* it. It's out. One down, three to go.

You must also be sure to use the same level of rigor with each answer choice you read. If you eliminate answer (A) because you don't like the word *surpris-*

ing, and (B) also contains *surprising*, you should either eliminate it, too, or go back and reconsider (A). Just because an answer is further down the page doesn't mean it gets more breaks than those that come before it. Be sure as well that you don't inadvertently change what you're looking for between answer choices.

THE THREE VERBAL QUESTION FORMATS

Critical Reasoning

Each Critical Reasoning question you will see on the GMAT is composed of three parts: a **Prompt**, a brief question about that prompt (which we will call the **Question Stem**), and five **Answer Choices**.

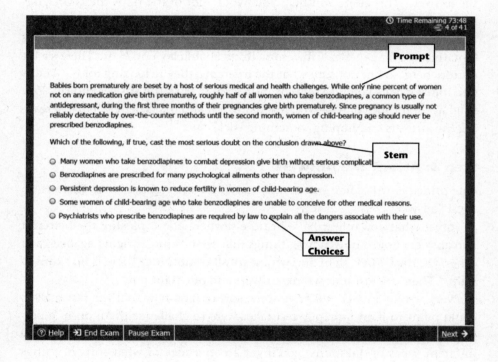

The **Prompt** contains a set of facts, opinions, and observations that create a scenario, a little self-contained world with only a handful of details sketching it out. For most of the questions, these details will be used to make an argument; for some, there will only be a series of related pieces of information. The only facts that you need to understand to find the answer can be found in the prompt. The test maker never asks you to rely on your outside expertise.

The typical Critical Reasoning prompt is about 100 words long, so you won't have to scroll to see the prompt all at once, although occasionally you will need to scroll down the page to see the fifth answer choice.

Unlike the Reading Comprehension questions, the Critical Reasoning questions will not reuse the same prompt to ask multiple questions. Each question has a unique scenario attached to it.

The information in the prompts is drawn from many different subject areas, including the arts, philosophy, the sciences, law, and business. You're not expected to know any of the material beforehand, and you should be careful if the subject happens to be one you're personally familiar with. There's no guarantee that the things presented as facts in these passages are actually true, and often the test maker will bend the truth in order to make the subject fit into the narrow constraints of a Critical Reasoning scenario.

The **Question Stem** that follows contains instructions from the test makers detailing what they expect us to do with the information in the prompt. In the chapters that follow, you will learn the language that test makers typically use to indicate the task they wish you to perform. Ninety-five percent of the questions reuse the same handful of phrasings, and with time and practice, you will almost always be able to tell immediately what the question demands of you.

The Answer Choices will always come in sets of five. Four of them will be incorrect for definite reasons, usually because of specific wording used in the original prompt. Only one will be correct.

Note: On the test, answer choices don't have letters (A), (B), etc. We'll use them in the printed questions, however, to avoid confusion.

Critical Reasoning Question Types

All in all, there are 13 different types of Critical Reasoning questions, more types of questions than the number of Critical Reasoning questions you'll probably see in total on the day of your test! That's the bad news. But the good news is that these 13 questions are just slight variations on three far simpler questions:

1. What does this argument take for granted?
2. What is the structure of this argument?
3. If all of these facts are true, what else must be true?

Notice that the first two questions ask you about an **argument**. That's why we're going to classify them in the broad, cleverly named category, **Argument-Based Questions**, which we're going to immediately divide into the **Assumption Family** and the **Structure Family**, depending on whether the question asks you what the argument takes for granted (its **assumptions**) or how it's organized (its **structure**). The other Critical Reasoning questions ask you to work with a loose collection of facts, so we'll classify those as **Fact-Based Questions**.

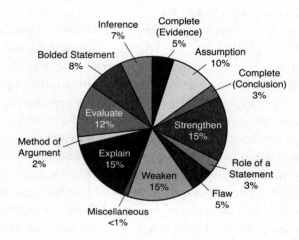

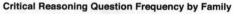

Critical Reasoning Question Frequency by Family

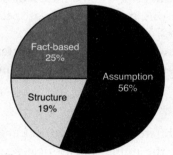

These question types will be discussed in detail in the Critical Reasoning chapter, but here's a quick rundown:

Argument-Based Questions

Argument-Based Questions make up about three-fourths of the questions on the GMAT, so you'll see about eight in a single test sitting. Your initial approach to all of these will be the same, breaking the information in the argument down into its component parts: its **conclusion** and its **evidence**.

The Assumption Family

ASSUMPTION—In Assumption questions, an argument is given, and you must identify something that the argument relies upon but that is not stated explicitly, something that, if not true, means the argument itself must not be true.

STRENGTHEN—Here, you go one step beyond the Assumption question to find a new piece of information in the answer choices that would make one of the argument's unstated assumptions more likely to be true or that would answer a possible objection to one of those unstated assumptions.

WEAKEN—The Weaken question is the flip side of the Strengthen question. Here you would find a piece of information in the answers that, if true, would call into question or present an objection to one of the arguments' assumptions.

EVALUATE—In Evaluate questions, which are closely related to Strengthen and Weaken questions, you must select an answer choice that describe some unknown information or a question that, if known, has the potential to either weaken or strengthen the argument.

FLAW—The stem of Flaw questions calls out the speaker in the argument prompt for making a mistake and asks you to find the answer choice that best describes it. Invariably, the mistake is assuming something that shouldn't be assumed.

The Structure Family

BOLDED STATEMENT—Here, an argument is given, with two sentences or phrases in **bold type**, and you are asked to identify the part that each plays in the argument as a whole.

METHOD OF ARGUMENT—An argument is given, occasionally written as a dialogue between two people, and you must explain how the argument works (i.e., what sort of evidence the author uses such as invoking a general principle or providing a counter example) and whether that case is for or against something.

ROLE OF A STATEMENT—These questions are essentially Bolded Statement questions in which nothing is bolded. They, too, ask you to identify the role a particular part plays in the argument.

PARALLEL ARGUMENT—Very rare on the GMAT, this question contains five arguments for the price of one! You must match the argument in the prompt with the one in the answer choices that has the same structure.

Fact-Based Questions

The remaining quarter of Critical Reasoning questions do not ask about arguments. Their prompts almost always have no conclusion and no evidence. As Sgt. Joe Friday said, they want "Just the facts, ma'am." You'll probably see four or five of them in the Critical Reasoning section (SPOILER ALERT! **Inference** questions will make an appearance in the Reading Comprehension, too).

INFERENCE—These questions ask you to find the answer choice that must be true if the information in the prompt is true. (If the prompt tells you that *all dogs go to heaven* and that *Rusty is a dog*, then the correct answer could be that *Rusty will go to heaven*.)

EXPLAIN—The prompt that accompanies these questions contains an anomalous situation like "demand's up, but prices have stayed the same" or "after the law changed to require seatbelts, automobile injuries went up." The correct answer provides an additional fact that can explain why the *apparent* weirdness really isn't weird at all.

Complete the Argument Questions

Wait a minute, didn't we just say there were three categories? What's with this fourth? **Complete** questions are just a different way of asking you to do one of the two question types we've already discussed. They're easy to spot because their question stem is placed above their prompt, rather than below, and because there's a big empty blank (like this: _____) somewhere in the text. You're asked to insert something into the blank that will somehow complete the argument.

COMPLETE (EVIDENCE)—If an evidence keyword precedes the blank (e.g., *for example, because, since, after all),* the **Complete** question is essentially a weirdly worded **Assumption** question. The only piece of evidence that could complete the argument is a piece that fills in the gap that is its unstated assumption.

COMPLETE (CONCLUSION)—If a conclusion keyword precedes the blank (e.g., *thus, therefore, hence, in conclusion),* the Complete question can be treated as a form of the **Inference** question. The answer choice that fills the blank will be a certainty if all the information in the prompt is taken as true.

Sentence Correction

Each Sentence Correction question you see on the GMAT will look the same: a sentence will be either partially or completely **underlined** and followed by five **answer choices** that give different possible versions of the underlined section.

Sentence Correction Question Types

After the 14 Critical Reasoning variations, it should come as welcome news to learn that there is, strictly speaking, just the one type of Sentence Correction question. Sure, there's some variation in how much is underlined or where the underlined section is placed in relation to the rest of the sentence, but the fundamental task is still the same each time: eliminate the answer choices that contain an obvious error until you're down to one.

Thankfully, even though the English language has numerous multivolume textbooks filled with rules and variations on those rules, the GMAT limits itself to a very small collection of errors to test in Sentence Correction questions. Six major categories of error dominate the questions; at least one of them appears in just about every question, and most questions contain two or three of them. They are:

SUBJECT/PREDICATE AGREEMENT—The subject of the sentence (a noun) must match the predicate (the verb); singular subjects get singular predicates, and plural subjects take plural predicates.

PRONOUN REFERENCE—Pronouns must refer unambiguously to a single noun, and they must also match the noun they replace in number, gender, and case.

MODIFICATION—Modifying elements, such as adjectives, adverbs, and prepositional phrases, must be placed so that it's clear what they're supposed to modify and so that the modification makes logical sense.

PARALLELISM—Parts of a sentence that play the same role must be put into matching forms. This includes words in lists, in comparisons, and in other multipart constructions.

CLAUSES AND CONNECTORS—Clauses can be either independent or dependent. Linking them incorrectly can result in a run-on sentence or a sentence fragment.

IDIOMATIC CONSTRUCTION—Certain words are paired with other words in English not because of any logical rule but because that's just the way they're expected to be. Usually, this involves preposition choice (i.e., you sleep in a bed, not at a bed).

In the sections that follow, we will discuss each of these frequently tested errors, explaining both the formal rules and the ways that the rules tend to be tested in the context of a question. For now, let's see how to apply the Four-Step Verbal Method to all Sentence Correction questions, no matter what error they contain.

Reading Comprehension

You will know that you are dealing with a Reading Comprehension question set the moment the screen switches to a two-paned display with a scroll bar in the middle of the screen:

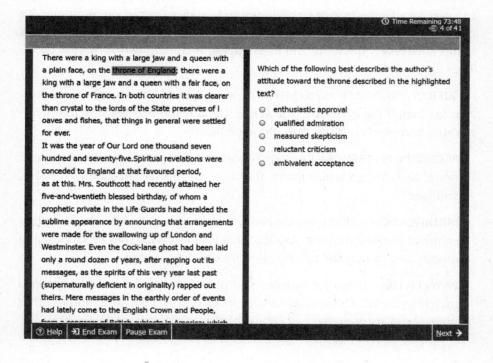

Like the other two formats, Reading Comprehension questions can appear at any point in the Verbal section, but they do cluster into sets every time. There's never a one-off single-question passage. Indeed, nearly every Reading Comprehension set is composed of three or four questions.

Thus, every Reading Comprehension set will be composed of a **passage** in the left-hand window on your screen and a **question** in the right. The **passage** will remain until all the questions in the set are completed. You can't skip questions; even though they're part of a set, they still appear one at a time. Each **question** is composed of a **stem** and **five answer choices**, four incorrect and one correct.

The lines of text are not numbered, as they are in a paper-and-pencil GMAT (such as those you'll encounter in the *Official Guides* and in this book). When a question makes a reference to a specific part of the passage, instead of line numbers, the interface will highlight that part of the passage in yellow for as long as the question is on your screen.

> There were a king with a large jaw and a queen with a plain face, on the throne of England; there were a king with a large jaw and a queen with a fair face, on the throne of France. In both countries it was clearer than crystal to the lords of the State preserves of l

The vast majority of test takers see four total passage and question sets during their test. Two of the passages will be on the short side, between 150 and 200 words long; two will be longer, between 250 and 350 words.

The number of questions doesn't necessarily correspond to the length of the passage. You might be asked four questions about a single-paragraph passage and later only get three with a passage twice that size.

You should try to keep track of how many Reading Comprehension questions you've seen so far as you progress through the test because you need to leave extra room in your time budget to read the passages. So if you're on question 25 but you've not seen any Reading Comprehension questions yet (a *very* unlikely situation), you'd know that almost every remaining question was going to be Reading Comprehension. To be on pace, you'd still have the majority of your time remaining, even though you'd be over two-thirds of your way through the section.

The biggest mistake that novice GMAT test takers make with Reading Comprehension is reading the passages as though they were just any old piece of text they've just happened to have come upon. "Oh, that's interesting," they might think while reading the passage, or "Really? I didn't know that," when what they should be thinking is "Whose side is the author on?" and "This example is meant to prove which theory, exactly?"

Just as with the Critical Reasoning questions, the information in a Reading Comprehension passage is drawn from many different subject areas, including the arts, philosophy, the sciences, law, and business. You're not expected to know any of the material beforehand, and you should be careful if the subject happens to be one you're personally familiar with because there's no guarantee that the things presented as facts in these passages are actually true.

Sure, the test maker generally starts with a journal article or a newspaper or magazine report, but in order to make it into a GMAT Reading Comprehension passage, the facts are tweaked and the descriptions of things changed so that the passage will fit into the specific logic they use to determine which of the five answers is right and to ensure that there are four tempting but wrong answers.

Thus, the key to mastering Reading Comprehension questions will be learning to organize the information in the passage in your head (or on your noteboard) in such a way that you can answer the sorts of questions the GMAT asks about these passages. You're not reading for fun or just to say you've read the passage. You're reading in preparation for a very narrow range of possible tasks you might be called upon to perform.

Reading Comprehension Question Types

Remember the most important ground rule for the Reading Comprehension section: every answer must be based on **specific** pieces of **information found in the passage**. You are not required to know anything about the passages nor are you expected (or allowed) to justify picking an answer because of information you know from any other source.

Now, consider how limiting that is for the test makers and how hard it makes their job. They can present information from anywhere, from any source or subject under the sun, but they can only ask you to do things with that information that someone could reasonably be expected to do solely on the basis of that information and that information alone. Thus, a lot of the things that you're accustomed to doing with a piece of text or a chunk of an article are explicitly out of bounds. So what's left for them to do?

Recall Questions

One question the test maker can still ask is simply "Hey, what did this guy say about this particular subject?" Or, to put it in the context of the question, "Which of these five different things did the passage you just read actually say?" We call this general category of questions **Recall** questions because they ask you to do just that: recall a single piece of information from the passage. There are two ways this question can be asked:

DETAIL—These questions ask you to recall or locate a piece of information that was explicitly written in the text of the passage.

INFERENCE—These questions ask you to recall or locate a piece of information that was not explicitly written in the passage but that MUST BE TRUE if you take all the information in the passage as true.

Global Questions

The test maker can also ask you, "What was the reason this passage was written?" or, phrased another way, "What did the author do with this information? Was there some sort of point to it all? Or was it just a bunch of random facts?"

MAIN POINT—These questions ask you to identify the author's agenda or the overall point of the passage.

Nearly every single passage on the GMAT will have some sort of agenda or direction to it. Something is at stake. It might be as simple as, "People used to think this, but now they think that, **and it is right to think that instead of this** for these reasons." Most often the author is explicitly siding with one of two parties or one of two interpretations. In this way, they're a lot more like Critical Reasoning questions than they might seem.

On the rare occasions that the passage does not have a point, then that means that the test maker is even more constrained than usual. The only questions in bounds would be **Detail** and **Inference** questions.

The other type of **Global** question singles out a specific piece of information presented in the passage and asks, "Why did the author mention this?" The answer to that question must always involve the author's overall goal.

FUNCTION—These questions ask you to identify the role that a particular piece of information plays in the author's overall agenda.

And that's it. There are just four questions.

RECALL QUESTIONS (ask you "What?")
Detail: "Did the author say this or that?"
Inference: "Which of these has to be true because of something the author said?"

GLOBAL QUESTIONS (ask you "Why?")
Main Point: "Why did the author write this?"
Function: "Why did the author say this here?"

Critical Reasoning Questions

Didn't we already cover Critical Reasoning questions two sections ago? Yes, but they also show up from time to time in the Reading Comprehension question sets. When one does pop up, you will treat it according to the method appropriate to whatever type of Critical Reasoning question it happens to be. If it's a **Weaken** question, then weaken; a **Strengthen** question, strengthen. That's that.

THE KEY TO KEYWORDS

As you read any chunk of GMAT text, you should be on the alert, waiting for **keywords** that will allow you to break the information contained in the text into smaller, more useful chunks. **Keywords** come in many different flavors, each with their own use.

Timing Keys	First, second, finally, in the end, in the 1850s, later, earlier, was once
Illustrating Keys	For example, to illustrate, this can be seen in, which shows, such
Emphasis Keys	Fortunately, crucially, most important, disastrously, even goes so far as
Concluding Keys	Therefore, thus, consequently, from this we can, in conclusion
Doubt Keys	Appears, seems, was even once, some critics contend, might be taken to
Continuing Keys	Moreover, additionally, also, as well as, and, further, not only
Contrasting Keys	However, nevertheless, despite, yet, although, but, rather
Place Holding Keys	This, that, these, those, such as, such a, the latter, the former

Be careful! It's very easy to misuse keywords. When doing pencil-and-paper practice problems, people often underline and circle these words as they read them and stop there, treating the passage like some sort of word jumble search. *Finding* the keys is only the first step to understanding the passage. It's how you *use* them that counts.

So how do we use the keywords? When you see a keyword, pause long enough to figure out what the keyword tells you about the relationship between the pieces of information that surround it in the passage. GMAT questions are, at their core, built on the relationships between details. In action, the process would go something like this:

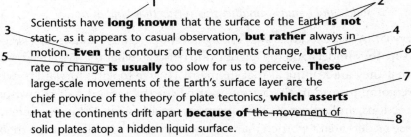

Scientists have **long known** that the surface of the Earth is not static, as it appears to casual observation, **but rather** always in motion. **Even** the contours of the continents change, **but** the rate of change **is usually** too slow for us to perceive. **These** large-scale movements of the Earth's surface layer are the chief province of the theory of plate tectonics, **which asserts** that the continents drift apart **because of** the movement of solid plates atop a hidden liquid surface.

Some early models of plate tectonics treated the motion of plates as though it were similar to a flat piece of lumber riding on top of a conveyor belt, the convection cells in

1 Sets up a contrast between old and new info? No new info in this ¶. Keep in mind for later.

2 Another contrast. What are the two parts? (1) appears static, but isn't and (2) is in motion (though slow). What's the contrast about? Earth's surface.

3 More info about (2) from before.

4 Contrast: actual vs. perceived. What's the contrast about? Movement of continents.

5 Hanging contrast. No exceptions given.

6 "these" what? Connect the dots … this describes earlier "contours of continents changing."

7 Definition of what? The theory of plate tectonics.

8 What causes what? Drift caused by movement of solid on liquid.

If we could get inside the head of the GMAT test taker using this approach, we'd hear an inner monologue not too different from what we saw when we didn't know what the content was:

> *OK, so there's a phenomenon that appears one way but is another: the Earth's surface appears still but actually moves. And now more about this: blah, blah, OK I get it, it seems still because of how slow it is. Hmmm hmmm—wait, **these** large-scale movements? Which ones were those? Ah, right, the ones that are hard to see because they're slow. The continent ones. So those movements are described by a theory. And now we get the theory's definition. And it's about a cause. Something about solids and liquids—another this versus that kind of thing.*

Savvy GMAT readers are always asking questions, always double checking to make sure they understand the relationship between what they've already read and what they are reading at that moment. They're looking forward to what they're going to read in the future, waiting for the second half of two-part constructions, and noticing when questions are asked but left unanswered.

These readers aren't worried that they need to know exactly how the theory of plate tectonics works, though. They're confident that should they run across the question:

> According to the passage, which of the following is a
> central claim of plate tectonics?

All they will have to do is go back to the part of the passage where they know the definition lies and reread it to make sure they can recognize the correct answer when they read the answer choices.

Critical Reasoning | 14

A ccording to what GMAT and ACT say elsewhere, Critical Reasoning questions target three different cognitive skills:

ARGUMENT CONSTRUCTION: Questions of this type may ask you to recognize the basic structure of an argument, properly drawn conclusions, underlying assumptions, well-supported explanatory hypotheses, or parallels between structurally similar arguments.

ARGUMENT EVALUATION: Questions of this type may ask you to analyze a given argument, recognize factors that would strengthen or weaken an argument, reasoning errors committed in making an argument, or aspects of the methods by which an argument proceeds.

FORMULATING AND EVALUATING A PLAN OF ACTION: Questions of this type may ask you to recognize the relative appropriateness, effectiveness, or efficiency of different plans of action; factors that would strengthen or weaken a proposed plan of action; or assumptions underlying a proposed plan of action.

—"The GMAT—Test Structure and Overview—Verbal Section," *MBA.Com*

ARGUMENTS AND FACTS

Arguments

When the test makers use the word "argument," they mean the logician's definition: a series of connected premises meant to demonstrate the truth of a proposition.

Argument—An attempt to support a claim by giving reasons for it.

Conclusion—The claim that an argument attempts to support.

Evidence—The reasons given in support of an argument's conclusion.

The evidence explains the conclusion. The conclusion is explained by the evidence. When you have both, you have an argument.

Does that seem a little circular to you? It should. Logically speaking, **evidence** and **conclusion** only exist as a pair. If you don't have at least two pieces of information, it's impossible to have an **argument**. If you simply say *ABC Cola is the best cola in the world*, you have not made an argument. You've only made a claim.

And even when you have two pieces of information, if one doesn't explain why you should believe the other, then you *still* don't have an argument.

Evidence	Evidence	Conclusion
Socrates is a man.	All men are mortal.	Socrates is mortal.
Celery is gross.	You shouldn't eat gross things.	You shouldn't eat celery.
If it's Tuesday, we should eat by 12.	It's Tuesday, and it's 12:30!	We should have eaten by now.
Words in columns look cool.	These words are in columns.	How cool!

The arguments you'll encounter on the GMAT usually have only one or two pieces of evidence, and sometimes the test makers go out of their way to disguise the evidence, but whatever the trick being played, every single argument on the GMAT can be put into the form **conclusion** *because* **evidence**.

When you finish reading a Critical Reasoning prompt that has an argument in it, try to rephrase the argument into that basic template before going on to the answer choices. That's your spot check to make sure you understood what you just read.

Also, don't think that the argument's conclusion has to come at the end of the argument or the evidence at the beginning. You can scramble them up however you want. As long as there's something being explained and something doing some explaining, you have an argument.

You might not have a *good* argument, though, which brings us to valid and invalid arguments!

Valid and Invalid Arguments

Valid Arguments

Once in a while (for Argument Structure questions), the GMAT lets you stop once you've identified the parts of the argument, but more often the test also asks you to say something about whether the argument is *good* or *bad*—or to use more formal-sounding words, *valid* or *invalid*. But what makes an argument valid?

Earlier we described an argument as a "series of connected premises meant to demonstrate the truth of a proposition." The keyword there was "connected." When an argument is valid, the evidence and conclusion form a chain, a series of reasonable little steps from one idea to the next.

FUN WITH SYNONYMS!

Good arguments are valid, properly drawn, supported, logical, sound, logically correct, convincing.

Bad arguments are invalid, improperly drawn, flawed, unsound, illogical, unconvincing.

Invalid Arguments

There are lots of reasons an argument might be bad. Earlier, when we professed our undying love of ABC Cola, you probably found yourself thinking "Come on, no survey's going to show 100 percent agreement. That's crazy." In effect, you were thinking, "That's a pretty terrible argument." Maybe, getting into the spirit of this section's heading, you even thought, "That argument is invalid!" Not so fast! **Invalid** is not the same as **incorrect**.

Arguments aren't invalid because their evidence is wrong. They're invalid because their evidence, as stated, does not give enough reason *on its own* for you to believe the conclusion.

Assumptions

Earlier, you learned that arguments have two parts, evidence and conclusion. To this we add a final part that is never written out explicitly: the argument's **assumptions**. In one sense, assumptions are pieces of evidence that are left *unstated*. To put it another way, an argument's assumptions consist of everything else that needs to be true in order for the argument to be true.

Assumptions—The information an argument does not state explicitly but that is required for the argument to be true.

Facts

What is a fact? In the world outside the GMAT, that's a thorny question, but for our purposes it couldn't be simpler: a fact is any piece of information that we are asked to take as true without being given an argument to explain why.

Fact—Any piece of information that you're told to take as true on the GMAT.

Every piece of evidence in a GMAT argument is something we'll be told to treat as though it were true. Thus, all GMAT arguments are built out of facts—but not all facts on the GMAT are found in arguments.

Paradoxically, that means that a lot of things that we think of in real life as opinions, on the GMAT we're going to be taking as facts. Other than the conclusion, everything found in a prompt is, to us, simply true. A fact.

Making Inferences from Facts

Primarily, the GMAT expects us to be able to make valid **inferences** from facts.

In our day-to-day lives, we make a lot of inferences.

> If someone comes back from vacation with a sunburn, we think, "I'll bet they went to the beach."

> If we hear a crash in another room followed by the pitter pat of paws beating a hasty retreat, we think, "That darn cat broke something again."

When you start from something you know and make a guess or a prediction about something you don't know, you're making an inference.

However, if somehow these examples appeared in GMAT Critical Reasoning questions, we would have just missed these questions in a row. Each of these inferences would be considered invalid according to the GMAT's rules for inferences.

On the GMAT, the only inferences allowable are those that are 100 percent certain, things that absolutely, positively, without a doubt and without any extra information beyond what is found in the prompt MUST BE TRUE.

Arguments preceded by *probably, possibly, maybe,* and *more than likely* all fail to make the GMAT inference cut.

THE FOUR-STEP METHOD FOR CRITICAL REASONING QUESTIONS

Time to see the **Four-Step General Verbal Method** in action on a Critical Reasoning question. We'll use the sample question from the Verbal Introduction:

> Babies born prematurely are beset by a host of serious medical and health challenges. While only nine percent of women not on any medication give birth prematurely, roughly half of all women who take benzodiazepines, a common type of antidepressant, during the first three months of their pregnancies give birth prematurely. Since pregnancy is usually not reliably detectable by over-the-counter methods until the second month, women of child-bearing age should never be prescribed benzodiazepines.
>
> Which of the following, if true, casts the most serious doubt on the conclusion drawn above?

Step 1: Identify the Question Type

The first step of the **Four-Step Verbal Method** is to **Identify the Task**. The task in a Critical Reasoning question always depends on the question's **type**. The **question stem** will contain keywords that signal the question's type and thus the task demanded.

After you've read the stem, first decide whether the question is **Fact-Based** or **Argument-Based**. Then narrow it down to the particular question type.

If we take a look at the stem of this question, three words allow us to decide:

> Which of the following, if true, casts the most serious doubt on the conclusion drawn above?

When a question asks us to *cast doubt* on an argument's *conclusion*, it's a **Weaken** question, part of the **Assumption** family of **Argument-Based** questions.

Step 2: Identify the Parts of the Argument (for Argument-Based Questions)

Because our question is **Argument-Based**, the best way to **Process** the information is to identify the parts of the argument.

The two basic parts of an argument are the **conclusion**, the thing that the speaker in the prompt is trying to prove, and the **evidence**, the reasons the speaker provides as proof. Start by locating the argument's conclusion.

This argument's conclusion happens to be where you might expect conclusions to come, at the very end:

> [...] counter methods until the second month, women
> of child-bearing age should never be prescribed
> benzodiazepines.

Take note of how **extreme** the argument's conclusion is—by which we don't mean that it's provocative or the sort of thing an extremist might say, rather that this argument's conclusion is not qualified in any way. There is no hedging, no *maybe* this or *possibly* that. According to this speaker, there is absolutely no reason—none, nada, zero, zilch—why these benzodiazepines should be prescribed to women in the indicated age group. Such a far-reaching conclusion would require similarly far-reaching evidence to back up—indeed, far more evidence than you could ever fit in a 100-word GMAT prompt.

Extreme—On the GMAT, something that applies to 100 percent of cases, without exception.

Once we have the conclusion, we need to take an **inventory** of the rest of the passage. After you've found the conclusion, what remains will almost always be some kind of **evidence**. Here, we should be able to tease out these pieces of evidence:

- ✔ It can sometimes be hard to tell a pregnancy has started.
- ✔ The drug whose name starts with a *b* is an antidepressant.
- ✔ The *b*-drug causes women to give birth prematurely.
- ✔ Being born prematurely is bad.

Your description of the evidence can be as general or as specific as you need; the important thing is to understand what things the speaker actually said and what was left to the speaker's audience to fill in. You can jot your evidence **inventory** down in a more abbreviated shorthand on your noteboard, or you could just keep it in your head.

Now, does all this **evidence** add up to a compelling case that benzodiazepines should *never* be prescribed to any women in this age group? Certainly not. The argument establishes only that there is *one disadvantage* associated with the drug and then makes a big leap to claim that the drug should *never* be prescribed. In other words, we've found a gap, the gap between *one disadvantage* and *never prescribing*.

Note: When you're doing a Fact-Based Question, this step is going to look a little different. Instead of breaking the argument down into parts, you'll be searching the prompt for the most definite pieces of information. See page 230.

Step 3: Prephrase the Answer

The third step of the **General Verbal Method** is to plan out your approach to the answers. Ideally, for Argument-Based questions we should have a concrete prediction in mind of what the right answer will look like.

For a **Weaken** question the right answer will contain new information about something in the argument that makes us less likely to believe the argument's **assumptions**.

We already know where this argument's assumptions lie, in that gap between finding out that this drug *has one disadvantage* and concluding that it should *never be used*. If the conclusion is correct, the speaker must assume that

> There are no possible advantages or other considerations
> that could outweigh the one disadvantage given.

So what sort of thing would make us less likely to believe that there are no other advantages? We might be moved by an answer choice that mentions an advantage the speaker neglected to bring up. Or perhaps information that defangs the disadvantage could change our mind, something showing that the disadvantage is not as bad as the speaker seems to think. As we move into the answer choices, we'll be looking for something that can change the **advantage/disadvantage balance**.

Step 4: Evaluate the Answer Choices

Let's take it from the top:

> (A) Many women who take benzodiazepines to combat
> depression give birth without serious complications.

This answer choice offers nothing new. The argument only claimed that the side effects were experienced by *roughly half of all women*, which is to say, not all of them. Thus, we already knew that there were some women who didn't experience the side effects (the roughly less than half). Something taken into account by the evidence already present can never weaken a GMAT argument. In other words, this is a **closed issue**. Eliminate.

> (B) Psychiatrists who prescribe benzodiazepines are required by law to explain all the dangers associated with their use.

This answer choice hopes to lead you astray by bringing up something **reasonable but irrelevant** to the situation presented in the prompt. You can probably think of several instances of required warning legislation that was passed in the real world. But there's no indication in the prompt that a patient's knowing about the dangers or not knowing would change the rate of negative outcomes significantly. (And that's why we try, whenever possible, to avoid **real-world thinking**. Limit yourself to the facts explicitly stated in the prompt.) Cross this one out.

> (C) Persistent depression is known to reduce fertility in women of child-bearing age.

But for the word *persistent*, this answer choice might require more thought. As it stands, we don't know anything about how benzodiazepines work or about what specific kinds of depressions they're used to treat or whether other treatments might be able to be used for the same thing. So how could we possibly say whether benzodiazepines could provide a benefit to people suffering this specific type of depression (the persistent kind)? Since we have to know more to know whether this answer choice would be relevant, we'd say it's **one step removed** from the argument we're dealing with. Out it goes.

> (D) Some of the women of child-bearing age who take benzodiazepines are unable to conceive for other medical reasons.

Aha! Finally, we have an answer choice that affects the balance of advantage and disadvantage because it both blunts the force of the disadvantage and suggests a possible advantage. The argument's conclusion, as stated, applies to all women of a certain age because of things that are dangerous only to a subset of those women—namely, the subset who can conceive. Those unable to conceive will not be directly affected by the cited disadvantage, so it might prove advantageous to allow benzodiazepines to still be prescribed, just only to those who cannot be harmed by their negative side effect. (D) is the correct answer.

    (E) Benzodiazepines have been prescribed for many years
         by doctors for most common forms of depression.

There is one answer choice left, but we've already found one that must be right. On the day of the test, you might only spare (E) a courtesy glance to make sure you didn't misread something in answers (A) through (D).

After reading (E), we could be reasonably certain that we didn't make any mistakes earlier, as it's clearly a **closed issue** like (A). We already know that *benzodiazepines* are *a common type of antidepressant.*

Click the oval by the answer choice, hit Next and Confirm. It's on to the next question.

Speaking of questions. It's time for you to try some GMAT questions on your own . . .

Remember these **common types of wrong answers**. You'll definitely see them again.

closed issue—Something the evidence in the prompt already takes into account or which is explicitly excluded by the conclusion.

reasonable but irrelevant—The answer choice test takers tend to default to when they don't understand the question, something that's reasonable or familiar from a different context.

one step removed—Something that would be relevant to the argument, if a second fact unmentioned by the prompt was true.

THE ARGUMENT STRUCTURE FAMILY OF QUESTIONS

Anatomy of an Argument Structure Question

Prompt

Some managers believe that the hourly wage that an employee receives ought to be proportional to the effort required by that job's typical duties, but it would be terrible if a business actually followed this advice, as it would mean that those employees with the least ability to perform their jobs adequately would be entitled to the highest hourly wages, a perverse incentive.

Stem

The claim that employees with the least ability to perform their job adequately would be entitled to the highest hourly wages is used in the argument as

Answer Choices

(A) a general principle that provides a reason in favor of adopting a disagreeable practice illustrated elsewhere in the argument.

(B) a potentially unpopular general principle that is illustrated by a list of reasons that its adoption would be favorable.

(C) an undesirable consequence that would follow from the adoption of a general principle described elsewhere in the argument.

(D) a piece of evidence that discredits a general principle under consideration by showing that the principle could not be uniformly applied.

(E) a possible consequence said to follow from a general principle's adoption that some incorrectly describe as inevitable.

Prompt

- All contain an **argument** that has a specific **conclusion** and one or more pieces of **evidence**.
- Keywords like *therefore* or *thus* are often absent or used misleadingly.
- Often the prompt contains more than one point of view—someone is **responding** to someone else or to a **commonly held** belief.

Stem

- Most include the actual word **argument** or a close synonym like **reasoning**.
- Will make reference to the **function, role**, or how a piece is **used in** or **factors into** the argument.

Answer Choices

- Abstract descriptive terms and answers that differ in only small ways are the norm.
- Can often be grouped into twos and threes that share the same part.

Identifying Argument Structure Questions

There are four different ways that a GMAT question might ask about an argument's structure. Sometimes, the question will ask only about a part of the argument and the role it plays in the argument as a whole. If the part is highlighted in **boldface**, we call it a **Bolded Statement** question. If there's no boldface, but you're still only looking at a part of the argument, then you're dealing with a **Role of a Statement** question. Most Bolded Statement questions are just two Role of a Statement questions stitched together. You're asked about two roles for the price of one argument.

The other two types of structural questions ask you to describe the argument as a whole, how it comes to its evidence is used to come to its conclusion. **Method of Argument** questions ask for that description directly, whereas **Parallel Argument** questions ask you to find the argument in the answer choices that has the same structure as the one in the prompt.

Because of the specific ways each of the four questions is phrased, you'll be able to identify the task just by looking at the stem.

Role of a Statement

A few ways Role of a Statement stems might be phrased:

- In the argument above, the statement that all wolves born in the wild are able to recognize their pack's leader plays which of the following roles
- The claim that the comptroller has overlooked the value of the finance department is used in the auditor's response as a
- In the passage above, the reference to a possible reduction in foreign oil production serves primarily to

Occasionally, a Role of a Statement question works in the opposite direction, naming a role and asking you to find the statement that plays that role:

- Which of the following states the main conclusion of the argument above?
- In defending the position above, the inspector offers which of the following as evidence?

Method of Argument

The most common stems for Method of Argument questions include:

- In the passage, the author **develops** the **argument** by
- Which of the following best describes the **rhetorical strategy** used above?
- The statement that X **plays which role** in the **argument** above?
- In making his **claim**, the judge's use of Y **serves to**

A second style of Method of Argument stem usually occurs with prompts that contain more than one point of view and uses some synonym of the word *responds*:

- The farmer **responds** to the rancher's argument by
- The rancher **addresses** the issue by

Bolded Statement

Look for the **bolded parts**. Enough said!

Parallel Argument

Parallel Argument stems describe both the prompt and the answer choices as containing arguments and ask you to find the two that are *similar* or *parallel*:

- The reasoning above is most similar to that found in which of the following?
- The argument above contains reasoning most similar to which of the following answer choices?
- The argument above most closely parallels which of the following arguments?

Attacking Argument Structure Answer Choices

Recognizing the right answer choice will depend on your ability to describe the argument's parts using abstract terminology and descriptions rather than content. Answers, both wrong and right, will look more like

> The author rebuts a potential criticism to a general rule by showing the criticism to apply only to a small minority of instances in which that rule might be applied.

than

> The author argues that buying flea collars for your dog
> is still a good idea even though some particularly inbred
> poodles are allergic to flea collars.

The same argument is being described in each; the first is just using abstract vocabulary to do so.

IDENTIFYING CONCLUSIONS AND EVIDENCE

The first step to every Argument-Based question is to locate the conclusion of the argument given in the prompt. If you can't find the conclusion, you won't be able to identify the argument's structure, nor will you be able to consider the assumptions that underlie the argument. So how do you go about finding it?

Technique #1: Look for the Keywords

Sometimes, the speaker in the prompt just comes out and says, "Hey, lookie here, this is my conclusion." OK, so they don't put it that way, exactly, but they might as well. Instead, speakers direct your attention to their conclusion by tagging it with "therefore," or "thus," or, our personal favorite, "in conclusion." These are conclusion keywords, and about half the arguments on the test have them.

Of course, not every prompt is so nice. Sometimes you can find the conclusion by looking for *evidence* keywords, eliminating everything following them; what you have left is likely your conclusion. This is most often the case when the conclusion comes at the beginning of the argument.

Technique #2: The Types of Conclusion and Evidence

Suppose an argument lacks any identifying keywords (or that it has too many). What would you do then? One way to find the conclusion is to look for "the most conclusionary part."

While there's an infinite number of possible arguments that could be made in English, all argument conclusions can be sorted into a handful of categories that describe the *type* of claim the conclusion makes. Not just anything can be a conclusion.

The Most Common GMAT Conclusion Types

PREDICTION—A conclusion about what *will* happen, what *is going to* happen, what *ought to* occur, what *can be expected*, etc.

> The Hendersons will arrive tomorrow. Winning the bid will make a profit for the company. If Thomas enters the race, he will lose.

RECOMMENDATION—A conclusion about what someone *should* or *ought* to do, often phrased as a plan or proposal to meet a goal spelled out earlier.

> The company should invest in new machinery. People who want to be loved should learn to love others. The best way to get to Carnegie Hall is to practice.

BARE ASSERTION—A conclusion about what *is* the case, what *is true* about a situation or phenomenon, what someone *should believe* about a particular case. This is the most common type of conclusion.

> Petra is an excellent dancer. The building is structurally unsound. Hydrogen indicates contamination.

VALUE JUDGMENT—A conclusion about what is right or wrong and what is moral or immoral. These are relatively rare on the GMAT and can usually be treated as a more specific type of recommendation.

> One should never lie. Pol Pot was history's worst dictator.

CAUSAL CONNECTION—A conclusion that asserts that one thing *is responsible for*, *brought about*, or *caused* some other thing. These are usually established on the basis of a correlation between two things.

> Rain makes the flowers grow. The earthquake knocked the buildings down. Static electricity is responsible for your hair being so hard to manage.

Technique #3: Further Characterizing the Evidence and Conclusion

Both **Role of a Statement** and **Bolded Statement** questions single out part of an argument and ask what role it plays. Since there is little to no fluff or filler in a GMAT Critical Reasoning prompt, everything that appears in the prompt of an Argument-Based question is either part of the **evidence** or part of the **conclusion**.

As you sort through answer choices, look for the words that indicate what type of evidence is used:

> finding, explanation, objection, judgment, standards, methods, data, etc.

or what type of conclusion:

> position, explanation, prediction, recommendation, hypothesis, interpretation, objection, contrary conclusion, implication, etc.

Is the Conclusion Positive or Negative?

Sometimes the difference between the right answer and the wrong ones comes down to a simple word like *not*. Some authors arrive at positive conclusions; others reach negative conclusions.

How Definite is the Evidence or Conclusion?

The basic parts of an argument can be **extreme** or **qualified**.

Extreme evidence takes the form of rules that are always true, characteristics that are never shared, things that are impossible or the only way to proceed:

> The shark, as scientists have long known, is **unable** to survive if it remains still.

> ... because there **can be only one** definition for a word in the Burundi language.

> **No** Ps are Qs, but **all** Qs are Js.

Qualified evidence leaves wiggle room:

> There was a forty percent **likelihood** that the participants would not survive.

> **Many** fields of study require specialized lingo or jargon.

> It **occasionally** can be seen from the north side of the mountain.

Extreme conclusions make all-encompassing claims that admit no exception:

> Therefore, **everything** in the universe is composed of either energy or matter.
>
> Thus, **all** the items on this table are edible.
>
> Hence, **there is only one** way to skin a cat.

Qualified conclusions hedge with weasel words like *some, probably, to an extent, in many cases.*

> So, the mail **will likely** be here by Tuesday.
>
> The researchers concluded that heart disease **is often** linked to diet.
>
> Consequently, **at least some of** the food in the refrigerator is rotten.

To determine if the evidence and conclusion are qualified or definite, be on the lookout for keywords like:

> all, every, most, many, some, several, few, only, never, probably, not necessarily, rarely, etc.

Is the Scope Limited?

Sometimes, the argument throws out a limitation on the applicability of its evidence or its conclusion, admitting that there are some cases to which it doesn't apply or some exceptions to the rule:

> This research, **if accurate**, suggests that people form opinions on such subjects immediately.
>
> **To the extent that** a species' range is limited, it will always adopt this behavior.
>
> **Inasmuch as** the goal of such programs is financial stability ...
>
> **If** you want to secure a seat by Tuesday, you must act now.

Is the Evidence Used to Prove or Disprove Something?

Most of the time, evidence presented on the GMAT is positive.

> this shows, this confirms, an example would be, etc.

On the other hand, sometimes a fact is used as a counter example or an evidence to disprove a claim, often accompanied by keywords such as:

> but, yet, however, admittedly, by way of contrast,
> although, even still, whereas, despite this, in spite of, after
> all, and our favorite, on the other hand

How Many Pieces of Evidence Are Used?

Does the author cite only one rule or are multiple rules linked together? Does the author add a second premise that supports the conclusion indirectly, eliminates some possible misinterpretation, or answers an objection?

In these cases, you'll often see keywords like:

> furthermore, as well, besides, after all, moreover, in addi-
> tion, what's more

How Many Conclusions Are There?

The most common way to complicate an argument in a Structure question is to present two arguments that oppose one another within the same prompt. This can be done implicitly:

> **There are those who say** that contentment is
> impossible if desire persists; **however, ...**
>
> **Some argue** that we always hurt the ones we love, **but ...**
>
> **A number of students** often maintain that they cannot
> arrive on time, **but ...**

Another way to throw more than one conclusion into an argument is to tack an **additional implication** or suggestion onto the **end** of an argument.

> **Because** Chemical X harms small children, it should be
> banned. **Further**, those who developed it should be fined.

These extra conclusions are almost always present only to set up a wrong answer choice, not to be a part of the right one.

The final way an argument might have more than one conclusion is if the argument has a **complex** or **nested** structure. By this, we mean that it arrives at an **intermediate conclusion**, taking that conclusion as evidence for a **final conclusion** given later. An example:

> Because no other military in the world possesses even a
> single "supercarrier," there exists no real threat to any
> naval operation. Consequently, the suggestion that we
> increase the Navy's budget to allow the purchase of three
> additional "supercarriers" is absurd.

The first sentence presents a miniargument with both a conclusion and evidence:

> **Evidence:** No one else has a supercarrier.
> **Conclusion:** No one can threaten our naval operations.

This conclusion is itself used as evidence for the argument's final conclusion:

> **Evidence:** No one can threaten our naval operations.
> **Conclusion:** We shouldn't buy three new supercarriers.

If you're having trouble sorting evidence from conclusion because it seems like two different parts are being explained by evidence, you're likely facing a complex argument with a nested structure.

THE ARGUMENT ASSUMPTION FAMILY OF QUESTIONS

Anatomy of an Argument Assumption Question

Prompt

The most famous protagonists in literature have always been at odds with societal norms, but it has been increasingly fashionable for postcolonial literature to glorify these iconoclastic protagonists much more than any previous genre of literature has. By presenting these characters as being worthy of emulation, postcolonial authors subtly endorse their outsider ethos and may convince their readers to adopt it. Thus, postcolonial literature can be harmful to at least some of its readers, and thereby to society itself.

Stem

Which of the following is an assumption on which the argument above depends?

Answer Choices

(A) Some protagonists from earlier literature were better role models than any found in postcolonial literature.

(B) It is beneficial for some readers to avoid adopting an outsider ethos or to avoid emulating iconoclasts.

(C) Postcolonial protagonists who adopt an outsider ethos will harm readers more now than if they did not adopt that ethos.

(D) The aesthetic merit of some literary works cannot be judged without considering their moral implications.

(E) Postcolonial literature presents a greater number of outsider characters than did the literature of earlier eras.

Prompt

- All contain an **argument** that has a specific **conclusion** and one or more pieces of **evidence**.
- You can usually trust a *thus* or *therefore* will point to the actual conclusion.
- Usually there's only one speaker in the prompt, although about a third of the time there's still a "those who say" that the speaker opposes.

Stem

- Look for *assumption* or an obvious stand-in like *unstated premise* paired with *required, necessary,* or *underlies.*

Answer Choices

- The answers to Assumption questions tend to bounce around from topic to topic; there's often no major theme or splits to grab onto. Prephrasing becomes key.

Assumption Questions

Mastering the **Assumption** family of **Argument-Based** questions begins with the "pure" **Assumption** question, which asks you to recognize in the answer choices something that must be true if the argument in the prompt is taken to be valid.

Identifying Assumption Questions

A few examples of the way a "pure" **Assumption** question might be phrased:

- The argument depends on which of the following assumptions?
- Which of the following is an assumption made in drawing the conclusion above?
- The argument presupposes

Identifying Assumptions

Ironically, the main reason that finding an argument's assumptions can be difficult is that, as reasonable people, we fill in the holes in an argument that makes no sense with reasonable information. Suppose someone were to come up to you in the hall at work and tell you that

> Anna is going to be fired tomorrow because Imran saw
> her stealing from the supply cabinet.

Though you might not necessarily think, "Oh, this person is making an argument," they are.

> Conclusion: Anna is going to be **fired** tomorrow.
>
> because
>
> Evidence: Imran saw her **stealing** from the supply cabinet.

Seems reasonable, right? Stealing is often the sort of thing that makes a company unhappy with you, and unhappy companies tend to fire employees. But the evidence did not explicitly tell us those things—we *assumed* that they were true because if they weren't, the person coming to us in the hallway would be kind of crazy to conclude that Anna's getting fired.

Put simply, then, assumptions are everything that needs to be true so that the person making the argument isn't crazy.

Technique #4: Look for the Three Main Types of Assumptions

We can divide these "non-crazy-making-things" into three basic categories: Connecting Assumptions, Defending Assumptions, and Feasibility Assumptions. When in doubt, use these three categories as a quick checklist of things an argument needs to assume in order for it to be valid.

Connecting Assumptions

If an argument is valid, the reasons given as evidence are directly relevant to the conclusion. But unless an argument is just a tautology, there will be *some* difference between what the evidence states and what the conclusion claims. For Imran and Anna.

> Conclusion: Anna is going to be **fired** tomorrow.
>
> Evidence: Imran saw her **stealing** from the supply cabinet.
>
> Assumption: Stealing results in firing. (There is a connection between **stealing** and **firing**.)

Thus, when you are analyzing an argument in an Assumption family question, look carefully at the terms used in the conclusion and those used in the evidence. If they differ (and they usually will), then the argument assumes a connection between them.

Defending Assumptions

We defined arguments originally as "a series of connected statements that demonstrate the truth of a proposition." Connecting assumptions fills in the gaps where a connection is left unstated. Conversely, defending assumptions protect the connections against possible objections or weaknesses.

For example, if it's true that Anna is going to be fired because Imran saw her stealing, it needs to be the case not only that stealing is a fire-able offense at the company, but also that Anna is the sort of employee who can get fired. There's nothing *special* about Anna that might protect her from what is generally the case.

> Assumption: Anna isn't exempt from normal rules about firing.

The test maker will generally test these assumptions by presenting specific scenarios in which the assumption would be tested and then ruling them out.

> Anna is not the only one at the company who can make firing decisions.

> Anna is not the daughter of a boss who never fires family members.

> If this is Anna's first offense, there is no "free pass" given to first time offenders.

Defending assumptions also cover all the things that might render a piece of evidence irrelevant to the specific case at hand. For example, even if it's true that stealing does get you fired at this company and even if it's true that Anna is fire-able, we sill need to assume that

> Whoever does the firing at this company knows about what Imran saw.

If Imran never told anyone and is the only person who knows about what happened that day at the supply cabinet, then it doesn't matter whether stealing is punishable by firing.

Feasibility Assumptions

Feasibility assumptions concern unstated facts about the scenario presented that would make the argument possible. For example, if it's true that Anna is going to be fired **tomorrow**, then we must assume

> Anna is still working at the company today.

If Anna has already been fired for some other offense, then the argument that she'll be fired tomorrow is incorrect. In the same vein, we also must assume that

> Anna won't be fired tomorrow for cooking the books
> instead of stealing.

Remember, conclusions and arguments are not the same thing. If we found out that Anna's being fired for some reason other than what Imran saw, the argument that she'll be fired for stealing is incorrect. That argument's conclusion *is* correct, however. Anna's still getting fired. But the evidence presented in the original case does not explain why the conclusion is true anymore, so the argument based on that evidence is wrong.

Technique #5: The "Opposite Day" Test

An assumption is something that MUST BE TRUE if the argument as a whole is true. Therefore, if you are uncertain about whether an answer choice contains something that MUST BE TRUE, you can ask yourself, "What if this answer choice *wasn't* true?"

Remember our argument about postcolonial protagonists?

> The most famous protagonists in literature have always
> been at odds with societal norms, but it has been
> increasingly fashionable for postcolonial literature to
> glorify these iconoclastic protagonists much more than
> any previous genre of literature has. By presenting these
> characters as being worthy of emulation, postcolonial
> authors subtly endorse their outsider ethos and may
> convince their readers to adopt it. Thus, postcolonial
> literature can be harmful to at least some of its readers,
> and thereby to society itself.

If on Opposite Day, the argument can still work, then the answer choice is not an assumption required for the argument. Consider tricky Answer Choice (C):

> Postcolonial protagonists who adopt an outsider ethos will
> harm readers more now than if they did not adopt that
> ethos.

What if that *wasn't* the case? Indeed, what if the *opposite* were the case? What if postcolonial protagonists who adopt an outsider ethos (whatever that is) don't harm readers *more*? What if they just harmed them *some*?

The argument's conclusion was that postcolonial literature *sometimes* harms its readers. On Answer Choice (C)'s Opposite Day, then, the readers still get harmed *some*. The argument can survive even when the opposite of Answer Choice (C) is true, so (C) fails the test. It's not required for the argument to be true, so it's not an assumption in the argument.

Technique #6: Use the Common Argument Patterns for Assumption Questions

Content is never king on the GMAT. The structure and function of the pieces of information is far more important to finding the right answer than the content itself. Consider these two arguments:

The city council of Belleville has enacted a new ordinance allowing police officers to issue a ticket for loitering to anyone lingering longer than five minutes outside a storefront. We can expect a general decrease in crime to follow, as vagrants will now have less opportunity to commit street crimes such as mugging or vandalism.

When salmon migrate from ocean to fresh water, they make a transition between environments few other aquatic species can manage. Significant energy resources are invested swimming upstream, and the salmon that mate after migration ultimately die. Yet the practice is to the species' advantage overall, as it allows the salmon to lay their eggs in streams unmolested by predators that threaten them in the ocean.

But for the content, they are essentially the same argument, a **net benefit** calculation: on balance, doing a thing would offer more good than harm (or harm than good). Consequently, you'll see big improvements in your GMAT Verbal subscore if you can learn to see the basic structures of arguments and the patterns that recur across many different types of question.

Obviously, since they ask you *directly* about an argument's structure, this skill is most vital in tackling Structure family questions, but the Assumption family draws heavily on it as well. If you recognize a common pattern to the evidence and conclusion, it is often a shortcut to the argument's assumptions.

Pattern #1: The Applied Rule

Evidence:	A general rule.	All men are mortal.
	A specific case.	Socrates is a man.
Conclusion:	The rule applies to the case.	Socrates is mortal.

In these arguments, the evidence will do two things: (1) present a **general rule** and (2) establish that there is a **specific case** to which the rule is said to apply—not necessarily in that order.

Granted, the test maker can sneak a rule into the evidence in a lot of ways so that it might not always feel "rule-like" on first reading. But the pattern is possible any time an argument presents evidence establishing either (1) a **guarantee** that something will happen (or is true) if that thing means one criterion or (2) a **requirement** that something is needed for something else to happen (or to be true). For example:

> Works of art that are designed to appeal to the senses cannot be made with an eye towards the utility of the work. There is no work of art that has more visual impact than the ceiling of the Sistine Chapel. [...]

According to the **general rule** stated in the first sentence, if I show you something that we can agree is *a work of art designed to the appeal to the senses*, then we will also have to agree that that work couldn't have been *made with an eye towards utility*. (In other words, if you set out to make some pretty art, you can't also set out to make something useful.)

The second sentence presents a **specific case**: the Sistine Chapel. If we can agree that the Sistine Chapel fits the criteria of the rule, that it is *a work of art designed to appeal to the senses*, then clearly the rule's **application** must apply, and we could safely conclude that *the Sistine Chapel was not made with an eye towards its utility*. The conclusion that would be attached to our example evidence above would likely read:

> Therefore, no matter what the current use to which Michelangelo's masterpiece is put in the Apostolic Palace, that use was not part of his original artistic conception.

If this argument had appeared in a **Structure** family question like the **Method of Argument** question, we might expect the right answer to be something like

> It proceeds from a general principle to make a claim about what is necessarily true in a particular instance to which that principle applies.

If you recognized this pattern in an **Assumption** family question, you would instantly know at least one of the argument's assumptions. If the argument above were true, we would need to assume that

✔ having lots of "visual impact" is the same as being "designed to appeal to the senses," and

✔ an "original artistic conception" is the same as the "design" of a work of art.

And thus, the right answer to an Assumption question about what the argument depends upon might be

> If a goal is not one that an artist originally intended an artwork to meet, that goal cannot be said to be part of the artist's conception of the work.

Departing from the specifics of the argument above, we could say that the main assumption that all arguments that follow the **applied rule** pattern will assume is

✔ There is nothing **special about the case** that would keep the rule from applying or

✔ The rule applies to this case.

Thus, in **Weaken, Strengthen,** and **Evaluate** questions, correct answers would provide new information that addresses the link between case and rule, making it weaker, stronger, or just pointing out that it's an open question, respectively.

Flaw questions featuring invalid versions of this pattern usually involve someone mistaking a **guarantee** for a **requirement**.

> If all men are mortal, and my dog is not a man, he must not be mortal.

In other words, just because all men are mortal, it doesn't mean that men are the only things that are mortal. A possible correct phrasing for an answer choice pointing this out:

> (A) the argument treats a condition found among all members of a group as though it were exclusive to that group

You might also see a speaker sneakily swapping words as the argument moves from evidence to conclusion in a **Flaw** question, in essence assuming because a word sounds like another word or because two groups tend to be associated with each other that rules that apply to the first apply to the second:

> Car owners must register their cars with the city before they are allowed to park in this lot. Since many of the cars here clearly have expired registration stickers, their drivers should be ticketed.

In this case, the right answer could be that the argument is flawed because it

> (A) fails to establish that something true of one group is necessarily true of another.

The people who drove those cars are not necessarily the same people as the cars' owners.

Pattern #2: Cause and Effect

Evidence:	**correlation**:	1. X happened/is true	Fan sales rise during the summer.
		2. Y happened/is true	It is hot during the summer.
Conclusion:	**causation**:	3. X caused Y	The heat causes the increased fan sales.

From our discussion above, you already know that a **Causal Connection** is a type of conclusion. When you spot an argument concluding that something *is responsible for* something else or that one thing *brought about* another, you will find that the evidence is composed of two statements establishing only that two different things happened (or are true). The two things would be said to be **correlated**—they tend to happen at the same time or in the same place.

You've probably heard the maxim "correlation does not imply causation," often accompanied by a story like this one:

> According to folklore, there once was a czar who learned that the most disease-ridden province in his empire was also the province where the most doctors lived and worked. Accordingly, he ordered all doctors throughout his empire shot on sight in order to end the threat of plague once and for all.

Flaw questions often turn on "the czar's mistake," assuming that because there were more doctors in the diseased district (doctors and disease were correlated), it was the doctors who caused the spread of disease—and not that more doctors flocked to that district because of all the sick people to treat! Thus:

Which of the following best describes the error in the czar's reasoning?

(A) The evidence used to conclude a phenomenon is the cause of another is equally consistent with its occurrence being an effect of the other.

Certainly, there are cases where a causal connection is the likeliest explanation for two things occurring together, such as

> Runners often report that a feeling of euphoria follows a long run. When runners experiencing this heightened sense of well-being have submitted to blood tests, those tests have revealed an unusually high concentration of endorphins to be present. Therefore, it is reasonable to believe that some cases of such euphoria are brought on by the release of chemicals in the brain.

The difference between the flawed argument and the convincing one all comes down to a matter of assumptions. Causal arguments all assume:

✔ There is no other factor that might have been the cause.

✔ There is a plausible mechanism by which the cause could have brought about the effect.

✔ The correlation between the cause and effect is not coincidental.

If all these considerations check out, then the argument for a causal connection is strong. Thus, each of these answer choices would **Weaken** the argument:

(A) Runners typically have heightened amounts of endorphins in their blood, as these chemicals are released when muscles regenerate from any sustained exercise.

(B) Blood tests also reveal that runners who experience euphoria following a run have unusually high concentrations of certain minerals and nonchemical agents in their bloodstream.

(C) Blood tests for endorphins are highly inaccurate.

(D) Throughout the day, the body's concentration of mood-altering chemicals fluctuates wildly, particularly in runners.

And this one would **Strengthen** it:

> (E) Runners who report never experiencing postrun euphoria have been shown in MRI tests to lack a particular receptor in the brain that mediates the effect of endorphins.

Similarly, an **Assumption** question's correct answer often states the assumption directly:

> (A) It is unlikely that a blood test would record high concentrations of a mood-altering chemical in the blood unless the person tested had recently experienced a change in mood.

Spot a **causal connection** as an argument's conclusion and you can be certain that you know at least three of its assumptions.

Pattern #3: Representativeness

Evidence:	Something is true of one party.	Toy poodles present no threat to children.
Conclusion:	The same thing is true of another.	Dogs make safe pets if you have children.

In these arguments, the evidence establishes that there is a quality that members of one group have, like *all dogs go to heaven* or *participants in the survey were more likely to report satisfaction*. From this, the argument concludes that some other group shares this quality—usually a larger group, and often the group extends to *"everybody"* or *"people in general."* Other times, the conclusion group is a group of one, a single individual.

Any time an argument relies on an analogy between two things or the similarity between two groups, or uses as its evidence a poll, a survey, an experiment, or some other way of measuring a big effect by looking only at specific cases, the argument will contain an assumption that

> ✔ the evidence group is not different from the conclusion group in a way that would be relevant to the specific quality being discussed.

Thus, a prompt built on this pattern might look like this:

> Children who live within easy walking distance of a well-maintained public playground are much more likely to be physically fit than those who must be driven to a playground further from their homes, according to a new study of children's fitness nationwide. Thus, in order to combat obesity in the very young, more playgrounds ought to be built.

Were the question attached to this prompt an **Assumption** question, this would be a credited response:

> (A) There are no other significant demographic differences between the two groups of children that would account for their differing levels of fitness.

We might **Strengthen** it by eliminating a possible difference, like

> (B) Neighborhoods with public playgrounds do not typically have more recreational sports leagues for children than those without.

And to **Weaken** it, we could point out a difference, such as

> (C) Most often, it is only young parents vigorous enough to engage with their children in physical activities that walk their children to public playgrounds.

If asked to identify the **Flaw**, we might well see:

> (D) The argument relies on the overall similarity of two groups not shown to be similar in all relevant respects

Polls and surveys are, in particular, sticking points in Critical Reasoning prompts. Because we all know that polls need to be conducted in such a way that no unintended bias creeps in, we may often suspect bias where there is no evidence of it.

Whenever we employ statistical methods to draw conclusions, it is true that we must assume many things about the polls or surveys employed if we're going to believe those conclusions.

> ✔ The sample size of the poll (or survey, etc., was large enough to draw conclusions from.

> ✔ The people selected for polling were selected in a random enough fashion to avoid bias.

But we must be careful on the GMAT that we don't assume things about answer choices that they don't say. Suppose you saw an answer choice in a Flaw question that said

> (A) Because of the risk to participants' lives, only a dozen
> patients were involved in the clinical trial.

You might be tempted to choose it, as 12 doesn't sound like a very big sample size. But the keyword in each of the assumptions above is *enough*. The poll must be large *enough*, and random *enough*. You're not allowed to use outside information to make decisions in Critical Reasoning, and the answer choice doesn't explicitly tell you that 12 is not big *enough* to draw conclusions from. Thus, it would NOT be the credited answer.

When the GMAT tests these two assumptions, they have to be very specific in their wording so that the *enough* is buried in there somewhere.

> (B) The incidence of the disease is one per ten thousand
> individuals, requiring at least one hundred trials to
> evaluate the vaccine's efficacy reliably.

The same goes for the original assumption, that the two groups are similar *enough with respect to the quality in question*. If you don't spot the *enough*, then just any old difference between the two groups is not sufficient to strengthen, weaken, or evaluate. In our original playground question, this would NOT be a credited answer:

> (E) Families that live near public playgrounds tend to be
> poorer, on average, than those who live further away.

Sounds reasonable, right? But the answer choice never hints at why wealth might affect a child's physical fitness, unlike the *recreational sports league* or the *young parents* who engage in other *physical* activities with their children. Thus, there's no way for you to know what effect wealth would have on the children's levels of physical fitness.

Just think, wealthy parents might be able to afford better coaches for their kids, but they also might tend to keep their children quiet by feeding them lots of expensive sweets and plying them with video games and other sedentary activities.

Finally, there's one special flavor of the **representativeness** pattern that often slips under the test taker's radar: **predictions**. Whenever you make a claim about what will happen in the future based on evidence about what has happened in the past, you are making a kind of **representativeness assumption**, namely that

✔ things that are true of the past can be taken as
   representative of things that will be true of the future.

Or put another way, you assume

✔ nothing on which the prediction is based will change
   materially in the future.

or

✔ the future will resemble the past in all relevant ways.

Thus, credited answer choices for questions involving a prediction often introduce information that indicates that the future will or won't resemble the past in some important way.

And don't forget, **plans** and **proposals** are often themselves claims about what *will* work or what *should* be done in the future—they're predictions, too! Thus, these arguments likewise assume that the conditions which the plan or proposal was built to address won't change in some material way in the future.

Pattern #4: Net Benefit/Net Harm

This is in all likelihood the most common argument pattern on the test. Remember the example we began with?

> The city council of Belleville has enacted a new ordinance
> allowing police officers to issue a ticket for loitering to
> anyone lingering longer than five minutes outside a store-
> front. We can expect a general decrease in crime to fol-
> low, as vagrants will now have less opportunity to commit
> street crimes such as mugging or vandalism.

The evidence in this argument is that **one factor** that contributes to crime **has been reduced** by the plan; therefore, the plan will bring about an **overall reduction**. But what about all the other factors that might increase or decrease crime? Will they remain the same? We must assume they will. Indeed, all arguments that fit this pattern must assume

✔ the thing said to be beneficial or harmful will not
   indirectly cause a harm or benefit that **outweighs** its
   stated effect.

Consider this the old law of unintended consequences. What if we found out, for instance,

(A) Vagrants who usually spend their time loitering will,
    when unable to do so, often engage in criminal activity.

Exactly. The argument would be **Weakened**. On the other hand, we can **Strengthen** such an argument by eliminating a possible side effect that would **change the balance** between the plan's advantages and any possible disadvantages.

> (B) Reducing the number of people on the street outside a business will not make that business more likely to be the target of an armed robbery.

What does *armed robbery* have to do with anything? It's a crime that might have increased due to one of the effects of the new loitering law. Since the stated prediction was that crime would go down, any crime is within the argument's **scope**.

The pattern of a **net benefit** or a **net harm** can be found attached to virtually any type of conclusion, so in most arguments, we should be on the lookout for indirect effects that are clearly relevant to the goals stated by the speaker or the benefit said to accrue from a plan.

Technique #7: Argument Diagramming

Remember, your wet erase noteboard isn't taken up after the break following the Quantitative section. It's still there for you to use during the Verbal section.

One thing you might consider doing with that board is using it to diagram tricky arguments in Critical Reasoning questions. You might just spot a common pattern you've missed or make a connection that you didn't realize already existed in the argument as stated.

Since the most important thing you need in order to understand an argument is to be able to state the conclusion (and distinguish the conclusion from the evidence), you'll need some symbol for keeping track of which is which.

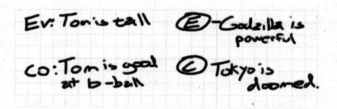

The next thing you'll need is some way to indicate "this is directly connected to that." Connections, after all, are what make an argument valid or invalid.

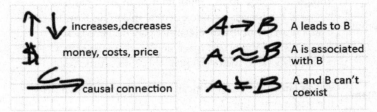

After that, you'll want to make sure you have a consistent shorthand for concepts that you see again and again. Here are a few to get you started:

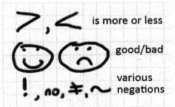

And now, here are a few final tips for diagramming:

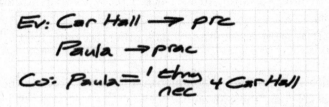

Don't "Pronounce" Your Symbols in Your Head

If you write something like this:

$$Ev: Car\ Hall \rightarrow prc$$
$$Paula \rightarrow prac$$
$$Co: Paula = '\ \underset{nec}{thg}\ 4\ Car\ Hall$$

Don't read it back to yourself as "Car Hall then per-eck, Paula then per-eck, so Paula is one thig neck for Car Hall."

Instead, translate as you read. "Practice is necessary for going to Carnegie Hall; Paula has practiced; so, Paula has one thing necessary for Carnegie Hall." No caveman-speak, no gibberish—always use your diagrams as shorthand for your thoughts about the argument, not to replace those thoughts. If you let the notes take over, they become an extra step between you and understanding.

FACT-BASED QUESTIONS

Anatomy of a Fact-Based Question

Prompt
> Ironically, George Lucas's reputation as an artist has been hindered by the very technology that makes his films so dazzling. Many of the theaters that play his films lack top of the line projection machinery. Such machinery is absolutely vital to the full display of Lucas's artistic skill.

Stem
> Which one of the following can be properly inferred from the statements above?

Answer Choices
> (A) Some theaters that play Lucas's films provide support for Lucas's reputation as an artist.
> (B) All theaters that play Lucas's films and that possess top of the line projection machinery display Lucas's artistic skill fully.
> (C) All of the showings of Lucas's films that do not display his full artistic skill lack top of the line projection machinery.
> (D) If a theater possesses top of the line projection facilities, it will provide a full display of an artist's skill.
> (E) At least some of the theaters that play Lucas's films fail to display fully Lucas's skills as an artist.

Prompt
- There is more variation in Fact-Based prompts than Argument-Based prompts.
- Some are as short as a line and a half; others are quite long.

Stem
- Instead of using the word argument, stems often describe the prompt as "the passage" or "the statements."
- Explain and Inference work in opposite directions. Explain adds to the prompt; Inference deduces from it.

Answer Choices
- Pay attention to words that indicate that facts are qualified or extreme.
- Double-check the language of the answer choice to make sure you aren't glossing over a small detail.

Identifying Fact-Based Questions

Inference questions account for all but a tiny slice of the remaining Critical Reasoning questions, and they also show up among the Reading Comprehension questions.

Remember the test maker's definition of inference, which is something that **MUST BE TRUE** on the basis of some specific, definite piece of information. *Might be true, could be true,* and *really, really, really likely to be true* don't make the inference cut.

Complete (Conclusion) questions are just another form of **Inference**, as the only conclusion you are allowed to complete an argument with is one that is inferable (that MUST BE TRUE) from the facts presented.

For both, when you read the prompt, you are searching for the most definite, specific information present. Inferences come out of such information.

Explain questions rely on the same sorts of prompts—facts rather than arguments—but the task is different from that in **Inference** questions. Instead of adding the information in the prompt together to say what must be true, these questions ask you to add a piece of information *to* the prompt so that what seems like it can't possibly be true will be revealed to be sensible and sound.

As always, the stem will guide you. Possible stems for each follow.

Inference Questions
- Which of the following conclusions can most properly be drawn from the information on the previous page?
- If the facts stated in the passage above are true, which of the following must be true on the basis of them?
- The claims above, if true, most strongly support which of the following conclusions?

Complete (Conclusion) Questions
- The stems for these questions are always found above the prompt.
- Which of the following most logically completes the passage?
- Which of the following most logically completes the argument?
- Which of the following best completes the passage below?

Be sure not to mistake them for **Complete (Evidence)** questions. Look for the **conclusion keyword** in front of the blank (or nearby).

Explain Questions

- Which of the following, if true, most helps to explain the surprising finding?
- Which of the following, if true, does most to explain the phenomenon previously described?
- Which of the following, if true, best accounts for the race's anomalous results?

Processing the Prompts of Fact-Based Questions

In Argument-Based questions, your first step to untangling the prompt is the hunt for the conclusion. With Fact-Based questions, you're also on a hunt, just for different things.

Inference Prompts

We begin with **Inference** questions, which require you to find the "most inferency part" of the prompt—the definite rule, the principle, the thing that is *always true*, etc. The more you practice with Official Guide or GMATPrep questions, the more you will come to appreciate the way that the test maker sets up an inference question.

Technique #8: Recognize the Common Inference Keys

The content of an Inference prompt may vary, but there are certain things you learn to recognize as the test maker's way of saying "Hey, look here, we're going to build an Inference off of this!"

Inference Pattern #1: Untangle the Double Negatives

The test maker loves hiding information under tortuously constructive double negatives. Or perhaps we should say instead, the test maker doesn't not love hiding it there.

Thus, you might see something like this in an Inference prompt:

> No one is incapable of everything.

What can you infer from that? Well, if *no one* is *incapable of everything*, then everyone (the opposite of no one) must be capable (i.e., not *incapable*) of something. Notice that negatives can be found both in little words like *no*, *not*, *nor*, and *none*, but also *inside* words through prefixes like *in-*, *un-*, and *im-*.

Combine the two, and you end up with all kinds of places in which to hide inferences.

> If everything that is not material is imperfect, then it's also true that everything that is immaterial is not perfect, and also that nothing that is not material lacks perfection.

Inference Pattern #2: Keep Track of "So and So" and "Such and Such"

Another way to hide an inference is to separate two facts about the same thing in different parts of the prompt. The prompt starts out by talking about one thing:

> The detention of hostile combatants without specific charge has become commonplace during the modern struggle against fanaticism [...]

Then it switches gears to something else.

> [...] Throughout the era following the first two World Wars, nations generally fought other nations, rather than disparate loosely affiliated groups united only by ideology. [...]

Then sneakily switch back to the first topic.

> [...] These new methods, their proponents contend, are justified by the same principles that allow for nations to combat each other.

Take piece A and piece C, put them together, and you have the credited answer to an Inference question.

> (A) Established principles allow for some to defend the practice of detention even when that detention is not accompanied by a formal charge.

Kind of silly, right? Just remember that the right answer to an Inference question must be 100 percent justified, not merely likely or sensible. The test maker's hands are bound by this limitation, so they have to resort to some pretty silly tactics to cloud your ability to see the credited answer.

Thus, look for demonstrative pronouns like *this*, *that*, and *these*, along with place holder words like *such*, *one*, *it*, *there*, or the *latter* and the *former*. Trace the pronoun back to its referent and you'll often have your Inference.

Inference Pattern #3: Group Information by Category

Names are important. Sometimes, you're given two names for the same concept. Other times, you're told that two concepts can both be described by a single named. Either way, keeping track of what details are said to be true of which concepts is often the key to another sort of Inference. For example:

> Disruptive thinking challenges the status quo by
> advocating for change; some disruptive thinkers work
> within existing institutions, others from without.
> Regardless, in their efforts to bring about a new social
> consciousness, those intellectual elites who would break
> with the establishment are aided by the public's growing
> consensus that institutions no longer work as they should.

Keep track of which group is which. Here, we have one group, *disruptive thinkers*, who can also be called *intellectual elites* and *people who break with establishment*. That group is further subdivided into two groups, those who work *within* institutions, and those who work *outside* them. Nothing is told to us about the individual halves; rather, another two facts are added to the original group: they *try to bring about a new social consciousness* and when they do, they're *aided by the public's consensus that institutions are broken.*

The difference between a correct inference

> (A) The success of disruptive thinkers outside an institution
> can be influenced by attitudes toward that institution.

and an incorrect one

> (B) The public's distrust of institutions allows disruptive
> thinkers to form a consensus for social change.

is just lining up the details with the right party.

Inference Pattern #4: But That's Too Obvious!

Take a look back at Answer Choice (A) above and notice how modest the claim contained in it is. Success *can* be influenced—not *will*, not *is always*, not *is never*, merely *can*. Sometimes Inference prompts contain little to no definite information, no rules, no conditional statements, nothing that will allow an impressive inference to be drawn.

In those cases—when the Inference prompt lacks concrete, definite information—the correct answer is most often phrased very weakly.

(A) The atmosphere plays **some role** in the transmission of radio waves.
(B) The success of a venture is determined, **in part**, by factors beyond a capitalist's control.
(C) The ultimate temperature reached by a chemical reaction **is influenced by** the permeability of the outer valence.
(D) Cholesterol **plays a part** in blood pressure assessment.
(E) **At least one** of the factors that **contribute** to a gene's expression occurs after the organism has developed.

When the GMAT gives you lemons, make very small, very limited claims about those lemons, the sort of thing that's so bland and timid that it would be consistent with nearly any specific scenario.

Inference Pattern #5: Formal Logic Part 1—
Inferring the Contrapositive

We've told you throughout this chapter that you are not required to understand the complicated or arcane rules that logicians and philosophy professors concern themselves with, and we stand by that. The most complicated logical principle you're ever asked to handle on the GMAT is the sort of thing that's covered during the first week of a Symbolic Logic or Formal Logic class.

In truth, the only "formal logic" that appears on the test concerns **conditional statements** and what can be *inferred* from them. A conditional statement consists of two concepts, one of which is **sufficient** to bring the other about, the other of which is **necessary** for the other to occur. For example, there is a specific conditional relationship between automobiles with gasoline-powered engines and gasoline. If a car has no gas, then it will not run.

If we wanted to express this relationship formally, we would place the **sufficient condition** on the left side of an arrow and the **necessary condition** on the right side. Gas is necessary for your car to run, thus:

Sufficient	**Necessary**
If your car is running,	then it must have gas.
Run $\rightarrow$	Gas

Every conditional statement can be written two ways. If we call the way we just wrote it *the positive*, then the other way is called the *contrapositive*. The contrapositive of our statement would look like this:

Sufficient		Necessary
If your car has no gas,		then it must not be running.
No Gas	→	No Run

If the positive is true, the contrapositive must also be true. Or, to put a finer point on it, they're the same statement just expressed two different but equally correct ways.

Transforming a simple conditional statement from the positive to the contrapositive (and back again), is a two-step process: (1) reverse the order the elements are written in, and (2) negate the elements. Thus:

Sufficient			Necessary
Positive:	If your car is running,		then it must have gas.
	Run	→	Gas
Step 1: Reverse	Gas	→	Run
Step 2: Negate	no Gas	→	no Run
Contrapositive:	If your car has no gas,		then it must not be running.
	no Gas	→	no Run

If the statement is complicated—that is, if it includes more than two connected ideas—then a third step is added: (3) any *ands* become *ors* and any *ors* become *ands*.

Here's a complicated formal logic statement:

Sufficient		Necessary
If you are not wearing shoes **or** not wearing a shirt,		then you will not be given service.
no Shirt or no Shoes	→	no Service

To transform this complicated statement into its contrapositive, just follow the 3-step process:

Sufficient		Necessary	
Positive:	If you are not wearing shoes **or** not wearing a shirt,	then you will not be given service.	
	no Shirt or no Shoes	→	no Service
Step 1: Reverse	*no Service*	→	*no Shirt or no Shoes*
Step 2: Negate	*Service*	→	*Shirt or Shoes*
	(no no Service)		*(no no Shirt)*
			(no no Shoes)
Step 3: Or/And	*Service*	→	*Shirt and Shoes*
Contrapositive:	If you are getting service,		then you must be wearing a shirt AND shoes.

That's as difficult as the logic gets on the GMAT. But understanding how to do this little transformation does play into a sizeable minority of GMAT Critical Reasoning questions, particularly Inference questions. Whenever you see a definite, conditional rule in the prompt of an Inference question, the correct inference may just be as simple as recognizing the contrapositive—something *always* inferable from a conditional rule.

Inference Pattern #6: Formal Logic Part 2—Connecting Conditionals

When two or more conditional statements appear in an Inference prompt, that's usually a clue that you should try to combine the two. For example:

> If it rains tomorrow, then the fair will be canceled. But since it's August, days when it doesn't rain are invariably so hot that cotton candy melts.

In shorthand, the statements and their contrapositives would look like this:

Rain → no Fair   no Rain → no Cotton Candy

Fair → no Rain   Cotton Candy → Rain

The necessary condition for one set becomes the sufficient condition for the other, and vice versa. Thus:

Fair → no Rain → no Cotton Candy

Cotton Candy → Rain → no Fair

What can we infer from these two linked conditionals? If the fair is open, then no one will be able to eat any cotton candy. Also, if people are able to eat cotton candy, they won't be eating it at the fair because the fair will be closed. Each way of phrasing this relationship between the fair and cotton candy is 100 percent true if the original two conditionals are true, the very definition of an Inference.

Recognizing Conditional Statements

If the test maker would always use the *if ... then ...* construction, then recognizing conditionals would be a lot easier. Alas, there are many ways to invoke a conditional relationship. Here are the most common:

If X, then Y.	$X \rightarrow Y$	If you call me, then I'll be there. If I didn't come, then you didn't call me.
When X, Y	$X \rightarrow Y$	When you call me, I'll be there. When I'm not there, you didn't call me.
Whenever X, Y	$X \rightarrow Y$	Whenever you call me, I'll be there. Whenever I'm not there, you didn't call me.
Every X is Y.	$X \rightarrow Y$	Every owl is able to fly. Every flightless thing (e.g., my desk) is not an owl.
All Xs are Ys	$X \rightarrow Y$	All owls are birds. All nonbirds (mammals, for example) are not owls.
People who X, Y	$X \rightarrow Y$	People who like birds like cool things. People who don't like cool things don't like birds.
Only Xs are Ys	$Y \rightarrow X$	Only people who are cool like birds. Only people who don't like birds aren't cool.
X, only if Y	$X \rightarrow Y$	You are cool only if you like birds.
X must Y	$X \rightarrow Y$	Legal drivers must have a current license. Drivers who don't have licenses must not be legal.

X is required for Y	Y → X	Being 18 is required for voting.
X, unless Y	X → no Y	I will go to the store, unless it rains.
Can't be X unless Y	X → Y	You can't be a legal driver unless you have a license.
X, except Y	X → no Y	People are terrible, except for children.
X until Y	Y → no X	You can talk until the bell rings.
No X without Y	X → Y	You can't do well without studying. You can't (always) avoid studying without (later) failing.

Explain Prompts

Even though Inference prompts and Explain prompts both contain information, you are asked to treat as true at face value, what you do with that information differs greatly between the two. Remember, Explain questions ask you to *resolve* or *explain* an apparent dilemma. Your job when attacking these prompts will be to find the two "horns" of the dilemma. Called the "horns" from the idea that a bull has two horns, and the choice between being gored by one is no better than being gored by the other. After all, if you don't know what the two things that need to be brought together are, how are you ever going to find the answer that brings them together?

Technique #9: Finding the "Horns" of the Dilemma

Explain questions present you with all kinds of weird situations. The most common are:

THE RULE VIOLATION—The prompt presents two things: (1) a **general rule** and (2) a case that seems like the rule should be applied to it, but in which **the rule *seems* to be violated**. The correct answer will usually either show that the rule **doesn't actually apply** or that the violation is itself just **further demonstration** of the rule applying.

THE FLOUTED TREND—Similar to the rule violation, in these prompts (1) **a general trend** is cited but then (2) **a specific case** that seems **counter to the trend** is given. It, too, is usually solved by the introduction of information that shows that the trend **isn't relevant to this specific case**, or that, when another factor is considered, the specific case is just **further demonstration** of the general trend.

THE UNREALIZED EXPECTATION—These prompts present (1) an **expectation** or **prediction**, but then state that it (2) **never happened** or that the **opposite happened**. Usually, the right answer will show that the expectation was based on an **assumption that doesn't apply** in this case, sometimes by showing that there was an extra **unconsidered factor** that explains things.

THE REJECTED ADVICE—These prompts establish that, in general, (1) using **one strategy is a good idea**, but that some group or actor that has been given the facts has (2) **chosen otherwise**. These paradoxes are usually explained by answer choices that provide, again, an **unconsidered factor** that show that in *this case* the advice would be bad.

When you have identified an **Explain** question, read the prompt and then try to rephrase it into either

(1), but (2) or on the one hand X, but on the other hand Y.

Only when you hold the two "horns" of the dilemma in your hand will you be able to bridge the gap between them.

Also, keep in mind that the wrong answer choices to explain questions usually fall into two camps, things that are **irrelevant to the dilemma**—that is, things that wouldn't change things at all if you knew them—or things that actually *worsen the dilemma*, by making the weirdness in the prompt even weirder.

CRITICAL REASONING PRACTICE SETS

Argument Structure

500- to 600-Level Argument Structure Practice Set

1. The global increase in standard of living is the driving force behind the increased carbon dioxide emissions of the last three decades, and it is this increase that contributes the most to global climate change. As wages rise, more of the world's population can afford luxuries that, while agreeable, require substantially more energy to maintain, which causes more carbon dioxide to be emitted. Moreover, when the standard of living declined over the last few years because of the financial crisis, carbon dioxide emissions declined in turn.

   Which of the following best describes the role played in the argument above by the statement that the global increase in standard of living is the driving force behind increased carbon dioxide emissions?

   (A) It is a phenomenon whose existence is taken as evidence for a prediction later proposed.

   (B) It is the main conclusion that the remainder of the argument provides reasons to accept.

   (C) It is a phenomenon that can only be understood if all of the facts that follow are true.

   (D) It is a premise the argument presents in order to make a recommendation for conservation.

   (E) It is used to limit the extent of possible phenomenon to which a subsequent explanation can be applied.

2. Despite what they profess to believe, **atheists clearly believe in a higher power**. A prominent religious activist has posted a bounty on his website offering $10 to anyone who would sign a piece of paper that says that he owns their soul, and yet after many months, there have been no takers. Why would anyone be unwilling to part with something that they do not believe exists to begin with?

Which of the following best describes the role played in the argument by the portion in **bold**?

(A) It is a statement that the author believes is valid to hold for reasons given later.

(B) It is an observation that the author uses to support a position given later.

(C) It is a pattern of cause and effect that the author believes holds true for reasons given later.

(D) It is a conclusion that the author presents in order to discredit later.

(E) It is a relationship that the author does not believe holds true in a case described later.

3. Spokesperson: **We recommend that our clients prepare today for the inevitable consequences of technological development**. The current pace of advancement is such that in less than a decade, most of the technologies currently in use will have been superseded by more efficient, lower cost alternatives. **The cost of replacing outdated technologies need not outweigh the savings these alternatives will allow**, so long as businesses take steps now to streamline their processes so that replacement innovations can be integrated seamlessly into their day-to-day activities.

In the spokesperson's argument above, the two portions in **boldface** play which of the following roles?

(A) The first is evidence offered in support of an opinion that the spokesperson rejects; the second offers information that contradicts that evidence.

(B) The first is a premise that the spokesperson partially accepts; the second offers evidence that explains why that acceptance is not complete.

(C) The first is a position that the spokesperson argues against; the second is the position that the spokesperson defends.

(D) The first is a generalization accepted as accurate and used as a premise in favor of the spokesperson's conclusion; the second is a consideration that further supports the spokesperson's conclusion.

(E) The first is the main conclusion that the spokesperson asserts; the second suggests a potential objection the spokesperson's argument later addresses.

600- to 700-Level Argument Structure Practice Set

1. Last month, The Olde Tyme Creamery introduced a new milkshake flavor, Gravely Choctastic. Within a week, its main competitor, Shakez, announced an almost identical flavor named Ghastly Chocolate. Neither company has accused the other of copying its design, but **the similarity is too close to be coincidental**. Each is equal parts fruit sorbet and Rocky Road, an unorthodox combination. Moreover, **it is absurd to think that two companies working in isolation would simultaneously launch identical products with nearly identical names**.

   In the argument above, the two statements in **bold** play which of the following roles?

   (A) The first is the argument's main conclusion; the second is a condition sufficient for that conclusion to be true.

   (B) The first is a secondary conclusion used to argue in favor of the argument's final conclusion; the second is likewise evidence for the main conclusion.

   (C) Both statements are evidence given to support the argument's main conclusion.

   (D) Both statements are an explanation that the argument concludes is more likely than one the argument opposes.

   (E) Both statements are conclusions; the first is used as evidence demonstrating the truth of the second.

2. The Maillard reaction, first described in the 19th century by a French physician, is the process by which meat turns brown and crispy when cooked. Indeed, applying heat to a food is the key technique to cooking, which means that cooking should be seen as an example of applied physics, rather than as an art. Even though qualities like tastiness of browned meat or the appropriate level of crispiness may be hard to define, this difficulty alone would not relegate cooking to the ranks of the practical arts.

Which of the following is the main conclusion in the argument above?

(A) The Maillard reaction is the process by which meat turns brown and crispy when cooked.

(B) It may be hard to define some qualities that are considered relevant to cooking, like crispiness and tastiness.

(C) Something that is a practical art can never be properly considered an example of an applied science.

(D) Cooking is better classified as an example of applied physics than as an art.

(E) Applying heat to a food is the key technique to cooking.

3. Estragon: Our friend sent word that he would not arrive by train, but by carriage. Almost all of our friends come by train. Our friend who is coming today is like our other friends in most respects. How can he be different in this one? He must no longer be our friend.

    Vladimir: Our friends usually come by train because we usually arrange to meet them at the train station, rather than at our home. Our friend who is coming today knows where we live, so we did not make such arrangements.

    Vladimir responds to Estragon's reasoning by

    (A) offering an alternative explanation for the evidence Estragon cites.
    (B) undermining some of Estragon's evidence while agreeing with his conclusion.
    (C) drawing attention to an inconsistency between two of Estragon's claims.
    (D) pointing out that Estragon's use of the term "friend" is excessively vague.
    (E) presenting evidence that directly contradicts Estragon's evidence.

700- to 800-Level Argument Structure Practice Set

1. **The dividends that shareholders were expecting MegaBiz to pay this quarter were reduced at the last minute,** a sign that many analysts claim does not bode well for MegaBiz's stock price over the short-to-medium term. This analysis is not necessarily correct, however, as **often dividends are reduced in order to conserve capital in preparation for an aggressive expansion**, something only companies otherwise equipped for long-term growth can undertake.

   In the argument above, the two **boldface** portions play which of the following roles?

   (A) The first is evidence for argument's conclusion; the second is that conclusion.

   (B) The first is a phenomenon the argument's conclusion explains; the second is a factor contributing to the likelihood of that explanation being correct.

   (C) The first is a phenomenon the argument's conclusion addresses; the second is an alternate hypothesis the argument rejects.

   (D) The first is a fact that the argument seeks to explain; the second is an alternate explanation the argument proposes.

   (E) The first is a prediction that the argument seeks to explain; the second is the hypothesis the argument presents as the likeliest evidence for that prediction.

2. Eddie: You won't be able to understand the true themes beneath the surface of the most popular alternative music of the 1990s because you were only a child when it was released. Popular music is always aimed at people in their late teens and early twenties.

Mark: You were not alive during the ancient Roman era, nor were any of us now living, but you trust that professor Bullfinch's interpretations of the *Aeneid* do, in fact, capture that work's deepest meaning. Why should alternative music require what Roman poetry does not?

Mark responds to Eddie's claim by

(A) using an example from classical culture in order to delegitimize contemporary culture.
(B) presenting an analogous situation that suggests Eddie relies on unsupported premises.
(C) contradicting a key piece of evidence that Eddie's argument relies upon.
(D) specifying a definition that Eddie's argument relies upon but leaves implicit.
(E) questioning Eddie's own qualification to make judgments about a similar phenomenon.

3. Minor increases in sea temperature, such as those brought on by human activity, can adversely affect fish and seabird populations, even if the resulting temperature is well within the tolerances of these complex species. Phytoplankton depend upon the vertical mixing of the different strata of sea water in order to obtain nutrients from the lower levels. Without phytoplankton, zooplankton will starve, and zooplankton are critical to the rest of the food chain that ends in seabirds and the fish they eat.

In the argument above, which of the following best describes the role played by the information that without phytoplankton, zooplankton will starve?

(A) It is a hypothesis for which support is offered elsewhere in the argument.

(B) It is an example that illustrates the phenomenon of vertical mixing of sea water.

(C) It is a premise that taken jointly with other premises establishes the argument's validity.

(D) It is offered in support of the conclusion that global warming should be avoided.

(E) It supports the conclusion that temperature change harms all species equally.

Argument Assumption

500- to 600-Level Argument Assumption Practice Set

1. Because of a sharp increase in the number of commercial fishing vessels plying the waters off the coast of Peru in the past decade, the anchovy population there was largely depleted. If the stock of anchovies is ever to recover, the number of fishing vessels must be reduced by at least 50 percent. Since the Peruvian government has recently closed loopholes that allowed foreign fishing vessels to enter its waters without permits, it is likely that the population of anchovies will rise significantly in the coming decade.

   Which of the following would it be most useful to establish in evaluating the argument?

   (A) Whether high demand for anchovies in Peru or in foreign markets led to the overfishing
   (B) Whether the foreign fishing vessels use the same methods and equipment as Peruvian vessels
   (C) Whether the Peruvian government was influenced unduly by environmental lobbyists
   (D) Whether fishing vessels that previously entered without permits will be able to obtain them in the future
   (E) Whether other fish stocks have declined substantially in recent years

2. Some believe that there are a large number of gun-related homicides in the U.S., but they are simply misinformed, as this belief is itself based primarily upon the frequency with which gun-related homicides appear in news reports on television in the U.S. It is precisely because gun-related homicides are such a rare occurrence in the U.S. that they are so frequently the subject of television news.

The argument above is most vulnerable to the objection that

(A) it presupposes that most television news reports are about gun-related homicides.

(B) it presupposes, without warrant, that the television news reports are not biased.

(C) it presupposes the truth of the conclusion that it purports to demonstrate.

(D) it uncritically draws an inference from what is often the case to what will occur in the future.

(E) it uncritically assumes that a characteristic of one member of a group is shared by all members of that group.

3. On some cruises, the *Princess Anne*'s entertainment selection includes performances by members of the cast of popular Broadway shows, and on some cruises, their entertainment selection includes "Alternative" bands last popular during the 1990s. Therefore, on some of the *Princess Anne*'s cruises, at least two different types of musical entertainment are available.

The reasoning in the argument is flawed in that the argument

(A) mistakes a condition that sometimes accompanies the presence of one type of musical act with something that necessarily accompanies it.

(B) fails to recognize that one set might overlap with each of the two others even though those two other sets do not overlap with each other.

(C) fails to consider that the fan bases of the two types of musical acts mentioned would rarely overlap.

(D) presupposes the truth of the conclusion that it purports to elsewhere explain.

(E) infers a causal relationship from a situation in which two groups are merely correlated with one another.

600- to 700-Level Argument Assumption Practice Set

1. Experts have long been puzzled by how a craftsman of humble origins like Stradivarius could have developed a technique for making such exquisitely perfect violins, but a new hypothesis offers a different explanation. A drought during Stradivarius' lifetime affected the growth of Italian willow and maple trees, resulting in wood with superior acoustic properties, and thus the reputation of these violins owes more to the materials used than the man using them.

    Which of the following is an assumption upon which the hypothesis in the argument above relies?

    (A) No other Italian violin makers produced violins from the same materials as Stradivarius used.
    (B) No violin that is made with different materials could ever match the quality of a Stradivarius.
    (C) A violin made from the wood of trees whose growth was unaffected by drought would be less perfect than a Stradivarius.
    (D) The reputation of Stradivarius violins rests mostly on the name alone and not the qualities of the violin itself.
    (E) The violins made by Stradivarius were not made entirely of wood harvested before he was born.

2. Recently, a study of donations to the city's public radio station found that, on average, the dollar value of each pledged donation was higher during the winter drive than during the one held midsummer. The study was funded by the station itself and from it the station's owners concluded that in order to increase the amount of money donated to the station, the winter drive should be extended an extra week.

    Which of the following, if true, casts doubt on the station owners' plan?

    (A) A study conducted by an independent group found that donations to the station are down 10 percent this year.
    (B) Those who pledge donations to the station during the winter often do so in order to obtain an income tax deduction.
    (C) People who donate money to public radio typically do so only once per calendar year.
    (D) Neither the midsummer drive nor the winter drive are as successful at securing donations as the late fall drive.
    (E) Though people may pledge to donate money during a drive, they are under no obligation to actually donate that money.

3. Cornell University's Center for Hospitality Research has conducted many studies of tipping behavior over the past decade. Their research shows that, in general, women receive higher tips than men and that women in their thirties receive better tips than younger or older women. Susan is an attractive single mother in her mid-thirties, so it is reasonable for her to expect to be tipped well.

Which of the following indicates the most serious problem with the reasoning above?

(A) The studies do not provide a basis to expect that an attractive person will receive better tips than an unattractive person.
(B) A general rule is drawn from a series of cases that may be atypical.
(C) No information is given concerning the manner in which the Cornell Center conducted its research.
(D) The studies do not address the question of whether age also affects the tips received by men.
(E) An average trend need not hold true in any particular case.

700- to 800-Level Argument Assumption Practice Set

1. In a typical circus troupe, acrobats perform for one fifth of the show's duration, are involved in one fourth of all performance-related accidents, and account for one third of the cost of insurance premiums paid by the show. In order to remain in business, a circus cannot afford to spend more than one-fourth of its budget on any one type of performer.

Each of the following, if true, would provide support for a ringleader's decision to reduce the performance time of a troupe's acrobats EXCEPT?

(A) The longer a performer performs, the more likely a costly accident will occur.
(B) Insurance premiums for circuses are primarily paid to insure its performers against accidents.
(C) The single biggest cost a circus pays is the cost of insuring its performers against accidents.
(D) Ticket sales for a circus's performances would not decline if acrobats performed less.
(E) The accidents that an acrobat is likely to suffer do not occur primarily at the beginning of a performance.

2. In the famous 1971 Stanford prison experiment, participants were sent to a derelict prison where they were randomly assigned roles as either jailor or prisoner. After a week, the experiment was ended, as in that time those acting as jailors had become so cruel to their "charges" that it was deemed unethical to risk continuing any longer.

Which of the following is an assumption underlying the decision to end the experiment?

(A) Whenever people are given unequal amounts of power, those with more power will abuse it.

(B) Practical considerations are not the only grounds by which to evaluate an experiment.

(C) If an experiment is damaging to its participants, it must be ended immediately.

(D) Experimental methods that damage the participants of an experiment unequally are unethical.

(E) It is possible to determine whether an experiment's results will be unethical after only a week.

3. Without a deep, still body of water, the most popular sport fish cannot survive. Such bodies of water inevitably attract substantial beachfront development when those who fish for sport frequent the area. Building a dam on a shallow river is one way to create such a body, but maintaining a dam is economical only if there is also a market for hydroelectric power nearby. Thus, towns with no nearby market for hydroelectric power will tend not to build dams, so they will also be unlikely to have the most popular sport fish in their rivers.

Which of the following most accurately describes a flaw in the reasoning of the argument?

(A) The argument confuses what is necessary for substantial beachfront development with what would guarantee it.

(B) The argument fails to consider that deep, still pools of water might be present even in the absence of a particular condition that would ensure their presence.

(C) The argument confuses what is necessary for the most popular sport fish to survive with what is usually conducive to it.

(D) The argument fails to consider the possibility that hydroelectric power is only one of several advantages of a dam.

(E) The argument bases a claim that there is a causal connection between the presence of deep, still bodies of water and substantial beachfront development on a mere association between them.

Fact-Based Questions

500- to 600-Level Fact-Based Question Practice Set

1. Cement is composed primarily of two ingredients, calcium and silicon, mixed with small amounts of aluminum and iron. Sources of these ingredients are common—shale, limestone, basalt, and even industrial slag may be used—are not expensive, and can easily be substituted with other sources. The price of cement is, however, tightly connected to the price of oil, at least in the modern era, because the process of combining these ingredients into cement requires large amounts of energy.

   If the statements above are true, which of the following is most likely to also be true?

   (A) Oil should be considered one of cement's basic ingredients.
   (B) Oil is the primary source of the energy used in combining ingredients into cement.
   (C) If the price of shale were to increase, the price of cement would rise.
   (D) When the price of oil rises, cement manufacturers lower their overall costs by using cheaper substitutes as ingredients.
   (E) The cement necessary to build a parking garage costs more than the total cost of its basic ingredients.

2. Without the presence of Jupiter in our solar system, Earth would likely not be inhabited. Planets in solar systems with sizeable asteroid belts are subject periodically to meteor strikes that eradicate the biological precursors required for life to develop. The gravitational pull of a large gas giant such as Jupiter protects the other planets in its system from meteor strikes by attracting asteroid debris.

If the statements above are true, which of the following must also be true?

(A) If a solar system does not have a large gas giant such as Jupiter, no planet in it will be inhabited.

(B) If Jupiter were somehow destroyed by meteor strikes, life on Earth would cease to be.

(C) If Jupiter were somehow destroyed by meteor strikes, life would be less likely to develop on currently uninhabited planets in our solar system.

(D) Any planet that is found in a system with an asteroid belt cannot support life unless it is near to a gas giant such as Jupiter.

(E) No planet that is found in a system with more than one asteroid belt can support life.

3. The presence of sugar in the bloodstream directly affects the release of insulin; when more sugar is present, more insulin is released into the body. Yet those who regularly consume large amounts of sugar often have below-average levels of insulin in their blood.

Which of the following, if true, most helps contribute to an explanation of the anomalous phenomenon described above?

(A) The more overweight a person is, the lower the level of insulin in that person's blood.

(B) Though considered healthier diet choices, many fruits contain as much sugar as candy does.

(C) Consuming large amounts of sugar causes the receptors that trigger the release of insulin to become less sensitive to sugar.

(D) Consuming large amounts of processed sugar can be much more dangerous than sugar found naturally in foods.

(E) Insulin does not directly metabolize sugar, but instead triggers the process that metabolizes it.

600- to 700-Level Fact-Based Question Practice Set

1. The years between 1880 and 1905 saw a boom in timber production in Mississippi, which, by 1905, produced as much as one billion board feet of timber per year. Compare that to the rather more meager 300,000 board feet of timber produced annually in 1880. Yet in that same period, the labor force employed by timber mills in Mississippi actually shrank by about 10 percent.

   Which of the following, if true, most helps to explain the apparent discrepancy in the timber industry in Mississippi during the period indicated?

   (A) The timber industry in Mississippi has never been so productive as it was during the three decades following 1880.

   (B) Between 1880 and 1905, the total number of acres of virgin timberland in Mississippi fell substantially.

   (C) Since 1905, the majority of lumber produced in Mississippi has relied upon young second-growth timber.

   (D) Between 1880 and 1905, timber was such a large part of Mississippi's economy that many new labor saving technologies were implemented by the industry.

   (E) Between 1850 and 1905, Mississippi's economy transitioned from primarily agrarian to primarily industrial, due in part to the timber industry's success.

2. Which of the following best completes the argument below?

    Moral philosophers contend that it is important for public officials to avoid even the appearance of wrong-doing. However, actions that appear wrong are not always wrong. The main reason that these philosophers give for their contention is that public officials will be unable to maintain public trust if they appear to be doing things that are considered wrong by the general public. Yet no one should be obligated to conform to the moral standards of the general public; therefore, _____.

    (A) no public official should be obligated to avoid the appearance of wrong-doing.
    (B) all public officials have, to a degree, an interest in maintaining the public's trust.
    (C) public officials who have scrupulously avoided even the appearance of wrong-doing will be trusted by the general public.
    (D) moral philosophers will never accept that the public might trust a public official who presents the appearance of wrong-doing.
    (E) public officials who abuse their power without the public's knowledge are morally wrong for hiding their wrong-doing.

3. Adjuvants are chemicals that farmers apply to plants in order to increase the penetration and adherence of pesticides. Regulators are considering banning the most popular adjuvant because it appears to cause birth defects. There are no substitutes, however, that are as easily applied or as economical to use. If the overall cost of applying pesticide to crops increases, many farmers will go out of business.

    Which of the following is most strongly supported by the information above?

    (A) If the information about the side-effects of the most popular adjuvant is true, many farmers will go out of business.
    (B) If the use of the most popular adjuvant is not banned, the incidence of birth defects will continue to climb.
    (C) If the regulators' ban is not enforced, then no farmers will go out of business.
    (D) If pesticides become harder to apply or less effective, most farmers will go out of business.
    (E) If the regulator's ban is successful, some farmers will go out of business unless they can otherwise reduce their pesticide-related costs.

700- to 800-Level Fact-Based Question Practice Set

1. We intuitively know that all acts that are morally wrong should not be done because our intuition senses that these acts violate our basic autonomy as rational human beings. Any violation of our basic autonomy as rational beings ought to be avoided to the same degree as any other violation and punished accordingly. Murder is certainly wrong, whether it be the murder of one elderly criminal or a bus full of innocent children.

    Which of the following judgments follows from the principles stated above?

    (A) If it is noble to risk one's life saving the lives of others, then it is no nobler to risk one's life saving many lives than to risk it saving one life.
    (B) If stealing is morally wrong and adultery is morally wrong, then lying about one's adultery ought to be twice as intuitively obvious as merely lying.
    (C) If murdering is morally wrong, then accidentally causing a person's death is as much a violation of our basic autonomy as murdering that person.
    (D) If lying is morally wrong, then falsely claiming to have murdered someone ought to be punished to the same degree as if the liar had actually committed the murder.
    (E) If asked to choose between killing someone or letting that person kill someone else, there is no choice that is morally correct.

2. The North Island trade federation is composed of three fully autonomous states: Llassu, Tragda, and Baflazam. Under their trade agreement, each of the members receives a share of the federation's total trade revenues proportional to the state's population as a percentage of the total population of the three states. Though originally Tragda received the greatest share, followed by Baflazam and then Llassu, after the most recent population survey, the federation adjusted the share of trade revenues received by Tragda downward, even though its population grew more than did Llassu's.

If the adjustment to trade revenues that followed the population survey was made in accordance with the trade federation's agreement, which of the following must be true of the three countries in the year surveyed?

(A) The three countries, if arranged from greatest population to least, would be listed Baflazam, Llassu, Tragda.

(B) The three countries, if arranged from greatest population change to least, would be listed Tragda, Baflazam, Llassu.

(C) The three countries, if arranged from greatest population growth to least, would be listed Baflazam, Tragda, Llassu.

(D) The three countries, if arranged from greatest population growth to least, would be listed Tragda, Llassu, Baflazam.

(E) The three countries, if arranged from least population growth to most, would be listed Baflazam, Tragda, Llassu.

3. In the early 1990s, only 10 percent of people in the United States reported that they personally knew someone who was HIV positive. By the end of the decade, that number jumped to 58 percent, even though the number of people suffering from diagnosed cases of HIV in the population of the United States was slightly less in 2000 than it had been in 1990.

Which of the following, if true, could account for the apparent discrepancy in the data above?

(A) Improved therapeutic options allowed many people suffering from HIV to live well beyond initial estimates.

(B) In the decade between 1990 and 2000, several prominent celebrities revealed they had been diagnosed with HIV.

(C) Many of those diagnosed with HIV before 1990 died from complications related to the disease before 2000.

(D) Those with HIV often failed to be diagnosed properly until new techniques were developed in the early 1990s.

(E) The number of treatment options available to people suffering from diagnosed cases of HIV expanded greatly between 1990 and 2000.

Answer Key

500- to 600-Level Argument Structure Practice Set

1. **(B)**　　　　2. **(A)**　　　　3. **(E)**

600- to 700-Level Argument Structure Practice Set

1. **(D)**　　　　2. **(D)**　　　　3. **(A)**

700- to 800-Level Argument Structure Practice Set

1. **(D)**　　　　2. **(B)**　　　　3. **(C)**

500- to 600-Level Argument Assumption Practice Set

1. **(D)**　　　　2. **(C)**　　　　3. **(B)**

600- to 700-Level Argument Assumption Practice Set

1. **(E)**　　　　2. **(C)**　　　　3. **(E)**

700- to 800-Level Argument Assumption Practice Set

1. **(C)**　　　　2. **(B)**　　　　3. **(B)**

500- to 600-Level Fact-Based Question Practice Set

1. **(E)**　　　　2. **(C)**　　　　3. **(C)**

600- to 700-Level Fact-Based Question Practice Set

1. **(D)**　　　　2. **(A)**　　　　3. **(E)**

700- to 800-Level Fact-Based Question Practice Set

1. **(D)**　　　　2. **(C)**　　　　3. **(C)**

Explanations

500- to 600-Level Argument Structure Practice Set

1. **Argument:** The first sentence contains the conclusion (also the statement we are asked to find the role of), *increased standards of living contribute the most to global warming by increasing carbon dioxide*, **a causal connection**, supported by the evidence that luxuries require energy, and energy requires carbon dioxide and the evidence that when standards of living fell, the amount of carbon dioxide in the atmosphere fell. The correct role for the statement is thus described by Answer Choice (B).

   (B) The answers split 2/2/1 in the beginning: Answer Choices (A) and (C) label the statement a *phenomenon*, but the phenomenon being explained is global climate change, not the increase in standard of living itself. Answer Choices (D) and (E) label the statement as a sort of evidence, which is likewise incorrect.

2. **Argument:** This argument follows a familiar pattern, it's conclusion *some people say X and they're wrong*, with the people being *atheists* and the *X* that they don't believe in a higher power. The remainder of the argument is evidence for this claim. Through a bit of **double-negative** trickery, the bolded statement becomes the *and they're wrong (because this is right)*, which Answer Choice (A) nails.

   (A) Answer Choices (D) and (E) can be eliminated because they are the **exact opposite**, claiming the author opposes the bolded position. Answer Choice (C) brings up the **irrelevant** concept of *cause and effect*, the **right answer to the wrong question**, and Answer Choice (B) gets the explanation backwards; the argument explains the bolded statement.

3. **Argument:** The conclusion is found in the first bolded statement, which helpfully is labeled as a **recommendation**: clients should prepare today for technological development. This conclusion is supported by an explanation of how development works; then in the second bolded statement, a prediction that might seem counter to the conclusion, but that is shown later to be avoidable if precautions are taken, just as Answer Choice (E) describes.

(E) The answers split off evidence/conclusion 3/2, allowing Answer Choices (A), (B), and (D) to be eliminated. Answer Choice (C), which understands the first bolded statement's role as a conclusion, is out because it says the conclusion is one the author opposes.

600- to 700-Level Argument Structure Practice Set

1. **Argument:** The argument as presented is partially flawed, as the two bolded statements are just restatements of the same conclusion, that the two companies' certainly influenced each other somehow, as Answer Choice (D) correctly points out.

    (D) The answers split 2/3 over whether the two statements play different roles. Answer Choices (A) and (B) say they are different, and can thus be eliminated. Answer Choice (C) calls the statements evidence, rather than conclusion, and Answer Choice (E) misses that the two are not *different* conclusions; the second one is just a restatement.

2. **Argument:** Rare **Role of a Statement** questions name the role and ask for the part that plays it. Here, the main conclusion is wanted, and that conclusion is *cooking should be seen as an example of applied physics, rather than as an art.* "Should" is always a good sign of a conclusion, as "should" needs support, and conclusions are supported by evidence.

    (D) The correct answer is just a slightly reworded version of the conclusion. Answer Choices (A) and (E) are evidence, and Answer Choices (B) and (C) are **misused details**, things the argument never actually said—so there's no way they could be the argument's conclusion!

3. **Argument:** Two speakers argue over the best way to take their absent friend's recent behavior. The first says it means he is no longer their friend; the second rebuts that the behavior (which he agrees did occur) doesn't have to mean that and provides an **alternate explanation**, as Answer Choice (A) describes.

    (A) All the remaining answer choices describe the second speaker taking some sort of issue with the *evidence*, not with the *interpretation of the evidence*.

700- to 800-Level Argument Structure Practice Set

1. **Argument:** The argument begins with a phenomenon (the first bolded statement); dividends were reduced at the last minute by MegaBiz. This is followed by an explanation attributed to "analysts" who think it's bad news. The author concludes otherwise, or at least points out another explanation is possible, which is the second bolded statement. Answer Choice (D) nails this relationship of *phenomenon and new interpretation/ explanation.*

   (D) Answer Choice (A) is the only answer choice that doesn't get that the first statement is the thing being explained. Of the rest, they split over whether the second is a conclusion/alternate explanation or evidence for that explanation. Answer Choices (B) and (E) wrongly treat the second statement as evidence. Answer Choice (C) can be eliminated because it claims the speaker rejects the conclusion actually supported by the argument.

2. **Argument:** In this two-party prompt, Eddie claims that Mark won't be able to understand alternative music because he wasn't born when it was made; Mark counters by using the example of something neither of them were alive to see, but which Eddie thinks he can understand (or that he can understand through the professor's interpretations, at least). Answer Choice (B) calls the example an *analogous situation* (which it is) and describes the way it's used (to weaken Eddie's assumptions, just like a good GMAT test taker would).

   (B) Answer Choice (A) **misuses details** from the counterexample, in a way that might be tempting to those who didn't have time to read the original (as this is an argument we hear in the **real world** all the time). Answer Choice (C) is out because Mark doesn't contradict evidence; he merely introduces additional evidence. Answer Choice (D) would be fine if it didn't say *definition*, as Mark's evidence doesn't take the form of a definition, and Answer Choice (E) is another **real-world** trap, since Mark doesn't make personal attacks (even though in this situation a person might be expected to).

3. **Argument:** Lots of science jargon is used here to distract you from the fairly straightforward argument structure. The first sentence is a long claim: temperature can hurt birds even if they can stand the heat. The remaining information is evidence to support that claim which

establishes a chain of X affects Y affects Z. Answer Choice (C) correctly identifies the statement's role in that chain.

(C) Answer Choice (A) confuses evidence for conclusion; (B) is a **misused detail**, hoping to distract you with something mentioned but not relevant; (D) gets the overall argument's conclusion wrong, hoping for a little tempting **reasonable but irrelevant** action; and (E) likewise gets the conclusion wrong, presenting something **too extreme** in any event, but also never said in the argument.

500- to 600-Level Argument Assumption Practice Set

1. **Argument:** The argument's conclusion comes at the end of the prompt, though there is an **intermediate conclusion** in the middle, the **bare assertion** of a **requirement** for something to come about: If the anchovy population (specifically, the population off the cost of Peru) is ever to recover (and the speaker is not saying its recovery is definite or even possible), then it must be that the number of fishing vessels is reduced by 50 percent (the requirement). This intermediate conclusion is supported by a single piece of evidence, the **explanation** of the current reduction (a **causal connection**): a sharp increase in the *number* of fishing vessels. In a sense, the initial evidence is a miniargument for a **net calculation**: more vessels = more anchovy deaths. The speaker adds another piece of evidence (that recently loopholes allowed foreign fishing vessels to ply Peruvian waters). The speaker's final conclusion is found at the end, a **prediction**: the population of anchovies is going to rebound, thanks to this loophole change.

(D) Clearly, then, the speaker assumes that all the factors that went into the net calculation before, whatever they were, will continue, whereas no other factors that could change the calculation will emerge. The speaker also must assume that the **plan** will not meet with any hurdles. Answer Choice (D) would be relevant to that assumption, as it raises a possible problem with the plan. If the formerly unlicensed ships could re-enter with fresh licenses, the plan would not block the old factors that caused the decrease in anchovies from reoccurring.

Answer Choices (A), (B), and (C) are meant to mislead by bringing up things that are often relevant to fishing in the **real world**, but that don't matter in this specific case. Answer Choice (B) is **one step removed** from being relevant, as we don't know what would matter about the specific methods used. Answer Choice (E) is likewise **one**

step removed, suggesting an **irrelevant comparison** to other fish species—whatever's happening with them, we don't know that similar things are in play with anchovies.

2. **Argument:** It might have been hard for you to find the conclusion because the speaker essentially says it twice, phrasing it differently each time. Why are people wrong to say that there are lots of gun-related homicides? Because gun-related homicides are a rare occurrence. When an argument's conclusion is the same as its evidence, the argument is said to be **circular**, and Answer Choice (C) is just one way the test maker might phrase that flaw—though it should be noted that most often circular arguments appear as distracting wrong answers on the GMAT.

   (C) Answer Choice (A) is **too extreme** to describe this argument, which merely states that there are *a lot* of TV reports on guns, not that *most* TV reports are on guns. The issue of bias, raised in Answer Choice (B) is a **real-world** distraction, the sort of accusation often thrown around when gun control comes up. There's no prediction about the future, so (D) doesn't apply, nor is there a conclusion made about a group, so Answer Choice (E) is irrelevant as well.

3. **Argument:** Any two different majorities drawn from the same group must overlap at least once because you can't fit two majorities into the same whole without some overlap. This argument is structured to look like an inference drawn from overlapping majorities, but it fails because the evidence is built on things true of *some* members of the group, not on *most* members of the group. Answer Choice (B) describes this flaw exactly. (For example, it's possible that the Alternative bands only show up on cruises in June, the Broadway groups in March, and the rest of the year neither is present.)

   (B) Answer Choices (A) and (E) are restatements of the same general problem not found here, confusing **necessity and sufficiency/cause and effect**. Answer Choice (C) is a bit of **real-world** thinking (because you probably *don't* associate Broadway fans with Alternative fans). And Answer Choice (D) describes a **circular argument**, which this speaker doesn't make.

600- to 700-Level Argument Assumption Practice Set

1. **Argument:** The argument's conclusion is that *the reputation of Stradivarius violins is **more** due to the materials they're built from than the person who built them.* In support, the speaker offers evidence about how awesome the materials are and a **hypothesis** about what makes them so. There are two major assumptions here, first that such special wood requires no special artistry to work with, and second, brought out in Answer Choice (E), that *Stradivarius violins are actually made out of this special wood.* (Note that the evidence only says that this wood was *available* in Stradivarius's lifetime, not that he used it.)

   (E) Answer Choice (A) lies somewhere between the two assumptions, but it doesn't quite nail either, as the Opposite Day test would reveal. (Even if other violin makers used the same materials as Stradivarius, it wouldn't mean that Stradivarius used the special wood or that Stradivarius's techniques were *more important* than the materials.) Since the argument is limited only to explaining why Stradivarius violins are impressive, other violins aren't relevant, so Answer Choices (B) and (C) aren't required assumptions. Answer Choice (D) contradicts the conclusion, so couldn't possibly be an assumption in the argument.

2. **Argument:** The argument consists of a **plan** whose **stated goal** is to increase the amount of money donated to the station. The plan is to lengthen the winter pledge drive, which currently receives higher average pledges than does the midsummer drive. Since it features a plan, if the argument is to be true, we must assume that there is nothing that will prevent the plan from being put into effect; additionally, because it is built upon a comparison between two different pledges, we must assume that there's nothing special about one group that would change conclusions drawn about the other. Answer Choice (C) casts doubt on the first assumption. If people only donate once a year, it doesn't matter how long the winter pledge drive is. Those who donate will either have already donated in midsummer or would have already donated during the shorter drive.

   (C) Answer Choice (A) doesn't cast doubt on the plan; it just intensifies the need for the plan. Answer Choice (B) is probably true in the **real world**, but wouldn't really have any effect on the success of a longer winter drive. Answer Choice (D) presents an **irrelevant comparison** that might be mistaken for an **alternate method**; the conclusion of the argument is not, however, that lengthening the winter drive is the *best method* or the *only one* that will succeed, it is just that it will definitely increase the amount of money made by the station. And finally, Answer Choice (E) is also true in the **real world**, but here it is **one step removed** from weakening the argument, since it doesn't tell us that the winter drive is more susceptible to this problem than any other, or that a longer winter drive would be more susceptible to it than a shorter one would.

3. **Argument:** This argument commits the flaw of assuming that something true of one group is true of all members of that group. Indeed, it commits the flaw several times over! Just because women in general get higher tips, doesn't mean any single woman is likely to get higher tips. The same is true for any given woman in her thirties or any given attractive woman. Answer Choice (E) points this out, using the synonym of *trend* for *fact true of a group*.

(E) Answer Choice (A) actually **contradicts the evidence**, never the right answer on the GMAT. Answer Choice (B) is the **exact opposite** of what we want. Answer Choice (C) seems to suggest some sort of bias in the study, but it never actually presents us with a reason to believe it was biased. Finally, Answer Choice (D) is something you might be interested in knowing, but which isn't relevant to this particular argument either way.

700- to 800-Level Argument Assumption Practice Set

1. **Argument:** This argument presents a **plan** (sneakily presented in the stem, rather than the prompt), reducing the *performance time* of acrobats in a circus, with the **stated goal** of reducing the portion of the circus's *total budget* that is given over to *insurance premiums for the acrobats*. Thus, the argument has two major assumptions: (1) *performance time is in some way related to insurance premium costs* and (2) *insurance premiums are a big part of the budget overall*. Answer Choices (A) and (B) directly support the first assumption. Answer Choice (E) also supports the first, though a bit more obliquely. If accidents to acrobats tended to happen at the beginning of their performance, cutting time from the end wouldn't necessarily reduce the number of accidents. Answer Choice (D) is instead the confirmation of a **defending assumption**, protecting against the **unintended harm** that the budget might suffer

from reducing the amount of time that acrobats perform (driving away its paying customers).

(C) The evidence says only that a single cost cannot rise above one-fourth of the budget. Answer Choice (C) doesn't strengthen the argument because insurance could still be smaller than one-fourth if it was the largest line item in the budget.

2. **Argument:** The stem of this question warns us to be very careful. The conclusion we're interested in is the *decision to end the experiment*, which we're told was based on the idea that it would be *unethical to risk continuing any longer*. Thus, the argument assumes that an experiment's being *unethical* is a good reason to end it. Answer Choice (B) says this, though in a roundabout way, substituting *nonpractical considerations* for *ethical considerations*.

(B) Answer Choice (A) is wrong because it doesn't affect the decision to end the experiment but is instead something we'd likely conclude from the behavior of the participants. Answer Choice (C) is **too extreme** for this situation, since the experiment wasn't ended *immediately* as soon as someone was damaged, only when the jailers had become "so cruel" that it was unethical. Answer Choice (D) might seem tempting, but nowhere does the argument state that the participants were damaged unequally—it merely mentions one sort of damage; there could have been other, equal damages elsewhere. And Answer Choice (E) confuses the experiment's *results* with *conducting* or *continuing* the experiment.

3. **Argument:** Treating this argument as a series of connected Formal Logic statements is the surest path to spotting the missing assumption. According to the prompt:

Sport fish → deep, still bodies of water (no dsb of water → no sport fish)
Deep, still bodies of water → beachfront development (no development → no dsb of water)
Dam → deep, still bodies of water (no dsb of water → no dam)
Dam economical → market for hydro power (no market → no economical dam)
Therefore, no market for hydro power → no dam → no sport fish

Notice the gap? From the evidence, we could correctly conclude lots of things, but not that the lack of a dam will guarantee the lack of the deep, still pools of water that sport fish need. A dam is said to be *one way* of ensuring the pools will be there, not the only way: a classic **necessity versus sufficiency** flaw. Answer Choice (B) correctly states this.

(B) Answer Choices (A), (B), (C), and (D) are all different ways of stating **necessity versus sufficiency**, but only Answer Choice (B) concerns the right sufficient thing being mistaken for a necessary one. Answer Choice (E) brings up a flaw not made here, a **causation versus correlation** mistake.

500- to 600-Level Fact-Based Question Practice Set

1. **Facts:** With **Inference** questions, always seek the most definite information in the prompt. Here, there's only one, found in the final sentence: *cement requires large amounts of energy to make*. The correct inference will need to involve this fact.

   (E) Careful with the answer choices. Only Answer Choice (B) directly mentions energy, but it is **too extreme** a claim to infer from what we have. Sentence three tells us that oil is *connected* to the energy requirement, but not that it is the main source of that energy. Answer Choice (A) is **reasonable but unsupported**, since we don't really know what the definition of an ingredient ought or ought not to include. Answer Choice (C) is **directly contradicted** by information about cheap replacements in sentence two. Answer Choice (D) is consistent with the same information about replacements, but we're never given any information about the business practices of cement makers. This leaves only Answer Choice (E), which indirectly connects to the one fact we know. Energy costs are required parts of making cement, so the cost of cement isn't entirely found in the cost of its basic ingredients.

2. **Facts:** We know from sentence one that *Without Jupiter, the chances of life developing on Earth would have been less*. The second sentence explains why in general this would be true: *something that hurts the chances of life developing (the meteor strikes) happens when there are asteroid belts*. And the third sentence ties this explanation to Jupiter: *without something like Jupiter, there'd be nothing stopping the meteor strikes*. By connecting these facts, we can infer Answer Choice (C): Without Jupiter, the chances of life developing in our solar system would be lowered. Don't be frightened by the absurd situation given in Answer Choice (C). It doesn't matter *why* or *how* Jupiter gets destroyed.

(C) Answer Choices (A) and (D) are both **too extreme**, as our information only says the chances of developing life are *lowered* without a gas giant, not lowered to zero. Answer Choice (B) is **one step removed** from the information we have, since we don't know what causes life to continue, only what affects its chances of starting. Answer Choice (E) is both **too extreme** and a case of **mixed details** because the prompt never gives information about multiple asteroid belts.

3. **Dilemma: On the one hand**, *in general, the more sugar in the blood, the more insulin,* **but on the other hand**, *when there is **lots** of sugar in the blood **regularly**, insulin levels are below average.* Answer Choice (C) explains what's different about this **specific case**: lots of sugar eaten regularly wears the insulin release system out.

   (C) Answer Choices (A), (B), and (D) all present us with **real-world distractions**. Answer Choice (A) only **worsens the dilemma**, since it shows the weirdness that happens if our specific case happens consistently. Answer Choices (B) and (D) are both **irrelevant to the dilemma** for the same reason, since we don't know that the source of sugar is relevant to insulin. Answer Choice (E) just further explains how insulin works, without tying this explanation to the relevant distinction, the *level of sugar*.

600- to 700-Level Fact-Based Question Practice Set

1. **Dilemma:** The dilemma here is that two things we might assume are connected seem to be unconnected: (1) timber production went up during the period but (2) labor employed by timber mills went down. Answer Choice (D) presents the **unconsidered factor** that reconciles the two trends: labor-saving technologies were introduced during the period in question.

   (D) Answer Choices (A) and (C) are both **irrelevant to the dilemma** because they concern different time periods than the one we're interested in. Answer Choices (B) and (E) give us extra facts about the time period, but neither would account directly for a difference between production and labor.

2. **Facts:** The *therefore* in front of the blank flags this question as close cousin to the **Inference** question, since the only thing we are allowed to put in that blank is something inferable from the definite information

in the prompt. Here, the correct answer, (A), is inferable by applying the definite piece of formal logic rule right before the semicolon (*no one should be obligated to conform to the moral standards of the public*) to the specific case of *public officials*. As part of "anyone," public officials, too, should not be obligated.

(A) Answer Choice (B) could be inferred if only we knew that the moral philosophers are definitely right (and the speaker doesn't seem to think they are, anyway). Answer Choice (C) confuses **necessity and sufficiency**. Answer Choice (D) seems reasonable (if you agree with the speaker), but it is unsupported here, as we know only what moral philosophers have said before, not what they will always and forever say. And Answer Choice (E), while a laudable sentiment in the real world, is not specifically addressed here.

3. **Facts:** Build out from the most definite piece of information to find the credited inference. Here, that piece comes at the very end: *if the overall cost of applying adjuvants goes up, many farmers will go out of business.* Add to that the second definite fact, found in the middle of the prompt: *there are no substitutes as easy to apply or as economical to use as the most popular adjuvant*, the one that will be banned if the proposals go through. Thus, if the ban goes through, one of the costs of pesticide use—the adjuvants—will go up. Answer Choice (E) says this directly while adding the helpful loophole closer caveat that this will only be true so long as these farmers don't find some other way to reduce their costs.

(E) Answer Choices (A) and (D) both forget the loophole that Answer Choice (E) covers. Answer Choice (B) forgets a different loophole— that it might be possible to reduce birth defects some other way than banning this one adjuvant. Answer Choice (C) confuses **necessity and sufficiency**—the ban will be sufficient to drive farmers out of business, but it's not the only possible way their businesses might fail.

700- to 800-Level Fact-Based Question Practice Set

1. **Facts:** The first two sentences of this prompt consist of two Formal Logic statements that can be connected: morally wrong → violates autonomy → should be avoided and punished the same. The prompt also tells us that murder is morally wrong. Each of the answer choices provide an if, but the only if that will "trigger" the chain of logic will be "If <something> is morally wrong." Answer Choice (D) begins just this

way and correctly concludes that if lying and murder are both morally wrong, then they should be punished equally.

(D) Answer Choice (A) is out because the prompt provides no rules to judge whether something is *noble* or not, and the same is true for Answer Choice (E) because there are no rules about what is morally *correct*. Answer Choice (B) concludes that something is *twice as obvious*, but all the information in the prompt is about things being *equally wrong*. Answer Choice (C) would be right if we knew that accidentally causing a person's death were morally wrong, but neither the answer nor the prompt contain this information.

2. **Facts:** Beneath this question lies one of the GMAT's favorite facts, the difference between **percentages and numbers**. According to the prompt, the trade federation's members split revenues proportional to the size of their populations. Originally, the sizes were Tragda > Baflazam > Llassu. After the census, Tragda lost revenue, which means that, as a percentage, its population was no longer as large as it had been. We're also told that Llassu's population grew *less* than Tragda's, meaning that the reason for Tragda's decrease can't be Llassu's population increase. Therefore, it must be Baflazam's increase that reduced Tragda's share. And if Baflazam grew more than Tragda, it must also have grown more than Llassu. Thus, Answer Choice (C) is inferable, the order of population *growth* (not absolute population number) must be Baflazam, Tragda, Llassu.

(C) Answer Choice (A) concerns total population, not rate of population growth. Answer Choices (B) and (D) get the nations out of order, and Answer Choice (E) pulls a **but for one word** trick by changing the list to *least to most* instead of *most to least*.

3. **Facts:** This is such a depressing topic! It is also another version of the old **percent versus number** problem. This time, the dilemma is that from 1990–2000 (1) the absolute number of people with HIV has gone down, even as the overall population has gone up, but (2) the percentage of people who say they personally knew someone who is *suffering* from HIV has gone way up. How can fewer people be suffering, yet more people say they *knew* someone suffering? The obvious answer is that the cases of suffering have been better publicized—but this doesn't show up as an answer choice. Instead, Answer Choice (C) explains how the number

of sufferers could go down while the number of *known sufferers* could go up: if lots of known sufferers are now dead, they are not *currently suffering.*

(C) Answer Choice (A) is **one step removed** from the dilemma because it is not limited to the right timeframe. Answer Choice (B) is meant to seem like the obvious answer, but note that it is about *celebrities*, not necessarily people that Americans *personally know*. Answer Choice (D) **worsens the dilemma**, because it should increase the number of people suffering from *diagnosed* cases. Answer Choice (E) likewise **worsens the dilemma** because increased treatment should be slowing down the death rate, causing there to be more, rather than fewer, diagnosed sufferers for Americans to learn about.

Sentence Correction | 15

According to the GMAC, Sentence Correction questions are meant to test three general areas of English language proficiency: "correct expression, effective expression, and proper diction."

Much of the time, the quickest path to the credited answer will lie in selecting the answer choice that matches the GMAT house style or that "sounds like the GMAT"—which is rarely the same as the choice that "sounds right" in your head. Indeed, the GMAT loves throwing weird but grammatically correct things into the correct answer choice precisely because the weirdness will "sound wrong" and send the unwary test taker on a wild goose chase for a better answer choice that simply does not exist.

GMAT GRAMMAR 101

This chapter will go more smoothly if we take a few pages first to refresh your memory of the most basic grammatical terms. We promise that no unnecessarily complicated jargon lies ahead, only the bare bones necessary for us all to be on the same page as you learn the best ways to dominate GMAT Sentence Correction questions.

The Parts of Speech

Words can be classified many different ways; when you classify a word according to its **function** in communication, you assign it to one of the categories together called the **parts of speech**. For the GMAT, it is necessary to be able to recognize only a few: **nouns**, **verbs**, **pronouns**, **prepositions**, **adjectives**, **adverbs**, and **conjunctions**.

Nouns

As you probably heard back in first grade, a noun is "the name of a person, place, or thing." *Dog, cat, mom, Albuquerque, sandwich, kettle, CD, elevator, Abraham Lincoln*—all are nouns.

So, too, ideas such as *love, marriage, correctness, number, sluggishness, justice,* and *symmetry*.

Verbs

Verbs are a bit trickier than nouns. We usually define them as either "an action" or "a state of being." Actions include *walk, run, sing, sit, bark,* and *love.* States of being are instead things like *is, was, will, does, shall, could, might.*

The most common way a verb changes is in relation to what is called its **tense**, forms that allow us to keep track of the different times an action occurs. The simple tenses include **present**, **past**, **and future**: *I walk today, I walked yesterday, I will walk tomorrow,* and so on. But tenses can get complicated quickly. Special ones exist for actions that are ongoing (the continuous: *I am walking now*), that occurred in the past but continue into the present (the present perfect: *I have walked for some time*), that occurred frequently in the past (the past habitual: *I used to walk*), and even that occurred in the past but that we worry might be doubted (the emphatic: *I did walk*).

Pronouns

While not as complicated as verbs, nouns do have one special added consideration: **pronouns**. A pronoun is a word that is allowed to "stand in for" or "replace" another noun. The noun that's being swapped for the pronoun also has a special name that we should add to our vocabulary for convenience's sake. We call these referenced nouns the **antecedents** of the pronoun.

Notice that pronouns change their form depending on the sort of noun they're replacing: people get pronouns like *he* and *us, objects use it* and *its; singular nouns get his* and *it, plural their* and *those,* and so on. That's because in order to be clear about a pronoun's antecedent we give the pronoun characteristics to match it.

Take comfort in knowing that on the GMAT pronouns are directly tested in just two ways: (1) whether a pronoun agrees with its antecedent and (2) whether its antecedent is clear enough or left ambiguous.

Prepositions

Prepositions come in many different varieties, depending on the way that they describe the noun or verb they've been attached to:

Time and duration: *at, on, in, during, until, after*

Movement: *to, toward, through, across, over, into, onto, after*

Agency: *by, with*

Manner or instrument: *with, by*

Location: *above, below, in*

Adjective

Some words can describe another word directly, without needing a word like a preposition to help them. These **modifiers** come in two different varieties, classified by the things that they are able to modify. The easiest and most limited of the two are called **adjectives**, words that can directly describe nouns. In the sample sentence, *noisy* was an adjective. *Small, weird, tight, gigantic, outstanding*, and *squeaky* are all adjectives.

Adverbs

Adverbs are much more flexible than adjectives. While adjectives can only be used to describe nouns and pronouns, adverbs can be used to modify verbs, adjectives, and even other adverbs. For example:

The dogs bark **loudly**.
(*loudly* describes the verb *bark)*

The dogs have a **very** loud bark.
(*very* describes the adjective *loud)*

The dogs bark **very** loudly.
(*very* describes the adverb *loudly)*

Conjunctions

Conjunctions are the grammatical "glue" that allows us to move beyond words to the larger combinations called **phrases**, **clauses**, and **sentences**. Depending on the type of words being connected and on the type of connection made, we can further classify them.

Cats **and** dogs hate baths.
(*And* coordinates the two subjects in the sentence.)

Both cats **and** dogs make good pets.
(*Both … and* are used to correlate cats and dogs.)

Although dogs hate baths, they are easier to bathe than cats.
(*Although* subordinates the first clause to the second.)

Subjects and Predicates

As it turns out, you can't just use any old noun or verb you'd like when making a sentence. *Dogs to bark* is nonsense because *to bark*, the infinitive form of the verb, can't anchor a sentence. The noun also has to be of the type that can describe an action doer when linked to an action-describing verb. Grammarians helpfully gave these "sentence type of nouns" and "verb type of nouns" names: **subject** and **predicate**. We'll borrow them for our GMAT Grammar vocabulary list.

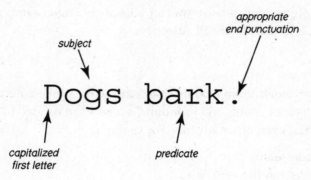

Phrases

A **sentence** is a special type of arrangement of nouns and verbs, one we often say "expresses a complete thought." A **phrase** is just an arrangement of words that makes sense; completeness is optional. In addition to all the sentences we've used thus far, all these count as **phrases**, too:

> the noisy dogs
> the long and winding road
> without so much as a word
> eating all the porridge before it got cold

Noun and Verb Phrases

The most important thing about phrases is that any part of a sentence that can be occupied by a word can be occupied instead by a multiword phrase with that word as its head.

So far, we only know two parts of a sentence, **subject** and **predicate**. Swap out our single words for phrases and you can build a more respectable looking sentence like *The noisy dogs are always barking*. Subjects can thus be nouns *or* noun phrases; predicates can be verbs *or* verb phrases.

Phrases are the secret to how the test maker can build a question around the simple concept while pretending that something more complicated is happening.

The test maker expands *dogs*, the subject, into the longer **noun phrase** *the violent, noisome, obnoxious dogs*. The verb is similarly expanded from *barks* to *barks constantly*. Yet no matter how much is piled onto the dogs or their barking, the core of the sentence remains the same: a subject and a predicate. Everything else is just some form of **modifier** or **modification**.

Modifying Phrases

English has many different types of modifiers, but the GMAT is most interested in testing your ability to handle modifying phrases, phrases that—like our noun and verb phrases—are built on a single head word and used in the sentence in some way to further describe or characterize the subject and predicate. We've already discussed one type of modifying phrase, the **prepositional phrase**:

prepositional phrases

> **after** the fox
> **in** the woods

Just like nouns, verbs, and prepositions, adjectives and adverbs can be used as a phrase's head word to create adjective phrases and adverb phrases.

adverb phrases

> much more **efficiently**

adjective phrases

> **desperate** with fear
> **previous** even more brutal

Such phrases can be used in a sentence any way that the head adjective or adverb could when alone.

Thus, it would be equally grammatically correct to say:

> The dogs bark until their ***desperate*** prey has been run to exhaustion ***efficiently***.

and

> The dogs bark until their prey, ***desperate with fear***, has been run to exhaustion ***much more efficiently***.

You may have noticed that in the second sentence the adjective phrase is set off from the thing it modifies by commas, whereas the adjective in the first is attached directly to and in front of the noun.

If the sentence were instead

The dogs bark until desperate with fear their prey has been ....

it would be hard to tell whether the dogs are barking until *the dogs* are desperate with fear or whether they chase their prey until *their prey* is desperate with fear. In this revised sentence, *desperate with fear* is stranded between the dogs and their prey, rendering the thing that the modifier is meant to modify unclear.

Since "the thing the modifier is meant to modify" is a bit long, we can use that term from our discussion of prepositional phrases, **antecedent**, to indicate it.

Direct and Indirect Objects

Just as prepositions have a bit that follows them, which we say "receives" the effect the preposition provides, a sentence's predicate can have a bit that "receives" the action described by the predicate's verb. The **direct object** gets acted upon, usually in a way that completes that idea of the verb's action. Some verbs almost require objects in order to make sense. We don't often say *the dog bit* without adding what or who was bitten, or *I saw* without saying what was seen. The thing bitten or seen would be the verb's **direct object**.

Other verbs can get by perfectly well without direct objects but can take them if need be. *We danced* and *the police left* could stay as they are, or we could add that *we danced **a waltz*** and *the police left **the building***. Either works.

The **indirect objects** are rarer creatures and require that there already be a direct object in the sentence before they can appear at all. The **indirect object** is typically the recipient not of the verb but of the direct object. Usually a preposition is involved.

Clauses

Phrases that have subjects and verbs are called **clauses**. As we already know, to be a complete sentence, a sentence must have both a **subject** and a **predicate**. Taken together, we call this **subject-predicate** pair an **independent clause**. It can "stand on its own" or "express a complete thought."

> The dog is very tall.
> They built the boat quickly.

Some clauses can't stand on their own; they aren't in and of themselves complete sentences. We call such clauses **dependent clauses**. What makes a clause dependent? Primarily, a clause is "demoted" to dependent status through the use of a **subordinating conjunction** (such as *unless*, *after*, *where*, *when*, *since*, *though*, *as*, and *if*). Thus, these clauses do not count as sentences on their own:

> before they built the boat
> because the dog is very tall
> unless you do as I say

For a dependent clause to become a sentence, it has to be attached to an independent clause with a conjunction and a comma. Without the independent clause, the dependent all by its lonesome gets labeled a **sentence fragment**.

THE FOUR-STEP METHOD FOR SENTENCE CORRECTION QUESTIONS

Step 1: Read the Original Sentence

The task is the same in every Sentence Correction question. Eliminate answer choices that contain obvious grammatical errors until you are left with one. Start by reading the sentence looking for an error. There's usually more than one error in a question, so if you spot multiple errors, just focus on the one that you know the most about. That's the error you're going to carry forward into the next step.

If nothing sticks out, that's fine, too. Answer Choice (A) is there for cases when the sentence is fine as originally written. But at this point, you shouldn't just select (A) and move to the next question. There are undoubtedly some errors that don't seem obviously wrong on the first pass. In order to make sure there aren't any lurking in this potentially correct question, you'll still want to eliminate down to (A).

Here's the sentence as originally written:

> As a vocalist and, just as importantly, as a
> songwriter, <u>Dolly Parton is one of the most
> successful cross-over artists of all time who
> inspired many of the singer-songwriters who
> today routinely top</u> the country and rock and
> roll charts simultaneously.

Step 2: Scan the Answers

In Sentence Correction questions, the most important information to process is found in those **Decision Points**, the places where the answer choices clump together in groups of two and three that all share the same feature. These are the possible errors we must vet in order to find the credited answer choice. So Step 2 of the Sentence Correction method is to pick one **Decision Point** and compare your options.

We've already directed your attention to one possible **Decision Point**. There's a long descriptive phrase, *who inspired many of the singer-songwriters who today …*, that's clearly meant to describe Dolly Parton, the subject of the sentence. Three answer choices keep Dolly on the other side of the long **Distractor** *is one of the most successful …*, and two of them move her. Pause to consider whether there is a grammatical reason to favor one way over the other.

Step 3: Eliminate

As it turns out, there's not really a grammatical reason why Dolly needs to be at the front of the sentence. Answer Choices (D) and (E) probably feel clunkier than the others, but grammatically speaking, they're in the clear on this issue. The first **Decision Point** was a dud, but that's not a problem. Not every difference between the answer choices is something you need to settle. We just move on to the next step.

Step 4: Repeat

When you've done all you can with one **Decision Point**, go back up to Step 2 and scan for another one.

THE BIG 6: ERRORS MOST COMMONLY TESTED

As we mentioned back in the *Verbal Introduction,* the number of errors that have shown up on the GMAT is actually quite small—approximately 30 in the many decades during which the test has included some sort of grammar question. And of those 30 or so errors, only about a dozen appear with any regularity, so that the lion's share of Sentence Correction questions involve one or more of a group of just six errors. Ninety-five percent involve one of the six; about 60 percent test two or more. They are:

SUBJECT/PREDICATE AGREEMENT—The subject of the sentence (a noun) must match the predicate (the verb); singular subjects get singular predicates, and plural subjects get plural predicates.

PRONOUN REFERENCE—Pronouns must refer unambiguously to a single noun, and they must also match the noun they replace in number, gender, and case.

PARALLELISM—Parts of a sentence that play the same role must be put into matching forms. This includes words in lists, in comparisons, and in other multipart constructions.

CLAUSES AND CONNECTORS—Clauses can be either independent or dependent. Linking them incorrectly can result in a run-on sentence or a sentence fragment.

MODIFICATION—Modifying elements, such as adjectives, adverbs, and prepositional phrases, must be placed so that it's clear what they're supposed to modify and so that the modification makes logical sense.

IDIOMATIC CONSTRUCTION—Certain words are paired with other words in English not because of any logical rule, but because that's just the way they're expected to be. Usually, this involves preposition choice (i.e., you sleep *in* a bed, not *at* a bed).

Agreement Errors

The first three of The Big 6 errors—verbs, pronouns, and parallelism—all involve selecting the right *form* for a word so that it matches up with some other word.

Big Error #1: Subject/Predicate Agreement

The **subject** of the sentence (a noun) must **match** its **predicate** (the verb); singular subjects get singular predicates, and plural subjects get plural predicates.

> Teacher: Would you kindly give me a sentence starting with the word "I"?
>
> Student: I is...
>
> Teacher: No, no! Always say, "I am."
>
> Student: All right ... I am the ninth letter of the alphabet.

Subject-Predicate Variation #1: The Separated Subject-Predicate Pair

It is easy to disguise the subject of the sentence by either burying it under modifiers or separating it from its predicate with the same.

distractor   **subject**   distractor   **predicate**
The oldest fossil **organisms** presently known **has been dated** [...]

subject   distractor
[...] **incumbent politicians,** including such once popular politicians
as Charlie Crist, Florida's two-term governor, **has elected** [...]
                                        predicate

In the first sentence, the plural *organisms* requires the plural form *have been dated*, but if you mistook the first distractor, *fossil*, for the subject, you would have gone with the singular *has been dated*.

In the second sentence, the subject *incumbent politicians*, again plural, is separated from its predicate by 12 words and two lines! Notice how the nouns closest to the predicate—*Charlie Crist, Florida, governor*—are all singular? The predicate *has elected* agrees with these singular distractors; *have elected* agrees with the plural *incumbent politicians*.

Subject-Predicate Variation #2: The "Placeholder" or "Dummy" Subject

The phrases *there are, there is,* and *it is* can be used to delay the subject in a sentence. Even though the word *there* or *it* starts the sentence, the sentence's real subject follows the predicate verb. Suppose the test maker hit you with

There are, without a doubt, a wealth of good reasons to
invest early in one's own retirement.

you'd look after the verb (and after another distractor) to find the real subject of the sentence, the singular *a wealth*—and not the plural *reasons*. *Are* must change to *is*.

There is, without a doubt, a wealth of good reasons
to invest

In a sense, *there* and *it* are just "dummy" subjects that are holding the spot for the subject of the sentence that will be introduced later.

Exception 1: A small number of indefinite pronouns are singular or plural depending on whether the noun they're replacing is countable or not. These include *all* and *some*. (More on this under *Error #6: Idioms*.)

Some of the hovercrafts **are** full of eels. (You can count
hovercrafts, so they are plural.)
All of the milk **was drunk** yesterday. (You can't count milk,
so it is singular.)

Exception 2: A small number of indefinite pronouns are always plural. They're easy to remember, since they all clearly describe multiple things: *both, few, others,* and *several.*

Exception 3: The word *none* switches between singular and plural depending on whether the *none* is being used by the writer to mean *not any* or *not one.* Since you can't read the test maker's mind, it doesn't really matter which one you use; either is correct. Hooray!

She looked in the cupboard for lights, but there
were none. (How many lights? *Not any.*)
He looked in the cupboard for a flashlight, but there
was none. (How many flashlights? *Not one.*)

Subject-Predicate Variation #3: Compound Subjects

The word *and* has a special quirk in English. When you link two subject nouns with the word *and*, you create what is known as a "compound subject," and **compound subjects are always treated as plural**, no matter whether the individual items linked by the *and* are plural or singular.

few landmarks and little available water exists

Subject-predicate pairs that appear in dependent clauses must agree, just as the pairs that appear in independent clauses, so here the *and* in this dependent clause means that the plural verb *exist* is needed instead of the singular *exists*— even though the singular word *water* is closer to the verb.

You can also expect the compound subject rule to be tested in the negative, too. That is, only the word *and* can create a compound subject. The word *or* does not. When *or* is used to link two subjects, the predicate agrees with whichever subject is **closest**, so it is usually the second item in an *either... or* or *neither... nor* list. This issue was also tested in Question 9, where Answer Choice (D) read

little available water or landmarks exists

Big Error #2: Pronoun Reference

> Teacher: Beavis, name two pronouns!
> Beavis: Uh … who, me?

Pronouns must (1) refer unambiguously to a single noun, and they must also (2) **match the noun they replace** (or refer to) in number, person, gender, and case.

Pronouns are words that stand in for nouns. We call the word that the pronoun stands in for its **antecedent**. Pronouns must agree with their antecedents, just as subjects must agree with predicates.

As far as agreement is concerned, subjects and predicates get off easy. They merely have to agree in number (singular versus plural), but there is a whole host of ways that pronouns and antecedents must agree.

Pronoun Variation #1: Basic Pronoun Agreement

Agreement by Number

Simply put, singular pronouns must replace singular nouns, plural pronouns plural nouns, regardless of what type of pronoun is involved.

> Anyone who uses this miter saw must put it back where they got it from.

Anyone is singular, but *they* is plural. Thus, the credited answer to the question above might be:

> (B) All who use this miter saw must put it back where they got it from.

Agreement by Person and Gender

In grammar, "person" refers to the relationship between a subject and its verb. First-person (*I, me, we*) is used for those talking or speaking about themselves; second, for direct address (*you*); third, for speaking about an absent party (*him, her, he, they, it*).

Agreement by person is rare but does occasionally get tested, usually as a misplaced *you*. If we found both gender and person in a question, it might look like this:

INCORRECT 2nd person **you**	As Dorothy Parker observed, if a woman wants to succeed in this world, you have to play the game better than a man.
CORRECT 3rd person feminine **she**	she has to play the game better than a man

Agreement by Case

Of all the pronoun agreement error flavors, agreement by case is the one most likely to worry test takers, even though it appears much less frequently than agreement by number—probably because nobody quite remembers what "case" means anymore. Let us curse you with this rare knowledge:

> **Case:** The grammatical role that a noun or pronoun plays in a sentence.

Nouns in English look the same in most cases.

If *Rusty* is the subject of the sentence, you use the **subjective case** *Rusty*.

> *Rusty* is the subject of this sentence.

If *the flag* is the object of a sentence's predicate verb, you use the **objective case** *the flag*.

> We raised *the flag* to half-mast.

Only in the **plural** and the **possessive** do we change the form of a noun, and most of the time all we do then is add an *-s*, an *-es*, or a *-'s* (*apostrophe + s*).

> The *record player's* needle is broken, and who stocks *needles* for *record players* anymore?

Pronouns retain a few more case distinctions. **She** *went to the store,* but *Yoshiko went with* **her.**

The GMAT expects you to be familiar with these distinctions, but only passingly so:

If the subject of the sentence is replaced by a pronoun, you use the *subjective case.*

> *Rusty* is the subject of this sentence, and what the predicate says *he* does.

If the object of the sentence is replaced by a pronoun, you use the *objective case.*

> Throw the ball to *Regina*? Of course I'm going to throw it to *her*!

If a noun that's possessive is replaced by a pronoun, you use the *possessive case.*

> Which of the record players is *Xian's*? That one over there is *her* record player.

If both the owner and the owned noun are replaced by a pronoun, you use the *absolute possessive case*.

> Which of these is *Xian's record player*? That one over there is *hers*.

Pronoun Variation #2: Lots and Lots of Pronouns

This variation is less a grammar rule and more a matter of bookkeeping. The GMAT often gives test takers a question with a long underlined section that contains multiple pronouns, several of which agree correctly, save one that the test makers hope is overlooked.

If a GMAT question contained this sentence:

> Every **one** of the great chef's recipes were catalogued and filed according to **their** country of origin, **its** required ingredients, and **their** reception by the critics.

the correct and credited answer would be

> Every **one** of the great chef's recipes was catalogued and filed according to **its** country of origin, **its** required ingredients, and **its** reception by the critics.

because the antecedent *one* is singular, demanding a possessive singular *its* for each of the three items in the list that follows.

The more places to hide a pronoun, the more vigilant we must be.

Pronoun Variation #3: Ambiguous Pronoun Reference

Just as the test makers like to quiz you on pronoun agreement, they also like to give you sentences in which there are too many possible antecedents for the pronoun. In these cases, the trick is to replace the pronoun with a more specific word or phrase.

Faced with

> The government launched an attack on the rogue nation after **it** violated UN airspace.

we would select

> after **that nation** violated UN airspace.

You'll even see the ambiguous pronoun slipped into a single answer choice in a question that doesn't otherwise concern pronouns, most often when the answer choices are long and involve a lot of reorganizing of clauses and phrases. If you're having trouble finding a grammatical reason to choose between two answer choices, do a quick scan for a stray *they* or *it*.

Big Error #3: Parallelism

There are two main relationships that elements in a sentence may have to each other. Take our simple sentence we used back in "GMAT Grammar 101" again: *Dogs bark*.

Suppose we wanted to add a second barker to the sentence, to have two subjects but only one predicate. Easy: *Dogs **and** seals bark*.

When two elements both play the same role in a sentence, we say that they are **coordinated**. Any part of a sentence can be expanded by coordinating two words or phrases.

Coordinated Subjects

> **The dogs and the three seals** barked at the waves.

Coordinated Predicates

> The dogs **barked and growled** at the mailman.

Coordinated Objects

> The dogs barked **at the mailman and his partner**.

> The dogs bit the **one mailman but not the other one**.

Parallelism Variation #1: Basic Lists and Other Compound Sentence Parts

Parallelism is most easily demonstrated with a simple sentence that would never appear on the GMAT:

> I like to hop, skip, and jump.

Here we have a simple list of things that *I like to (do)*. Each of the elements—in this case, the actions *hop*, *skip*, and *jump*—is a verb in the **infinitive** form, and they all share the same relationship to that little accompanying word *to*.

When a sentence is properly parallel, you could separate it into multiple sentences with the same form that all make sense:

I like to hop, skip, and jump → I like to hop. I like to skip. I like to jump.

We're not allowed to mix and match our parts of speech in a coordinated list. So this sentence isn't parallel:

I like to hop, skipping, and to jump.

Infinitive, noun, infinitive isn't allowed.

We are, however, allowed to change the part of speech of members of a list, so long as we change each element. So it would still be correct for a sentence to say

I like hopping, skipping, and jumping.

Now the list is composed of three different nouns that *I like*: (1) *hopping*, (2) *skipping*, and (3) *jumping*.

And even if we were to return to our infinitive verb list, we could still change the list a different way and be in the clear—the *to* can be attached to each infinitive if we so desire. Thus:

I like to hop, to skip, and to jump.

Parallelism Variation #2: Multipart Constructions

All of the coordinating conjunctions (FANBOYS) require parallelism between the things they coordinate:

Apples *and* **peaches** will sell well.
[noun] *and* [noun]

The treasure was hidden **under Henderson's mattress** *or* **beneath the big X.**
[prepositional phrase] *or* [prepositional phrase]

What he promised *and* **what he delivered** were markedly different.
[dependent clause] *and* [dependent clause]

Tomas ate all the Ramen, *so* **Harry kicked him out of the apartmen**t.
[independent clause], *so* [independent clause]

Parallelism Variation #3: Comparisons

Comparisons are a special type of multipart construction that requires parallelism on two different levels. The first level you're already familiar with: compared items must be expressed as the same part of speech. Thus, regardless of what you may have heard elsewhere, it's perfectly acceptable (on the GMAT and in real life) to compare apples and oranges. Just make sure that you phrase both parts of the comparison as the same part of speech.

> Apples are denser than oranges and are more fun to throw.
>
> Oranges grow better in the winter than apples do.
>
> I like oranges just as much as apples.

But on top of being grammatically parallel, items in comparisons must also be **logically parallel**.

Because apples and oranges are both fruits, they pass the logical parallelism requirement easily. Trouble arises when you do something like this, instead:

> I like **apples** more than I like **the taste of oranges**.
>
> **Apples' skin** is thinner than **an orange**.
>
> The farmer grew more apples than in the nearby farmer's fields.

In the first sentence, a kind of fruit (apples) is compared with a particular quality (taste) that another fruit has. In the second, part of a fruit (the skin of an apple) is compared with the whole of different fruit. In the last sentence, many things might be the subject of the comparison, it's so completely muddled.

Parallelism Variation #4: I'm Sorry, You're Not on the List

Sometimes, the test maker will try to trip you up by putting something in a parallel list that actually doesn't make sense there:

> In order to improve his golf game, Mr. Morton <u>began a regimen of stretching exercises, added weight training to his daily workout, and seeing a consequent</u> substantial change within weeks.

There are three actions in this sentence, which might suggest that you need to create a parallel three-item list:

X	began a regimen […]	→	began a regimen […]
Y	added weight training […]	→	added weight training […]
Z	**seeing** a substantial change	→	**saw** a substantial change.

Now look back at that modifying phrase in the first nonunderlined section, *in order to improve his golf game.* Would it make sense to say "In order to improve his golf game, Mr. Morton saw a substantial change within weeks?" Of course not. The change Mr. Morton saw is not part of the plan to improve but rather the improvement that followed the plan. Instead, the credited answer contains a two-item list and makes it clear that the last part of the sentence is a separate thought.

> began a regimen of stretching exercises and added
> weight training to his daily workout, and consequently
> he saw a

SENTENCE ORGANIZATION ERRORS

While *agreement errors* involved the forms of individual **words**, *sentence organization* errors are built on **phrases** and **clauses**.

The larger the portion of the sentence that's underlined, the more likely it is that large chunks of the sentence (its phrases and clauses) will get moved around and reorganized in the answer choices. If the entire sentence is underlined, it's pretty much a foregone conclusion: at least one of the next two of our Big 6 will be the key to the credited answer.

Big Error #4: Modification

Everything that isn't the subject or predicate of a sentence is, in some way, a **modifier**: it adds descriptive information to either the subject or the predicate (or to some *other* modifier). Consider the corrected version of the following sentence.

> The oldest fossil organisms presently known have
> been dated at 3.4 billion years old and thus are taken
> as evidence that life evolved soon after a planetary
> bombardment 3.8 billion years ago that would have
> sterilized Earth of any incipient life.

When you **drilled down** to the core of the sentence, you realized that it had a simple subject (*organisms*) and a compound predicate (*have been dated* and *are taken*).

Organisms have been dated and are taken. The remaining 34 words all provide some sort of description of what kind of *organisms* we are talking about (the subject):

> **The oldest fossil** organisms
> organisms **presently known**

or of how they *have been dated* and what they *have been taken* to be (the compound predicate):

> have been dated **at 3.4 billion years old**
> are taken **as evidence**

or of one of the previous modifiers:

> evidence **that life evolved**
> evolved **soon after a planetary bombardment**
> evolved **3.8 billion years ago**
> bombardment **that would have sterilized Earth**
> sterilized **of any incipient life**

There are so many modifiers! And so many varieties! Adjectives, adverbs, participial phrases, verbal adjuncts, direct objects, etc.

However many modifiers appear in a GMAT sentence and whatever kind of modifier you're dealing with, the key is to make sure that the modifying element clearly and unambiguously modifies only one possible thing in the sentence (AKA **the modifier's antecedent**) and to make sure that the modifying element modifies (AKA **whatever it modifies**) in a logical way.

In other words, when organizing the sentence, make sure that the modifiers all make sense in their new contexts.

Incorrect:	Dangled over the precipice, the climber's hands nearly slipped.
	*It's **not clear** who's dangling over the precipice and **illogical** to think it's the climber's hands.*
Correct:	While the climber dangled over the precipice, his hands nearly slipped.
	Ah, it was clearly the climber dangling and not his hands.

Big Error #5: Clauses and Connectors

> Q: What does a grammar teacher call Santa's helpers?
> A: Subordinate Clauses.

Errors of parallelism crops up whenever two parts of a sentence are **coordinated**, that is, whenever two parts of a sentence play the same role. **Clause and connector** errors, instead involve cases where one part of the sentence is attached to or made dependent on another—not coordinated, but **subordinated**.

There are three levels of organization within a sentence:

Sentences are made of clauses. Clauses are made of phrases. And phrases are made of words.

Think of these levels as a hierarchy. Subordinate one word to another word and you get a phrase. In "GMAT Grammar 101," we called the main word in a phrase its "head word." Phrases can be "stacked" so that one phrase is itself subordinate to another head word.

head word + other words = phrase

Ex: the + Secretary	of + the Interior
noun phrase	**prepositional phrase**

phrase + phrase = bigger phrase
Ex: the Secretary of the Interior
noun phrase

Big Error #6: Idioms

> The bit about applying the glaze to the shapely jug—
> that's where I tend to stumble.
>
> In English, it's easy enough—"I put this on that"—but
> in French, such things have a way of [coming back to
> bite you]. I might have to say, "Do you like the glaze
> the shapely jug accepted from me?" or "Do you like the
> shapely jug in the glaze of which I earlier applied?"
>
> —David Sedaris, *When You Are Engulfed in Flames*

id·i·om ('i-dē-əm) n. 1. An ordering of words that relies on custom rather than grammar or logic for its meaning and correctness.
2. A colloquial expression in a language that cannot be understood from the individual meanings of its elements, as in *keep tabs on* or *raining cats and dogs*.

The final member of The Big 6 is in a class all by itself: errors of **idiomatic construction**.

As anyone trying to learn a new language for the first time quickly discovers, languages are *weird*. English is no exception.

You sleep *in* a bed, not *at* a bed, but why exactly is that? Things happen *at* a party, not *in* a party, but why is it that you're *in* the Army, not *at* the Army? You *get up* from your bed in the morning, but you don't *get down* when you fall asleep. We call these and other expected word combinations **idiomatic constructions** or simply **idioms**.

Logic goes out the window with idioms. There's no reason for most other than "because that's how we say it." This can be particularly galling for GMAT test takers whose first language is something other than English. But even for those who've spoken English all their lives, it can seem like there's always going to be one more idiom you've never heard of in the next Sentence Correction question that pops up on the CAT screen.

Some students react to this worry by trying to cram as many idioms into their brains as possible, which does sometimes work, but is also a lot of effort for very little reward. You've probably seen lists of 100, 200, even 1000 "Essential" GMAT Idioms floating around on the Internet. If you haven't, don't bother tracking them down, and if you have, know that there are many better ways to spend your Sentence Correction prep time.

The most important thing about idioms is that the test maker rarely makes a question whose credited answer turns *solely* on a correct idiom. Most often, incorrect idioms appear in answer choices that are wrong for some other reason, too.

Think of idioms as shortcuts. Don't make your first cut on an idiomatic issue, but when you spot something you think doesn't work idiomatically, use that feeling as a cue to look for an error elsewhere in the sentence.

SENTENCE CORRECTION PRACTICE SETS

500- to 600-Level Sentence Correction Practice Set

1. Tokyo, though visited by many millions of tourists each year, remains inwardly focused, largely because of having such strict expectations of its residents' public behavior.

   (A) because of having
   (B) because it has
   (C) because they have
   (D) on account of having
   (E) on account of their having

2. When attacked, slugs contract their bodies, making themselves harder and more compact.

   (A) themselves harder and more compact
   (B) themselves hard and the more compact
   (C) their selves harder and more compact
   (D) itself harder and more compact
   (E) it become harder and the more compact

3. Without the adequate amounts of supervision, children in daycare facilities can come to resemble nineteenth-century mad houses.

   (A) Without the adequate amounts of supervision, children in
   (B) Without an adequate amount of supervision, children's
   (C) If children do not get adequate amounts of supervision they need, children's
   (D) If children do not get the adequate amount of supervision, they have
   (E) If they do not have an adequate amount of supervision, children at

4. Except for being adamantly against Chicago, not one of our mutual friends have an opinion on whether I ought to move to a big city or a small one.

   (A) have an opinion on whether I ought to
   (B) have opinions on whether I should
   (C) have no opinions about if I ought to
   (D) has an opinion on if I should be
   (E) has an opinion on whether I ought to

5. Never before the advent of the firearm has a single person had the power to do such substantial harm.

   (A) Never before the advent of the firearm has a single person had
   (B) The advent of the firearm has never before had a single person
   (C) Before the advent of the firearm a single person has not had ever
   (D) Before the advent of the firearm, never did a single person have had
   (E) Never before has one person had since the advent of the firearm

Answers and Explanations for these questions can be found at the end of the chapter.

600- to 700-Level Sentence Correction Practice Set

1. On average 15 Americans die each year due to violence related to terrorism—less by far than are killed by falling television sets in their own homes.

   (A) terrorism—less by far than are
   (B) terrorism—fewer by far than are
   (C) terrorism, which is by far less than those
   (D) terrorism, a number lower by far than the people
   (E) terrorism, by far fewer than the ones

2. In spite of centuries of critical inattention, Aphra Behn's long-form prose *Oroonoko* had been recently come to being regarded as an important precursor to the novel for many, a milestone of early feminist literature.

   (A) had been recently come to being regarded as an important precursor to the novel
   (B) had recently come to be regarded as an important precursor to the novel that
   (C) has recently come to be regarded as an important precursor to the novel, and
   (D) has been recently regarded as coming as an important precursor to the novel
   (E) has recently come to be regarded an important precursor to the novel, and,

3. A much anticipated addition to the "extreme" candy scene is the world's largest gummy worm that is 128 times more massive than its smaller brethren, measuring 36 inches long and weighing in at approximately 3 pounds.

    (A) A much anticipated addition to the "extreme" candy scene is the world's largest gummy worm that is

    (B) As much-anticipated addition to the "extreme" candy scene, the world's largest gummy worm that is

    (C) A much-anticipated addition to the "extreme" candy scene, the world's largest gummy worm is

    (D) As much anticipated as an addition to the "extreme" candy scene, the world's largest gummy worm is

    (E) Much-anticipated as an addition to the scene of "extreme" candy, is the world's largest gummy worm

4. Big product launches and their coincident costs are one thread at this year's industrial fastener convention, however supply chain considerations and materials sourcing still occupy its core.

    (A) however supply chain considerations and

    (B) however, supply chain considerations along with

    (C) as supply chain considerations and their

    (D) but as supply chain considerations or

    (E) but supply chain considerations and

5. The artist secretly recorded passengers in his taxi and created an audio collage that he played looped over loudspeakers at the museum installation.

    (A) secretly recorded passengers in his taxi and created

    (B) having secretly recorded passengers in his taxi and created

    (C) secretly recording passengers in his taxi, creating

    (D) and his secret recordings of his taxi's passengers created

    (E) with his secret recording passengers in his taxi created

Answers and Explanations for these questions can be found at the end of the chapter.

700- to 800-Level Sentence Correction Practice Set

1. Much of the recent musical's regard among critics <u>are due to its topical subject matter—a feature typical of musicals of the 2000s and that</u> will hinder subsequent revival.

   (A) are due to its topical subject matter—a feature typical of musicals of the 2000s and that
   (B) are due to its topical subject matter—a feature that is typical of musicals of the 2000s and they
   (C) is due to its topical subject matter—a feature typical of musicals of the 2000s, and
   (D) is due to its topical subject matter—a feature that is typical of musicals of the 2000s and that
   (E) is due to its topical subject matter—a feature typical of musicals of the 2000s and they

2. Ironically, successful candidates for a party's presidential nomination have found victory in the subsequent general election all but impossible <u>if there is an absence of support from those who directly opposed them during</u> the primary.

   (A) if there is an absence of support from those who directly opposed them during
   (B) if there is an absence of support from the direct opposition to them during
   (C) with an absence of direct support of those who were their opponents from
   (D) without the support of the direct opposition during
   (E) without the support of those who opposed them directly during

3. Once smart-phones were considered luxury items, limited to no more than an 8 percent share of the market, but today <u>the percentage is nearly seven times higher.</u>

   (A) the percentage is nearly seven times higher
   (B) their share is nearly seven times higher
   (C) their share is nearly seven times higher than that
   (D) their numbers are nearly seven times greater
   (E) the percentage is nearly seven times as great as that

4. Although Congress's proposed ban on the use of anabolic steroids by Major League Baseball players is currently the subject of much discussion in the popular press, <u>significant revision is to be expected before it is to be passed by either chamber.</u>

   (A) significant revision is to be expected before it is to be passed by either chamber
   (B) either chamber does not expect to pass it without significantly revising it
   (C) either chamber expects significant revision to pass it
   (D) it is not expected to be passed by either chamber without it being revised significantly
   (E) it is not expected to pass in either chamber without significant revision

5. A majority of paleontologists contend <u>nearly all of the thousands of extinct driven species at the beginning of the Triassic were driven</u> by one single extinction event, rather than by a series of minor catastrophes.

   (A) nearly all of the thousands of extinct driven species at the beginning of the Triassic were driven
   (B) the thousands of species all nearly driven extinct had been so at the beginning of the Triassic
   (C) at the beginning of the Triassic that thousands of species were nearly all driven so extinct and
   (D) that nearly all of the thousands of species driven extinct at the beginning of the Triassic were so driven
   (E) the extinction that nearly all of the thousand species at the beginning of the Triassic were driven was

Answers and Explanations for these questions can be found at the end of the chapter.

Answer Keys

500- to 600-Level Sentence Correction Practice Set

1. **(B)**   2. **(A)**   4. **(E)**

3. **(B)**   5. **(A)**

600- to 700-Level Sentence Correction Practice Set

1. **(B)**   3. **(C)**   5. **(A)**

2. **(C)**   4. **(E)**

700- to 800-Level Sentence Correction Practice Set

1. **(D)**   2. **(E)**   4. **(E)**

3. **(A)**   5. **(D)**

Explanations

500- to 600-Level Sentence Correction Practice Set

1. Issues: **idiomatic construction** (*because*), **pronoun choice** (*it*), **connecting clauses** (*remains inwardly focused, because it*)

   (B) Both *because of having* in Answer Choice (A) and *on account of having* in Answer Choices (D) and (E) fall short of the correct *because*, doubly required here because *because* is both the correct **idiom** and is needed as a **subordinating conjunction** to render the second half of the sentence a **dependent clause** to the **independent** *Tokyo … remains inwardly focused*. The only difference between Answer Choices (B) and (C) is the pronoun whose antecedent is the singular *Tokyo*; Answer Choice (B)'s *it* is singular; Answer Choice (C)'s *they* is incorrectly plural.

2. Issues: **pronoun choice** (reflexive pronoun *themselves*), **coordination** (the comparative adjectives *harder* and *more compact*)

   (A) A compound object for the verb *making* is found in the sentence as originally written. Slugs make themselves harder and more compact. Answer Choice (B) ruins the neat **coordinated compound** with an extra *the*, as does Answer Choice (E). Answer Choices (C) and (D) introduce a pronoun error. *Themselves* already properly refers to the plural antecedent slugs, and it is in the proper case (objective) to boot. *Their selves* in Answer Choice (C) isn't a real pronoun, though it might be mistaken for one, and *itself* in Answer Choice (D) is singular. The already eliminated Answer Choice (E) also contains a singular, so it's doubly wrong.

3. **Issues: comparisons** (*daycare facilities resemble mad houses*), **modification** (the adverb phrase *without ... supervision* describes *facilities*), **pronoun choice** (the answers introduce ambiguous *they*)

(B) Whether the children require plural amounts or a singular amount of supervision is a distractor; both are acceptable. In fact, the question of the initial modifying phrase's antecedent doesn't work as a decision point, as we could describe both the children and the daycare as lacking enough supervision. The comparison begun at the end of the line is the key; the end of the two-part comparison (*mad houses*) is not up for grabs, so the beginning must be changed to match it. Answer Choices (A) and (E) compare the *mad houses* to *children*, Answer Choice (D) to an unspecified *they*. The choice between (B) and (C) is easy: Answer Choice (C)'s *adequate amounts of supervision they need* doesn't work as the object of the verb that precedes it, *get*. It's also redundant.

4. **Issues: idiomatic construction** (*has an opinion on*), **subject-predicate agreement** (*not one ... has*), **word choice** (*whether*, not *if* for options)

(E) The idiom *has an opinion on* eliminates Answer Choice (C) and its *opinions about if*. The choice between ***whether*** and *if* eliminates (D) [and (C) *again!*]; on the GMAT, *whether* is used to describe options (*whether I do this or that*), and *if* is for conditional statements (*if I were the king of the forest*). The **subject-predicate agreement** is the most useful decision point, eliminating Answer Choices (A), (B), and (C) (one more time); all contain the plural verb *have* instead of the singular *has* that would agree with the subject pronoun *one*. One is clearly singular. *Friends* is part of a prepositional phrase that modifies *one* and thus can't be the subject. (But it makes a good distractor.)

5. **Issues: idiomatic construction** (*never before X has Y + verb*), **subject-predicate agreement** (*has a single person had*),

(A) Reverse the word order and the idiom makes more sense: *A single person has never had the kind of power* ... (that they have today, now that firearms are available)—weird, but acceptable. On the easier end of the difficulty spectrum, you will still see the occasional odd, infrequently used idiom like this one, but not paired with very attractive alternative answers. Here, the others answers are just shy of gibberish.

Answer Choice (B) swaps the subject and object creating nonsense (the advent can't have a person); the *ever* in Answer Choice (C)'s *has not had ever [the power]*, a stranded modifier, is also nonsensical; Answer Choice (D)'s *did ... have had* is nonsense as a verb (and fails the **subject-predicate agreement test**, too); and Answer Choice (E) strands *since the advent of the firearm* in the middle of a clause and *never before* at the beginning, each where they have no clear antecedent.

600- to 700-Level Sentence Correction Practice Set

1. **Issues: comparisons** (*15 Americans die due to ... fewer than are killed by*), **modification** (the choice of a dash or comma), **quantities and counts** (*fewer/less*)

   (B) The alternating *less* and *fewer* in the answer choices signals that a **quantities and counts** rule is being tested, and, as usual, tested alongside a comparison rule. Comparisons are usually easier to check than other errors and reward us with more eliminated answers. As always, items compared must be parallel: *15 die* in the unchangeable part of the sentence, so the second half of the comparison must also be verb like *die*. Answer Choice (E) compares the noun *ones,* so it's out, and Answer Choice (D) changes the comparison to one between *number* and *people,* both nouns, but not logically parallel. Answer Choices (A) and (B) both have *are,* acceptable verbs, leaving the **quantities and counts** question as the tie-breaker. Fifteen Americans can be counted, so they must be compared with *fewer,* not *less.* (Of the other answers, only the already eliminated Answer Choice (E) gets this second issue correct.)

2. **Issues: verb tense** (had/has), **idiomatic construction** (*X is regarded as Y*), **word-phrase-clause problems** (the choice in comma placement and conjunction after *novel*)

   (C) This question contains the idiom *X is regarded as Y,* which Answer Choices (B), (C), and (D) use correctly. The verb at the beginning of the underlined section must agree with the subject. While it might not be clear what *Oroonoko* is meant to be at first, but the rest of the sentence clues us in to the fact that it's a book, and thus singular. *Has* is demanded, and *have* eliminates Answer Choices (A) and (B). The choice between Answer Choices (C) and (D) comes down to the end of the underlined section, whose form will determine whether the remainder of the sentence forms a compound object of *regarded as*, as it would in Answer Choice (D), or an **appositive phrase**, a rarer form of coordination that starts showing up on the test's more difficult questions.

Appositives link the phrases on either side of the comma, treating the comma like an equals sign, sort of. Like in comparisons, the phrases on either side of the comma need to be the same part of speech as the other and make logical sense. Logic kills Answer Choice (E). The placement of the comma would indicate that coming to be regarded by lots of people as a precursor to the novel counts as a milestone of early feminist literature. The **coordination** in Answer Choice (C) is preferable: the book has come to be regarded as two things, a feminist milestone and a precursor to the novel. The *for many* set off by commas is used here as—surprise, surprise—a distractor, meant to make it harder to see the coordination it's interrupting.

3. <u>Issues</u>: **modification** (choosing an antecedent for *A much anticipated* ...), **connecting clauses** (**coordinating** the first two clauses)

   (C) The switch between *that is* and *is* across the end of the answer choices would be an easy decision point to start with. *That* would serve as a conjunction, making one long phrase out of the two *is* phrases, resulting in the circular statement that this giant gummy worm is the largest worm that is 128 times as big as a normal worm, or, in other words, the largest worm that is the size that it is. Out go Answer Choices (A) and (B). The remaining answer choices turn the last clause in the sentence into some sort of modifying phrase.

4. <u>Issues</u>: **idiomatic construction** (punctuating *however*), **connecting clauses** (**coordination** with two layers of *ands* and *buts*), **subject-predicate agreement** (*supply chains and materials sourcing occupy*)

   (E) *However* can be used in two ways: at the beginning of a sentence followed by a comma or separating two clauses, with a semicolon before and a comma after. Neither is found in Answer Choice (A) or (B), so *however* must be removed. *But* wins as a replacement option over *as* because the two clauses are establishing a contrast—"these new things are one thread, but these others are still there,"—eliminating Answer Choice (C). Finally, the plural verb *occupies* means that the subject of the clause following *but* must be compound, linked with an *and* instead of an *or*, eliminating Answer Choice (D).

5. **Issues: connecting clauses** (**coordination:** *recorded* and *created*), **modification** (avoiding unclear modifiers)

(A) The artist did two things, *recorded* and *created*, the two verbs linked by an *and* must be parallel, as they are in Answer Choice (A) but not in (B). Answer Choice (C)'s *recording* and *creating* would count as parallel, but they're not linked by an *and*, the comma instead turning them into the verbs of two dependent clauses, resulting in a sentence fragment. Answer Choice (D) and (E) introduce another error, trying to turn *recorded* into a noun and linking that noun to *the artist*. Answer Choice (D) uses *and* to create a compound subject, resulting in the nonsensical statement that the (presumably inanimate) *recordings created* the *collage*. Answer Choice (E) does the same thing, its *with* making the *secret recordings* into equal partners with the *artist*, rather than things the artist used to make the collage out of.

700- to 800-Level Sentence Correction Practice Set

1. **Issues: subject-predicate agreement** (*much ... is*), **connecting clauses** (constructing a descriptive phrase after the dash)

(D) The tricky subject *much* is singular, demanding *is*, instead of the *are* found in Answer Choices (A) and (B).

Additionally, the tail end of the underlined section is mislinked with what follows it in all but Answer Choice (D). The correct answer coordinates two descriptions of the *feature*. It is one *that is typical ... and that will hinder*. Answer Choice (A) drops the first *that*, and (B) turns the second into a *they*. Answer Choice (C) turns the second half of the coordinated description into a verb phrase, which doesn't match the adjective phrase *typical ...*, and Answer Choice (E) turns the second one into an independent clause, incorrectly linked to what precedes it with an *and*, instead of the *and* and a comma that would be needed.

2. **Issues: idiomatic construction** (*X is all but impossible without Y2*), **modifiers** (the migrating *direct* and *during*), **word-phrase-clause errors** (*if* versus *with* or *without*)

(E) A slightly more obscure idiom than on easier questions, (*X is all but impossible without Y*) eliminates the *if*'s in Answer Choices (A) and(B) as well as the *with* in Answer Choice (C). The words *during* and *direct* move around a great deal from answer choice to answer choice, and the movement results in various nonsensical meanings for the incorrect choices. Answer Choice (A)'s arrangement is perfectly acceptable, but Answer Choice (B) is ambiguous (it's not clear whether the opposition happened during the primary or whether the victory is impossible during the primary). Answer Choice (C) tries to avoid the error with *from*, but the resulting phrase *were their opponents from the primary* is itself idiomatically incorrect. Answer Choice (D)'s *during* is as ambiguous as Answer Choice (B)'s. (How can the opposition support the nominee *during* the primary, the time when they are the opposition?).

3. <u>Issues</u>: **numbers and amounts** (*percentage/share is higher/greater*), **comparisons** (the *percentage* now is seven times higher *than 8 percent*), **idiomatic constructions** (*X is higher than Y* [*was*])

(A) A complicated comparison between two percentages presents itself. Since a *percentage* can be counted, it is *higher* rather than the *greater* found in Answer Choices (D) and (E). The comparison must be made between like things. The *share* can't be compared with a *percentage of the share*, thus eliminating Answer Choices (B) and (C). Answer Choice (D)'s *numbers* is trickier, but still wrong, as the specific number of cell phones shouldn't be compared with the earlier percentage. Answer Choices (C) and (E) introduce a *that* at the end of the underlined section, ruining the comparing idiom *X is higher than Y*.

4. <u>Issues</u>: **word-phrase-clause problems** (deciding what type of clauses make sense together), **idiomatic constructions** (*pass in a chamber*)

(E) Another obscure idiom appears, as they tend to do in the upper reaches of GMAT difficulty: bills *pass in Congress* (and other legislative bodies), rather than being *passed by*.

The major challenge of the sentence is organizing the subjects and predicates of the clauses so that they make sense. The bill should be the one passing or not, and the chambers aren't the ones expecting the passage.

5. Issues: idiomatic construction (two: *contend that* and *so driven by*), **modification** (placement of *so*)

(D) Two idiomatic constructions combine to form a thorny mess. The easiest idiom to track would be *contend that*. Answer Choices (A), (B), and (E) have no *that*. The organization of modifiers in Answer Choice (C), which has a *that*, suggests that the contention happened at the beginning of the Triassic, instead of the extinction.

So driven is used in the correct answer to drive the unwary away from the otherwise clearly correct Answer Choice (D), and moving the *so* around in the other answer choices only results in awkward or nonsensical phrasings. (In particular, the *so* doesn't work as an intensifier for *extinct*; nothing can be driven *so extinct*, as extinction is an all-or-nothing kind of thing.)

Reading Comprehension

16

Reading Comprehension questions will make up about a third of the 41 Verbal questions you'll see on the day of your GMAT—about 14 in all, mixed in among the rest. Unlike Sentence Correction or Critical Reasoning questions, Reading Comprehension questions are grouped in sets of three to four that draw on the same 200- to 400-word passage.

The screen splits into two columns when Reading Comprehension questions appear, with the passage on the left and questions on the right, so it's unlikely you'll mistake them for any other type of question.

SUBJECTS COVERED

GMAT Reading Comprehension passages are drawn from three major subject areas in about equal proportions:

1. **SOCIAL SCIENCE**—History, philosophy, economics, sociology, linguistics, etc.—the "soft sciences" built on statistical analysis and studies, surveys, and other experiments involving people.
2. **PHYSICAL SCIENCE**—Biology, physics, astronomy, chemistry, etc.—the "hard sciences" where data and experiments built on physical phenomena (gravity, plate tectonics, recombinant DNA, and so on) are king.
3. **BUSINESS**—Marketing, strategic planning, sales techniques, taxation, profit margins—all the things you'd expect from a test related to the MBA.

What the GMAT *Says* Reading Comprehension Tests

According to the MBA.com, Reading Comprehension questions break into three categories, "interpretive, applied, and inferential"—whatever those mean! How do you apply or infer without interpreting? Yeah, we don't know either.

On the other hand, the *Official Guide* uses a slightly different classification with twice as many categories: main idea, supporting idea(s), logical structure, inference, evaluation, application. But when you read the explanations that accompany the questions in the *Official Guide*, it's clear that the choice between "supporting ideas" and "logical structure" is almost random. (How could it be otherwise? Unless you understand the passage's logical structure, how could you understand how an idea supports the main idea?)

What's the reason for all the categories and jargon? It's all smoke and mirrors meant to disguise the very simple tasks being called for and the rigorous limitations the questions must operate under.

Truth is, the reason most people do poorly on Reading Comprehension is that they give the test maker too much credit. Test takers overthink the questions, avoiding the simpler answers because, surely, a test of comprehension requires a lot of subtle upper-level thinking. If only that were true!

ADAPTIVE DIFFICULTY IN READING COMPREHENSION

It's not been clearly established whether the GMAT algorithm continues "adapting" during each three-to four-question Reading Comprehension passage and question set. It's likely that the test maker has a smaller subpool of questions available for each passage, so that if you were to get the first two questions attached to a passage correct, the final question would be statistically harder than the previous two. It's also possible that the test maker assigns difficulty to the entire passage plus question set—so that missing the first two of three questions wouldn't noticeably reduce the difficulty on the third.

It's hard to tell which of these two models the test maker uses because part of what makes a question hard or easy is the passage it's attached to, and that can't change once you start a set. So, it's probably best to just not think about it. Do each question as it comes, and don't worry about whether one "feels" harder or easier.

PASSIVE VERSUS ACTIVE READING

To succeed at GMAT Reading Comprehension, you have to force yourself to read a new way, to **read actively, rather than passively**. This means that you need to read with an eye toward the specific tasks that the test maker can ask you to do.

Thus, as you read, you **interrogate the author**, taking in each piece of information one at a time. As each bit of information comes in, ask yourself, "What does this have to do with what the author already said?" and "Why is the author talking about this now?" and "Is this something new or just the continuation of a previous thought?"

Start slowly. The first sentence of a passage is not necessarily the most important. It might be a relatively meaningless bit of contextual flavor meant to throw you off the scent of the real purpose of the passage. Or it might be the author's main point, laid out as clear as day. Whichever it is, you're not going to know immediately because you have no context to put that first sentence into. The context will grow as you read each new sentence, and with that growing context, you'll be able to pick up speed.

Don't be afraid to circle back and reread a sentence or even a paragraph if something you read doesn't make sense. If you find yourself saying, "Wait, I thought this was about otters and how they clean their food, so why is the author talking about whales?" then go back and reread the otter bit. The relationship will always be spelled out somewhere.

This doesn't mean you have to understand each new bit of information completely. It's far more important to **understand the *relationship* to the author's overall point** and to the information you've already read. Your understanding of that relationship will only need to be specific enough to answer the sorts of questions that the test maker asks. (We'll discuss this more momentarily.)

Don't rush on to the next paragraph until you know what to make of the first. The second paragraph will usually go faster, and the third (if there is one) will go faster still. Build momentum by being an active reader!

When you're done reading, you won't have every answer to every possible question committed to memory or summarized in your notes, but you will know the general "shape" of the passage and the locations of the various kinds of details, and, most importantly, you will have a grasp on what the different parts of the passage contribute to the author's overall agenda.

Reading for Structure

Knowing the structure of a passage is much more important than knowing all the nitty-gritty details of its content. Being able to say, "in the first paragraph, the author introduced this one guy's theory, and in the second, he attacked it by giving counterexamples" will get you a lot further than trying to commit each detail of the first theory and each detail of the second to memory because **the details will stay on the screen**. If you're faced with a **Detail** question that asks

> According to the passage, the first theoretical model of
> tectonic plate movement relied on the analogy that

you can always just go back to the paragraph that talks about the first theoretical model and confirm the answer—provided your notes helped you divide up the passage into its component parts. Now, how do we find those parts?

Structural Keywords

Just as with the Critical Reasoning questions, structural keywords will help you immensely as you answer Reading Comprehension questions if you know what to do when you see them. The most important of these keywords you can think of as the "road signs" that will help you navigate the passage, telling you either "Caution: things get tricky ahead, slow down," or "Nothing to see here, move along." These are the keywords that indicate **continuation** or **contrast**.

Continuation Keywords

These words let you know that the author is continuing the same line of thought. There's no contradiction, no change in direction, no additional considerations. Some examples include:

moreover	as well as	in addition
likewise	further	by the same token
additionally	not only	along the same lines
also	thus	

However you are taking notes on the passage, continuation keywords tell you that the same note will cover what you've already read and what you're about to read. You don't need to slow down to make sure you've got a handle on a subtle distinction because *there won't be any*. Not here, at least.

Contrast Keywords

On the other hand, **contrast keywords** are signals that the author of the passage either just has or soon will make a distinction, so *slow down and be careful until you understand it*. Some examples:

however	but	except
nevertheless	rather	unless
despite	in spite of	on the other hand
yet	notwithstanding	
although	while	

Reading for Argument

When you break a passage down into its component parts, when you understand its basic structure, then the argument is easy to understand. Here, the author isn't really arguing directly with anyone. The "drama" of the passage lies in the small tweaks to the theory of plate tectonics that the author says are necessary and important. As a whole, the author seems to agree that the theory is correct, so long as the tweaks are considered.

We probably would need to add very little to our notes in order to capture this author's argument. The words "better" and "even better" already indicate where the author's sympathies lie.

Don't Look for Topic Sentences

Back in high school, you probably learned the three-part thesis statement/ five-paragraph model for writing essays; consequently, you might expect that reading comprehension passages will follow something similar. Strike that thought from your mind!

The main point of a Reading Comprehension passage can be found at any point in the passage—first sentence, last sentence, thirteenth sentence, fourth-from-last-sentence, etc. There's no secret place to look, no place where the author always says, as you were once taught to do, "in this essay, I will prove that A is true, for X, Y, and Z reasons." There are, sadly, many superstitions about where to look to find the passage's topic, and if you've come across any in some other GMAT book, it's time to let it go.

In fact, the test maker *exploits* the fact that many people believe there's a "topic sentence" by often putting concise, easy-to-understand sentences that are only tangential to the main topic in those spots. The test maker is always one step ahead of the bone-headed test taker (which is why we try hard not to be one). The topic may well be expressed in the first or last sentence. It's just not always there.

THE SIX-STEP METHOD FOR TACKLING QUESTIONS

Step 1: Read and Take Notes on the Passage

What do you know? That's exactly what we've been doing these past few pages. But there's still one final thing to do before you head into the questions.

Step 2: Restate the Author's Agenda to Yourself

Most Reading Comprehension questions demand that you be able to take a step back from the passage's details and understand the author's overall agenda. So, before attempting any of the questions, take a moment and ask yourself "What was the author trying to do here?"

Step 3: Identify the Question (Based on the Stem)

Just like Critical Reasoning questions, Reading Comprehension questions have a stem and five answer choices. You'll learn (in the coming chapter) to recognize the tell-tale words and phrases the test maker uses to delineate each.

Let's tackle the question we've been flirting with this whole chapter:

> According to the passage, the first theoretical model of tectonic plate movement relied on the analogy that
>
> (A) the solid plates that compose the Earth's crust are similar to the contours of the continents.
> (B) the brittle skin of the crust is wrapped around a surging molten layer.
> (C) the materials that compose the crust and mantle are not physically separate.
> (D) the liquid mantle is like a conveyor carrying the solid crust by friction.
> (E) the crust is like a solid, dense plate that sinks into the liquid core beneath.

In this question, the phrase "According to the passage" followed by the word "relied" indicates that the test maker wants us to find a specific **detail** somewhere in the passage that corresponds to one of the five answer choices, a question you'll soon learn to call a **Detail** question.

Step 4: Research the Relevant Text

Never be afraid to reread the passage before looking at the answer choices. Remember, the answers are *designed* to make you uncertain about what you've read. Most of the wrong answer traps rely on your not quite remembering and jumping at an answer that seems familiar but is ultimately wrong.

Don't avoid rereading the passage; just avoid aimlessly rereading. The notes you take while reading the passage will be your guide as to where to look. Our notes tell us that there was an "earlier version" of the theory described in the first part of the second paragraph, so that is what we should reread. When we do, we'd see:

> ...Some early models of plate tectonics treated the motion of plates as though it were similar to a flat piece of lumber riding on top of a conveyor belt, the convection cells in the molten magma gradually moving the continents apart. This analogy...

Step 5: Prephrase or Predict an Answer

The best way to avoid the various wrong answer traps that the test maker has laid is to know what you're looking for in the answer choices before you go looking. Based on what we just read, we'd say something like "the solid bits were like planks, and the liquid bit was like a conveyor belt."

Step 6: Evaluate the Answer Choices

Take the answer choices one at a time, keeping in mind that the correct answer usually doesn't use the exact same words as the passage originally did.

> (A) the solid plates that compose the Earth's crust are similar to the contours of the continents.

Answer Choice (A) might seem familiar from a misreading of the first paragraph, where the "contours of the continents" phrase appears. This doesn't match our prediction, and it's a bit of nonsense. The plates aren't *similar* to the contours of the continents. They're what causes the contours to change. We'll later learn to call this a **distortion**—when the test maker purposely garbles something from the passage but uses familiar phrasing to make it seem tempting.

> (B) the brittle skin of the crust is wrapped around a surging molten layer.

Here is something else that should be familiar: a near direct restatement of an analogy in the passage, but not one attributed to the earlier version of the theory. It's found in the third paragraph and seems to be referring to the second version of the explanation, not the first. You'll soon come to recognize this as a **wrong party** trap—a true fact, but one that belongs to someone or something the current question isn't asking you about.

> (C) the materials that compose the crust and mantle are not physically separate.

Here is yet another distortion, taking pieces from the very end of the passage and repeating them incorrectly. Since the discussion of the separation of the mantle and core on either side of the isotherm came at the very end of the passage, it might trip up those test takers who didn't bother to do a little targeted rereading of the passage before looking at the answer choices.

> (D) the liquid mantle is like a conveyor carrying the solid crust by friction.

Jackpot! Even though it starts with the conveyor belt and doesn't mention the planks on the belt, this is still the analogy we predicted.

If you find an answer choice that matches your prediction so closely, you might be able to click and confirm without even reading the rest. For completion's sake, what's wrong with Answer Choice (E)?

> (E) the crust is like a solid, dense plate that sinks into the liquid core beneath.

It's another **wrong party** trap, taking details from the second explanation in the passage, the one that's used to correct the original interpretation.

READING COMPREHENSION QUESTION TYPES

The nice thing about GMAT Reading Comprehension questions (and Reading Comprehension questions on any standardized test, for that matter), is the limited question selection. Even though the questions might be dressed up in distracting language, at heart they boil down to two questions: (1) **what** does the author say? and (2) **why** did the author say it? Or, to use our fancy lingo: **Recall** questions and **Global** questions. Let's handle them one at a time, starting with the trickier of the two, **Global** questions.

GLOBAL QUESTIONS

Main Point

Almost every passage you see on the GMAT will have one **Global** question in which the test maker asks about the main point of the passage as a whole. Accordingly, we'll call these **Main Point** questions.

You'll recognize them easily, because their stems will usually be phrased like this:

- The **primary purpose** of the passage is to
- Which of the following best states the **main idea** of the passage as a whole?
- The author's **overall goal** can best be described as

Note the clues: some synonym for the word **primary** and another for the word **purpose** combined with some hint that you should be thinking about the **entire passage**, not just a part.

FUNCTION

Function questions ask you why the author includes a particular fact or part of the passage. Why bring up the Duchess of York there in the second paragraph? Why call the critics "small-minded nitwits"? To answer Function questions, you must understand the passage's underlying logic and how the author develops the passage's main argument.

In some way, then, Function questions involve "why?"—though they don't all use the word "why." For example:

- The author refers to the Declaration of Independence primarily **in order to**
- Which of the following best describes the **relationship of the third paragraph** to the rest of the passage?

Before you head into the answer choices to a Function question, stop, refer to your notes, and, if necessary, reread the relevant portions of text. The key to the right answer is to keep the author's overall purpose in mind—so the final step of the Reading Comprehension method proves critical here as well as in **Main Point** questions. If you don't recall the author's overall agenda, it's impossible to say what part a certain bit of the passage plays in that agenda.

RECALL QUESTIONS

The remaining two types of GMAT questions are "little picture" tasks. Instead of focusing on the author's overall point, these questions just ask about something small that the author said explicitly at some point in the passage. The trick is finding that specific point and matching it up to the corresponding answer choice.

Detail Questions

Most **Recall** questions begin with the magic phrase "According to the passage/author...." You'll be able to distinguish a **Detail** question from its close cousin the **Inference** question by paying attention to the verb used in the part of the stem that comes after that "According to...."

INFERENCE

The second type of **Recall** question and the final GMAT Reading Comprehension question type will seem familiar if you've already read the Critical Reasoning chapter: **Inference** questions. Just like their Critical Reasoning brethren, Reading Comprehension **Inference** questions ask you to select an answer choice that is directly deducible from information given in the passage but never said explicitly.

Inference questions are thus similar to **Detail** questions in that they both require you to stick religiously to the actual text of the passage; inference just asks you to go that one extra step further, to take two facts and add them together or to turn a double negative into a positive.

Both **Inference** and **Detail** questions tend to use the phrase "According to the passage/the author"; however, rather than speaking in the *is/was/says/did* voice of **Detail** questions, **Inference** questions deal in *likelihoods* and *possibilities*, things that the *author would most likely agree with*, things that are *inferred*, *suggested*, or *implied*. For example:

- The passage provides support for which of the following statements?
- Which of the following can be inferred from the passage about the study participants?
- The passage implies that which of the following steps must first be taken in order to achieve Olympic-level competitiveness?

Reading Comprehension Practice Set

Questions 1–3 are based on the following passage.

Josephus, the first-century Romano-Jewish historian notes that when the Romans destroyed Jerusalem in 70 C.E., there were so many slaves on the market that they could not be sold, even at fire-sale
Line prices. But why not buy a slave at no cost? There was certainly no
(5) ethical compunction involved; slavery was then and would remain a long-standing and popular facet of Roman life. The law of supply and demand would suggest that even as the available stock of human chattel rose, the market would find the appropriate lower (but still positive) price point. The answer, presumably, is that potential buyers
(10) owned so many slaves already that any addition to their workforce would be so marginal as to fall short of the cost of the slave's upkeep. In other words, the variable cost of maintaining the slave would have exceeded his or her output. Josephus notes in the same chapter that nearly eleven thousand men and women died from want of food, and
(15) that even the lowest forms of wheat (barley and rye, likely) used to feed the poor and servile classes were in short supply. The true price of slave ownership had, in effect, become negative and would remain there until new fields could be cleared for tillage and mills constructed to be worked. The large, sudden influx of available workers could not
(20) be matched in the near term by the meager rate of expansion of agriculture and industry.

1. What of the following best describes the main point of the passage?

   (A) To argue against slavery, given the conditions imposed upon its victims
   (B) To examine the reason for the unusually low price at which slaves were sold
   (C) To review Josephus' analysis of the slave trade in Jerusalem in 70 C.E.
   (D) To explore the applications of economics to a common problem in ancient morality
   (E) To examine the reasons for which slaves were introduced to Jerusalem

2. According to the passage, what is a reason for the low prices at which slaves were sold?

   (A) Otherwise usual food was scarce.
   (B) Ancient Romans were averse to the idea of owning slaves.
   (C) Not even the poor and servile classes could be fed.
   (D) Jerusalem's citizens were viewed as unworthy of being sold at higher prices.
   (E) Most slaves were of a working quality insufficient to merit higher sale prices.

3. The author mentions that "there was certainly no ethical compunction involved" (lines 4–5) primarily in order to

   (A) lend a historical background to the discussion at hand.
   (B) tug at the reader's ethical heartstrings.
   (C) eliminate an alternative, reasonable explanation for a phenomenon.
   (D) criticize the Romans for the cruelty inherent to their slave trade.
   (E) introduce a claim that the second paragraph will support.

Questions 4–7 are based on the following passage.

For the past ten years, the world has been experiencing a commodity price boom. From coffee to coal and platinum to pork, the general
rule has been that if you took the trouble to mine it from the ground
Line or grow it on a farm, you would likely make money selling it, with
(5) one glaring exception: lobster. In 2005, Maine lobster sold for just
under six dollars a pound wholesale, yet by 2013 lobster off the boat
was selling for as little as two dollars a pound, less than the price of
ground chuck in the supermarket. Huge lobster harvests, believed by
many to be a consequence of global climate change, have glutted the
(10) market, flooding supermarkets with so much lobster that many Maine
lobstermen must wonder how they can possibly remain afloat.

Paradoxically, even as the wholesale price of lobster has collapsed,
the price for lobster tails in high-end restaurants has remained stable
and, in many cases, increased over the same span of time. Even the less
(15) glamorous lobster roll sold at roadside stands throughout the Northeast has resisted the downward pricing trend. While restaurateurs are
generally slow to reduce prices even as the cost of ingredients falls,
such a substantial and extended decline in commodity prices almost
invariably results in lower priced dishes. One possible explanation is
(20) that over the past fifty years, lobster has become more a luxury good
than a commodity. During previous decades in which overharvesting
depleted lobster supplies, it came to be associated chiefly with the
wealthy, the only ones who could continue to afford it.

Moreover, restaurants rightly worry about the message that price
(25) cuts send. Studies from as far back as the 1940s strongly suggest that
people wrongly assume a correlation between a product's price and
quality, particularly when they cannot objectively evaluate the product before they buy it. Since few consumers follow the commodity
market closely enough to know what's been happening to the whole-
(30) sale price of lobster, cheaper lobster tails could convince customers
that your lobster is inferior to that at the expensive white tablecloth
establishment down the street.

4. The primary purpose of the passage is

   (A) to discuss the state of the lobster industry and the consequences for those involved.
   (B) to compare the commercial success of lobster and pork in the last decade.
   (C) to examine the consequences of the collapsing wholesale price of lobster for restaurateurs.
   (D) to argue against over-harvesting and other scarce marine life in Maine.
   (E) to argue that prices have declined not solely in Maine but throughout the Northeast.

5. The author mentions "ground chuck" primarily in order to

   (A) mention another good that has steadily been declining in price.
   (B) emphasize just how low the price of lobster is, given its value.
   (C) provide readers with another way of approximating the price of lobster.
   (D) showcase that lobster prices remain elevated in comparison to the prices of some other goods.
   (E) contrast lobster with a good whose price has steadily been climbing.

6. According to the passage, what sort of product might retain its price even when wholesale prices are declining?

   (A) Products that proceed through a middleman business (e.g., a distributor of fish who sells lobsters to restaurants)
   (B) Goods that were previously regarded as luxurious
   (C) An everyday necessity consumed by a large quantity of people (e.g., coffee)
   (D) Food crafted and sold at high-end establishments
   (E) Lobster caught and sold in small, independent markets

7. According to the passage, what can be inferred about "luxury goods" (line 20)?

(A) Lobster is not the only luxury good whose price may have rapidly fallen in one scenario while remaining relatively elevated in another.

(B) They include all of the previously described goods: pork, coffee, and lobster, specifically.

(C) They experience declines in price according to the regions in which they are sold.

(D) There is an inconsistent demand for them even among those who can afford them.

(E) Their prices are inflated for no foreseeable reason.

ANSWER KEYS

READING COMPREHENSION TARGETED REVIEW

1. **(B)**	3. **(C)**	5. **(B)**	7. **(A)**
2. **(A)**	4. **(A)**	6. **(D)**	

Reading Comprehension Targeted Review

1. "The main point" signals that, not surprisingly, we are looking at a **Main Point** question. This passage proceeds by introducing a Romano-Jewish historian (Josephus) who observed that Romans were unable to sell slaves on the market for high prices. It then discusses assorted possible reasons for the extremely low prices, and culminates by hypothesizing that food was insufficient to support slaves. Cumulatively, then, the passage "examines the reason for the unusually low price at which slaves were sold"— Answer Choice (B).

(B) Answer Choice (A) is not clearly done anywhere within the passage— the other, quite contrastingly, seems to just acknowledge slavery as a normal facet of Roman life. Answer Choice (C) suggests that Josephus affected an analysis that this passage is geared at critiquing, which isn't true. The main point of the passage is to explain a specific situation, too, not to explore economics [Answer Choice (D), therefore, fails]. Answer Choice (E) is not mentioned anywhere in the passage.

2. "According to the passage" points us to a **Detail** question. Reading over the passage, it is constantly emphasized that there was a food shortage—the answer to the question of low slave selling prices "presumably, is that potential buyers [would] fall short of the slave's upkeep," and we are told right after that about the thousands of men and women of even the servile classes dying without food and of agriculture's being stagnant. All this points to the idea that a food shortage would be responsible and leaves us with Answer Choice (A).

(A) We are told that Romans did not object to owning slaves, so Answer Choice (B) is invalidated. Even though Answer Choice (C) is true, this is a Critical Reasoning-esque logic trap—to say that slaves were sold for low prices *exactly because* not even the poor and servile classes could be fed is false. Both circumstances arise from a food shortage, but one does not cause the other. Answer Choices (D) and (E) aren't ever mentioned.

3. "In order to" signals a **Function** question! Look at the placement of this line inside the passage. It occurs just after we're asked why slave selling prices were so low. As such, it's highly likely that we're trying Answer Choice (C): to eliminate an alternative, reasonable explanation (moral concerns) for a phenomenon (the inability to sell slaves).

(C) Answer Choices (B), (D), and (A) are likely, reasonable answers, but they are not in any way supported by the passage. Answer Choice (E) is not true.

4. This is another **Main Point** question. Look over all of the paragraphs to arrive at the largest sense of what we're discussing: lobster, its decline (and, in some places, continued success), and the consequences of this decline. See Answer Choice (A)!

(A) Answer Choice (B) is far too specific—although both lobster and pork are mentioned, they are never compared. Answer Choice (C) is also too specific—even though we do briefly mention that restaurateurs will suffer, this is not elaborate enough to be our main point. Answer Choices (D) and (E) are completely irrelevant.

5. Here is another "in order to," another Function question. Look, again, at the part of the passage in which you find "ground chuck" (which, by the way, is a form of beef). Just after saying how glaringly lobster prices have fallen, the author mentions that lobster can cost less than ground chuck—there's an "even less" hanging in the air there. This allows us to infer that we would typically see lobster costing more than ground chuck, and that Answer Choice (B) is a good choice.

(B) Answer Choices (A) and (E) are not mentioned, and Answer Choice (C) is useless, given that we are told a precise amount. Answer Choice (D) is untrue, as ground chuck presumably costs less than lobster.

6. "Might" signals an **Inference** question. Search the passage for details that help you make a generalization. We're told in the passage that, sure, even though wholesale prices are dropping, the lobster being sold at high-end establishments is still comparatively expensive. There's our Answer Choice (D).

(D) Answer Choices (A), (B), (C), and (E) cannot be supported on the basis of passage assertions.

7. We're directly told that this one is an **Inference** question. Look, again, for "luxury goods" inside the passage. We're told that the paradoxical state of lobster prices might be explained by the fact that lobster is a luxury good toward the end of Paragraph Two. It's not unreasonable, therefore, to think that we know this because other "luxury goods" have experienced similar patterns in pricing. See Answer Choice (A).

(A) Answer Choices (B) and (C) are never stated; while region is mentioned in the passage, it is not used to prove what Answer Choice (D) claims. Answer Choice (E) is definitely not true, as the whole passage is dedicated to finding a reason for the changes in price.

Sample Test with Answers and Analysis

ANSWER SHEET

Integrated Reasoning Section

1 i. Ⓐ Ⓑ Ⓒ Ⓓ

   ii. Ⓐ Ⓑ Ⓒ Ⓓ

2	Could Be Classified	Could Not Be Classified	Animal
	◯	◯	Penguin
	◯	◯	Flamingo
	◯	◯	Flying Squirrel
	◯	◯	Pterodactyl
	◯	◯	Eagle

3	Yes	No
	◯	◯
	◯	◯
	◯	◯

4	Yes	No
	◯	◯
	◯	◯
	◯	◯
	◯	◯

5 Ⓐ Ⓑ Ⓒ Ⓓ Ⓔ

6	Either Day	Neither Day	Speaker
	◯	◯	Branson, male, U.K.
	◯	◯	Robinson, female, U.K.
	◯	◯	D'Agostino, female, Brazil
	◯	◯	Miller, female, Canada
	◯	◯	Soares, male, India

7 i. Ⓐ Ⓑ Ⓒ Ⓓ

   ii. Ⓐ Ⓑ Ⓒ Ⓓ

8 Ⓐ Ⓑ Ⓒ Ⓓ Ⓔ

9   True   False
      ◯   ◯
      ◯   ◯
      ◯   ◯

10 i. Ⓐ Ⓑ Ⓒ Ⓓ

    ii. Ⓐ Ⓑ Ⓒ Ⓓ

11   True   False
      ◯   ◯
      ◯   ◯
      ◯   ◯

12   Would   Would Not
      Help   Help
      Explain   Explain
      ◯   ◯
      ◯   ◯
      ◯   ◯

Quantitative Section

1 Ⓐ Ⓑ Ⓒ Ⓓ Ⓔ	11 Ⓐ Ⓑ Ⓒ Ⓓ Ⓔ	21 Ⓐ Ⓑ Ⓒ Ⓓ Ⓔ	31 Ⓐ Ⓑ Ⓒ Ⓓ Ⓔ
2 Ⓐ Ⓑ Ⓒ Ⓓ Ⓔ	12 Ⓐ Ⓑ Ⓒ Ⓓ Ⓔ	22 Ⓐ Ⓑ Ⓒ Ⓓ Ⓔ	32 Ⓐ Ⓑ Ⓒ Ⓓ Ⓔ
3 Ⓐ Ⓑ Ⓒ Ⓓ Ⓔ	13 Ⓐ Ⓑ Ⓒ Ⓓ Ⓔ	23 Ⓐ Ⓑ Ⓒ Ⓓ Ⓔ	33 Ⓐ Ⓑ Ⓒ Ⓓ Ⓔ
4 Ⓐ Ⓑ Ⓒ Ⓓ Ⓔ	14 Ⓐ Ⓑ Ⓒ Ⓓ Ⓔ	24 Ⓐ Ⓑ Ⓒ Ⓓ Ⓔ	34 Ⓐ Ⓑ Ⓒ Ⓓ Ⓔ
5 Ⓐ Ⓑ Ⓒ Ⓓ Ⓔ	15 Ⓐ Ⓑ Ⓒ Ⓓ Ⓔ	25 Ⓐ Ⓑ Ⓒ Ⓓ Ⓔ	35 Ⓐ Ⓑ Ⓒ Ⓓ Ⓔ
6 Ⓐ Ⓑ Ⓒ Ⓓ Ⓔ	16 Ⓐ Ⓑ Ⓒ Ⓓ Ⓔ	26 Ⓐ Ⓑ Ⓒ Ⓓ Ⓔ	36 Ⓐ Ⓑ Ⓒ Ⓓ Ⓔ
7 Ⓐ Ⓑ Ⓒ Ⓓ Ⓔ	17 Ⓐ Ⓑ Ⓒ Ⓓ Ⓔ	27 Ⓐ Ⓑ Ⓒ Ⓓ Ⓔ	37 Ⓐ Ⓑ Ⓒ Ⓓ Ⓔ
8 Ⓐ Ⓑ Ⓒ Ⓓ Ⓔ	18 Ⓐ Ⓑ Ⓒ Ⓓ Ⓔ	28 Ⓐ Ⓑ Ⓒ Ⓓ Ⓔ	
9 Ⓐ Ⓑ Ⓒ Ⓓ Ⓔ	19 Ⓐ Ⓑ Ⓒ Ⓓ Ⓔ	29 Ⓐ Ⓑ Ⓒ Ⓓ Ⓔ	
10 Ⓐ Ⓑ Ⓒ Ⓓ Ⓔ	20 Ⓐ Ⓑ Ⓒ Ⓓ Ⓔ	30 Ⓐ Ⓑ Ⓒ Ⓓ Ⓔ	

Verbal Section

1 Ⓐ Ⓑ Ⓒ Ⓓ Ⓔ	12 Ⓐ Ⓑ Ⓒ Ⓓ Ⓔ	23 Ⓐ Ⓑ Ⓒ Ⓓ Ⓔ	34 Ⓐ Ⓑ Ⓒ Ⓓ Ⓔ
2 Ⓐ Ⓑ Ⓒ Ⓓ Ⓔ	13 Ⓐ Ⓑ Ⓒ Ⓓ Ⓔ	24 Ⓐ Ⓑ Ⓒ Ⓓ Ⓔ	35 Ⓐ Ⓑ Ⓒ Ⓓ Ⓔ
3 Ⓐ Ⓑ Ⓒ Ⓓ Ⓔ	14 Ⓐ Ⓑ Ⓒ Ⓓ Ⓔ	25 Ⓐ Ⓑ Ⓒ Ⓓ Ⓔ	36 Ⓐ Ⓑ Ⓒ Ⓓ Ⓔ
4 Ⓐ Ⓑ Ⓒ Ⓓ Ⓔ	15 Ⓐ Ⓑ Ⓒ Ⓓ Ⓔ	26 Ⓐ Ⓑ Ⓒ Ⓓ Ⓔ	37 Ⓐ Ⓑ Ⓒ Ⓓ Ⓔ
5 Ⓐ Ⓑ Ⓒ Ⓓ Ⓔ	16 Ⓐ Ⓑ Ⓒ Ⓓ Ⓔ	27 Ⓐ Ⓑ Ⓒ Ⓓ Ⓔ	38 Ⓐ Ⓑ Ⓒ Ⓓ Ⓔ
6 Ⓐ Ⓑ Ⓒ Ⓓ Ⓔ	17 Ⓐ Ⓑ Ⓒ Ⓓ Ⓔ	28 Ⓐ Ⓑ Ⓒ Ⓓ Ⓔ	39 Ⓐ Ⓑ Ⓒ Ⓓ Ⓔ
7 Ⓐ Ⓑ Ⓒ Ⓓ Ⓔ	18 Ⓐ Ⓑ Ⓒ Ⓓ Ⓔ	29 Ⓐ Ⓑ Ⓒ Ⓓ Ⓔ	40 Ⓐ Ⓑ Ⓒ Ⓓ Ⓔ
8 Ⓐ Ⓑ Ⓒ Ⓓ Ⓔ	19 Ⓐ Ⓑ Ⓒ Ⓓ Ⓔ	30 Ⓐ Ⓑ Ⓒ Ⓓ Ⓔ	41 Ⓐ Ⓑ Ⓒ Ⓓ Ⓔ
9 Ⓐ Ⓑ Ⓒ Ⓓ Ⓔ	20 Ⓐ Ⓑ Ⓒ Ⓓ Ⓔ	31 Ⓐ Ⓑ Ⓒ Ⓓ Ⓔ	
10 Ⓐ Ⓑ Ⓒ Ⓓ Ⓔ	21 Ⓐ Ⓑ Ⓒ Ⓓ Ⓔ	32 Ⓐ Ⓑ Ⓒ Ⓓ Ⓔ	
11 Ⓐ Ⓑ Ⓒ Ⓓ Ⓔ	22 Ⓐ Ⓑ Ⓒ Ⓓ Ⓔ	33 Ⓐ Ⓑ Ⓒ Ⓓ Ⓔ	

Analytical Writing Analysis

Time: 30 minutes

> **DIRECTIONS:** In this section, you will be asked to write a critique of the argument presented. You are NOT being asked to present your own views on the subject.
>
> **WRITING YOUR RESPONSE:** Take a few minutes to evaluate the argument and plan a response before you begin writing. Be sure to organize your ideas and develop them fully, but leave time to reread your response and make any revisions that you think are necessary.
>
> **EVALUATION OF YOUR RESPONSE:** College and university faculty members from various subject matter areas, including management education, will evaluate the overall quality of your thinking and writing. They will consider how well you: organize, develop, and express your ideas about the argument presented; provide relevant supporting reasons and examples; and control the elements of standard written English.

Question: The following appeared in the editorial section of a local daily newspaper:

> "Although forecasts of elections based on opinion polls measure current voter preference, many voters keep changing their minds about whom they prefer until the last few days before the balloting. Some do not even make a final decision until they enter the voting booth. Forecasts based on opinion polls are therefore little better at predicting election outcomes than a random guess would be."

Discuss how well reasoned you find this argument. In your discussion be sure to analyze the line of reasoning and the use of evidence in the argument. For example, you may need to consider what questionable assumptions underlie the thinking and what alternative explanations or counterexamples might weaken the conclusion. You can also discuss what sort of evidence would strengthen or refute the argument, what changes in the argument would make it more logically sound, and what, if anything, would help you better evaluate its conclusion.

ON THE ACTUAL GMAT,
AFTER YOU HAVE CONFIRMED YOUR ANSWER,
YOU CANNOT RETURN TO IT.

INTEGRATED REASONING SECTION

Time: 30 minutes
12 questions

This section consists of four types of questions: Graphics Interpretation, Table Analysis, Two-part Analysis, and Multi-Source Reasoning.

> **DIRECTIONS:** The new Integrated Reasoning section consists of four question types. Some require the use of both quantitative and verbal skills. Others involve the use of graphics, tables, or text material. The questions also use various response formats.
>
> For each question, review the text, graphic, or text material provided and respond to the task that is presented. *Note: An onscreen calculator is available in this section on the actual test.*

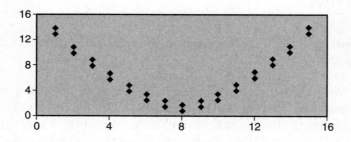

1. The scatter plot above shows the relationship between two variables.

    Complete each statement according to the information presented in the diagram.

    i. Which of the following statements is the only one that can be said to be true based on the chart?

    (A) The slope is positive.
    (B) The relationship is strong.
    (C) The slope is negative.
    (D) The slope is linear.

ii. If you plotted the absolute difference between the two variables at each point in the chart, what slope would the graph have?

(A) a positive slope
(B) a slope of zero
(C) a negative slope
(D) a parabolic slope

2. Birds are a class of vertebrate animals. Birds (class Aves) are a more homogeneous group than many other vertebrate classes, such as mammals. Birds possess very distinct characteristics. The top two are as follows:

(i) **The beak or bill** is a bony, toothless structure that extends from the jawbone. It is used primarily for eating, grooming, and feeding young.

(ii) **The wings**, which are a pair of forelimbs, are uniquely adapted for flying.

Based on the information above and ignoring all other characteristics of birds, which of the following could be classified as a "Bird" and which could not?

Could Be Classified	Could Not Be Classified	Animal
○	○	Penguin
○	○	Flamingo
○	○	Flying squirrel
○	○	Pterodactyl
○	○	Eagle

3. The table below displays data concerning UltraMart stores in Canada.

Store Number	City	Province	# of Employees	Grocery Section
3145	Concord	Ontario	27	N
3004	Brandon	Manitoba	28	N
3149	Mascouche	Quebec	31	N
3122	Belleville	Ontario	36	N
3065	Orleans	Ontario	38	N
3148	Levis	Quebec	42	N
3007	Brossard	Quebec	44	N
3134	Kanata	Ontario	44	N
3063	North Bay	Ontario	48	N
3097	Sudbury	Ontario	48	N
3140	Saint Bruno	Quebec	49	N
3000	Agincourt	Ontario	50	N
3080	Rosemere	Quebec	53	N
3642	St. Constant	Quebec	55	N
3046	La Salle	Quebec	59	N
3090	St. Jean	Quebec	59	Y
3161	Oshawa	Ontario	60	Y
3039	Joliette	Quebec	61	Y
3044	Kirkland	Quebec	64	Y
3189	Laval	Quebec	65	Y
3047	Laval	Quebec	66	N
3146	St. Foy	Quebec	66	Y
3053	Markham	Ontario	68	Y
3084	Saskatoon	Saskatchewan	68	Y
3135	Brampton	Ontario	70	N
3195	Richmond Hill	Ontario	70	Y
3130	Brampton	Ontario	72	Y
3186	Pickering	Ontario	72	Y
3054	Meadowvale	Ontario	77	Y
3159	Scarborough	Ontario	79	Y
3125	Gatineau	Quebec	80	Y
3131	Ottawa	Ontario	82	Y
3111	Scarborough	Ontario	83	N
3051	London	Ontario	84	N
3029	Edmonton	Alberta	86	Y
3656	Montreal	Quebec	86	Y
3635	Scarborough	Ontario	87	Y
3043	Kingston	Ontario	88	Y
3012	Calgary	Alberta	98	N
3074	Quebec City	Quebec	98	Y

Store Number	City	Province	# of Employees	Grocery Section
3050	London	Ontario	99	Y
3119	Winnipeg	Manitoba	102	Y
3654	Mississauga	Ontario	103	N
3055	Mississauga	Ontario	107	Y
3009	Calgary	Alberta	112	Y
3106	Toronto	Ontario	119	Y
3165	Montreal	Quebec	121	Y
3105	Toronto	Ontario	128	N
3740	Toronto	Ontario	131	Y
3031	Etobicoke	Ontario	142	Y

For each of the following statements, select *Yes* if the statement can be shown to be true based on the information in the table. Otherwise, select *No*.

Yes No

○ ○   The median number of employees in a store in Quebec is higher than the median number of employees in a store in Ontario.

○ ○   If a store has less than 60 employees, it does not have enough resources to support a grocery section.

○ ○   More than seven cities have at least two stores.

Questions 4 and 5 refer to the following articles.

Article 1: From an environmental journal

> February 28—Given the global increase of deforestation, some experts predict that in 50 years, Earth may lose over 20% of wildlife species to extinction. In addition, the destruction of forests provokes further global warming. CO_2 levels are predicted to rise by 100% in the same time period, which could have disastrous effects. Lastly, the loss of trees in an area also decreases the amount of water within that region, thus affecting the world's water supply. Governments and industry have failed to put sufficient restrictions and regulations in place. Although recycling programs have made a significant dent in reducing paper use, there is still much more work to be done. However, one of the challenges is that many citizens vote down proposals for recycling program expansion or regulations on industry.

Article 2: Interview with a well-known scientist

> March 6—Dr. James Finnegan, special advisor to the New York City Mayor's Program on Environment Sustainability, has been most critical of the forest industry, which continually hires and utilizes aggressive lobbyists to ensure that expanded recycling program proposals are defeated. He advises that without a significant increase in recycling programs, the rate of global warming could soon quadruple in the next generation.
>
> "It's true that most voters keep rejecting costly measures to reduce paper and lumber usage, such as more aggressive 'reduce, reuse, and recycle' programs. Worse yet, CEOs are unsurprisingly going to avoid taking huge risks for unpopular policies among their key stockholders. However, if something isn't done soon, by 2060, a bottle of water may become so expensive that only the rich can afford it as a luxury item."

Article 3: From a forestry magazine

April 2—The price of bottled water over the last two decades has increased by 200% as a decrease in supply has met with an increased demand. Despite an increase in recycled paper products available to the public, most paper companies charge a premium for them. This has encouraged some companies to exploit many large natural water resources around the world. This has also motivated many companies to continue using nonrecycled paper products. Several American environmental groups have expressed concern that certain pulp and paper companies choose the economics of extraction and manufacturing over the well-being of the ecosystem. Some North American scientists have called for an increase in regulations to protect deforestation and water sources. However, companies from both industries caution that this may dramatically increase the cost of both recycled paper and fresh water.

4. Consider each of the following statements. Does the information in the three articles support the inferences as stated?

Yes No

○ ○ Deforestation is the most significant cause of increasing CO_2 levels in the atmosphere.

○ ○ Citizens tend to vote down environmentally friendly proposals due to the strong lobbying of the forestry industry.

○ ○ Dr. James Finnegan would prefer to pass legislation to regulate the forestry industry than legislation to regulate the bottled-water industry.

○ ○ Business leaders in environmentally affected industries may not always agree with science experts on environmental sustainability.

5. Each of the following is true based on the passage EXCEPT:

(A) at least 15% of Earth's wildlife species may become extinct within 50 years.

(B) a bottle of water will cost the same as a bottle of premium vodka by the year 2060.

(C) bottled water has doubled in price over the past 20 years.

(D) for most consumers, recycled paper can cost more to purchase than nonrecycled paper.

(E) CO_2 levels are expected to double before the end of the 21st century.

An organization of technology leaders is arranging a two-day business conference in California that will bring together the top minds in leadership and development from around the world. The conference organizers want to get a diverse range of speakers for the event. Each day will have six speakers. To reflect the global diversity, one day will have a majority of international speakers (i.e., not from North America) and the other day will have a majority of female speakers. Neither day should have more than 2 speakers from the same country unless they are from the United States. So far, 10 speakers have already booked. The list of speakers for each day, including the speaker's country of origin, is as follows:

Day 1 (Majority International)	Day 2 (Majority Female)
Smith, female, U.K.	Fiorina, female, U.S.A.
Dalton, female, U.K.	Godin, male, U.S.A.
Xiang, male, China	Rodrigues, male, Brazil
Sharma, male, Spain	Hayek, female, Mexico
Robbins, male, U.S.A.	Valentino, female, Brazil

6. Select a speaker who could be added to the schedule for either day. Then select a speaker who could not be added to either day. Make only two selections, one in each column.

Either Day	Neither Day	Speaker
◯	◯	Branson, male, U.K.
◯	◯	Robinson, female, U.K.
◯	◯	D'Agostino, female, Brazil
◯	◯	Miller, female, Canada
◯	◯	Soares, male, India

Question 7 refers to the following graphs and information.

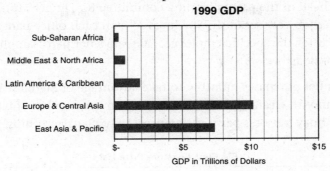

Graph 1

1999 GDP

Graph 2

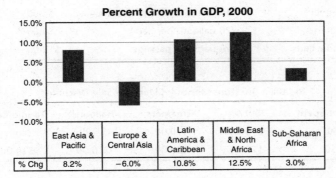

Percent Growth in GDP, 2000

	East Asia & Pacific	Europe & Central Asia	Latin America & Caribbean	Middle East & North Africa	Sub-Saharan Africa
% Chg	8.2%	−6.0%	10.8%	12.5%	3.0%

7. Complete each statement according to the information presented in the diagram.

i. What is the approximate dollar amount by which Europe and Central Asia's GDP increased from 1999 to 2000?

(A) −$610 billion
(B) −$439 billion
(C) −$6 billion
(D) $610 billion

ii. Which is closest to the combined growth in GDP in 2000 for all five regions?

(A) −3%
(B) 0%
(C) 4%
(D) 8%

Questions 8 and 9 refer to the following information and tables.

Sally is the head of the party planning committee for Dinder Mufflin. She takes her job very seriously. She loves to plan each office party and personalize it for the specific employee. Sally buys her party supplies from the Big Blast Boxstore.

Sally makes her purchases monthly to take advantage of Big Blast Boxstore's end-of-the-month clearance sales. Depending on the number of birthdays and the birthday person's party preferences, Sally plans accordingly.

Big Blast Boxstore Price List

Party Supply	Packaging	Cost
Ribbon	8 feet rolls, 6 per package	$8.00
Streamers	10 feet rolls, 10 per package	$6.00
Balloons	20 balloons per bag	$4.00
Goodie bags	24 bags per package	$12.00

Big Blast Boxstore Monthly Clearance Sale Discounts

Amount Spent	Ribbon	Streamers	Balloons	Goodie Bags
$30–$50	$15.00	$10.00	$5.00	None
Over $50	$25.00	$20.00	$10.00	$10.00

8. Which of the following options would result in the lowest cost?

   (A) August has 3 birthdays. Sally needs 180 feet of ribbon, 300 feet of streamers, 50 balloons, and 100 goodie bags.

   (B) February has 3 birthdays. Sally needs 300 feet of ribbon, 200 feet of streamers, 30 balloons, and 60 goodie bags.

   (C) September has 4 birthdays. Sally needs 300 feet of ribbon, 300 feet of streamers, 150 balloons, and 120 goodie bags.

   (D) December has 5 birthdays. Sally needs 360 feet of ribbon, 400 feet of streamers, 100 balloons, and 30 goodie bags.

   (E) April has 6 birthdays. Sally needs 336 feet of ribbon, 900 feet of streamers, 260 balloons, and 120 goodie bags

9. Answer the following True or False statements.

   True False

   ○   ○   If Sally was able to put leftover party supplies in storage, it would be cheaper to purchase 9 packages of streamers and 7 packages of ribbon instead of 8 packages of streamers and 6 packages of ribbon.

   ○   ○   It is cheaper for Sally to purchase 300 feet of ribbon and 900 feet of streamers than to purchase 144 goodie bags and 24 balloons.

   ○   ○   In order to get the maximum discount possible from purchasing all four products, Sally needs to spend at least $222.00.

The scatter plot below charts the test scores for an English exam and a math exam for 22 students in Mrs. Rosenblatt's class.

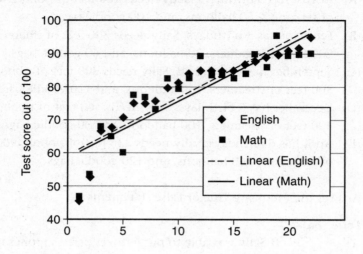

10. Complete each statement according to the information given by the graph.

i. How does the slope of the regression line for the English exam compare with the slope of the regression line for the math exam?

(A) The slope of the regression line for the English exam is greater than the regression line for the math exam.

(B) The slope of the regression line for the English exam is less than the regression line for the math exam.

(C) The slope of the regression line for the English exam is equal to the regression line for the math exam.

(D) The slope of the regression line for the English exam is undefined and cannot be compared with the slope of the regression line for the math exam.

ii. How do Mrs. Rosenblatt's students tend to score in math as compared with English?

(A) They tend to score better in math than in English.

(B) They tend to score worse in math than in English.

(C) They tend to score the same in math than in English.

(D) Since each student is an individual, the scores of the entire class cannot be compared with each other.

Questions 11 and 12 refer to the following table.

The table below shows data for the major types of sliced deli cheeses.

Type of Sliced Deli Cheese	Share of Market (lb.)	Change in Sales vs. Last Year (lb.)	Change in % Volume (lb.)	Share of Market ($)	Sales vs. Last Year ($)	Change in % Volume ($)
King Light Swiss	0	−17,489	−100	0	−168,120	-100
King Light Havarti	0	−17,893	−100	0	−172,403	-100
King Havarti	0	−22,860	−100	0	−218,829	-100
King Swiss	0	−27,648	−100	0	−265,065	-100
Kruger Mozzarella	16.2	8,547	4.2	14.7	124,537	7.6
King Swiss w/Zipper	11.5	64,852	74	11.9	641,205	81
Kruger Swiss	7.4	−10,292	−9.5	8.5	−58,444	-5.4
King Swiss Light w/Zipper	6.8	38,301	73.1	7.9	428,774	81.3
Aggio Jarlsberg	4.5	1,345	2.3	6.3	55,857	7.9
King Mozzarella w/Zipper	4.1	25,302	85.3	3.8	224,430	94.3
Davinci Swiss w/Zipper	3.4	44,729	NA	4.0	485,913	NA
Kruger Cheddar Mild	2.9	27,184	247.3	1.6	136,576	258
Davinci Havarti	2.7	26,911	290.2	3.2	292,398	320
Davinci Part Skim Mozzarella	2.6	7,797	29.2	2.4	92,119	45.4
Davinci Provolone	2.3	13,019	73.7	2.5	146,653	98.3
Norway Jarlsberg	2.1	361	1.3	1.8	7,186	3.5
Norway Jarlsberg Light	2.0	7,584	40.6	2.8	107,464	45.8
Kruger Part Skim Mozzarella	1.9	−14,941	−37.3	1.7	−121,058	-36.7
King Provolone w/Zipper	1.6	13,236	176	1.8	143,205	188
King Havarti w/Zipper	1.6	10,326	90.7	1.7	103,554	103
King Raclette w/Zipper	1.3	4,205	33.3	1.7	55,905	37.2

11. Consider each of the following statements. For each statement, indicate whether the statement is true or false based on the information provided in the table.

True False

○   ○   Cheddar and mozzarella cheese slices have a higher in-store price point than Swiss or Havarti cheese slices.

○   ○   Swiss cheese slices accounted for more dollar sales than any other type of cheese slice.

○   ○   King's cheese slices have had the largest overall absolute growth per pound since last year.

12. For each of the following statements, select *Would help explain* if it would, if true, help explain some of the information in the table. Otherwise select *Would not help explain*.

Would   Would Not
Help   Help
Explain   Explain

○   ○   Consumers tend to prefer cheese slices packages with zippers versus packages with no zipper.

○   ○   King discontinued some of their SKU's (stock keeping units) and replaced them with products that were packaged with zippers.

○   ○   Light cheese slices are more expensive to manufacture than regular cheese slices.

ON THE ACTUAL GMAT,
AFTER YOU HAVE CONFIRMED YOUR ANSWER,
YOU CANNOT RETURN TO IT.

QUANTITATIVE SECTION

Time: 75 minutes
37 questions

This section consists of two types of questions: Problem Solving and Data Sufficiency.

Problem Solving

DIRECTIONS: Solve each of the following problems; then indicate the correct answer.

NOTE: A figure that appears with a problem is drawn as accurately as possible so as to provide information that may help in answering the question.

Numbers in this test are real numbers.

Data Sufficiency

DIRECTIONS: Each of the following problems has a question and two statements that are labeled (1) and (2). Use the data given in (1) and (2) together with other available information (such as the number of hours in a day, the definition of *clockwise*, mathematical facts, etc.) to decide whether the statements are *sufficient* to answer the question. Then fill in space

(A) If you can get the answer from **(1) ALONE** but not from (2) alone
(B) If you can get the answer from **(2) ALONE** but not from (1) alone
(C) If you can get the answer from **BOTH (1)** and **(2) TOGETHER** but not from (1) alone or (2) alone
(D) If **EITHER** statement **(1) ALONE OR** statement **(2) ALONE** suffices
(E) If you **CANNOT** get the answer from statements (1) and (2) **TOGETHER** but need even more data

All numbers used in this section are real numbers.

A figure given for a problem is intended to provide information consistent with that in the question, but not necessarily with the additional information contained in the statements.

All figures lie in the plane unless you are told otherwise.

Figures are drawn as accurately as possible; straight lines may not appear straight on the screen.

> **(A)** If you can get the answer from **(1) ALONE** but not from (2) alone
> **(B)** If you can get the answer from **(2) ALONE** but not from (1) alone
> **(C)** If you can get the answer from **BOTH (1)** and **(2) TOGETHER** but not from (1) alone or (2) alone
> **(D)** If **EITHER** statement **(1) ALONE OR** statement **(2) ALONE** suffices
> **(E)** If you **CANNOT** get the answer from statements (1) and (2) **TOGETHER** but need even more data

1. What is the remainder when 320 is divided by 400?

   (A) $\frac{4}{5}$

   (B) 40

   (C) 80

   (D) 320

   (E) 400

2. Which of the following is a factor of both 21 and 24 but not of 50?

   (A) 2

   (B) 3

   (C) 4

   (D) 5

   (E) 7

3. Which of the following must be odd?

   (A) The sum of an odd and an even number

   (B) The sum of a positive and negative number

   (C) The difference between two even numbers

   (D) The quotient of two even numbers

   (E) The product of an odd and an even number

4. A store owner marked an item for $50. When he sold the item at a 10% discount, he made a 20% profit. What was the original cost of the item?

   (A) $36.00

   (B) $37.50

   (C) $39.00

   (D) $40.00

   (E) $40.09

5. If $1000 is placed into account X, yielding 10% interest compounded annually and $1000 is placed into account Y using 10% simple annual interest, how much more will be in account X than in account Y at the end of 5 years?

    (A) $0
    (B) $100
    (C) $110.51
    (D) $133.31
    (E) $146.41

6. May and June both work for April, who owns a used-car dealership. May sold 18 cars in August, and June sold 12 cars in July. Of the cars that May sold, the range of the selling price was $16,000 and the lowest selling price was $5500. Of the cars that June sold, the range of the selling price was $17,500, and the lowest selling price was $7200. What was the range of the selling prices of the 30 cars sold by May and June for April?

    (A) $16,200
    (B) $18,700
    (C) $19,200
    (D) $21,500
    (E) $22,700

7. If $st + u = u$, and s does not equal 0, which of the following must be true?

    (A) $|s - t| = 0$
    (B) $t = 0$
    (C) $s > t$
    (D) $st = 1$
    (E) $s + t = 0$

(A) If you can get the answer from **(1) ALONE** but not from (2) alone

(B) If you can get the answer from **(2) ALONE** but not from (1) alone

(C) If you can get the answer from **BOTH (1)** and **(2) TOGETHER** but not from (1) alone or (2) alone

(D) If **EITHER** statement **(1) ALONE OR** statement **(2) ALONE** suffices

(E) If you **CANNOT** get the answer from statements (1) and (2) **TOGETHER** but need even more data

---

8. What is the ratio of the number of teaspoons of baking soda to the number of cups of chocolate chips required in a certain brownie recipe?

   (1) The number of cups of chocolate chips required in the recipe is 350 percent of the number of teaspoons of baking soda required in the recipe.

   (2) $2\frac{1}{2}$ more cups of chocolate chips than teaspoons of baking soda are required in the recipe.

9. A certain list consists of many different integers. Is the product of all the integers in that list positive?

   (1) When you multiply the smallest and the largest integers in the list, you get a positive number.

   (2) There are an even number of integers in the list.

10. If T is a line in the xy-plane, what is the slope of T?

   (1) The y-intercept of T is 4.

   (2) The x-intercept of T is 5.

11. Is positive integer y divisible by 3?

   (1) $\dfrac{144}{y^2}$ is an integer

   (2) $\dfrac{y^2}{36}$ is an integer

12. How many more worker compensation insurance claims were filed in month *V* than in month *Z*?

   (1) For months *W, X, Y, Z,* the average number of first-time insurance claims filed was 272,000.
   (2) For months *V, W, X, Y,* the average number of first-time insurance claims filed was 277,250.

13. Machine A produces 1000 widgets in 5 hours. Machine B produces 450 widgets in 3 hours. While working together at their respective rates, how long will it take the machines to produce 2000 widgets?

   (A) $4\frac{4}{9}$ hours

   (B) 5 hours

   (C) $5\frac{9}{20}$ hours

   (D) $5\frac{5}{7}$ hours

   (E) 6 hours

14. Leonardo da Vinci was invited to exhibit 3 new paintings, 4 new sculptures, and 2 new inventions at the local museum. If Leonardo has 5 new paintings, 5 new sculptures, and 3 new inventions from which he must choose, how many different combinations of paintings, sculptures, and inventions are available to him?

   (A) 24
   (B) 150
   (C) 300
   (D) 450
   (E) 1050

15. If *T* is a set of six positive, distinct integers with an average (arithmetic mean) of 12 and a median of 8, what is the smallest possible value of the largest number in the set?

   (A) 19
   (B) 20
   (C) 21
   (D) 22
   (E) 23

(A) If you can get the answer from **(1) ALONE** but not from (2) alone
(B) If you can get the answer from **(2) ALONE** but not from (1) alone
(C) If you can get the answer from **BOTH (1)** and **(2) TOGETHER** but not from
     (1) alone or (2) alone
(D) If **EITHER** statement **(1) ALONE OR** statement **(2) ALONE** suffices
(E) If you **CANNOT** get the answer from statements (1) and (2) **TOGETHER** but
     need even more data

16. A certain granola mix is made up of raisins, bran flakes, and pecans.
     The mixture contains 30% bran flakes by weight and 40% pecans by
     weight. The bran flakes cost twice as much as the raisins per pound,
     and the pecans costs $2\frac{1}{2}$ times as much as the bran flakes per
     pound. Approximately what percent of the cost of the granola mix
     do the bran flakes contribute?

     (A) 18%
     (B) 20.7%
     (C) 22.5%
     (D) 24%
     (E) 25%

17. In a rectangular coordinate system, what is the x-intercept of a line
     passing through (4, 3) and (6, 9)?

     (A) (–3, 0)
     (B) (0, 3)
     (C) (–3, –3)
     (D) (1, 0)
     (E) (3, 0)

18. At what speed must a runner return from the gymnasium to home,
     a distance of 30 km, if the trip there took 2.5 hours and she wishes
     to average 15 km/h for the entire trip?

     (A) 12 km/h
     (B) 15 km/h
     (C) 18 km/h
     (D) 20 km/h
     (E) 24 km/h

19. If Jonathan is 12 years younger than Sebastian, how old is Sebastian today?

    (1) In three years from now, the combined ages of Sebastian and Jonathan will be 11 times the current age of Jonathan.
    (2) Four years from today, Jonathan will be one-third the age of Sebastian.

20. The upscale restaurant Sassafras adds an 18% gratuity to all bills with groups of 6 or more but adds no gratuity for groups with fewer than 6 people. If a group of friends ate at this restaurant, what was their total bill, not including any gratuity?

    (1) There were 6 people in the group of friends.
    (2) The total gratuity for the meal was $16.30.

21. A square lawn is reduced in size by removing 3 feet from one dimension and 5 feet from the other. By what percentage did these changes reduce the area of the original lawn?

    (1) The area of the lawn was 35 square feet after the changes.
    (2) After the changes, the longer dimension was three-tenths shorter than before the changes.

22. Is x an integer?

    (1) $4x$ is an integer.
    (2) $x - 1$ is not an integer.

23. For any triangle Q in the xy-coordinate plane, the center of Q is defined to be the point whose y-coordinate is the average of the y-coordinates of the vertices of Q and whose x-coordinate is the average of the x-coordinates of the vertices of Q. If a certain triangle has vertices on the points (0, 0) and (10, 0) and center at the point (5, 4), what are the coordinates of the remaining vertex?

    (A) (5, 12)
    (B) (5, 8)
    (C) (10, 5)
    (D) (7.5, 6)
    (E) (6, 10)

(A) If you can get the answer from **(1) ALONE** but not from (2) alone

(B) If you can get the answer from **(2) ALONE** but not from (1) alone

(C) If you can get the answer from **BOTH (1)** and **(2) TOGETHER** but not from (1) alone or (2) alone

(D) If **EITHER** statement **(1) ALONE OR** statement **(2) ALONE** suffices

(E) If you **CANNOT** get the answer from statements (1) and (2) **TOGETHER** but need even more data

---

Province	Amount of Organic Waste Collected Normally	Amount of Organic Waste Extracted From Regular Garbage
New Brunswick	21,400	4100
Nova Scotia	49,100	8900
Prince Edward Island	17,200	3400
Quebec	112,600	17,800
Ontario	62,500	14,100

24. The table above shows the amount of organic waste, in metric tons, collected by five provinces in Canada and the amount of organic waste extracted from regular garbage in a certain year. Which province has the highest ratio of normal organic waste collected to extracted organic waste collected?

(A) New Brunswick
(B) Nova Scotia
(C) Prince Edward Island
(D) Ontario
(E) Québec

25. The equilateral triangle above has sides of length x, and the square has sides of length y. If the two regions have the same area, what is the ratio of $x : y$?

    (A) $\dfrac{2}{3}$

    (B) $\dfrac{4}{3}$

    (C) $\dfrac{2}{\sqrt{3}}$

    (D) $\dfrac{2}{\sqrt[4]{3}}$

    (E) $\dfrac{4}{\sqrt[4]{3}}$

26. The marketing team at Alpha Company decides to go to lunch to celebrate Jim's birthday. The lunch costs a total of L dollars, and there are C members on the marketing team, not including Jim. If F of the team members forget their wallets, which of the following represents the extra amount, in dollars, that each of the remaining team members would have to pay?

    (A) $\dfrac{FL}{(C(C-F))}$

    (B) $\dfrac{L(C-F)}{C}$

    (C) $\dfrac{L}{(C-F)}$

    (D) $\dfrac{FL}{(C-F)}$

    (E) $\dfrac{L}{C}$

(A) If you can get the answer from **(1) ALONE** but not from (2) alone

(B) If you can get the answer from **(2) ALONE** but not from (1) alone

(C) If you can get the answer from **BOTH (1)** and **(2) TOGETHER** but not from (1) alone or (2) alone

(D) If **EITHER** statement **(1) ALONE OR** statement **(2) ALONE** suffices

(E) If you **CANNOT** get the answer from statements (1) and (2) **TOGETHER** but need even more data

27. Is $\dfrac{1}{x} > \dfrac{y}{(y^2 + 2)}$?

    (1) $y > 0$

    (2) $x = y$

28. The operation Ω is defined for all positive integers a and b by $a \, \Omega \, b = \dfrac{2^a}{2^b}$. What does $(4 \, \Omega \, 2) \, \Omega \, 5$ equal?

    (A) 0

    (B) 2^{-2}

    (C) 2^{-1}

    (D) 4

    (E) 2^5

29. What is the greatest prime factor of $4^{23} - 2^{40}$?

    (A) 3

    (B) 5

    (C) 7

    (D) 11

    (E) 13

30. If $z + y < 0$, is $z - x > 0$?

    (1) $x < y < z$

    (2) $x + y = 0$

31. A teacher creates a test with x statements, each of which is true or false. What is the smallest value for x where the probability is less than $\frac{1}{1000}$ that a person who randomly guesses every question could get them all right?

    (A) 10
    (B) 20
    (C) 25
    (D) 50
    (E) 100

32. Machines A, B, and C can each print the required number of magazines in 12, 15, and 18 hours, respectively. What is the ratio of the time it takes machines C and B working together to print the required magazines to the time it takes all three machines working together to print them?

    (A) $\frac{11}{90} : \frac{7}{30}$

    (B) $\frac{11}{60} : \frac{9}{30}$

    (C) $\frac{1}{11} : \frac{2}{37}$

    (D) $\frac{90}{7} : \frac{30}{9}$

    (E) $\frac{60}{14} : \frac{90}{22}$

33. There are 500 delegates at a leadership conference. During the day, breakout sessions are offered. Participants can attend workshops on networking, social media, or business plans. 80% of the delegates attend the workshops. 310 delegates attend the networking session. 250 delegates attend the business plan session. At least 45 delegates that attended at least one session do not attend either of the networking or the business plan sessions. The number of delegates that attend both the networking and business plan workshops must be between:

    (A) 160 and 205
    (B) 205 and 250
    (C) 160 and 250
    (D) 205 and 310
    (E) 250 and 310

(A) If you can get the answer from **(1) ALONE** but not from (2) alone

(B) If you can get the answer from **(2) ALONE** but not from (1) alone

(C) If you can get the answer from **BOTH (1)** and **(2) TOGETHER** but not from (1) alone or (2) alone

(D) If **EITHER** statement **(1) ALONE OR** statement **(2) ALONE** suffices

(E) If you **CANNOT** get the answer from statements (1) and (2) **TOGETHER** but need even more data

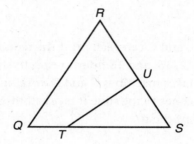

34. Equilateral triangle *QRS* has sides of length 6. The line *UT* is perpendicular to *RS*. If the length of *UR* is 4, what is the area of the quadrilateral *QRUT*?

(A) $\dfrac{7}{3}$

(B) $\dfrac{7}{\sqrt{3}}$

(C) $7\sqrt{3}$

(D) $9\sqrt{3}$

(E) $7 - 2\sqrt{3}$

35. Sheriff Roscoe travels from Hazzard County to Beaufort County by car in 35 minutes with a 5-minute bathroom stop on the way. He wants to shave his driving time on the way back by half. What average rate does Sheriff Roscoe need to reach on his way back?

    (1) Sheriff Roscoe's average speed traveling from Hazzard County to Beaufort County was 40 miles per hour.
    (2) The distance between Hazzard County and Jethro County, where Sheriff Roscoe made his bathroom stop, is 10 miles.

36. If sets x and y each have the same number of terms, is the standard deviation of set x greater than that of set y?

    (1) The first two terms and the last two terms of sets x and y are identical.
    (2) The range of set y is greater than the range of set x.

37. A jar contains g green marbles, r red marbles, and w white marbles. If one marble is chosen at random from the jar, is the probability that white will be chosen greater than the probability that red will be chosen?

    (1) $\dfrac{w}{(g+r)} > \dfrac{r}{(g+w)}$
    (2) $g - r > w$

STOP

VERBAL SECTION

Time: 75 minutes
41 questions

Reading Comprehension

DIRECTIONS: This section contains three reading passages. You are to read each one carefully. When answering the questions, you *will* be allowed to refer back to the passages. The questions are based on what is *stated* or *implied* in each passage.

Critical Reasoning

DIRECTIONS: For each question in this section, choose the best answer from among the listed alternatives.

Sentence Correction

DIRECTIONS: This part of the section consists of a number of sentences, in each of which some part or the whole is underlined. Each sentence is followed by five alternative versions of the underlined portion. Select the alternative you consider both most correct and most effective according to the requirements of standard written English. Answer (A) is the same as the original version; if you think the original version is best, select answer (A).

In considering the answer choices, be attentive to matters of grammar, diction, and syntax, as well as clarity, precision, and fluency. Do not select an answer that alters the meaning of the original sentence.

Questions 1–3 are based on the following passage.

Though the modern recycling movement did not percolate up into the public consciousness until the mid-1970s, recycling itself has been a feature of human society as long as there have been human societies.
Line Indeed, before the industrial age made a variety of goods available
(5) quickly and cheaply, virtually every consumer product was recycled after it was no longer fit for its original purpose. Long before large-scale recycling programs became the norm, thrifty households used clothing too frayed and threadbare to itself be salvaged to patch and repair clothing not quite so worn. Even sweaters so moth-eaten that
(10) they could neither be darned themselves nor serve as darning for other clothing were put to use, first to sop up spills of precious oils in the kitchen and garage, thereafter as kindling or fire starters in cooking and heating fires.

The need in recent decades for large-scale recycling programs can
(15) be traced to the otherwise beneficial advances in mass production brought about by industry. When a tablecloth can be produced and purchased for less than the cost of the food served upon it, it makes economic sense to simply throw it away when it becomes soiled or ripped. What once might have been pressed into service as, if nothing
(20) else, a cheap source of household cleaning rags, is consigned instead to a landfill, along with cleaning rags purchased new *as* cleaning rags—an innovation no eighteenth- or nineteenth-century maid would ever have predicted. Why ever would one be so foolish as to spend good money on something that one could easily make at home for free?

1. The passage is primarily concerned with

   (A) describing the beneficial effects of the industrial age upon consumer products.
   (B) explaining the need for programs to increase the amount of consumer goods recycled.
   (C) discussing how some practices considered modern are in fact much older.
   (D) explaining how harmful the unintentional side effects of mass production have been.
   (E) describing one manner in which technological progress has changed economic behavior.

2. Each of the following is given in the passage as an example of a premodern recycling program EXCEPT:

   (A) repairing damaged clothing with clothing too damaged to be repaired.

   (B) consigning household cleaning rags to a landfill only after using them repeatedly.

   (C) using the side products of food preparation to prepare other foods.

   (D) employing an item originally purchased as a household furnishing to maintain other furnishings.

   (E) extending the lifespan of personal accoutrements by patching or darning them.

3. The function of the rhetorical question given in the last line of the passage is primarily to

   (A) explain why many eighteenth- and nineteenth-century households were so frugal.

   (B) contrast modern large-scale recycling efforts with earlier smaller-scale ones.

   (C) suggest that what is now considered valuable was once considered useless.

   (D) illustrate one way in which a modern problem has been created by technological change.

   (E) emphasize the difference between impoverished and affluent households.

4. Employee morale is of tantamount importance to a business, as anything that reduces morale reduces the business's profitability. Thus, while it might seem like a prudent policy to reward exceptional employees with raises, parking spaces, and other perks, in practice this policy will backfire when those who do not receive such perks become aware of their existence.

Which of the following, if true, most strengthens the argument?

(A) Employee morale is generally reduced when compensation is unequal, even when performance is unequal.

(B) Of the things that reduce a business's profitability, damage to employee morale is the hardest to reverse.

(C) Businesses that reward performance with perks that do not include stock options are less profitable overall.

(D) Eliminating perks for employees is itself a way to increase the profitability of a company.

(E) When exceptional employees are rewarded with perks, their productivity and morale are both increased.

5. Only those with memberships at the Simon Island Country Club are allowed to use its golf course. Richard recently was admitted to membership at the Simon Island Country Club, so he will surely begin using the golf course.

The reasoning in the argument above is questionable because it

(A) confuses a policy that is regularly enforced with one that sometimes has exceptions.

(B) proceeds as though a fact that is required for the conclusion to be valid is also sufficient for it to be valid.

(C) asserts that in a given case only one of two options is possible, without eliminating other possible options.

(D) presupposes that a group of people who are alike in one respect must necessarily be alike in others.

(E) draws a conclusion that the premises of the argument, when taken to be true, explicitly contradict.

6. The Black Death (also known as the Bubonic Plague) <u>resulting in the death of about 75 million people, nearly one-third</u> of whom died in Europe alone.

   (A) resulting in the death of about 75 million people, nearly one-third

   (B) resulting in the death of nearly 75 million people, one-third nearly

   (C) resulted in the death of nearly 75 million people, nearing one-third

   (D) resulted in 75 million people having died, one nearly a third

   (E) resulted in the death of about 75 million people, nearly one-third

7. New research has enabled "bulk" silicon <u>to be able to emit broad-spectrum visible light and opening the possibility</u> of using the element in devices with both photonic and electronic components.

   (A) to be able to emit broad-spectrum visible light and opening the possibility

   (B) to emit broad-spectrum visible light and opening the possibility

   (C) to emit broad-spectrum visible light, opening the possibility

   (D) emit visible light and a broad-spectrum and open the possibility

   (E) be able to emit visible light in a broad-spectrum and to open the possibility

8. During the era of Jim Crow <u>many still were African-Americans treated like second-class citizens, even though they were freed</u> by the Emancipation Proclamation decades before.

   (A) many still were African-Americans treated like second-class citizens, even though they were freed

   (B) many African-Americans still were treated as second-class citizens, even though they had been free

   (C) many African-Americans were still treated as second-class citizens, despite having been freed

   (D) many African-Americans still were being treated as second-class citizens, even they had been freed

   (E) many second-class citizens still were treated, like African-Americans, even though they were freed

9. When Bogota's traffic problem grew too great to ignore, the mayor took an unorthodox step, firing many of the city's traffic officers and replacing them with mimes. These mimes followed traffic law violators and mimicked their behavior silently. In months, traffic had ceased to be a problem. This proves that sometimes the answer to a problem of compliance with the law is to shame law breakers rather than punishing them.

   Each of the following is an assumption required by the argument above EXCEPT:

   (A) the act of shaming someone for breaking a law should not be considered a form of punishment.

   (B) the mimes who followed traffic violators did not single out a few habitual breakers of the law to mimic.

   (C) the law breakers who were followed by mimes in Bogota afterward stopped breaking those law.

   (D) the traffic officers who were not fired did not markedly increase the rate at which they punished people for breaking traffic laws.

   (E) noncompliance with traffic laws in some way contributed to the traffic problem in Bogota.

10. In order to both reduce their overall insurance costs and provide extra compensation to their employees, many companies now offer to match funds that employees pay into flexible healthcare spending accounts. After a three-year analysis of this practice in the tech industry, researchers concluded that the benefits to the companies went well beyond these expectations. In that industry, companies matching employee contributions to flexible healthcare spending accounts could, on average, expect their employee absentee rate to be 20% lower than among companies who did not.

Which of the following would most weaken the conclusion of the three-year study?

(A) Those technology companies able to afford to match employee contributions to health accounts are usually so successful that they are able to be very selective about those they hire.

(B) At companies that offer flexible healthcare spending accounts, employees may use them to pay for eye and dental care not covered by the normal health plan.

(C) Starting a flexible healthcare spending account requires substantial effort for the employees who desire one.

(D) Other industries where companies match employee contributions to flexible healthcare accounts, similar improvements in absentee rate have been seen.

(E) In the technology companies that match employee contributions to flexible healthcare accounts, average worker productivity is also higher.

Questions 11–14 are based on the following passage.

Neuroscientists have for many years characterized sleep as a "whole brain phenomenon," a fully encompassing mental and biochemical state that is entirely distinct from those under which the brain operates
Line when awake or even when extremely fatigued. New research suggests,
(5) however, that the divide between wakefulness and sleep may not be so clear-cut as it once appeared.

Recently, a team led by Dr. Guilio Tononi conducted a series of experiments on sleeping rats in order to measure changes in activity in the brain as it slips from consciousness to unconsciousness and
(10) back again. Using a combination of scalp-mounted E.E.G. (or electroencephalography) and microwave arrays implanted directly in the frontal and parietal cortexes of the test subjects, the scientists were able to analyze both the sleeping and waking brain with a level of precision that had heretofore been unavailable. As expected, after
(15) falling asleep, the E.E.G. showed delta wave activity within the rats' brains, strong slow waves of electrical activity that are typical of deep, dreamless "slow wave sleep." The electrodes in the brain, however, told a different story. Although they recorded delta waves most of the time, they also revealed that there were episodes lasting from a few
(20) seconds to up to two minutes in which the motor cortex suddenly went into "waking mode." Delta waves disappeared and were replaced with fast, unpredictable activity.

Alternately, by recording the activity of many small populations of neurons while the rats had been kept awake artificially for a prolonged
(25) period, Tononi's team was also able to detect extremely brief, highly localized incidences of slow delta wave activity, the very hallmark of a brain in "sleeping mode." While the research remains in the early stages of completion, neuroscientists are cautiously optimistic that Tononi's research into the now increasingly nebulous border between
(30) these two modes of neural operation may help science arrive at a better understanding of the function of sleep itself.

11. Which of the following best describes the relationship between the experimental findings described in the second paragraph and those described in the third?

(A) The findings described in the second paragraph are revealed by the author to be anomalous when contrasted with those in the third.

(B) The findings described in the third paragraph are revealed by the author to be anomalous when contrasted with those in the second.

(C) Both sets of findings when taken together reveal that the experimental methodology of the researchers described in the passage is suspect.

(D) The findings described in the third paragraph each independently support the contention described by the author in the first paragraph.

(E) Neither set of findings independently support the researcher's original contention, but taken jointly suggest a new hypothesis worthy of further research.

12. Which of the following does the author indicate was true of the series of experiments performed by Tononi's lab?

(A) The researchers utilized technology that no rival lab could have fashioned with equal precision.

(B) The researchers utilized at least two sets of devices to obtain their experimental data.

(C) The highly localized incidence of slow delta wave activity detected could only be detected in test subjects that had been kept awake artificially.

(D) The delta waves detected by the first experiment interfered with the detection of other types of brain activity.

(E) Other labs lacking the unique combination of monitoring equipment used in the experiment will be unable to duplicate the experimental results.

13. Based on the passage, it can be inferred that prior to the work carried out by Tononi's research team, neuroscientists would have been surprised to detect

(A) slow wave delta activity in the brain of an unconscious test subject.

(B) microwave arrays implanted directly in the frontal and parietal cortexes of a waking test subject.

(C) two distinct biochemical states exhibited by a test subject before and after being awoken.

(D) fast, unpredictable activity within the motor cortex of a test subject whose brain is in "sleeping mode."

(E) a lack of activity other than delta waves in a sleeping test subject.

14. The primary purpose of the passage is to

(A) review research demonstrating the benefits of a new experimental technique and suggest future hurdles that it may bring about.

(B) present the findings of a group of researchers and the practical therapies their work will soon allow.

(C) describe the results of a recent set of experiments that challenge a significant assumption of a field of study.

(D) critique the callousness with which a provocative researcher conducts his clinical trials.

(E) lament the lack of practical applications for a series of experiments that were once thought to be promising.

---

15. By signing the Kyoto Protocol a nation is required to reduce their greenhouse gas emissions and to research an increase in technology to increase the absorption of these gases already present in the atmosphere.

(A) is required to reduce their greenhouse gas emissions and to research an increase

(B) is required to reduce its greenhouse gas emissions and to increase research

(C) is required to reduce their greenhouse gas emissions and to researching an increase

(D) requires to reduce their emitting of greenhouse gas and to increasing research

(E) required to reduce its greenhouse gas emissions and to research increasing

16. Traders <u>who predicted a continuing of the loss in value of the commodity</u> were surprised Wednesday when pig futures posted a strong rally.

   (A) who predicted a continuing of the loss in value of the commodity
   (B) who predicted continuing losses in the commodity's value
   (C) who had predicted the continuation of losses of the commodity's value
   (D) who had predicted continuing losses in value for the commodity
   (E) who had predicted a continuing loss for the value in the commodity

17. Researchers at the famous Copenhagen Institute <u>is working on developing new transgenic treatments and investigating the role played by tRNA in the spread of</u> cancer cells between tumorous sites within an individual.

   (A) is working on developing new transgenic treatments and investigating the role played by tRNA in the spread of
   (B) is working to develop new transgenic treatments and investigating the role played by tRNA in the spreading of
   (C) are working to develop new transgenic treatments and investigating the role played by tRNA in the spread of
   (D) are working on development of new transgenic treatments and the investigation of the role tRNA plays for the spread of
   (E) are working on developing new transgenic treatments and investigating the role played by tRNA in the spread of

18. To combat gun violence, restrictions on private handgun ownership are often proposed, the idea being that the fewer guns available, the fewer guns will be used in violent crimes. The problem with such proposals is not, as is often said, that **when guns are outlawed, only outlaws have guns**, but rather that not all guns have the same likelihood of being used in a violent crime. Unless gun legislation is tailored so that it primarily reduces the number of these more dangerous guns—ones currently in the hands of criminals, or those which criminals might easily obtain—**such legislation will fail to reduce the amount of gun violence in a society**.

In the argument above, the two portions in **boldface** play which of the following roles?

(A) The first is an observation that the author uses to support a particular position; the second is that position.

(B) The first is a position the author takes as inadequate to explain a phenomenon; the second is the author's conclusion about certain plans that would address the phenomenon.

(C) The first is a prediction that the author argues will not hold in a specific case; the second is the prediction the author argues is more likely.

(D) The first is a prediction that the author believes to be untrue; the second is a restatement of that prediction treated as though it were an independent conclusion.

(E) The first is a direct relationship that the author asserts will not hold in this case; the second offers evidence in support of the author's assertion.

Questions 19–21 are based on the following passage.

A collaborative artwork produced by Donatello and Michelozzo, the tomb monument of Antipope John XXIII is almost unanimously regarded among art historians as one of the earliest masterpieces produced during the Florentine Renaissance of the Fifteenth Century. Precisely which master is responsible for which piece is a subject on which there is far less agreement. Nearly every element of the tomb, from the gilded bronze recumbent effigy that adorns the papal sarcophagus to intricately designed marble reliefs of the personified Virtues in niches beneath, has been attributed to both Donatello and Michelozzo by different art historians at one time or another. In making such attributions, a critic or commentator often indicates more about what he or she finds to be valuable. Those things prized will inevitably be seen as the work of the master Donatello. Aspects attributed to Michelozzo will almost always be supported by the observation that they are "less well executed." In the end then, the many varied and extensive discussions of the iconography and design of the monument tomb are most valuable to historiographers, art historians who study the history of art history itself, and are far less useful for those seeking to understand the development of the techniques used by either artist.

Line (5)

(10)

(15)

(20)

19. The author's primary purpose is to

(A) refute the idea that particular features of the tomb of Antipope John XXIII can reliably be attributed.

(B) describe the characteristics of an early masterpiece of Renaissance art.

(C) argue that critical evaluations of a widely praised work of art are inevitably biased.

(D) assert that certain works of art history reveal more about the historian than about the art.

(E) rebut previous art historians who have incorrectly attributed the work of Donatello to Michelozzo.

20. If an art historian were to declare that one of the marble reliefs of personified Virtues found on the tomb of John XXIII required much more artistic skill to produce than the other two, the author would most likely take the assertion as evidence that

 (A) the relief in question was most likely the work of Donatello, rather than Michelozzo.

 (B) the more-skilled relief is equally likely to have been the work of either Donatello or Michelozzo.

 (C) the exact artist responsible for all three of the reliefs will never be reliably determined.

 (D) at least two of the reliefs should be considered to be the work of the same unknown artist.

 (E) the relief in question will provide insight into the qualities valued by the appraiser.

21. Which of the following can be inferred from the passage?

 (A) The observations about a work of art's execution that are the most valuable are those that do not attempt to determine that work's original artist.

 (B) Those works of art that cannot be reliably attributed to one artist are most likely to have been created by a collaboration between artists.

 (C) Some works of art history that are unable to provide valuable information on their stated subject may provide other valuable information.

 (D) Some works of history that are seen as more valuable by certain historians who study history are worthless to the general public.

 (E) Many of those features of the monument tomb that are currently attributed to Donatello were probably the work of someone else.

22. A researcher studying the habits of highly effective CEOs found that there was a positive correlation between those who described themselves as having "goal-oriented" personalities and those who were rated as most effective by annual surveys of their employees. The researcher concluded that people with "goal-oriented" personalities are more likely, on average, than those without to seek a job as a CEO.

    Each of the following, if true, would weaken the argument above EXCEPT:

    (A) CEOs and other top executives are unlikely to be able to describe their own personality accurately.
    (B) The annual surveys of employees are usually conducted immediately after the employees have been paid their annual bonuses.
    (C) The term "goal-oriented" is so vague as to be able to apply to nearly any set of personal characteristics.
    (D) CEOS who do not describe themselves as "goal-oriented" rarely remain CEOs for long.
    (E) The researcher made no effort to control for other variables that might have influenced the finding.

23. The U.S. Supreme Court recently ruled that the military commissions enacted as part of the response to global terrorism are not <u>constitutional; as they are violating</u> the separation of powers.

    (A) constitutional; as they are violating
    (B) constitutional; a violation of
    (C) constitutional, but rather they violate
    (D) constitutional; but rather that they violate
    (E) constitutional, but rather it violates

24. Analyst: Offshoot Records has weathered changes in the music marketplace for over sixty-four years. However, as customers become accustomed to purchasing music via downloadable file, rather than via physical media such as CDs and LPs, it will become increasingly difficult for locally owned music stores like Offshoot to remain profitable. Expect Offshoot to close its doors within the next year.

    Which of the following, if true, makes the analyst's prediction about the future viability of Offshoot Records more likely to be correct?

    (A) There are no other locally owned music stores that have successfully adapted to the challenge of digitally distributed music.

    (B) The only way that a music store can remain profitable is if its customers remain loyal and eschew general trends.

    (C) Sales at Offshoot Records have not been increasing over the past few months.

    (D) CDs and LPs make up the vast majority of the stock on sale at a locally owned music store like Offshoot Records.

    (E) The past sixty-four years has presented Offshoot with challenges largely dissimilar to the present shift toward digital distribution.

25. The newly elected board of regents must consider <u>whether to recommend that the disgraced head of the football program be released</u> from his contract.

    (A) whether to recommend that the disgraced head of the football program be released

    (B) whether to recommend that the disgraced head of the football program should be released

    (C) whether it should recommend that the disgraced head of the football program be released or not

    (D) if it should make the recommendation that the disgraced head of the football program should be released

    (E) if to recommend that the disgraced head of the football program should be released

26. After a decade that saw steep increases in the average price of cars aimed at the middle of the market, overall sales of cars in this category have finally begun to suffer. In an attempt to stem the loss of sales, one major Detroit automaker has reduced the price of its middle-tier cars by 12 percent. However, since few other automakers are likely to follow suit, the average price of a middle-tier car is unlikely to fall significantly.

Which of the following indicates the main conclusion of the argument above?

(A) The average price of cars aimed at the middle of the market has increased steeply over the past decade.

(B) One major Detroit automaker has reduced the price of its middle-tier cars by 12 percent.

(C) Few automakers are likely to adopt the price reduction that one automaker has recently announced.

(D) The sales of middle-tier cars have suffered significantly over the past decade.

(E) The actions of one automaker are not likely to affect the average price of cars aimed at the middle of the market.

27. You may know Martha Rose Shulman as a food critic, but in her kitchen she leads a double life as a ghost-writer of pastry cookbooks.

(A) You may know Martha Rose Shulman as a food critic, but

(B) You might know Martha Rose Shulman to be a food critic,

(C) Although you may know of Martha Rose Shulman as a food critic, still

(D) While you may know that Martha Rose Shulman is a food critic, although

(E) You might know Martha Rose Shulman as a food critic,

28. The Battle of Bull Run—or Manassas, as it was known in the South—was the first major ground engagement of the American Civil War <u>resulting in over 2,000 dead and nearly half again that number were wounded.</u>

   (A) resulting in over 2,000 dead and nearly half again that number were wounded
   (B) and resulting in over 2,000 dead and nearly that number and half wounded
   (C) resulted in over 2,000 dead and nearly that number plus half of the wounded
   (D) and resulted in over 2,000 dead and nearly half again that number wounded
   (E) and resulted in over 2,000 and nearly half again that number that were wounded

Questions 29–32 are based on the following passage.

The principles of economics, Guido Calabresi argues in his Cost of Accidents, suggest that we ought to reject the idea that the central aim of tort law should be the minimization of the harm
Line caused by accidents themselves, but rather the minimization of
(5) the costs associated with accidents, including the costs that accrue from minimizing the risks of harm that accidents cause. Since any economically fruitful endeavor will increase the risk of some accident, he contends, any risk reduction will reduce in turn some economically fruitful activity, which would itself entail a cost. If a
(10) society wishes to minimize the overall cost of accidents and apportion those costs fairly, it must consider the amount expended reducing risk. After all, no one would ever seriously argue for a 5 mph speed limit on all motorways; the lost time and productivity would be unfathomably costly, no matter the lives saved.
(15) Paradoxically, in order to make the case that the constraints faced by real-world actors necessitate the adoption of a legal analogue of the Neoclassical rational choice model of human agency—his chief and most influential contention—Calabresi resorts to the same idealized hypotheticals that he initially decries in previous critics
(20) when advocating this real-world turn toward economically driven legal analysis, a rhetorical weakness that is often noted. Nowhere is the tension between Calabresi's means and ends more evident than in the chapter concerning his insurance-incentive thesis, presented through hypothetical drivers Taney and Marshall and their carefully
(25) idealized decision whether to install a new kind of brake. The cost of installation is set by Calabresi's fiat at a flat $50, the cost of the accidents Taney would cause without it $25, Marshall $200.
As these intentionally oversimplified numbers nevertheless illustrate, a tort system that motivates Marshall to install the brake
(30) while allowing Taney to forgo it is clearly to be preferred, even though such a system would allow Taney to engage in risky behavior traditionally punished in civil courts. The proper venue for ensuring the desired outcome, Calabresi concludes, is the economic incentives inherent in the insurance system. If viewed as rational agents
(35) motivated by their own self-interest, as economists suggest, private insurers will set their premiums relative to the harm that drivers

can be expected to cause, as the insurers will bear the cost of those accidents that occur. Since Marshall is far more costly without the brake than Taney, the insurers will increase his insurance premium
(40) commensurately. Similarly, Marshall will, if rational, certainly choose to pay the lower cost of installing the brake.

The problem in Calabresi's use of hypotheticals in making his tidy case for the necessity of considering economic incentives when evaluating a legal system is, however, not simply a rhetorical one, for
(45) with them he avoids the central question he purports to answer: how to best determine the cost of accidents. In the real world governed by economic principles in which Taneys, Marshalls, and insurance companies must operate, who possesses the Calabresian insight to determine with such precision that one driver will cause $200
(50) of damage in accidents per year, another $25, and to take action accordingly?

29. Which of the following titles most accurately expresses the main point of the passage?

   (A) "Calabresi's Cost of Accidents: More Relevant Today Than Ever Before"
   (B) "Calabresi's Insight as Oversight: Implications of His Hypotheticals
   (C) "Calabresi's Folly Revisited: The Underappreciated Genius"
   (D) "When Marshall Met Taney: Real-World Data Confirms Calabresi"
   (E) "Guido Calabresi Reconsidered: The Influence of an Economic Titan"

30. If the author's appraisal of Calabresi's work is accurate, which of the following must he also believe?

   (A) When there arises a conflict between rational self-interest and the behavior traditionally punished by courts, economic considerations must be put aside.

   (B) A legal theory's use of economic calculations that are too simple to correspond closely to the real world is not alone cause to reject all the claims made by that theory.

   (C) Rhetorical weaknesses are usually the least serious defects that a theoretical framework is vulnerable to.

   (D) Whether an activity is economically fruitful is less important a consideration in its continuation than whether that activity causes substantial harm.

   (E) Only those theories that reconcile the competing self-interests of multiple rational agents will be able to accurately guide public policy concerning the cost of accidents.

31. Based on the passage's description of Calabresi's argument, each of the following would contradict at least one of Calabresi's theoretical commitments EXCEPT:

   (A) there are some real-world costs associated with the harm caused by attempts to minimize larger harms that we ought to ignore for the purposes of devising a legal theory.

   (B) in cases where a risk can be mitigated without government intervention, it is unlikely that there is any harm associated with that risk.

   (C) an agent acting in accord with the dictates of rational self-interest will often elect to ignore the costs that another party's behavior will later cause that agent.

   (D) the value of a human life is so great that attempts to create an economic theory robust enough to guide our behavior in most cases will always fail in those cases where many lives will inevitably be lost.

   (E) should an economic theory seem to imply that we engage in behavior that is currently considered improper, that is grounds enough to reject that theory's application.

32. With which of the following evaluations of Calabresi's theories is the author of the passage most likely to agree:

(A) Because of the tension between his theories' ends and means, it is unlikely to be accepted widely in society.

(B) Because his own theories insist upon the necessity of taking economic considerations into account when evaluating a legal theory, they display little insight into economic affairs more broadly.

(C) Because his theories share assumptions and methodologies with Neoclassical economic theory, they are less useful to lawyers than the theory of accident cost that they replaced.

(D) Even though his theories fail to provide a manner in which the exact costs associated with accidents may be determined, they are still correct in asserting that accident cost ought include the costs of risk aversion.

(E) Even though his theories sometimes appear to advocate outcomes that are at odds with current jurisprudence, they should be rejected only if they also fail to explain the economic component of those outcomes.

---

33. Unlike older televisions that used cathode ray tubes, which required heavy lead shielding to protect viewers, no shielding is needed by LED or LCD televisions, allowing them to be much lighter than their predecessors.

(A) to protect viewers, no shielding is needed by LED or LCD televisions, allowing them to be much lighter than their predecessors

(B) to protect viewers, LED or LCD televisions need no shielding that allows them to be much lighter than their predecessors were

(C) protecting viewers, LED or LCD televisions are allowed to be much lighter without shielding than their predecessors

(D) for viewers' protection, no shielding is needed by LED or LCD televisions to allow them to be much lighter than their predecessors

(E) for viewers' protection, LED or LCD televisions need no shielding, allowing them to be much lighter than their predecessors

34. Foreign aid is said to be "tied" when it is given with the stipulation that it may only be used to purchase items from the nation lending the aid. This practice has fallen out of favor in the international community, as it always results in economies more dependent on foreign money than before the aid. Even the relatively successful tied aid given by China to Singapore to rebuild in the wake of a devastating earthquake would today be frowned upon.

Which of the following can most reasonably be inferred from the passage?

(A) Even when ethical considerations outweigh a nation's self-interest, tied aid will not produce an ethical outcome.

(B) Countries that give tied aid most often do so out of a desire to benefit domestic businesses and industries.

(C) Even when tied aid is motivated by purely ethical concerns, it will exacerbate at least one economic problem in the receiving nation.

(D) China's actions would be more frowned upon if there had not been a recent earthquake in Singapore.

(E) Tied aid has caused more damage to the economies of the nations receiving it than most other economic factors.

35. Noble gases are inert because <u>the completion of their outer electron orbital makes these elements more stable and less reactive when in</u> the presence of other atoms and molecules.

(A) the completion of their outer electron orbital makes these elements more stable and less reactive when

(B) the completing of its outer electron orbital makes these elements more stable and less reactive when it is

(C) the completion of its outer electron orbitals making them more stable and less reactive within

(D) of completing their outer electron orbitals, which makes these elements more stable and less reactive if

(E) the completion of their outer electron orbital makes these elements more stable and less reactive if

36. When we read the histories written centuries ago, we must remember that many, if not most, works of history ever written have been lost, for histories must be transmitted in books, yet books are fragile things prone to much abuse even in one lifetime, unlikely to survive more than a handful of centuries. To combat this constant reduction of existing copies across the millennia, a history must be recopied, and no book will be recopied if it does not manage to speak across the centuries to those who would do that recopying. Thus, no matter how valueless an ancient history might seem to our modern sensibilities, its very existence is testament to its value.

Which of the following, if true, most strengthens the conclusion above?

(A) No work of ancient history would have been copied in sufficient quantities to allow a small fraction of its copies to remain without being recopied.

(B) No work of ancient history will be able to speak across the centuries unless it appeals equally to those living in each century.

(C) No work of ancient history that has failed to survive to the modern day would have appealed to modern sensibilities if it had survived.

(D) All works of ancient history that are valuable were recopied.

(E) All works of ancient history that speak across centuries are recopied in sufficient quantities to allow their survival.

37. Though the press releases and other official statements of oil companies take great pains to emphasize that the scientific community is not unanimous in the belief that global warming can be tied to the burning of fossil fuels and other human activities, oil companies clearly do not believe this to be the case. If there were actually credible, respected scientists who rejected human-caused climate change, these companies would surely spend more money to support the research done by these dissenting voices, for they have a vested interest in making sure debate on the issue continues indefinitely.

Which of the following best explains the apparent discrepancy described above?

(A) Oil companies have only recently begun investing in scientific research that addresses climate change.

(B) Unless a researcher can credibly claim independence from those whom their research might benefit, they will not be as successful as those who can.

(C) Oil companies typically earmark money spent on research for technologies that would directly benefit their profits.

(D) Oil companies spend substantial amounts circulating their press releases and publicizing their other official statements.

(E) If a company spends money to support one side of a contentious issue, such support will be taken as a sign that the issue is already decided.

38. Fertilizer runoff caused by industrial-scale farm practices <u>overwhelm streams and rivers with excess nitrogen and fertilizes blooms of algae, depleting oxygen and leaving</u> vast "dead zones" in their wake.

(A) overwhelm streams and rivers with excess nitrogen and fertilizes blooms of algae, depleting oxygen and leaving

(B) overwhelm streams and rivers, with excess nitrogen that fertilizes blooms of algae, depleting oxygen and leaving

(C) overwhelms streams and rivers with excess nitrogen, fertilizing blooms of algae that deplete oxygen and leave

(D) overwhelms streams and rivers with excess nitrogen that fertilize blooms of algae and deplete oxygen, leaving

(E) has overwhelmed streams and rivers with excess nitrogen and have fertilized blooms of algae, depleting oxygen and leaving

39. Consolidated Foodstuffs recently changed the ingredients to its infant formula recipe, replacing high-fructose corn syrup (HFC) with cane sugar, even though **the greater expense of the latter means that the company will make less profit**. Because cane sugar is much better for the developing infant than HFC, doctors have praised the move, saying that **Consolidated Foodstuffs has demonstrated that it places more value on the health of its customers than on purely financial considerations**, as well it should. Unfortunately, there is a more likely explanation for the change. Pending regulation will likely remove the subsidy that currently ensures that the price of HFC remains artificially low.

The two **boldfaced** portions play which of the following roles?

(A) The first supports the argument's conclusion; the second calls into question that conclusion.

(B) The first supports the doctors' conclusion; the second states that conclusion.

(C) The first states the conclusion of the argument; the second supports that conclusion.

(D) The first states the doctors' conclusion; the second provides evidence used to support that conclusion.

(E) Both statements support the primary conclusion of the argument, but the second does so indirectly.

40. Though crocodiles and alligators both possess rows of sharp teeth, <u>before their food reaches the stomach the gizzard has stones swallowed earlier which further grind it.</u>

   (A) before their food reaches the stomach the gizzard has stones swallowed earlier which further grind it
   (B) before it reaches the stomach, the gizzard in which stones they have swallowed earlier is used to further grind their food
   (C) before it reaches the stomach, the gizzard in which stones swallowed earlier further grinds their food
   (D) their food is further ground into pieces in their gizzards by stones swallowed earlier before it reaches their stomach
   (E) before reaching the stomach in their gizzards, in which stones they swallow earlier further grind their food into pieces

41. Purring, <u>though often thought to be a sign of a cat's good mood, is actually an involuntary response caused by the stimulation of certain nerves.</u>

   (A) Purring, though often thought to be a sign of a cat's good mood, is actually an involuntary response caused by the stimulation of certain nerves.
   (B) Though often it is thought that cats purr because of its good mood, it is actually involuntary and responds to the cause of nerve stimulation.
   (C) Though often thought that cats purr because they are in a good mood, it is actually an involuntary response caused by the stimulation of certain nerves.
   (D) A cat's purring, though often thought to signify a good mood, is actually involuntarily a response caused by the stimulation of certain nerves.
   (E) The purring of a cat, thought often as though a sign of a good mood, is actually caused by the involuntary stimulation of certain nerves.

ON THE ACTUAL GMAT,
AFTER YOU HAVE CONFIRMED YOUR ANSWER,
YOU CANNOT RETURN TO IT.

ANSWER KEY—SAMPLE TEST

Integrated Reasoning Section

1. i. B

ii. B

2.

Could Be Classified	Could Not Be Classified	Animal
○	●	Penguin
●	○	Flamingo
○	●	Flying Squirrel
●	○	Pterodactyl
●	○	Eagle

3.

Yes	No
○	●
○	●
●	○

4.

Yes	No
○	●
○	●
○	●
●	○

5. B

6.

Either Day	Neither Day	Speaker
○	●	Branson, male, U.K.
○	○	Robinson, female, U.K.
○	○	D'Agostino, female, Brazil
●	○	Miller, female, Canada
○	○	Soares, male, India

7. i. A

   ii. B

8. B

9. True   False

10. i. A

   ii. B

11. True   False

12. Would Help Explain   Would Not Help Explain

Quantitative Section

1.	D	**11.**	B	**21.**	D	**31.**	A
2.	B	**12.**	C	**22.**	B	**32.**	C
3.	A	**13.**	D	**23.**	A	**33.**	B
4.	B	**14.**	B	**24.**	E	**34.**	C
5.	C	**15.**	E	**25.**	D	**35.**	A
6.	C	**16.**	B	**26.**	A	**36.**	E
7.	B	**17.**	E	**27.**	C	**37.**	A
8.	A	**18.**	D	**28.**	C		
9.	C	**19.**	D	**29.**	C		
10.	C	**20.**	B	**30.**	A		

Verbal Section

1.	E	**12.**	B	**23.**	C	**34.**	C
2.	B	**13.**	D	**24.**	E	**35.**	A
3.	D	**14.**	C	**25.**	A	**36.**	A
4.	A	**15.**	B	**26.**	E	**37.**	E
5.	B	**16.**	D	**27.**	A	**38.**	C
6.	E	**17.**	E	**28.**	D	**39.**	B
7.	C	**18.**	B	**29.**	B	**40.**	D
8.	C	**19.**	D	**30.**	B	**41.**	A
9.	B	**20.**	E	**31.**	A		
10.	A	**21.**	C	**32.**	D		
11.	E	**22.**	B	**33.**	E		

ANALYSIS

SELF-SCORING GUIDE
Analytical Writing

Evaluate your essay (or have a friend or teacher evaluate it for you) on the following basis. Read your essay completely, paying special attention to its logical organization and use of examples and facts to buttress its claims or position. Assign a holistic score between 0 and 6, using the scale below.

6 OUTSTANDING: Cogent, well-articulated analysis of the issue or critique of the argument. Develops a position with insightful reasons and persuasive examples. Well organized. Superior command of language and variety of syntax. Only minor flaws in grammar, usage, and mechanics.

5 STRONG: Well-developed analysis or critique. Develops a position with well-chosen examples or reasons. Generally well organized. Clear control of language and variety of syntax. Minor flaws in grammar, usage, and mechanics.

4 ADEQUATE: Competent analysis or critique. Develops a position with relevant reasons or examples. Adequately organized. Adequate control of language, but may lack syntactic variety. May have some flaws in grammar, usage, and mechanics.

3 LIMITED: Competent but clearly flawed analysis or critique. Vague or limited in developing a position. Poorly organized. Weak in using relevant examples or reasons. Language used imprecisely or lacking in sentence variety. Contains major errors or frequent minor errors in grammar, usage, and mechanics.

2 SERIOUSLY FLAWED: Serious weaknesses in analysis and organization. Unclear or seriously limited in presenting or developing a position. Disorganized. Few relevant examples or reasons. Frequent serious problems in language and sentence structure. Numerous errors in grammar, usage, or mechanics that interfere with meaning.

1 FUNDAMENTALLY DEFICIENT: Little evidence of ability to organize and develop a coherent response to issue or argument. Severe and persistent errors in language and sentence structure. Pervasive pattern of errors in grammar, usage, and mechanics that severely interfere with meaning.

0 UNSCORABLE: Illegible or not written on the assigned topic.

ANSWERS EXPLAINED

Integrated Reasoning Section

1. i. **(B)** If you look at the scatter plot, you can see a distinct relationship between the two curved lines. Assuming that one variable is always a little bit more than the other variable at each point on the graph, the relationship is very strong. Even if you assume that one variable is larger than the other at some of the points and vice versa for the rest, the relationship is still strong given that the distance apart appears small and constant. Therefore, the correct answer is **B**.

   ii. **(B)** The absolute difference between the variables at each point in the chart is constant. Therefore, the graph would be plotted along the same number across, resulting in a straight line. Since the question doesn't say which variable is plotted on the x-axis and which is plotted on the y-axis, the only possible answer of the choices given is zero. Note that if "an undefined slope" was one of the choices instead of "a slope of zero," an undefined slope would be correct. Therefore, the answer is **B**.

2. **(Could Not Be Classified, Could Be Classified, Could Not Be Classified, Could Be Classified, Could Be Classified)**
   (i) Although the penguin has the appropriate beak, its forelimbs are not adapted for flying as described in the second criterion. Therefore a penguin **could not be classified** as a bird.
   (ii) The flamingo matches both criteria given: having a beak or bill and having wings adapted for flying. Therefore a flamingo **could be classified** as a bird.
   (iii) The flying squirrel's forelimbs could technically be said to have been adapted for flying. However, the flying squirrel clearly does not have a beak as defined in the first criterion. Therefore a flying squirrel **could not be classified** as a bird.
   (iv) The pterodactyl matches both criteria given: having a beak or bill and having wings adapted for flying. Therefore a pterodactyl **could be classified** as a bird.
   (v) The eagle matches both criteria given: having a beak or bill and having wings adapted for flying. Therefore an eagle **could be classified** as a bird.

3. **(No, No, Yes)**

(i) First you need to determine the median number of employees per stores in Quebec. If you sort the chart by province, you can see that Quebec has 16 stores. Then if you sort by number of employees, you can see that the 8th and 9th largest numbers are 61 and 64, respectively. Therefore the median is 62.5. If you look quickly at the Ontario stores, you can count 27 of them. Just by going down the chart, which is already sorted by number of employees, you can quickly estimate that the median is within a group of Ontario stores with numbers of employees in the 70s. More specifically, the median is the 14th number, which is 77. Therefore the answer is **No**.

(ii) If you sort by number of employees, you can see that the St. Jean store has 59 employees and also has a grocery section. Therefore the answer is **No**.

(iii) If you sort by city, you will find more than 7 cities that have either two or three locations. Therefore the answer is **Yes**.

4. **(No, No, No, Yes)**

(i) Article 1 does mention that deforestation affects CO_2 emissions. However, no direct link is given in any article suggesting that deforestation is the only or the major cause of increasing CO_2 levels. Therefore the answer is **No**.

(ii) Both articles 1 and 2 cite that citizens vote down some environmental proposals. There is also mention of aggressive lobbying by the forestry industry. However, no direct link between the lobbying and voters striking down environment proposals is provided. Lobbying may be a strong cause but is not necessarily the main reason. Therefore the answer is **No**.

(iii) Dr. Finnegan mentions both the forestry industry and bottled-water industry in article 2. However, there is no mention of where his focus is or whether he would support one type of legislation over another. Therefore the answer is **No**.

(iv) Both articles 2 and 3 imply that scientists, one of whom is Dr. Finnegan, have opinions that differ from those of leaders of both industries. So you can say that the two parties may not always agree. Therefore the answer is **Yes**.

5. **(B)** This question is a bit tougher because you are looking for support in the articles for four of the answer choices. Only one answer is

not supported by the articles. Answer choice A is fine because article 1 mentions 20% of wildlife may become extinct. Answer choice C is supported because article 3 mentions that the price has actually tripled over the past two decades. Answer choice D is supported in article 3. Answer choice E is supported by article 1 since levels are expected to double in 50 years, which is still within the 21st century. Only answer choice B is not supported since there is no mention of vodka. Article 2 does mention that bottled water may have a premium price as a luxury item, but no specifics are given in the passage. Therefore the answer choice is **B**.

6. **(Miller, Branson)**
This problem has 3 constraints.

- Four or more international speakers are needed on Day 1.
- Four or more female speakers are needed on Day 2.
- No more than two speakers from the same country can appear on either day.

Day 1 already has four international speakers, but two are from the U.K. Therefore the only constraint that applies is that you cannot add speakers from the U.K. on Day 1. This constraint eliminates Branson and Robinson from Day 1.

Day 2 already has three female speakers. In addition, two speakers are from the U.S.A. and two are from Brazil. Therefore, you cannot add any speakers who are male, from the U.S.A., or from Brazil. These constraints eliminate Branson, D'Agostino, and Soares.

Therefore Branson can attend on neither day and Miller can attend on either day.

7. i. **(A)** Graph 1 shows that Europe and Central Asia's GDP in 1999 was approximately $10 trillion. Graph 2 shows that Europe and Central Asia's growth in 2000 was –6.0%. The increase in GDP is approximately:

$$\text{\$10 trillion} \times -0.06 = -\$0.6 \text{ trillion}$$

This amount, which converts to –$600 billion, is close to –$610 billion. Therefore the answer is **A**.

ii. **(B)** You already know from question 7. i. that Europe and Central Asia's GDP decreased by approximately $600 billion. Graph 1 shows that East Asia and Pacific have the only other significant GDP, approximately $7.5 trillion. Use the information from graph 2 and the calculator to determine the increase in GDP in 2000 for East Asia and Pacific:

$$\$7.5 \text{ trillion} \times 0.082 = \$0.62 \text{ trillion}$$

This GDP increase for East Asia and Pacific almost matches the GDP decrease for Europe and Central Asia, so they cancel out each other. You can estimate Latin America GDP growth to be approximately $0.2 trillion. Similarly, Middle East and North Africa have an approximate GDP growth of $0.1 trillion. The increase in GDP for Sub-Saharan Africa is insignificant. This total increase of approximately $0.3 trillion in GDP for all five regions, which is a little over $20 trillion, works out to approximately 1.5% growth. Therefore the closest answer is **B**.

8. **(B)** First notice how the answer choices vary. Then determine which products have a greater effect on the total cost. Goodie bags are far more expensive and have the smallest discounts, so answer choices C and E are likely to be quite high, especially since the ribbon and streamer amounts are also quite high. Next notice how many feet of ribbon and streamers are in each package. The ribbon package yields 48 feet of ribbon, while the streamer package yields 100 feet of streamers. Calculate the costs for the other answer choices:

A: ($8 × 4) + ($6 × 3) + ($4 × 3) + ($12 × 5) = $122 subtotal
$122 – ($15 ribbon discount + $10 goodie bag discount) = $97 total

B: ($8 × 7) + ($6 × 2) + ($4 × 2) + ($12 × 3) = $112 subtotal
$112 – $25 ribbon discount = $87 total

D: ($8 × 8) + ($6 × 4) + ($4 × 5) + ($12 × 2) = $132 subtotal
$132 – $25 ribbon discount = $107 total

Therefore the answer is **B**.

9. **(True, True, False)**
(i) At first glance, this problem doesn't seem to make sense. However, the trick is to consider the discounts given for large-scale spending. Since 9 packages of streamers cost $54, a $20 discount is given. This results in a total cost of only $34. In contrast, 8 packages of streamers cost $48 before the $10 discount is applied. The total cost for 8 packages of streamers is $38. Similarly, 7 packages of ribbons cost $56 minus

the $25 discount, resulting in a total cost of only $31. In contrast, 6 packages of ribbons cost $48 before the $10 discount is applied. The total cost for 6 packages of ribbons is $38. Add the amounts:

9 streamers plus 7 ribbons: $34 + $31 = $65
8 streamers plus 6 ribbons: $38 + $33 = $71

Therefore the answer is **True**.

(ii) Calculate the cost of buying 300 feet of ribbon plus 900 feet of streamers and the cost of purchasing 144 goodie bags plus 24 balloons.

300 feet of ribbon: 7 packages × $8 = $56 subtotal
$56 − $25 discount = $31 total
900 feet of streamers: 9 packages × $6 = $54 subtotal
$54 − $20 discount = $34 total
300 feet of ribbon plus 900 feet of streamers: $31 + $34 = $65
144 goodie bags: 6 packages × $12 = 72 subtotal
$72 − $10 discount = $62 total

At this point, you can stop since you know a package of balloons will cost $4 and take the price of goodie bags and balloons above the price of the ribbons and streamers. Therefore the answer is **True**.

(iii) To get the maximum discount from all four products, Sally needs to spend more than $50 for each product. She would need:

- 7 packages of ribbons totaling $56
- 9 packages of streamers totaling $54
- 13 packages of balloons totaling $52
- 5 packages of goodie bags totaling $60

The total cost looks like it would be $222. Wait! Do not forget to include the discounts. When the discounts kick in, the total amount that Sally has to spend is reduced by $25 + $20 + $10 + $10 = $65. Therefore the total amount Sally spends is $157 and the answer is **False**.

10. i. **(A)** The regression lines for both math and English scores are very close to each other. However, you can see from the scatter plot that the dotted regression line (English) has a steeper slope than the solid regression line (math). Therefore the slope for the English score regression line is greater than the slope for the Math score regression line. The answer is **A**.

ii. **(B)** The easiest way to solve this is by looking at the scatter plot and counting how often a square (math) is above a diamond (English). Excluding the points where the square and diamond are too close to tell, you can find at least 13 diamonds that are higher than squares. This represents more than half of the 22 students. Therefore the students tend to score worse in math than in English. The answer is **B**.

11. **(False, True, False)**

(i) It's important to learn how to use the data given. In order to determine the in-store price points, look at the share of market in pounds (lb.) and the share of market in dollars ($). Calculate the average price per pound ($/lb.) just by dividing share in dollars by share in pounds. Determine the price per pound of the four cheeses:

Kruger Cheddar Mild: $\dfrac{\$1.60}{2.9 \text{ lb.}}$ = $0.55/lb.

Kruger Swiss: $\dfrac{\$8.50}{7.4 \text{ lb.}}$ = $1.15/lb.

Kruger Mozzarella: $\dfrac{\$14.70}{16.2 \text{ lb.}}$ = $0.91/lb.

Davinci Havarti: $\dfrac{\$3.20}{2.7 \text{ lb.}}$ $1.86/lb.

Both cheddar and mozzarella give values of less than $1/lb. Both Swiss and Havarti give values higher than $1/lb. Looking at the other examples of these cheeses would show the same relationship. Therefore the cheddar and mozzarella are not higher priced than the Swiss and Havarti. The answer is **False**.

(ii) The best way to figure this out is by sorting by the share of market ($). You can use the calculator to add up all the shares by dollar for Swiss cheese products:

$$11.9 + 8.5 + 7.9 + 4.0 = 32.3$$

The only other competitor would be mozzarella. Add up the shares by dollar for mozzarella:

$$14.7 + 5.9 + 3.8 + 2.4 + 1.7 = 28.5$$

Therefore the answer is **True**.

(iii) The easiest way to determine King's cheese slices growth per pound is to sort by product. Then look at the change in sales vs. last year (lb.). Instead of using the calculator for a long list of numbers, just estimate. Try matching up the negative and positive values for King brand products. You should be able to estimate a little less than 70,000 lb. Now do the same for Davinci products. You will get a ballpark figure of around 90,000 lb. for Davinci. This should be enough information for you to answer the question with confidence. The answer is **False**.

12. **(Would Help Explain, Would Help Explain, Would Not Help Explain)**
    (i) If you sort by change in % volume ($), you will see that most of the zippered packages are at the top of the list. This suggests a trend where consumers favor packages with zippers and would help to explain the statement. Therefore the answer is **Would Help Explain** the statement.
    (ii) If you sort by change in % volume (lb.) or by change in % volume ($), you will notice four King products that have decreased by 100%. This would imply that they were discontinued. You may also notice that the same flavors were replaced by packages with zippers. Therefore the table **Would Help Explain** the statement.
    (iii) The table does show that the price per pound of light cheese (e.g., King Swiss Light w/ Zipper) is higher than the price per pound of regular cheese (e.g., King Swiss w/ Zipper). However, no information is given regarding the manufacturing costs of any of the sliced cheeses. Therefore the table **Would Not Help Explain** the statement.

Quantitative Section

1. **(D)** In arithmetic, a remainder is what's left after dividing a divisor into a dividend. In this case, the divisor is 320 and the dividend is 400. When we divide through we get a quotient of 0 and a remainder of 320.

2. **(B)** The best way to do this problem is to break down the prime factors. We get

$$21 = 3 \bullet 7$$
$$24 = 2 \bullet 2 \bullet 2 \bullet 3$$
$$50 = 2 \bullet 5 \bullet 5$$

Both 21 and 24 have the factor 3, but 50 does not.

3. **(A)** This is a property of numbers question. The two main ways to do this are to use your understanding of the properties of numbers or just to pick numbers and prove the answer. By definition, when you add an odd and an even number together, you always get an odd number.
For example, $3 + 4 = 7$.

4. **(B)** Let the original cost of the item be x. At a 10% discount, the market item is now $45. In order to yield a 20% profit, we get

$$1.2x = 45$$
$$x = \$37.50$$

5. **(C)** A good way to handle this question is to use a chart and calculate the amounts for each subsequent year using the percent increases given in the question:

Year	Account X	Account Y
0	$1000	$1000
1	$1100	$1100
2	$1210	$1200
3	$1331	$1300
4	$1464.10	$1400
5	$1610.51	$1500

The difference between the year 5 amounts is $110.51.

6. **(C)** First look at the cars that May sold. If the lowest selling price was $5500 and the range was $16,000, then the highest selling price was $5500 + 16,000 = \$21,500$. Similarly for June, her highest selling price was

7200 + 17,500 = $24,700. Therefore, the range of all the car prices was $24,700 − $5500 = $19,200.

7. **(B)** If we subtract the u from both sides, we get $st = 0$. We know that either s or t must be zero. However, the question tells us that s cannot be zero. Therefore, t must be zero.

8. **(A)** We're looking for the ratio of teaspoons of baking soda to cups of chocolate chips. Statement 1 gives us exactly that, saying that if we had 1 teaspoon of baking soda, there would be 3.5 cups of chocolate chips. *Sufficient*

   Statement 2 gives us the difference between the numbers of cups of chocolate chips and the number of teaspoons of baking soda. This is not enough to give us a ratio because we don't know exactly how much of each ingredient there is. *Insufficient*

9. **(C)** Statement 1 tells us that there are either two positive numbers or two negative numbers, but we still don't know anything about the other numbers in the set. *Insufficient*

   Statement 2 doesn't tell anything about what those numbers are, either positive or negative. *Insufficient*

   When we combine both statements, we have two possibilities. If both numbers from statement 1 are positive, then all numbers in between are positive. Similarly, if both numbers are negative, then all the numbers in between are negative. Either way, with an even number of integers we will always have a positive product.

10. **(C)** This is a coordinate geometry question. Each statement by itself only gives us one point of line T and no idea what the slope is. When we combine the statements, we have two points on the graph, which is all we need to calculate the slope.

11. **(B)** The best way to handle this question is to break it down into prime factors.

    In statement 1, the number 144 breaks down into $12 \cdot 12 = 2 \cdot 2 \cdot 3 \cdot 2 \cdot 2 \cdot 3$. Since dividing by y is an integer, it's possible that y could be a multiple of 3 or a multiple of 2. *Insufficient*

    In statement 2, the number 36 breaks down into $2 \cdot 3 \cdot 2 \cdot 3$. Since y is now a multiplier of 36, y must have all of the prime factors that 36 has. Therefore, y is at least a multiple of 6 and y is divisible by 3. *Sufficient*

12. **(C)** Each statement by itself is insufficient because statement 1 mentions only month Z and not month V, while statement 2 does the reverse. When we put both statements together, we can see conceptually that there are more insurance claims in month V because the average went up.

13. **(D)** The best approach to solving any work rate problem is to create a unit rate. In this case

    Machine A: 1000 widgets/5 hours = 200 widgets/hour

    Machine B: 450 widgets/3 hours = 150 widgets/hour

    We find the combined rate by just adding these 2 rates together = 350 widgets/hour.

    To produce 2000 widgets, we get $\dfrac{2000}{350} = \dfrac{40}{7} = 5\dfrac{5}{7}$ hours.

14. **(B)** This is a combinations problem because the order doesn't matter. For each subgroup—paintings, sculptures, and inventions—we first calculate the separate combinations. Then we multiply them all together. We are given 5 paintings, 5 sculptures, and 3 inventions from which to choose 3 paintings, 4 sculptures, and 2 inventions. Using standard notation we get:

    $_NC_K$(paintings) • $_NC_K$(sculptures) • $_NC_K$(inventions) = $_5C_3$ • $_5C_4$ • $_3C_2$ = (5 • 4) • 5 • 3 = 150 possible combinations.

15. **(E)** The key to this question is the word "distinct" and the fact that there are an even number of integers in the set. If the average is 12 and there are 6 integers, then the sum of the terms must be 72. If the median is 8, then the two middle numbers are 7 and 9. We want to minimize the numbers on the right-hand side, so we should maximize numbers on the left-hand side. This gives us the integers 5 and 6. At this point, we have:

$$(5, 6, 7, 9, ?, ?)$$

    The sum of the first four terms is 27. To get to 72, the next two terms must add up to 45. To create the smallest possible value of the largest number in the set the numbers should be 22 and 23.

16. **(B)** When a question contains too much information to easily manage, consider using a chart. We can set up the following:

Ingredient	Weight (%)	Cost/lb.	Weighted Cost
Raisins	30	x	$0.3x$
Bran Flakes	30	$2x$	$0.6x$
Pecans	40	$5x$	$2.0x$

We can see that the relative weighted cost of the bran flakes is $0.6x$ and the total cost is $2.9x$. The percent of the cost would be $\frac{6}{29}$ = 20.7%.

17. **(E)** By using 2 points on a coordinate plane, we can calculate the slope, which is

$$\frac{(9-3)}{(6-4)} = \frac{6}{2} = 3$$

This means that every time the y-coordinate decreases by 3, the x-coordinate decreases by 1. So if we look at (4, 3), the x-intercept will be where $y = 0$, which would be at (3, 0).

18. **(D)** The best way to do distance-rate-time (DRT) problems is with a chart. We can input the information we are given as well as the information that is implied (in bold type).

	Trip to Gym	Trip to Home	Total
D	30 km	**30 km**	60 km
R			15 km/hr.
T	2.5 hrs.	**1.5 hrs.**	4 hrs.

Since we know the total distance and the average rate required for both of the trips combined, we get 4 hours total. This means that the time to go home takes 1.5 hours. Finally, we can calculate the rate for the trip home, which is $\frac{30}{1.5}$ = 20 km/hr.

19. **(D)** We know that $J = S - 12$. We need to solve for S. To do this, you will likely need another distinct equation with J and S.

   Statement 1 gives you a relationship between J and S. Note that we don't need to create the distinct algebraic equation because you already know conceptually that we have one. *Sufficient*

   In case you're curious, the equation would be

$$J + 3 + S + 3 = 11J$$

$10J = S + 6$, combining with the original equation $J = S - 12$, we can then subtract the equations to get $9J = 18$, $J = 2$. Therefore $S = 14$.

Note that in data sufficiency problems, we do not have to solve for the equation. We just have to know that we can. Two distinct equations and two unknowns is enough to know that this statement is sufficient to solve the problem.

Statement 2 also gives you a relationship between J and S. *Sufficient.*

The equation here would be $J + 4 = \left(\dfrac{1}{3}\right)(S + 4)$.

20. **(B)** Statement 1 tells us the number of people in the group but says nothing about the bill. *Insufficient*

Statement 2 gives us the total gratuity, from which you can use the 18% to calculate the total bill. The trick here is that it doesn't matter how many friends there are as a gratuity value is all we need. *Sufficient*

21. **(D)** A good way to proceed is to draw the square

A square of side s has an area of s^2. With the changes, the area becomes $(s - 3) \bullet (s - 5)$.

Statement 1 tells us $(s - 3) \bullet (s - 5) = 35$. If you pick numbers, you can see that if s = 10, then the equation becomes $7 \bullet 5 = 35$. Thus we can determine that $s = 10$. *Sufficient*

Statement 2 tells us that $s - 3 = \left(\dfrac{7}{10}\right) \bullet s$. We can solve this equation to get

$$s - \left(\dfrac{7}{10}\right) \bullet s = 3$$

$\left(\dfrac{3}{10}\right) \bullet s = 3$, which gives us $s = 10$. *Sufficient*

22. **(B)** Statement 1 tells us that x could be an integer such as 1 or 2 or a noninteger such as $\dfrac{1}{2}$ or $\dfrac{1}{4}$. *Insufficient*

Statement 2 tells us that x could only be a noninteger. Therefore, the answer to the macro data sufficiency question is no. *Sufficient*

23. **(A)** A lot of information is provided in this question. The key is that the triangle's center point is the average of the other 3 points on the triangle. So we would get $(0, 0)$, $(10, 0)$, (x, y), which averages out to $(5, 4)$.

   If we isolate the x- and y-values we get

$$0 + 10 + x = 3 \bullet 5, \text{ therefore } x = 5.$$

$$0 + 0 + y = 4 \bullet 3, \text{ therefore } y = 12.$$

24. **(E)** Whenever we see a table in problem solving, we can usually approximate the top few possibilities. Alternatively, we can just estimate the ratios to isolate our best choices quickly. If we look at answer choices A, B, and E, their ratios are approximately 5:1. Looking more closely at our two finalists shows us that Québec's ratio is little over 6:1 and Prince Edward Island's ratio is closer to 5:1. Be careful here not to be tricked by the shuffling of the answer choices!

25. **(D)** The area of the equilateral triangle is $\dfrac{(x^2\sqrt{3})}{4}$ and the area of the square is y^2. If we set them equal to each other, we get $\dfrac{(x^2\sqrt{3})}{4} = y^2$ $\dfrac{x^2}{y^2} = \dfrac{4}{\sqrt{3}}$. If we take the square root of both sides, we get $\dfrac{x}{y} = \dfrac{2}{\sqrt[4]{3}}$

26. **(A)** Determining the correct answer to this question involves algebra, so it's particularly important to keep track of what each variable means. We can break this down into 2 parts.

   The cost per team member $= \dfrac{L}{C}$

   The cost for each remaining member when F people can't pay $= \dfrac{L}{(C-F)}$

   The additional cost for those members who can pay is $\dfrac{L}{(C-F)} - \dfrac{L}{C}$

   When we manipulate this equation to have a common denominator, we get $\dfrac{[L \bullet C - L \bullet (C - F)]}{C(C - F)} = \dfrac{FL}{(C(C - F))}$.

27. **(C)** Statement 1 doesn't tell us anything about x. *Insufficient*

   Statement 2 looks sufficient, but the original equation is an inequality with variables. Whenever that happens, we must ask ourselves, "Are we multiplying or dividing by a negative number?" Since we don't know for sure, we cannot answer the question. *Insufficient*

   When we put both statements together, we know that y is positive. So we can manipulate the equation to reach a solution. *Sufficient*

28. **(C)** Many people find operation or symbol questions difficult. The key is to understand the function given and simply replace the values given for *a* and *b*. We proceed in two steps.

$$4 \, \Omega \, 2 = \frac{2^4}{2^2} = 4$$

$$4 \, \Omega \, 5 = \frac{2^4}{2^5} = 2^{-1}$$

29. **(C)** This question appears intimidating because the calculations would be very time consuming. We need a shortcut. Whenever exponents are being added or subtracted, look for common factors to take out of each term.

You should also work with the same prime factor base, in this case 2.

$$4^{23} - 2^{40} = 2^{46} - 2^{40} = 2^{40}(2^6 - 2^0) = 2^{40}(64 - 1)$$
$$= 2^{40}(63) = 2^{40}(3 \bullet 3 \bullet 7).$$

The highest prime factor here is 7.

30. **(A)** Whenever you see variables and inequalities in data sufficiency problems, consider using properties of numbers, algebraic manipulation, and picking numbers as strategies.

Let's jump ahead to statement 2, which has no mention of *z*. *Insufficient*

By examining the information provided in statement 1, we see that the question is really asking if $z > x$? Statement 1 tells us exactly that. *Sufficient*

31. **(A)** Suppose we have a true or false test with only one question. The probability that we will get the right answer is $\frac{1}{2}$. If the test had 2 questions, the probability of getting all questions right would be $\frac{1}{4}$. So using this construct, we should be able to see a pattern.

$$P(3 \text{ questions right}) = \frac{1}{8} \text{ or } \frac{1}{2^3}$$

$$P(4 \text{ questions right}) = \frac{1}{16} \text{ or } \frac{1}{2^4}$$

So the real question is what powers of 2 are greater than 1000? The answer is $2^{10} = 1024$.

32. **(C)** By looking at the answer choices, we can see that this problem has complicated values. We need to break it down into 2 sections. First, let's calculate the rates that this question requires.

$$R_B = \frac{1}{15} \text{ job/hr.}$$

$$R_C = \frac{1}{18} \text{ job/hr.}$$

$$R_{B\&C} = \frac{1}{15} + \frac{1}{18} = \frac{(6+5)}{90} = \frac{11}{90} \text{ job/hr.}$$

This means that the time it takes machines B and C working together is $\frac{90}{11}$ hours. Similarly, calculate the rate of all 3 machines working together.

$$\frac{11}{90} + \frac{1}{12} = \frac{(22+15)}{180} = \frac{37}{180} \text{ job/hr.}$$

So the time it takes all 3 machines to complete the job is $\frac{180}{37}$ hours. The ratio would reduce to $\frac{1}{11} : \frac{2}{37}$.

33. **(B)** This is a Venn diagram problem. Draw it out, and input the information that you know.

Total: 400

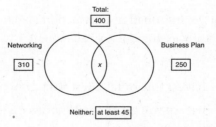

When we use the standard formula for Venn diagrams, we get

Total = Networking + Business Plan + Neither − Both

400 = 310 + 250 + at least 45 − x

x = at least 205

We can't have more than 250 people taking the business plan workshop since that is the total amount possible from our Venn diagram.

34. **(C)** Equilateral triangles have angles of 60° and UT is perpendicular to RS. Thus angle UTS is 30° and triangle UTS is a 30-60-90 triangle. Using 30-60-90 ratios, which are $1 : \sqrt{3} : 2$, we can calculate that $UT = 2\sqrt{3}$. Now we can calculate the area of both triangles.

$$\text{Area of equilateral triangle} = S\frac{2\sqrt{3}}{4} = \frac{(6^2 \sqrt{3})}{4} = 9\sqrt{3}$$

$$\text{Area of smaller triangle} = \frac{1}{2} b \bullet h$$

$$= \frac{1}{2} \bullet 2 \bullet 2\sqrt{3} = 2\sqrt{3}$$

Therefore the area of quadrilateral $QRUT$ is

$$9\sqrt{3} - 2\sqrt{3} = 7\sqrt{3} \, .$$

35. **(A)** The best way to solve DRT problems is with a chart. With data sufficiency questions, it's always good to sort out what we know, both direct and implied. Note that the bathroom break shouldn't matter because the question says driving time. If we fill in the chart, using hours instead of minutes for the time, we get the following. Given information is in bold type.

	Hazzard to Beaufort	**Beaufort to Hazzard**	**Total**
D			
R	**R = 40 miles/hr**		
T	0.5 hours	want 0.25 hours	

We want the time back to be 15 minutes. We need more information on the distance and rate that Sheriff Roscoe traveled on his trip from Hazzard County to Beaufort County.

Statement 1 gives us the average rate from Hazzard to Beaufort. From this, we can calculate the distance from Hazzard to Beaufort because $D = rt = (0.5) \bullet 40 = 20$ miles. We can then calculate the required rate to get back in half the time using 20 miles $= (R_{back}) \bullet (0.25 \text{ hours})$. This will give us that the rate would be 80 mph.

A simpler way to do this is to realize that once we know the original rate is 40 mph, then we just need to double the rate in order to half the time going back. *Sufficient*

Statement 2 gives us the rate from Hazzard to Jethro. There is no way to determine how far Jethro is from Beaufort. Be careful that you don't assume it is halfway there. Statement 1 may have told you the distance was 20 miles, but you can't take information from one statement and apply it to another statement. You need to look at each statement independently. *Insufficient*

36. **(E)** Statement 1 gives us no information about the middle elements in the set, so we have no idea how many elements are in sets x and y. *Insufficient*

    Even though statement 2 tells us that the range of set y is greater than the range of set x, we still do not know all of the actual elements. The average of the elements may vary greatly. Standard deviation is a measurement of the spread of numbers around the mean. *Insufficient*

    When we put both statements together, it appears that we have quite enough information for sufficiency. We know the first two terms and the last two terms are equal, and we know the range of y is greater than the range of x. However, depending on the number of elements in the set, the mean could vary significantly. Therefore, we cannot determine which set has the higher standard deviation. *Insufficient*

37. **(A)** To solve this, what we really need to know is if there are more white marbles than red marbles in the jar, or if $w > r$. What does statement 1 tell us? Well, we may assume that if g is the same on both sides of the denominator (say $g = 1$), then the equation implies that $w > r$. This would allow us to answer the question. Is it possible, though, that r, g, and w are negative? No, because you cannot have a negative number of marbles. Be careful about the assumptions you make in the question. Thus, we can answer the question. *Sufficient*

    For statement 2, we can rearrange the equation to get $g > r + w$.

    This only tells us that the jar has more green marbles than any other types of marbles. We don't know whether $r > w$ or $w > r$. Therefore, we are unable to answer the question. *Insufficient*

Verbal Section

The passage for questions 1–3 appears on page 361.

1. Main Point questions are often made easier with a firm understanding of the author's tone, but not in this case, as all the answer choices are neutral in tone. Luckily, the content of this passage is not hard to ascertain. Answer Choice (E) works, as long as we realize that the *one manner* is the use of disposable products (and the subsequent need for recycling) and the *technological progress* is the changes to consumer goods mentioned as following the Industrial Revolution.

   (E) The incorrect answers to this question are mostly of the "hoping to catch you sleeping" variety. Answer Choices (A) and (C) are mentioned, but they aren't the main idea (**part not the whole**), and Answer Choices (B) and (D) are both **real-world ideas** the test maker hopes you let bleed into your understanding of the passage.

2. Whenever a passage contains a list of examples or a list of features of some phenomenon, a Detail EXCEPT question is always a good bet to expect. Usually, three of the details are found right next to each other, while one requires a bit of hunting (and is disguised through the clever use of synonyms). Here, there's no hidden answer; instead, one example is stated in two different ways (another way to get four wrong answers from a list of three examples). The incorrect answer is usually a **distortion** or a **misused detail**, and Answer Choice (B) is both. Landfills are mentioned, though using them repeatedly is something said to have happened when there weren't any landfills.

   (B) Answer Choices (A) and (E) are both a restatement of the example of *clothing too frayed and threadbare to itself be salvaged [used] to patch and repair clothing not quite so worn*. Answer Choice (C) is an oblique way of saying that the rags used for sopping up spills of precious oils are later used as fire starters in cooking fires (the end of the first paragraph). And, finally, Answer Choice (D) is the example of the tablecloth from later in the passage, a furnishing later cut up to be used as cleaning rags.

3. While finding the function of an example usually requires reading a few lines up, there might as well have been a colon following the immediately previous sentence, since the rhetorical question is just an example of *an innovation no eighteenth- or nineteenth-century maid would ever have predicted*. Recognize that since the maids wouldn't have

understood the problem, it must be a modern one, and Answer Choice (D) becomes the clear choice.

(D) Beware of Answer Choice (A), a **distortion** placed earlier in the answer choice list in hopes of your not reading all the answers or reading the answers all the way through. The maids are here, but the question doesn't explain *why* they were frugal. Answer Choice (B) is an **irrelevant comparison** never made though suggested by the first line of the passage. Speaking of suggestions, our author never makes them, eliminating Answer Choice (C), which is probably also a **distortion**, since in this passage it's actually the things now considered useless (torn tablecloths) that were once considered valuable. Answer Choice (D) is actually almost the **opposite** of the passage's content, though reasonable if seen through modern prejudices. In this passage, something today seen as frugal (reusing every scrap) was just what you did, affluent and impoverished households alike, because there weren't any disposables available to anyone.

4. **Argument**: The conclusion is the **prediction** given at the end: *this practice (giving rewards to the best employees) will backfire when the other employees find out*, supported by a single piece of evidence (that's stated twice) that anything that reduces morale reduces profits. Thus, the argument must assume that *the policy will affect the morale of some employees negatively*. Strengthening the argument means supporting this assumption, which Answer Choice (A) does directly.

(A) Answer Choices (B) and (C) are **irrelevant comparisons** that do not concern the argument's assumptions; Answer Choice (D) is meant to seem reasonable, though it's **one step removed** from relevant and the **opposite** of what we want (as if it were true, *and* we knew that the increases were huge, it would weaken the argument). Answer Choice (E) is just additional **evidence for the evidence**, further explaining the positive effect the bonuses have on the employees who get raises; it's the ones that don't that really matter to us.

5. **Argument:** The conclusion is the **definite prediction** that *Richard will surely begin using the golf course*, supported by two pieces of evidence: (1) Richard is a member of the club and (2) membership is required in order to use the course. The evidence would make for a good **applied rule** argument, but the speaker instead **confuses**

necessity and sufficiency as Answer Choice (B) indicates by taking the fact that the meeting is a *requirement* (having a membership) is itself a *guarantee*.

(B) The answers would mostly be flaws if they had been done, but our speaker never did them. We have no evidence that there are any *exceptions* as in Answer Choice (A), no *multiple options* as in Answer Choice (C), no *group/whole confusions* as in Answer Choice (D), and no *contradiction* as in Answer Choice (E).

6. **Issues: subject/predicate agreement** (*The Black Death... resulted*), **modification** (the correct form of *nearly one-third*)

    (E) Though separated by the distracting parenthetical phrase, the subject *The Black Death* is *singular* and needs a verb in the **predicate form**, eliminating Answer Choices (A) and (B)'s *resulting*. The descriptive phrase after the *people,* needs the proper form to maintain the meaning that the *nearly one-third* is a subdivision of the *75 million*. Answer Choice (B)'s placement of *nearly* is wrong, Answer Choice (C)'s switch to *nearing* makes the *of whom* nonsensical, and Answer Choice (D)'s *one nearly a third* is a random **word salad**.

7. **Issues: idiom: redundant constructions** (*enabled... to be able*), **connecting clauses** (avoiding parallel but nonsensical constructions by eliminating the *and*), and **idiomatic construction** (of *enabled* + *infinitive*)

    (C) Because *enabled* already means *to be able*, the *able*s in Answer Choices (A) and (E) are redundant. The *and* in Answer Choices (A), (B), (D), and (E) sets up a two-part coordination of things that the research enabled silicon to do, which is nonsensical, as silicon can't open a possibility. Idiomatically, the word *enable* takes the infinitive *to emit* rather than Answer Choice (D)'s *emit* or (E)'s *be able to emit*.

8. **Issues: sequence of tenses** (*were treated... had been freed*), **passive voice** (the *by the Emancipation Proclamation* demands a verb in the passive), **connecting clauses** (making sensible the relationship between the clauses in the sentence)

    (C) As written, the sentence is a confused mess. The *African Americans* were *treated* as *second-class citizens*, not the other way around, as in Answer Choices (A) and (E). The *Emancipation Proclamation* in the non-underlined sentence is treated as the *instrument* by which the freeing was conducted, meaning that the final verb in the underlined section needs to be in the passive voice (X was verbed by Y); Answer Choice (B)'s *free by* makes no sense as an alternative. The relationship between the last clause and the rest of the sentence could work with either *even though* or *despite*, but Answer Choice (D)'s *even they had* won't work.

9. **Argument:** Since this is an EXCEPT question, we can expect an argument with *lots* of assumptions. The argument's conclusion is an **explanation** of what happened in a situation, or how a **plan** was successful. The situation was a city with a high traffic problem where mimes replaced traffic cops and the problem went down. The explanation has multiple parts, each of which requires an assumption: (1) the traffic problem was a problem of *compliance with the law* (and thus, we must assume *not something else*), (2) it was shame rather than punishment (so we assume that *mimes are shaming and not punishing*), (3) the mimes caused the reduction (requiring everything a **causal connection** must assume), and (4) the specific things the mimes did were relevant (assuming it was the *following and mimicking,* not something else). Answer Choice (B) has nothing to do with any of these assumptions; it is meant to appear as though it is addressing a **representativeness** assumption, which this argument does not require.

(B) Answer Choice (A) addresses the assumption in part 2; Answer Choice (C) is required for the **causal connection**; Answer Choice (D) eliminates an **alternate explanation** (again part of the causal connection); and Answer Choice (E) addresses part 1.

10. **Argument:** The stem points us to the argument's conclusion (the study's explanation): *the benefits (of matching funds paid to flexible healthcare accounts) did more than just what was expected (reduced insurance costs and extra compensation).* The evidence is mostly **setup information** that explains what happened in this situation: (1) the analysis took three years; (2) it concerned the tech industry only; (3) on average, studied companies that used the matching funds had a lower absentee rate than those that didn't. The correct answer weakens the argument by attacking the necessary assumption that the participants in the study were **representative**—or, in other words, there was nothing special about them, like what Answer Choice (A) describes. (Selective companies might be able to hire employees who are so good that they have a low absentee rate anyway.)

(A) Answer Choices (B) and (E) are the **exact opposite** of the answer, as they actually **strengthen** the argument, adding additional benefits to the practice said to be beneficial in other ways. Answer Choice (C) is **reasonable but irrelevant**, since however difficult it is for employees to take advantage of the program, that difficulty would be the case throughout the study's participants. Answer Choice (D) is an **irrelevant comparison** to other industries (also a **closed issue**, as the **setup** limits the study only to tech companies).

The passage for questions 11–14 appears on page 367.

11. **Question:** Because it asks us to relate two different facts in the passage, which goes beyond merely confirming a correct detail, this is a Function question. The function will accord with the author's overall goal, which, as indicated in Question 1 above, was to describe how two experiments suggest a new direction for research, which is almost exactly what Answer Choice (E) says.

    (E) Answer Choice (A) is out because there are no anomalous findings in the passage. Answer Choice (B) is the same as Answer Choice (A,) merely rearranging the order of the two experiments, but there are still no anomalous findings. The author never censures or otherwise casts doubt on the researchers, so Answer Choice (C) is a no-go. And Answer Choice (D) doesn't work because the author merely enthusiastically describes the experiments; no argument is made that says they're correct or that they prove anything.

12. **Question:** When the question asks what was true according to the author or passage, it is a Detail question. The correct answer (B).

    (B) Although the author does suggest that the researcher's equipment was more precise than previously available, the author does not state that the researchers were uniquely able to create it, so Answer Choice (A) is out. Answer Choice (C) is a **distortion**, a garbled account of the experiments, as is Answer Choice (D). Answer Choice (E) is meant to be **reasonable but unmentioned**, as the gear does come off as new and shiny, but there is no suggestion that the findings could not have been obtained without it.

13. **Question:** Answering this inference question requires keeping track of the details that are assigned to the brain in "waking mode" and "sleeping mode" as well as understanding that because Tononi's research is cited

as a revolutionary discovery in the field of neuroscience, anything first detected in his team's research would qualify as surprising to neuroscientists working prior to his team's effort. This allows Answer Choice (D) to be inferred.

(D) Answer Choice (A) would not be surprising because delta wave activity (lines 21–22) is the hallmark of a brain in sleeping mode (or unconscious as the question phrases it), so neuroscientists before Tononi would surely expect this. Answer Choice (B) is a **misused detail**, as the implantation of electrodes in the rats' brains is a technique employed by Tononi, not a discovery. Answer Choice (C) could never have been surprising, as we are told in lines 3–5 that neuroscientists have long thought this very thing. Answer Choice (E) is **too extreme** an inference from the information given; we know from the passage that delta wave activity is characteristic of the sleeping brain, but we do not know that it is the ONLY activity that could be detected.

14. **Question:** In the first paragraph, the author introduces a supposition held by neuroscientists who study sleep, namely that sleep is a "whole brain phenomenon," that being awake and being asleep are entirely different mental states. The author then presents the work of a scientist, Tononi, whose research challenges that supposition. He details the researchers' technique in the second and third paragraphs and concludes by suggesting that the work may one day have a highly sought after effect, increasing scientists' understanding of sleep itself. Overall, the author is mostly descriptive, though there is no hint of censure or disapproval of the research he describes, and thus Answer Choice (C) is the best match.

(C) Answer Choice (A) is **half-right/half-wrong** because nowhere does the author point to future hurdles or any other possible negative consequence to the research. Answer Choice (B) is another **half-right/half-wrong** because there are no practical therapies discussed in the passage. Answer Choice (D) has the **wrong tone**, as the author has no words of critique for anyone and remains neutral to positive on everything discussed in the passage. Likewise, Answer Choice (E) has the **wrong tone** because *lamenting* suggests disapproval, but the author never speaks in disapproving terms in the passage (additionally, practical applications and lost promise are not discussed in the passage).

15. **Issues: pronoun agreement** (*a nation… its*), **coordination** (creating a correctly coordinated list of things the nation *is required to [do]*), and **idiomatic construction** (picking a relationship between *research* and *increasing* that is both grammatically correct and that makes sense in context)

    (B) Because *a nation* is a singular noun phrase, *its* is required, eliminating the *theirs* in Answer Choices (A), (C), and (D). Whether it is the nation that requires or the Kyoto Protocol (though the latter makes more sense), the requirement is compound because of the later *and*, meaning **parallel** forms are needed for both the reducing of greenhouse gas emissions and the researching—Answer Choices (C) and (D) fail by having the first as a verb in the infinitive (*to reduce*) and the second as a prepositional followed by a gerund (*to increasing* or *to researching*). Answer Choice (E) fails to construct a correct idiom to connect the non-underlined *in technology* with its *research increasing in technology*.

16. **Issues: sequence of tenses** (*had predicted… were surprised*), **idiomatic construction** (*predicted for, losses in value*), **modification** (a sensible form for and placement of *continuing*)

    (D) Because the prediction happened at an earlier point in time than the rally, the **past perfect** *had predicted* is needed, the only tense prior to the non-underlined **past tense** *posted*, eliminating Answer Choices (A) and (B). Answer Choice (C)'s version of the *continuing losses* question is the only one that is absolutely wrong, and Answer Choice (E) has an unacceptable version of the idiom used to connect value and loss.

17. **Issues: parallelism** (the coordinated list of things the researchers *are working on* doing), **subject/predicate agreement** (*is/are working*), **idiomatic construction** (*working on* versus *working to*)

    (E) The subject of the sentence, *researchers*, is plural, requiring *are* and eliminating Answer Choices (A) and (B)'s *is*. The *and* creates a compound object for what the researchers are working on or working to do, and each element must be the same form and have the same complement of small words attached. Thus, Answer Choices (B) and (C)'s *to develop… investigating* are out, as is Answer Choice (D)'s *development… the investigation*.

Both *working on* and *working to* are correct idioms, but *working on* has to be followed by a noun like *development* (or a verb in the noun form called a **gerund** like *developing*), while the *to* in *working to* is generally part of an infinitive verb (*to develop*). You can't mix and match, as Answer Choice (C) tries to do.

18. **Argument:** The subject of the argument is probably familiar, so it is important not to let **real-world thinking** intrude. The argument's structure should also be familiar; **somebody says X (and they're wrong)**: somebody says the first bolded statement (that when guns are outlawed, only outlaws will have guns) is the best way to understand why gun legislation fails, and the speaker in the argument thinks this is wrong, preferring instead the explanation given in the unbolded section that follows. The prompt concludes by restating the thing that the two competing explanations are trying to explain, given in bold, which is why gun legislation will fail. Thus, Answer Choice (B) is the correct description of the roles of the statements, though it is tricky for one reason. The second statement is described as "a conclusion about certain plans"—which is not the same as saying the author's *overall conclusion*, but is a plausible way to describe what the author says.

    (B) If you realized that neither statement is *evidence* for a position (either the author's or the **somebody** who **says X**), Answer Choices (A) and (E) could be eliminated quickly. Answer Choices (C) and (D) both call the first statement a **prediction**, which it isn't—it's an **explanation** used as evidence to support a prediction (that gun legislation won't work).

The passage for questions 19–21 appears on page 372.

19. **Question:** With short dense passages like this one, it can often be difficult to spot the author's main idea. In such cases, you can fall back on your Critical Reasoning skills, knowing that Reading Comprehension passages are almost always an argument of some sort. Here, the author's conclusion comes at the very end of the passage (helpfully pointed out by the conclusory keywords "in the end"); thus, Answer Choice (D) is the correct answer.

    (D) Because the answer choices all begin with verbs, a **vertical scan** can assist your process of elimination on the first pass. Answer Choices (A) and (E) both have the **wrong tone**, since the author isn't directly attacking someone else's conclusion. Answer Choice (B) arguably has the wrong tone as well, but should be checked, since neutral verbs (like *describe*) can be used to mask positive tones—though that doesn't happen here, where it instead introduces a **part not the whole** (since characteristics of the tomb are in fact given in the passage). Choosing between Answer Choices (D) and (C) is the final task, and the *inevitably biased* is **too extreme** to describe our passage, so Answer Choice (C) is out.

20. **Question:** The complicated stem hides a simple and familiar **Inference** task. **Apply** the author's conclusion, which is a sort of **rule**, to a **specific case**. The author's rule says that when an art historian praises a feature as being objectively better, that usually reveals more about their personal values than about the artwork itself. Thus, Answer Choice (E) is the correct inference resulting from applying that rule to this particular case in which one of the three virtues is singled out as being better than the other two.

    (E) Answer Choices (A) and (B) exist to trick those who only skimmed the passage, ultimately the **exact opposite** of what our author believes, which is that historians' appraisals don't actually correspond to which artist likely made a particular piece of the tomb. Answer Choice (C) is, however, **too extreme**—though the author is skeptical of such evaluations, the passage doesn't go so far as to say these evaluations are *always* wrong. (D) brings up something possible in the real world, but for which there is no information here.

21. **Question:** More difficult passages often ask multiple **Inference** questions, so the later a passage comes in your test, the more you should be on the lookout as you read the passage for the common **Inference** clues. Here, you might have noticed that the only really definite information is the author's conclusion, and Answer Choice (C) is a **but that's too obvious!** restatement of that conclusion. The art historians' attributions aren't valuable for information about the work, but they are valuable to people studying art historians.

    (C) Answer Choice (A) is an **irrelevant comparison** that's ultimately unsupported by the passage's definite information. Answer Choices (B) and (E) are **reasonable but unsupported**, things we might conclude if we heard someone making this argument in real life but that will never be the correct answer to a GMAT Inference question. Answer

Choice (D) goes **too extreme** to the claim that there is *no worth* to these art historians' evaluations of the tomb.

22. **Argument: Weaken EXCEPT** sets up an argument with many assumptions or a single assumption with lots of ways to attack it. Here, it's sort of both at the same time, as the speaker concludes that *"goal-oriented" personalities* **cause** *people to become CEO's*, based on evidence of a **correlation** between the two found in a **study**. Answer Choices (A) and (C) attack the **feasibility assumptions** this study relies upon, that CEOs actually know what their own personalities are and could possibly describe them. Answer Choice (D) attacks the **causal connection** somewhat subtly, by showing the correlation might be coincidental (since the appearance of one of the two parts of the correlation is unpredictable and changes a lot), and Answer Choice (E) attacks another **feasibility assumption** that goes with **studies**, probably the most common assumption, which is that studies must be **representative**.

    (B) Answer Choice (B) fails to weaken the argument because though it suggest a sort of bias to the study, it's a bias that we would require more information to verify was in fact a bias. How do we know that bonuses change the evaluations of employees in one consistent way that would bias the results? Thus, the answer is **one step removed** from the assumption of **representativeness** of the **study**.

23. **Issues: connecting clauses** (semicolons and linking independent clauses with conjunctions), **pronoun reference** (*commissions... they*)

    (C) The semicolons in Answer Choices (A), (B), and (D) would require what followed to be an independent clause, but Answer Choices (A)'s *as* and (D)'s *that* both render the clauses attached **dependent**. Answer Choice (B)'s *a violation of* lacks a verb, so is essentially an unacceptable stray fragment. That leaves only Answer Choices (C) and (E), which both share the less often used compound conjunction *but rather* (used correctly with a comma to link two independent clauses) whose unfamiliarity is used to steer you away from the correct answer. Both Answer Choices (C) and (E) also introduce pronouns, but Answer Choice (E)'s singular *it* does not match the antecedent *commissions*, which is plural.

24. **Argument:** The argument concludes that Offshoot will close within the next year, a very specific **prediction**, based on the evidence that there

is **one problem** (one disadvantage) that Offshoot faces and information about the past. To strengthen this argument, we must support one of its assumptions; here, Answer Choice (E) supports the assumption that *the past will be representative of the future* (an assumption always implicit with **predictions**).

(E) Answer Choice (A) is **too extreme** and **irrelevant corroboration**. Answer Choice (B) relies on confusing this argument for one involving **formal logic**. Answer Choice (C) is meant to be tempting as it is something we might reasonably expect, but which doesn't actually strengthen the argument (and it might even **weaken** the prediction). Answer Choice (D) is **one step removed** from the argument's assumptions, since the argument never tells us that the reason Offshoot will fail has anything to do with how it makes *the majority* of its money (instead relying on the less extreme evidence that *part* of Offshoot's revenue stream will be endangered).

25. **Issues: idiomatic construction** (*if* versus *whether*), **the subjunctive** (of command, for *recommend* AND *consider*)

    (A) On the GMAT, if is always used for hypotheticals (*if it rains, we will get wet*), *whether* for choices or options, so Answer Choices (D) and (E) are out. The verbs *consider* and *recommend* require that a version of the subjunctive be used, the subjunctive of command, which requires either *consider/recommend* + *infinitive* or *consider/recommend* + *be* + *past participle*. Because they are command/demand verbs, *consider* and *recommend* also should not be followed by *should*, which eliminates Answer Choices (B), (C), (D), and (E) all in one fell swoop. Additionally, the *or not* is considered redundant by the GMAT when paired with *whether*, as in Answer Choice (C).

26. **Argument:** Be careful! Even though there is a **plan** given, the conclusion is a **prediction** about something that will (fail to) follow in the wake of the plan, not that the plan itself will or won't work. The prediction is that the average price of middle-tier cars won't fall significantly, based on the evidence that only the one major automaker will be reducing its prices. Answer Choice (E) states the conclusion directly, although it masks the conclusion through synonyms and the reordering of words.

    (E) Answer Choices (A), (B), and (D) are all pieces of **setup information** describing the little world in which the argument takes place. Answer Choice (C) is a piece of **evidence** used to support the conclusion.

27. <u>**Issues: connecting clauses**</u> (one dependent, one independent), **idiomatic construction** (here a distraction)

    (A) The sentence is correct as written. Later answer choices either add too many subordinating words, turning the sentence into two dependent clauses linked by a comma—as Answer Choices (C) and (D) do—or delete the *but* and turn the sentence into two independent clauses linked by a comma—Answer Choices (E) and (B). The former is a sentence fragment, the later a run-on, and both are incorrect. The choice between *may* and *might* and the various changes to *as a, to be,* etc. are simply distractions and there is no grammatical reason to rule any of them out.

28. <u>**Issues: idiomatic construction**</u> (the rare idiom *twice again that number*), **connecting clauses**

    (D) Though a bit obscure, *<some number> and nearly half again that number* is a correct English construction. The stray *that* in the middle of the idiom in Answer Choice (E), however, is not. The *were* in Answer Choice (A) does not ruin the idiom, but it does turn the sentence into a run-on, two independent clauses connected by a conjunction without a comma (*The battle was... and nearly half... were wounded*). Answer Choices (B) and (C) botch the idiom and make the sentence nonsensical.

The passage for questions 29–32 appears on page 378.

29. <u>**Question:**</u> Asking for a title to a passage is a way of asking about the passage as a whole, a less common variant on the standard Global question. The best title for a passage will be one reflecting the author's overall purpose. In the end, Answer Choice (B) proves the best title, concocting a clever play on words out of two things the author explicitly says in the passage that comprise his main point: (1) Calabresi's theories are insightful, and (2) his insufficient attention to the implications of his own hypothetical commitments is an oversight.

    Because the implication of specific words in a title may not always be immediately clear, it is often best to start these questions with a process of elimination.

(B) Answer Choice (A) is wrong because there is no indication that the relevance of Calabresi's work has changed over time; Answer Choice (C) is wrong because this title would be appropriate for something like the opposite of this passage. Our author takes a respected theory and shows it has a big hole (that doesn't completely invalidate its worth); the passage this title suits would take a theory thought to have a hole in it and show it should be respected; Answer Choice (D) can be eliminated because there is neither real-world data in the passage nor a confirmation of Calabresi's work; Answer Choice (E) is meant to be tempting, but it does not go far enough (the passage does represent a reconsideration of Calabresi; however, the point is not to prove his influence but to critique him).

30. **Question:** Asking what the author must believe, but did not "say" or "state" is asking us to make an Inference. The information necessary to eliminate the wrong answers is scattered across the passage, but the correct answer may be derived from the author's description of Calabresi's hypotheticals in line 25 and from his overall attitudes toward Calabresi's theories (that they have serious problems, but nevertheless provide valuable insights). Since the author both believes that Calabresi oversimplifies things in his analysis and that his theories should not be rejected outright, our author must believe Answer Choice (B).

(B) Answer Choice (A) is wrong because although both rational self-interest and behavior traditionally punished by courts are mentioned, they are not given as a reason to avoid economic considerations. Answer Choice (C) is built on a true fact that the author does seem dismissive of people who worry over rhetorical weaknesses, but they are never said to be the least important problems. There may be a great many problems that the author would be even more dismissive of. Answer Choice (D) is a confused and incorrect version of Calabresi's main argument. Answer Choice (E) should seem like a probable extension of Calabresi's work, and we do know that the author feels Calabresi's work is incomplete, but we do not know that the author would extend Calabresi in precisely this way, nor do we know that the author believes that only theories like Calabresi's will work.

31. **Question:** Because it asks us to make a determination based on Calabresi's argument, the question demands a correctly drawn Inference. And because it is an EXCEPT question, four of the answers correspond

directly to information presented in the passage. The question is further complicated by asking us for four contradictions to that information. The correct answer thus requires an exception to a contradiction, which could be either something that is necessarily true on the basis of something Calabresi said or something that we lack information about. To put it another way, if the passage lacks information on a subject, then we cannot say that subject is contradicted by the passage.

The correct answer (A) is a bit subtle. We do know from the author's description of Calabresi's theory in the first paragraph that Calabresi's legal theory involves weighing the costs of avoiding risks. The passage does not go so far as to say that Calabresi demands that every possible real world cost or real world harm should be included in our legal theories. Since it remains possible that there are some harms Calabresi allows to be excluded, this answer choice does not contradict Calabresi's theories.

(A) (B) is wrong because it contradicts lines 4–5 which clearly state that any mitigation of risk inevitably involves a harm of some sort under Calabresi's view. (C) is out because lines 30–33 indicate that according to Calabresi's theories, insurance companies will not ignore the costs associated with Marshall's behavior if they follow the dictates of rational self-interest. This answer says this should never happen. (D) won't work because we know from the author's explanation of Calabresi's theory in the first paragraph that it explains why we would not accept a 5mph speed limit in exchange for the many human lives that would be saved; thus, Calabresi doesn't believe theories that take the value of human life into account must fail, rather the opposite. (E) is the **exact opposite** of what we want: we are told Calabresi's theory insists society should incentivize behavior that is currently punished (thus, improper).

32. **Question:** When a question asks about what an author would agree with, rather than what is stated directly in the passage, we are dealing with an Inference question. The correct answer is (D). The author's approval of the general idea of using risk aversion costs in order to calculate accident costs can be found at the end of the first paragraph. That Calabresi's theories do not exactly explain how to determine these costs is the author's chief criticism of them. Nevertheless, this criticism does not mean that we ought to reject the general theory, just refine it somehow.

(D) Answer Choice (A) takes something the author says in passing, that there is a certain ends/means tension in Calabresi's view, and incorrectly concludes the author expects the theory to meet with popular disapproval, a **misused detail**. If anything, the author seems to take it as a given that Calabresi's theories have been widely accepted, even though they remain open for critique. Answer Choice (B) concerns what the author thinks about economic affairs broadly, which is not information included in this passage, so we may make no certain inferences about it. Answer Choice (C) is another **misused detail**, a **distortion**, as we know Calabresi's theory supplanted previous views and that he uses Neoclassical economic theory, but these two thoughts are not connected in any meaningful way by the author. Answer Choice (E) is out because even though Calabresi's theories do advocate outcomes that are counter to the current behavior of courts (their jurisprudence), the author does not connect this idea to a rule that demands we reject Calabresi's theories.

33. **Issues: comparisons, modification**

    (E) When a word such as *unlike* begins a sentence, it's a clear key to look for a comparison error. Entities compared must be parallel, both grammatically and logically. In Answer Choices (A) and (D), *older televisions* are compared with *shielding* (a property of TVs), which is incorrect. Answer Choices (B) and (C) add or change words that create peculiar nonsense—shielding doesn't allow something to be lighter, as (B) would have it, nor is there a person or entity that allows televisions to be a certain weight, as in (C).

34. **Facts:** Because this is an **Inference** prompt, you should read it on the lookout for **definite information** or other common **Inference** keys. The correct answer is a very safe inference (note the "at least one" language) based on the rule in the middle of the prompt: *it (tied aid) inevitably results in economies more dependent on foreign money* (the answer's "one economic problem" that is exacerbated). The first half of the answer is meant to distract you away from this simple **rule application** inference, as it is true that nowhere does the argument tell us that anyone is motivated "purely by ethical concerns," but the rule applies to any case in which tied aid is used (and thus even those cases not explicitly described in the passage).

(C) Answer Choice (A) is out because we have no rules by which to infer whether an outcome is *ethical* (just its economic effects); Answer Choice (B) is **reasonable but unsupported**, since the motives for aid aren't given to us in the prompt. Answer Choice (D) is an **irrelevant comparison**, as we have no rules explaining the *degree* to which anything will be frowned upon, and Answer Choice (E) is as well, since *other economic factors* are beyond the information given.

35. **Issues: pronoun** (both agreement and avoiding ambiguous *them*), **idiomatic construction** *(if* versus *when)*

    (A) The sentence is correct as written. Answer Choices (B) and (C) change the *their* to *it*, making the pronoun no longer agree with the plural *gasses*. Answer Choice (C) also introduces a stray *within* that would be ungrammatical preceding *in the presence*. Answer Choices (D) and (E) change the *when* to *if*, which makes the meaning of the sentence ambiguous (does the completion of the outer orbital only make them less reactive if there are other atoms around or less reactive if brought into contact with other atoms?). Answer Choice (D)'s switch to *comma-which* is not problematic, but also not necessary. And finally, Answer Choice (D)'s *because of completing* is almost never deemed acceptable by the GMAT.

36. **Argument:** The argument's conclusion is found in the confusingly worded final sentence, which we could rephrase as *ancient histories that survive must still be valuable even if we can't see the value.* This conclusion is supported by a chain of **formal logic** that might not apply to all situations. A book's being recopied is a guarantee that it spoke to people. But the argument still assumes that all histories that currently survive have been recopied, and Answer Choice (A) strengthens the argument by eliminating an **alternate explanation** for how a book could survive (that lots of copies were made in the book's "original print run," allowing for it to survive attrition without ever being recopied).

    (A) All the wrong answers are bits of formal logic that are either **irrelevant** to the relationship between conclusion and evidence or that are the **exact opposite** of what we'd need to assume.

37. **Dilemma:** The apparent discrepancy is a sort of **violated expectation.** Since (1) oil companies have an interest in making sure the debate over climate change keeps going, we would expect that they would fund any research that might be taken as credible

(and thus extend the debate), but (2) they don't. Answer Choice (E) resolves the discrepancy by providing information that shows that the apparent violation is itself a demonstration of the expectation. If the oil companies want the debate to continue, they can't fund this research because people will decide the issue is no longer debatable.

(E) Primarily, the question is designed as one long **reasonable but irrelevant** trap, as it is based on a situation often discussed these days and that most test takers will have an opinion on. Beware of your **real-world thinking**! Answer Choices (A) and (C) actually **worsen the dilemma**, giving further support to the claim that oil companies don't spend money in this way. Answer Choice (B) brings up the **one step removed** topic of whether a researcher is *successful*, whereas Answer Choice (D) does the same by addressing *press releases*.

38. **Issues: subject/predicate agreement** (*runoff… overwhelms*), **coordination and subordination** (at multiple points), **parallelism** (required between coordinated elements)

    (C) The easiest decision point to exploit is the agreement required for *overwhelms* (whose subject *runoff* is separated from it by the distractor phrase *caused by industrial-scale runoff*), which eliminates Answer Choices (A) and (B). Answer Choice (E) also fails the agreement test because the *and* before *have fertilizes* creates a compound predicate (so *has fertilized* or just *fertilized* would be needed). Answer Choice (D) fails a different agreement problem, the *that* connects *fertilize* and *deplete* with the singular *nitrogen* which requires *fertilizes* and *depletes*.

39. **Argument:** Like in many bolded statement questions, the prompt here is a **somebody says X (and they're wrong)**. The second bolded statement is the X, the conclusion being countered by the speaker's argument whereas the first is **setup information** that serves as **evidence** for the conclusion the speaker is arguing against, as Answer Choice (B) describes perfectly.

    (B) The answer choices split 3/2 over the first statement. Answer Choices (A), (B), and (E) all correctly peg the first statement as evidence, whereas Answer Choices (D) and (C) get it wrong. Answer Choice (E) can be eliminated because it treats both statements as evidence, and Answer Choice (A) describes the speaker's conclusion, not the conclusion of the **somebody** (here the doctors).

40. **Issues: pronoun reference** (ensuring only one plural antecedent for the *theirs* and one singular antecedent for the *its*), **modification** (making sense of all the prepositional phrases without creating dangling modifiers), **connecting clauses** (avoiding creating a run-on or a fragment)

    (D) Targeting individual small errors is probably the best way to handle these messy options, rather than trying to sort out the modification from the very beginning. Answer Choice (A) uses a *which* without a comma, and Answer Choice (E) uses a comma with *in which*, errors of connecting clauses. Answer Choices (A), (B), (C), and (E) all fail to correctly sort out their pronoun references, as well. The *it* in Answer Choices (A), (B), and (C) could refer to at least two singulars (*gizzard, stomach, food*), and Answer Choice (E)'s *they* could refer to multiple plurals (*gizzards, alligators and crocodiles*). Most of the incorrect answer choices also create illogical descriptions of one sort or another [for example, Answer Choice (E) puts the stomach inside the gizzards].

41. **Issues: clause organization** (actually a distracting issue here, as the various reorganizations are all correct in their own way), **modification** (the sensible placement and form of *actually* and *involuntary*), **pronoun** (avoiding **ambiguity** for *it*, but also **agreement** between the pronoun and its antecedent)

    (A) The sentence, though a little halting, is grammatically correct as written. Pronoun problems creep up in some answer choices: Answer Choices (B) and (C) have no clear antecedent for the *it* that starts the phrase *it is actually*, whereas Answer Choice (D) introduces a stray *they*. *Actually* and *involuntary* get confused in Answer Choice (D) by the switch to *involuntarily*. In Answer Choice (E) moving *involuntary* to describe the stimulation changes the meaning of the sentence [though a bigger problem with Answer Choice (E) is the **unidiomatic** *thought often as though a sign*].

EVALUATING YOUR SCORE

Tabulate your score for the Quantitative and Verbal sections of the Sample Test by giving yourself one point for every correct answer, and record the results in the Self-Scoring Table below. Then find your approximate rating for each score on the Self-Scoring Scale and record it in the appropriate blank.

SELF-SCORING TABLE		
Section	Score	Rating
Quantitative		
Verbal		

SELF-SCORING SCALE—RATING				
Section	Poor	Fair	Good	Excellent
Quantitative	0–12	13–20	21–29	30–37
Verbal	0–15	15–25	26–30	31–41

Study again the Review sections covering material in Sample Test 1 for which you had a rating of FAIR or POOR. Then go on to Sample Test 2.

*Important note: Up-to-date scoring guidelines for all sections of the GMAT can be found at *mba.com.*